The Z-Mail Handbook

Books That Help People Get More Out of Computers

Managing UUCP and Usenet, *8th Edition, 289 pages*
by Tim O'Reilly & Grace Todino

For all its widespread use, UUCP is one of the most difficult UNIX utilities to master. This book is for system administrators who want to install and manage UUCP and Usenet software. "Don't even TRY to install UUCP without it!" —Usenet message 456@nitrex.UUCP

Using UUCP and Usenet, *210 pages*
by Grace Todino & Dale Dougherty

Shows users how to communicate with both UNIX and non-UNIX systems using UUCP and *cu* or *tip*, and how to read news and post articles.

!%@:: A Directory of Electronic Mail Addressing & Networks, *2nd Edition, 438 pages*
by Donnalyn Frey & Rick Adams

Answers the problem of addressing mail to people you've never met, on networks you've never heard of. A general introduction to e-mail, followed by detailed reference sections for over 130 networks.

MH & xmh: E-mail for Users and Programmers, *598 pages*
by Jerry Peek

Learn how to customize your e-mail environment to save time and make communicating more enjoyable. MH commands are available on virtually any UNIX system; *xmh* is an X Window System client that runs MH programs.

The Z-Mail Handbook, *462 pages*
by Hanna Nelson

The complete, authoritative guide to Z-Mail, a powerful mail program that is a superset of the widely-used public-domain program, Mush. Z-Mail runs on UNIX terminals or on graphic workstations running the X Window System.

Contact us for a catalog of our books, for orders, or for more information.

O'Reilly & Associates, Inc.

103 Morris Street, Sebastopol CA 95472
(800) 338-6887 US/Canada   707-829-0515 overseas/local   707-829-0104 Fax

The Z-Mail Handbook

by Hanna Nelson

Dale Dougherty

Editor

The Z-Mail Handbook
by Hanna Nelson

Editor: Dale Dougherty

Printing History:

October 1991:   First printing.

ISBN 0-937175-76-5

Table of Contents

3 Reading and Managing Mail 23

5 Z-Mail Shortcuts, Bells, and Whistles 119

6 Using the Fullscreen Mode 163

8 Customizing Z-Mail

9 Writing Scripts and Functions 309

Figures

Tables

Preface

This book is about Z-Mail and, by extension, the program from which it was derived, MUSH, the Mail User's Shell. Z-Mail and MUSH are programs for sending, reading, manipulating, and managing electronic mail (e-mail) messages in the UNIX operating system environment.

Z-Mail is easy to use. Because Z-Mail provides an extensive online help facility with detailed information on each command and variable, first-time e-mail users will find it easier to learn than other mail programs provided on UNIX systems. If you're already familiar with another e-mail program, you should have no trouble switching to Z-Mail because it includes commands that are fully compatible with other UNIX system mail programs.

Z-Mail is flexible. You can customize existing commands and create your own using functions and command-line aliases. By adding custom message headers and signing your name automatically, you can personalize your outgoing mail messages. With scripts, filters, and functions, you can manipulate messages and folders automatically. As if that's not enough, Z-Mail provides three different interfaces to choose from (we'll explain more about the interfaces in Chapter 1, *Introduction to Z-Mail*).

Z-Mail is convenient. If new mail arrives during the current mail session, Z-Mail notifies you and automatically incorporates the new messages in your system mailbox; you don't have to quit and re-enter the program to read the new messages. In addition, Z-Mail includes features of the C shell, such as command history, filename completion, command-line aliases, and the ability to execute UNIX commands from within the program.

Z-Mail is fast. With one command, you can select all the messages from a particular person, on a certain subject, or sent on a specific date. You no longer have to search through all the message summaries in your mailbox for just one message.

This book is for anyone who uses (or plans to use) Z-Mail or MUSH. We cover all the features of these programs, beginning with a basic introduction on sending and receiving mail, through the more advanced commands and customization, including the fancy features and shortcuts, up to creating scripts and functions.

The main focus of this book is Z-Mail's *line-mode interface*; throughout the book we'll approach the features of Z-Mail from this interface. The reason for this is that the line mode is the basis for the other two interfaces, the *fullscreen* mode and the *Graphical User Interface* (GUI) mode. Once you understand how to perform tasks using the commands in line mode, you'll be able to apply this information and benefit more from the same features in the other modes. We explain how to use the other two interfaces in Chapter 6, *Using the Fullscreen Mode*, and Chapter 7, *Using the Graphical User Interface*, but in many instances, we'll refer back to the line-mode chapters to provide more extensive information.

It's not required that you learn the line mode first if you're only going to use (for example) the GUI. But, if you really want to understand, customize, and use Z-Mail to manage your mail most efficiently, you'll take our advice and spend some time with the line-mode interface.

Scope of This Book

Chapter 1,   *Introduction to Z-Mail*, presents an overview of the features of Z-Mail, the three interfaces, and the evolution of MUSH to Z-Mail.

Chapter 2,   *Getting Started*, gives a brief introduction to the Z-Mail line-mode interface for people who have never used an electronic mail program. This chapter explains the basics of using Z-Mail to send, read, save, and delete mail messages.

Chapter 3,   *Reading and Managing Mail*, describes the different commands you can use to read and manipulate your mail messages with Z-Mail and includes such tasks as selecting, marking, saving, and printing your messages. This chapter also introduces you to the concept of modifying Z-Mail by setting certain variables.

Chapter 4,   *Sending Mail with Z-Mail*, covers all the commands you can use to send mail with Z-Mail, including how to suspend and restart a message composition, send files and attachments, and create mail aliases.

Chapter 5,   *Z-Mail Shortcuts, Bells, and Whistles*, describes the shortcuts you can use to manage your mail more efficiently, including how to combine commands, create command-line aliases, use command history and file completion, manipulate folders, and access the UNIX shell from Z-Mail.

Chapter 6,   *Using the Fullscreen Mode*, describes how to use Z-Mail in the text-graphics, screen-oriented fullscreen mode.

Chapter 7,   *Using the Graphical User Interface*, explains the GUI mode X Window System interface.

Chapter 8,   *Customizing Z-Mail*, describes how to modify the behavior of Z-Mail at startup time by including commands and variable settings in your personal initialization file. This chapter also introduces you to the Z-Script scripting language.

Chapter 9,   *Writing Scripts and Functions*, explains how to use Z-Script to build your own scripts and functions to further customize the Z-Mail environment in each of the three modes. This chapter also covers the different ways to run scripts in Z-Mail.

Chapter 10,   *Creating and Using Macros*, describes how to create Z-Mail macros in line, compose, and fullscreen modes.

Chapter 11,   *Z-Mail Addressing*, discusses different kinds of mail addresses and how Z-Mail interprets them.

Appendix A, *Useful Tips and Hints*, is an index that collects in one place all the helpful tips for using Z-Mail presented throughout the book.

Appendix B, *Z-Mail Commands*, is a complete list of all the Z-Mail commands in alphabetical order.

Appendix C, *Z-Mail Variables*, describes each of the Z-Mail variables in alphabetical order.

Appendix D, *Tilde-escape Commands*, lists all the tilde-escape commands available with Z-Mail.

Appendix E, *Fullscreen-mode Commands and Bindings*, describes each of the fullscreen-mode commands and the default bindings.

Appendix F, *Command-line Options*, covers all the command-line options available with Z-Mail.

Appendix G, *Important Z-Mail Files*, lists the files and directories that Z-Mail uses.

Different Paths for Different Users

If you plan to use the Z-Mail line-mode interface to send and manage your mail, you should read through the chapters in order, beginning with Chapter 3, (or Chapter 2, if you've never used e-mail before). You can safely skip Chapters 6 and 7, if you don't plan to use these interfaces. When you're ready to learn more about customizing your Z-Mail environment, read Chapter 8 and Chapter 9.

If you want to use the fullscreen-mode interface, start with Chapter 6, and refer back to Chapters 3, 4, and 5, as necessary.

If you have a graphics display or an X terminal, and your UNIX computer runs the X Window System, you can use the GUI-mode interface. In this case, start by reading Chapter 7, (referring back to the line-mode chapters when necessary).

If you are using Z-Mail in the fullscreen or GUI mode and you want to learn to write your own functions to use in these modes, keep in mind that the Z-Script language depends on the line-mode commands. Before you can write scripts and functions, you will need to familiarize yourself with the Z-Mail line-mode commands. To do this, read through Chapters 3 through 5, before reading Chapter 8 and Chapter 9.

Finally, if you send mail to people on other machines and to people in other companies, be sure to read Chapter 11.

Ordering Z-Mail

To order Z-Mail, contact the software publisher at the following location:

Siren Software Corporation
750 Menlo Avenue, Suite 200
Menlo Park, CA 94025-9606
Telephone: 415/322-0600 or 1-800-45-SIREN
Fax: 415/322-4023
e-mail address: info@siren.com

Conventions Used in This Book

Bold	is used for Z-Mail commands, options, and variable names.
Italic	is used for filenames, directory names, and UNIX commands. Italic is also used in text to reference variables in syntax statements and to emphasize new terms when they are introduced.
`Constant Width`	is used in text for Z-Mail header fields and in examples to show the contents of files or the output from commands.
`Constant Bold`	is used in examples and syntax statements to show commands and options that should be typed literally. For example, **rm foo** means to type "rm foo" exactly as it appears in the text or example.
`Constant Italic`	is used in examples and syntax statements to show variables where you should make a context-dependent substitution. For example, replace the variable *filename* with an actual filename.
$	is the Bourne shell prompt.
%	is the C shell prompt.
_	indicates the position of the cursor.
[]	surround optional values in a description of program syntax. (The brackets themselves should never be typed.)
...	stands for text, usually computer output that's been omitted for clarity or to save space.
	indicates a useful tip or hint that you may wish to refer back to. A complete list of useful tips is found in Appendix A.

CTRL-*X* or *^X* indicates the use of *control* characters. This means, hold down the CTRL key while typing the (lowercase) "x" character. We denote other keys similarly (e.g., RETURN indicates a carriage return).

All command examples are followed by a RETURN unless otherwise indicated.

Acknowledgments

First of all, I want to thank Dan Heller, the author of MUSH and Z-Mail, who put me up to the daunting task of writing this book. Many thanks go to both Dan and Bart Schaefer (who co-wrote many pieces of MUSH and Z-Mail) who patiently answered hundreds of pieces of mail, reviewed drafts, provided examples, and dutifully sent updated copies of the software by UPS, Federal Express, and UUCP. And thanks to Bill "Rock" Petro for examples and reassurance as well as numerous other people on *comp.mail.mush* who consistently ask great questions.

Thanks to George Hoffer for his insightful and prompt review comments, Teresa Ellis for her splendid graphics, Tom Cuthbertson for his positive outlook and constant encouragement, Linda Gomish and Mark Taub and all my coworkers and friends at The Santa Cruz Operation, Inc. and beyond for support and assurance.

A great big thank you to David Neilson, who let me use his address in examples.

I want to thank everyone at O'Reilly and Associates. In particular, thanks to Tim O'Reilly for giving me the opportunity to write this book, Lenny Muellner for patiently answering all my questions, Eileen Kramer and Rosanne Wagger for copyediting and producing the book, and Ellie Cutler for producing the index. Very special thanks go to my editor, Dale Dougherty who, with his red pen and thorough review, has taught me more about technical writing in the last five months than I want to admit.

Finally, my undying gratitude goes to James Bohem. Without his knowledge, support, patience, confidence, inspiration, cappucino, and cooking, I never could have done this.

1
Introduction to Z-Mail

Even after almost ten years of working with different computers and operating systems, I continue to be amazed that I can send a message from Santa Cruz, California to my friend in Edinburgh, Scotland, and he'll read it the next morning when he gets to work (or the same evening, if he's working late).

Sending an electronic message (or "e-mail") with the computer is convenient; you don't have to get up from your desk to put a Post-it note on the other person's terminal. And the other person doesn't have to decipher your handwriting.

I've grown to depend on the convenience of this method of communicating to the point where I find myself wishing my parents had modems and computers running UNIX so I could send them e-mail instead of having to pick up the phone.

Communicating with E-mail

The UNIX operating system was conceived with the idea of making it easy for people to exchange information. One of the ways that was devised for people to communicate was through electronic mail. From the beginning, different UNIX computers came with their own electronic mail programs. For example, AT&T's UNIX system comes with *mailx* and Berkeley Software Distribution (BSD) UNIX comes with *Mail*.

There are actually two types of mail programs on UNIX systems. The mail program that you interact with to send and read mail is known as a *Mail User Agent* (MUA). The MUA doesn't actually deliver mail, but rather passes the message to another program (or group of programs), the *Mail Transport Agent* (MTA). The MTA takes care of routing the message to the other person. When we refer to a "mail program" in this book, we mean the mail program that you interact with, the MUA, not the MTA. MMDF, *sendmail*, and *smail* are three examples of MTAs. The MTA is a complex program maintained by your system administrator; you shouldn't need to interact with it directly.

As people use the mail programs provided with the UNIX system, they naturally come up with features that they wish were in the program. And, eventually, new (and improved) mail programs are developed. As a result, there are many other electronic mail programs available on UNIX today; these include such public domain mail programs as *MH* and *elm*. Also included in this list of alternate mail programs (although it's not in the public domain) is MUSH.

In this book, we'll explain how and why you should use the mail program called Z-Mail and in the process, we'll cover MUSH, the program from which it evolved. As we explain how to use the commands and variables in this book, we'll point out which features are specific to Z-Mail (and thus, not available with MUSH).

Evolution of Z-Mail

In 1985, Dan Heller created the Mail User's Shell (MUSH) (or "frankenmail" as it was then known); it was a friendlier, more versatile, and "backwards-compatible" electronic mail interface, more so than the ones commonly available on UNIX Systems. At that point, MUSH had only one interface that worked with SunWindows, but soon expanded to include the line and "curses" (or fullscreen) modes.

Bart Schaefer joined Dan in October of 1987 with MUSH Version 6.0. In 1989, the newsgroup *comp.mail.mush* was started on Usenet (along with it's companion mailing list *mush-users@apple.com*) to provide support and facilitate discussion of MUSH. The newsgroup and mailing list are identical in content. If you can't get the newsgroup at your site, you can join *mush-users* by sending a request to *mush-users-request@apple.com*.

The current version (at this writing) of MUSH, 7.2.3, is the culmination of efforts by Dan, Bart, and numerous contributors from Usenet.

In 1990, Dan and Bart decided to expand the features of MUSH, adding an X Window interface, to create a commercial product. As a result, Z-Mail includes everything and retains complete backwards-compatablity with MUSH. In the following sections, we'll describe the features of Z-Mail above and beyond MUSH.

What is Z-Mail?

Z-Mail is a program that you can use to send and read electronic mail messages on computers running the UNIX system. As mentioned earlier, Z-Mail is a Mail User Agent (MUA) that passes the mail message off to the Mail Transport Agent (MTA) which performs the actual mail delivery.

What's special about Z-Mail is that it has three different interfaces for reading and manipulating mail messages. Z-Mail also has a number of useful features, such as the ability to "attach" files and other messages to your message, support for multiple open folders and message compositions, the ability to select messages to read and manipulate based on different criteria, commands for creating command-line aliases and mailing lists, and Z-Script, a complete scripting language for customizing Z-Mail.

The Line-mode Interface

The default interface, called the *line mode*, is a standard command-line mode similar to other mail programs, such as AT&T's *mailx* and Berkeley Software Distribution (BSD) *Mail*.

In fact, the Z-Mail line-mode interface was designed to be backwards-compatible with these mail programs. In other words, if you're already using one of these programs, you can read the mail currently in your system mailbox by invoking Z-Mail instead. Z-Mail includes commands that accomplish the same things as the commands you're used to.

The line mode might not seem very user-friendly at first, so you might be tempted to use one of the other modes exclusively. I'm going to try to convince you that there are a lot of advantages to learning the line mode because the other two modes are built on this fundamental layer.

First of all, the line mode doesn't require anything special in terms of terminal display or operating system software. You don't need a graphics display or an X terminal to run Z-Mail in the line mode. Even if you use a graphics display at work, you can read your mail using Z-Mail on a terminal logged in over a modem. In addition, the line mode runs on many different versions of the UNIX operating system, including SunOS (Versions 2.0 and later), SCO Open Desktop, Berkeley Software Distribution UNIX (Versions 4.2 and later), UNIX System V, Version 7, System III and XENIX, without running extra software.

The line mode is basically the "engine" of Z-Mail. The other two interfaces are based on this mode. When you learn how the line-mode commands function, you'll have no trouble adapting to the other interfaces and you'll realize how much faster it is to manage your mail with this program.

If you know how to use these commands, you can manipulate messages and folders automatically by building scripts with Z-Mail's powerful scripting language Z-Script. Although this language uses line-mode commands, you can run the scripts in all three interfaces.

The scripting language, which was available in MUSH, has been expanded to include interactive commands, shell functions, and the ability to access functions from different interfaces. For example, you can now create a function that prompts the user for confirmation before executing the command. To run the function in line mode, you enter the function name at the line-mode prompt exactly as you run commands. In fullscreen mode, you select a new fullscreen-mode command to display a menu of available buttons at the bottom of the screen, then run the function by selecting the button. In GUI mode, Z-Mail displays buttons that are attached to functions in the main Z-Mail window; click the mouse button to run the function.

Unlike MUSH and other UNIX mail programs, Z-Mail allows you to open multiple folders and have more than one message composition in progress at any given time. So, if you're in the middle of composing a message and you have to do something else, such as check the contents of another message or folder, you can "suspend" the composition in line and fullscreen modes. In the GUI mode, simply open a new window. To finish composing the message, bring it to the foreground and then send it the usual way; in GUI mode, re-activate the Compose window.

In the following sections, we'll show you briefly how to perform the same simple mail management task from each of the different interfaces.

In this section, we'll invoke Z-Mail, read a message, and then quit the program using the line-mode interface. (Don't worry if you don't understand the terminology; we'll explain it further in the next chapter.)

First, enter this command at your UNIX system prompt:

```
$ zmail
```

Z-Mail reads your messages from the system mailbox and displays one-line *header summaries* of your messages in a list on your screen, as shown in the following example:

```
Z-Mail (2.0.0 7/1/91): Type '?' for help.
[0]+ "/usr/spool/mail/hanna": 6 messages, 6 new, 6 unread, 0 deleted
>  1  N  D Neilson          Aug  1 (83 ) Wild at Heart
   2  N  Eudora Moo         Aug  1 (12 ) more Z-Mail edits
   3  N  Eudora Moo         Aug  2 (18 ) Re: Chapter 7
   4  N  Mr. Dave           Aug  4 (198) Re: Chapter 7
   5  N  D Neilson          Aug  4 (10 ) $$
   6  N  Eudora Moo         Aug  4 (17 ) New Mail!!
Msg 1 of 6: _
```

To select a message and read it, enter **p** (for **print**) followed by the message number at the prompt, and press RETURN. For example, let's read message 2:

```
Msg 1 of 6: p 2
Message #2 (12 lines)
From eudora Fri Aug 2 13:06:11 1991
From: Eudora Moo <eudora>
Date: Fri,  2 Aug 1991 12:00:37 -0800
To: Hanna Nelson <hanna>
Subject: more Z-Mail edits

Those chapters you sent on Monday look great!
I'm looking forward to reading the rest of the
book.

-- Eudora
Msg 2 of 6: _
```

Now, quit Z-Mail by entering **q** (for **quit**) at the prompt:

```
Msg 2 of 6: q
```

Z-Mail tells you that it's "updating" the folder and returns you to the UNIX system prompt.

Because understanding the line mode is so important to using Z-Mail to the greatest advantage, we're going to spend much of the book discussing tasks, features, and customization in terms of running commands in the line mode.

The Fullscreen-mode Interface

The second mode supported by Z-Mail is a text-graphics interface called *fullscreen mode*. By default, the fullscreen-mode interface functions similarly to the *vi* visual editor—you press a key or sequence of keys to move the cursor around and perform certain actions. If you're not familiar with *vi*, you can configure the fullscreen mode to emulate another editor.

This interface doesn't require that your computer or terminal have any special graphics capabilities. However, to run Z-Mail in the fullscreen mode, your terminal must have the minimum capabilities required by any fullscreen editor like *vi*. (If you're not sure, you can try running Z-Mail in fullscreen mode or ask your system administrator.)

Using the fullscreen-mode interface, you can access commands and messages more quickly and intuitively than with line mode. What you gain in speed, you lose in some of the line-mode features, such as the ability to re-execute previous commands, combine Z-Mail commands with pipelines, and create your own command-line aliases, as well as the functionality of a few line-mode commands (we'll get to these commands in Chapter 3, *Reading and Managing Mail*, Chapter 4, *Sending Mail with Z-Mail*, and Chapter 5, *Z-Mail Shortcuts, Bells, and Whistles*). However, Z-Mail provides a way for you to "escape" to the line mode from fullscreen mode to run commands.

Again, if you know the line mode, you'll be able to get much more out of the fullscreen mode.

Now, let's look at our sample Z-Mail session using the fullscreen mode. To invoke Z-Mail in fullscreen mode, use the **–fullscreen** option to **zmail**, and type the following:

```
$ zmail —fullscreen
```

As with the line mode, Z-Mail reads in your messages and displays the header summaries on your screen:

```
Z-Mail (2.0.0 7/1/91): Type '?' for help.
[0]+ "/usr/spool/mail/hanna": 6 messages, 6 new, 6 unread, 0 deleted
   1  N  D Neilson          Aug  1 (83 ) Wild at Heart
   2  N  Eudora Moo         Aug  1 (12 ) more Z-Mail edits
   3  N  Eudora Moo         Aug  2 (18 ) Re: Chapter 7
   4  N  Mr. Dave           Aug  4 (198) Re: Chapter 7
   5  N  D Neilson          Aug  4 (10 ) $$
   6  N  Eudora Moo         Aug  4 (17 ) New Mail!!

(RET) display     (s) save        (m) mail          (r) reply
(j) next-msg      (k) back-msg     (z) screen-next   (Z) screen-back
```

This is known as the top-level screen in fullscreen mode.

The key to using fullscreen mode is remembering to select a message before entering the command to initiate the action that you want to perform on the message. Thus, to read message 2, use the **j** key on your keyboard to move the highlight bar to message 2 and then press RETURN:

```
Message #2 (12 lines)
From eudora Fri Aug 2 13:06:11 1991
From: Eudora Moo <eudora>
Date: Fri,  2 Aug 1991 12:00:37 —0800
```

```
To: Hanna Nelson <hanna>
Subject: more Z-Mail edits

Those chapters you sent on Monday look great!
I'm looking forward to reading the rest of the
book.

-- Eudora
    2       Eudora Moo          Aug  1 (12 ) more Z-Mail edits
Msg 2 of 6: ...continue... _
```

The `continue` prompt indicates that you are in continue mode; in this mode, you can enter a new fullscreen-mode command immediately without first returning to the top level. To quit continue mode and return to the top level, enter **q** (for **quit**) at this prompt:

```
Msg 2 of 6: ...continue... q
```

Z-Mail redisplays the header summaries; to quit the Z-Mail program, enter **q** again. You see the "updating" message again before you return to the UNIX prompt.

The Graphical User Interface

The third mode that Z-Mail supports is a Graphical User Interface for the X Window System. Z-Mail is an *X Client*, an application that runs under the X Window System. (Of course, MUSH does not support a graphical interface.)

The "look and feel" of Z-Mail depends on whether you're running the Motif or Open Look version of the software. The differences between the Motif and Open Look versions are minimal. For the most part, Z-Mail behaves the same, but looks slightly different. The examples in this book were created using the Motif version of Z-Mail; if you're running the Open Look version, your screen looks slightly different. This shouldn't affect the way you perform tasks and access commands.

In the GUI mode, you use a mouse to move a pointer in a window and then press the mouse button to select messages, commands, and options. Z-Mail includes *menus*, lists of options and commands that you select with the mouse pointer, and *icons* that, when selected, open windows for performing specific tasks. As with other X Clients, you can manipulate Z-Mail windows by resizing them, moving them around on your screen, and closing them.

Note that when you edit messages in GUI mode, Z-Mail uses the editing style defined by the Open Look or Motif interface. You can customize this in your X Window System defaults file.

Because of the nature of X, you can display multiple message compositions on the screen at the same time. However, with Z-Mail, you don't need an X Window System to open more than one folder or composition.

Here's our sample session again, this time from the GUI mode. Invoke Z-Mail in GUI mode using this command in an **xterm** window:

```
$ zmail —gui
```

The Z-Mail client starts up and you see the main Z-Mail window in Figure 1-1.

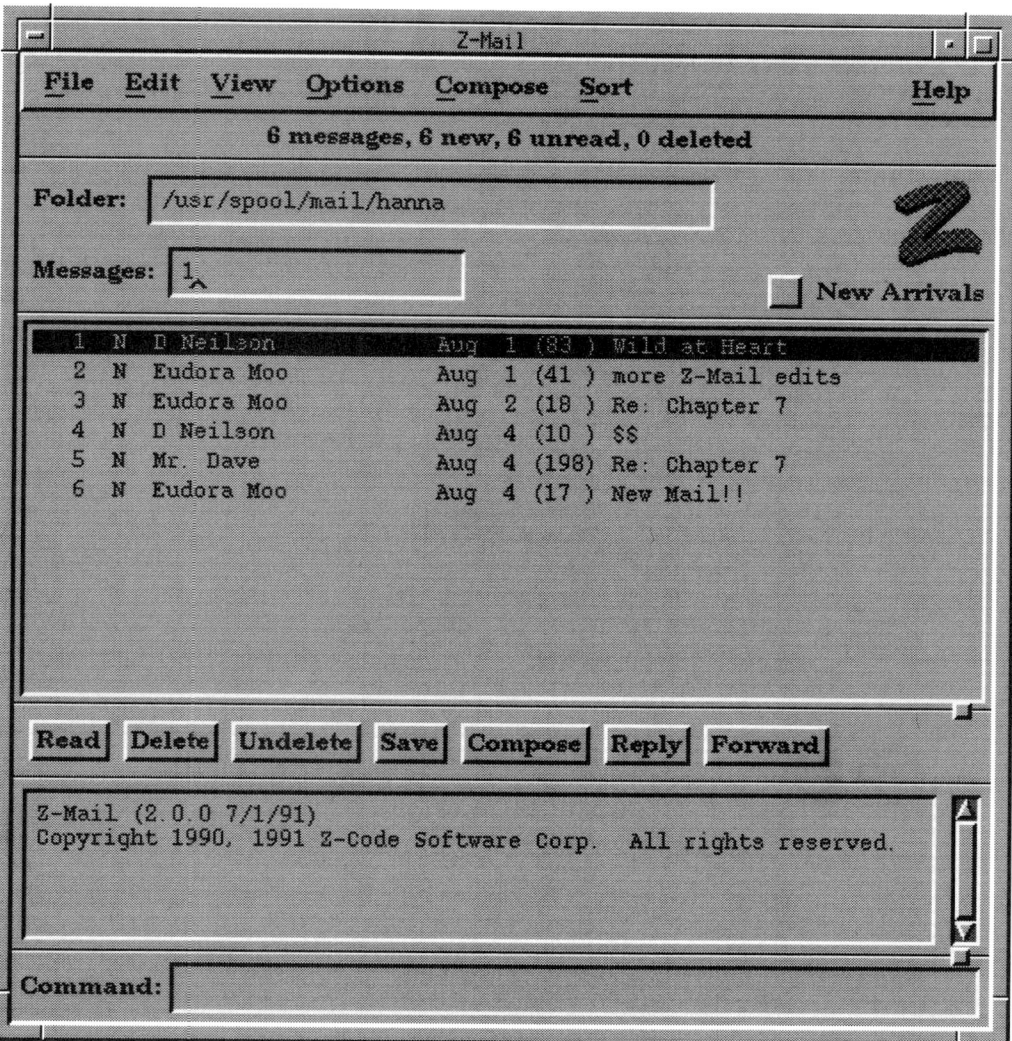

Figure 1-1. Main Z-Mail window

At the top of this window is the Menu Bar. Below this is the current folder and currently selected message. The list of header summaries appears in the middle of this window. Below the list are the main Z-Mail window buttons. At the bottom of the window, you see the Command field that you can use to enter line-mode commands.

You can select a message to read by double-clicking (in rapid succession) the left mouse button on the header summary. Z-Mail opens another window to display the message; Figure 1-2 shows what this looks like.

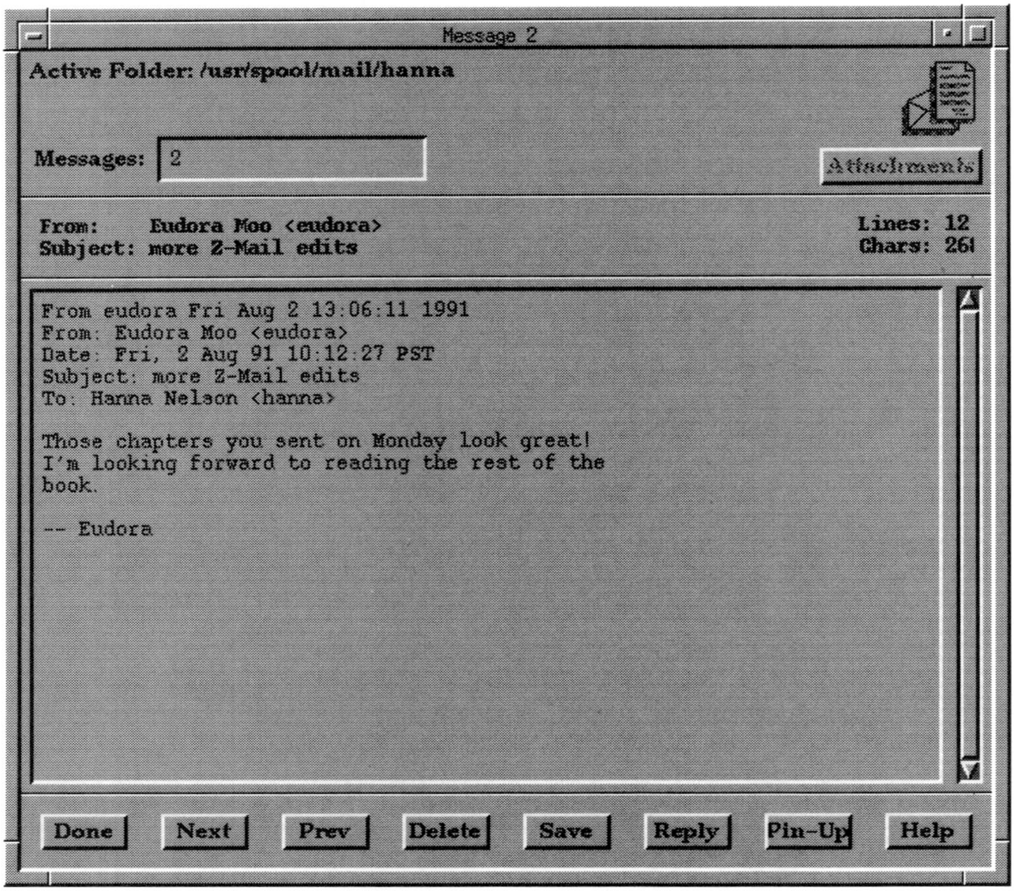

```
┌─────────────────────────────────────────────────────────────────────────┐
│ ─                              Message 2                           │ · │□│ │
│ ┌───────────────────────────────────────────────────────────────────────┐ │
│ │ Active Folder: /usr/spool/mail/hanna                          ╭─────╮   │ │
│ │                                                               │▒▒▒▒▒│   │ │
│ │                                                               │▒▒▒▒▒│   │ │
│ │  Messages:  ┌──────────────────────────────┐              ┌──────────┐ │ │
│ │             │ 2                            │              │Attachments│ │ │
│ │             └──────────────────────────────┘              └──────────┘ │ │
│ │                                                                         │ │
│ │  From:    Eudora Moo <eudora>                            Lines: 12      │ │
│ │  Subject: more Z-Mail edits                             Chars: 261      │ │
│ │  ┌───────────────────────────────────────────────────────────────┬──┐ │ │
│ │  │ From eudora Fri Aug 2 13:06:11 1991                            │▲ │ │ │
│ │  │ From: Eudora Moo <eudora>                                      │  │ │ │
│ │  │ Date: Fri, 2 Aug 91 10:12:27 PST                              │  │ │ │
│ │  │ Subject: more Z-Mail edits                                    │  │ │ │
│ │  │ To: Hanna Nelson <hanna>                                      │  │ │ │
│ │  │                                                               │  │ │ │
│ │  │ Those chapters you sent on Monday look great!                 │  │ │ │
│ │  │ I'm looking forward to reading the rest of the                │  │ │ │
│ │  │ book.                                                         │  │ │ │
│ │  │                                                               │  │ │ │
│ │  │ -- Eudora                                                     │  │ │ │
│ │  │                                                               │  │ │ │
│ │  │                                                               │  │ │ │
│ │  │                                                               │  │ │ │
│ │  │                                                               │▼ │ │ │
│ │  └───────────────────────────────────────────────────────────────┴──┘ │ │
│ │ ┌──────┐ ┌──────┐ ┌──────┐ ┌───────┐ ┌──────┐ ┌───────┐ ┌──────┐ ┌─────┐│ │
│ │ │ Done │ │ Next │ │ Prev │ │Delete │ │ Save │ │ Reply │ │Pin-Up│ │Help ││ │
│ │ └──────┘ └──────┘ └──────┘ └───────┘ └──────┘ └───────┘ └──────┘ └─────┘│ │
│ └───────────────────────────────────────────────────────────────────────┘ │
└─────────────────────────────────────────────────────────────────────────┘
```

Figure 1-2. Reading a message

To return to the main Z-Mail window by closing the Message Display window, click the Done button at the bottom of the screen in Figure 1-2. Now, exit Z-Mail by pulling down the File menu and selecting Quit. At the prompt to update the folder, click the Yes button.

Now that you've been introduced to each of the Z-Mail interfaces, you're ready to start using Z-Mail. For information on the line mode, start with Chapter 2, *Getting Started* (or Chapter 3, *Reading and Managing Mail*, if you're already familiar with e-mail). To use the fullscreen mode, turn to Chapter 6, *Using the Fullscreen Mode*. If you're going to use the GUI mode, start with Chapter 7, *Using the Graphical User Interface*.

2
Getting Started

This chapter is an introduction to Z-Mail for people who have never used electronic mail. This chapter covers the basics of sending, reading, saving, and deleting mail messages. If you are already familiar with another UNIX System mail application (such as UNIX System V *mailx* or Berkeley Software Distribution (BSD) UNIX *Mail*), you may want to skip this chapter and move on to Chapter 3, *Reading and Managing Mail*. On the other hand, if you're unfamiliar with Z-Mail's line mode, Chapter 2 is a good place to start learning it. The later chapters cover the more advanced commands and variables that allow you to customize your Z-Mail environment.

Basic Concepts

On UNIX systems, people read mail and send mail messages to other people on the computer (or other computers) using a mail program, such as *mailx*, *Mail*—or Z-Mail. When you invoke the Z-Mail program (either to send or read mail), Z-Mail reads a system-wide initialization file called *system.zmailrc*. (The MUSH system initialization file is *Mushrc*.) The system administrator sets up this file; it contains the default environment settings that control how Z-Mail works for all the users on the system.

You can override the system defaults by putting commands and variable settings in a file called *.zmailrc* in your home directory. (If you're using MUSH, your personal initialization file is called *.mushrc*.) Z-Mail reads this file *after* the system-wide initialization file, so your settings override the default settings. We'll explain more about this in Chapter 8, *Customizing Z-Mail*.

When you invoke Z-Mail to send mail, the program lets you compose and send a message. Then, the message is passed to the Mail Transport Agent (MTA) for transporting. To receive mail, the MTA uses a file (known as a mail folder) called the *system mailbox* to store messages for each person. Mail messages wait in the system mailbox until you invoke Z-Mail.

Figure 2-1 shows the path your mail message takes once you send it.

The name of the system mailbox folder is generally your login name and is located in the system spool directory */usr/spool/mail*. For example, my system mailbox is in */usr/spool/mail/hanna*. The location of your system mailbox depends on your MTA and

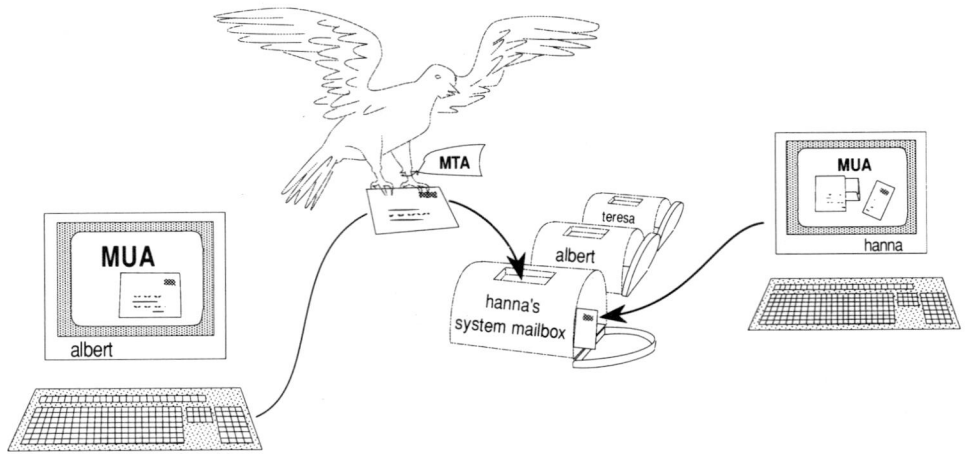

Figure 2-1. Path of a mail message

system configuration. You don't need to know where your system mailbox is because Z-Mail finds it automatically. The system mailbox file is also called the *spool folder*.

A folder is a file that contains one or more mail messages. You can think of folders as simple databases that allow you to select and manipulate mail messages. Z-Mail also uses another special folder, called the *main mailbox*, to store messages once you've read them. The main mailbox is also called the *mbox* folder and is generally located in your home directory. We'll explain more about folders in the next chapter.

If new mail arrives while you are logged in, your shell (the program that interprets the commands that you type at the UNIX prompt) might notify you by displaying a message like the following when you return to the system prompt:

```
You have new mail.
```

If you are not logged in when new mail arrives, the system alerts you the next time you log in. Depending on your system configuration, you might see the new mail message immediately before the prompt for terminal type at login time. For example:

```
You have new mail.
TERM = (wy60)
```

Sending Mail

To send a mail message, simply enter the **zmail** command followed by the *address* of the person to whom you want to send the message. The address is usually the person's login name on the computer where she receives mail. If you want to send mail to another person, you must first ask them for their login name or mail address. For example, my login name, on the machine *holycow*, is *hanna*. This is the address that people use to send me mail. An address can also be a sequence of letters or numbers. For example, I have a friend whose mail address is *erdb04*.

You can send mail to more than one person at a time by entering each address, separated by a space or comma character (,) at the UNIX prompt. For example, if you want to send a message to *albert* and *gordon*, enter the following at the UNIX system prompt:[1]

```
$ zmail albert gordon
```

When you press RETURN, you see the following:

```
$ zmail albert gordon
To: albert, gordon
Subject: _
```

Enter a line that describes the subject of your mail message and press RETURN.

Z-Mail normally prompts you for the message subject. You can choose to suppress this, so you might not see the `Subject` prompt. We'll explain more about this in Chapter 4, *Sending Mail with Z-Mail*.

Composing a Message

After you enter a `Subject`, Z-Mail moves to the next line and waits for you to compose your message. You are now in *compose mode*. In compose mode, you use a simple line editor to enter your message at the keyboard, pressing RETURN to start each new line. If you make a mistake on the line before pressing RETURN, use the BACKSPACE key, DEL, or CTRL-H to erase the previous character. To erase the previous word, press CTRL-W; to erase the entire line, press CTRL-U.

The simple line editor allows you to change words on the current line only. Once you press RETURN, you can't go back and edit previous lines. However, Z-Mail has other commands that let you back up and correct mistakes on the previous line or start up another editor to edit the entire message. We'll explain how to use these commands later in Chapter 4.

---

[1] Enter **mush** at the UNIX prompt to start MUSH.

Canceling a Message

If at any time you decide that you don't want to send the message, you can cancel the message by pressing the interrupt key (CTRL-C or DEL, depending on your system). If DEL is not the interrupt character, Z-Mail interprets it as BACKSPACE. When you press DEL, you see the following message:

```
** interrupt -- one more to kill letter **
```

If you press DEL again, you see:

```
Saving unfinished letter in ~/dead.letter.
exiting
```

When you cancel a message, Z-Mail saves it in a file called *dead.letter* in your home directory. Because this feature is configurable, Z-Mail might not save canceled messages; see Chapter 4 for more information.

Sending a Message

When you finish entering the message, press RETURN to move the cursor to a new line. To send the message, press CTRL-D or enter a dot (.) on a line by itself.

Sending a message by entering a dot is configurable; if this doesn't work, press CTRL-D.

Here's what your screen looks like after you compose and send a message:

```
$ zmail albert gordon
To: albert, gordon
Subject: Coffee after work?

Let's meet Harry at the Double-R for some
coffee and pie after work.

Dale
^D
$
```

Sending a File

If you have already composed your message in a file using a text editor such as *vi*, you can send the file with the left angle bracket character (<). This is known as *command-line redirection*. For example, if you want to send the file *coffee* in the current directory to *albert*, enter the following at the UNIX prompt:

```
$ zmail albert < coffee
```

Be careful with redirection; if you accidentally use the right angle bracket character (>), you can delete the contents of the file.

Reading Mail

To read the mail messages stored in your system mailbox, start up Z-Mail by entering **zmail** at the UNIX system prompt:

```
$ zmail
```

If you have mail, you see a list of header summaries followed by the Z-Mail prompt. If you don't have mail, you see a message like the following:

```
No mail for hanna
$ _
```

and you don't enter Z-Mail. To enter Z-Mail even if you don't have any mail, use the **–shell** (**–S**) option at the $ prompt as shown:

```
$ zmail —shell
```

Let's say I have mail in my system mailbox and I start up Z-Mail. Z-Mail retrieves the messages and displays the list of header summaries. Here's an example:

```
Z-Mail (2.0.0 7/1/91): Type '?' for help.
[0]+ "/usr/spool/mail/hanna": 5 messages, 5 new, 5 unread, 0 deleted
>  1  N  Dale Cooper       Jul  7 11:22 (14) Cherry pie
   2  N  Dale Cooper       Jul  7 12:00 (29) Re: Z-Mail Chapters
   3  N  Harry Truman      Jul 13 10:12 (42) Chapter 2
   4  N  Lucie             Jul 21  9:50 (84) phone message
   5  N  Albert            Jul 24 11:41 (49) Re: Great Coffee!!
Msg 1 of 5: _
```

Each line in the example above is a *header summary*. These lines are also referred to as message *headers*. However, because the people also use the term "headers" to refer to the lines that appear at the top of the message text when you read a message, we'll use "header summaries" for this list to distinguish between the two. We'll explain more about headers in the section "Reading a Message."

This example shows the default format that Z-Mail uses to display the header summaries. This format might be different on your system because it can be customized as described in Chapter 3. The > points to the current message.

By default, the prompt lists the time, your name, the current message, and the number of messages in your mailbox. Here's an example of what the default Z-Mail prompt looks like:

```
(6:41) hanna: #1 of 5>
```

To simplify the display, the examples in this book use the following prompt format:

```
Msg 1 of 5: _
```

You enter Z-Mail commands at this prompt. We discuss how to change the prompt in Chapter 3.

Header Summaries

Each field in a header summary contains information about the message. Figure 2-2 points out these fields.

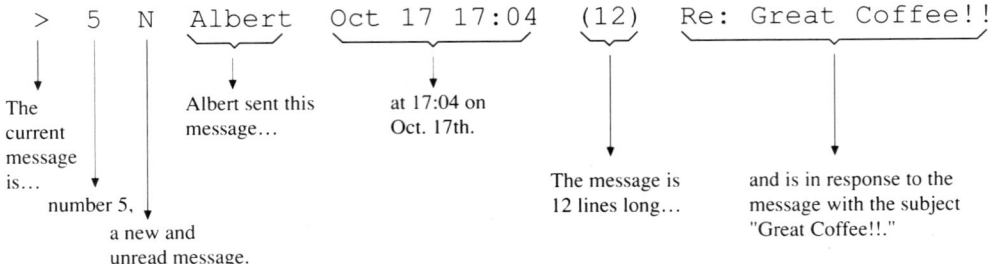

Figure 2-2. Header summary fields

We explain the header summary fields in more detail in Table 2-1.

Table 2-1. Header Summary Fields

Field	Description
Message number	The number that Z-Mail uses during this session to refer to the message.
Current message pointer	The right angle bracket character (>) indicates the *current message*. If you press RETURN, Z-Mail displays the contents of this message.
Status indicator	Contains one of the following characters:

	(blank)	read
	+	marked
	*	deleted
	!	newly arrived
	N	new and unread

Table 2-1. Header Summary Fields (continued)

Field	Description
	P preserved (read, but retained in your system mailbox)
	S saved to a file or folder
	U old and unread
	p printed
	f forwarded to another user
	r replied to
	Note that because **p**, **f**, and **r** appear in the same position, only one is visible. In MUSH, newly arrived messages are marked with **N** instead of !.
	In Figure 2-2, the message is marked with an "N", which indicates that it is new and unread; it arrived since the last time I invoked Z-Mail.
Author	The name of the person who sent the message.
Date	Lists the date and time that the author sent the mail message.
Size	The number of lines in the message.
Subject	Contains the subject of the message, if any. This field is optional; the author of the mail message can include a message subject, if she wants.

Because you can configure the summary display, your summaries might look different from the summaries in our examples. We'll explain how to use the **hdr_format** variable to configure your header summary display in Chapter 3, *Reading and Managing Mail*.

When New Mail Arrives

If new mail arrives while you are in the Z-Mail program (either at the header summary display or in compose mode while sending a mail message), Z-Mail displays a message like the following:

```
New mail in /usr/spool/mail/hanna:
  6  !  Harry Truman    Jul 14 10:12 (42) Re: Chapter 2
```

The exclamation mark character (!) in the status indicator field indicates that this message has arrived since you started Z-Mail.

Reading a Message

To read the first message (the message indicated by the current message pointer), enter **1** or the **print** (**p**) command and press RETURN. For example, if you press **p** with the message pointer at message number 1, you see the contents of the message:

```
Msg #1 (16 lines)
From cooper Sun Jul  7 11:22:01 1991
From: Dale Cooper <cooper>
```

```
Date: Sun,  7 Jul 1991 11:22:01
X-Mailer: Z-Mail (2.0.0 7/1/91)
To: Hanna Nelson <hanna>
Subject: Cherry pie

That cherry pie you sent over for the
party was excellent.

Where did you get it?

- The Coop

Msg 1 of 5: _
```

The lines at the top of the message are called *message headers*. They describe information about the message, such as the message number, who the message is from, when the message was sent, and the subject. Z-Mail uses this information when composing the list of header summaries that you see when you start the program.

The prompt shows the number of the message that you're currently reading. Continue reading the messages by pressing **p** followed by the message number and then RETURN. You can also use **next (n)** to display the next message in the list. So, to read message 2, enter **n** at the prompt:

```
Msg 1 of 5: n
```

Replying to a Message

To reply to the current message, use the **reply (r)** command. Entering **r** at the message number prompt sends a reply to the sender of the original mail only. You can include the other people on the **To** and **Cc** lists using the **replyall (R)** command.

When you use **r** or **R**, Z-Mail creates the **To** and **Subject** lines for you and then places you in compose mode. For example, if you reply to message 1 in the previous example, you see the following:

```
Msg 1 of 5: r
To: Dale Cooper <cooper>
Subject: Re: Great cherry pie!


—
```

Note that Z-Mail automatically inserts "Re:" in the **Subject** line to indicate that this message is a response to a message. If there is more than one person in the original **To** or **Cc** lists and you use **R** to respond to the message, these names appear on the **To** and **Cc** lines as well.

At this point, enter your response from the keyboard, as you do when composing a message, complete the letter and send it using CTRL-D.

You can include the message to which you are responding in your letter using the ˜i or ˜I *tilde-escapes*. We'll explain tilde-escapes and how to use them in Chapter 4, *Sending Mail with Z-Mail*.

Saving a Message

You can save the current message to a specific filename or to a folder called *mbox* in your home directory using the **save (s)** command. Remember: a folder is a file that contains mail messages. When you save messages to folders, you can access them just like the system mailbox.

To save another message, simply specify the message number. For example, if you want to save message number 3 to *mbox*, enter:

```
Msg 1 of 5: s 3
```

Z-Mail displays these messages:

```
Saving msg 3 ... (42 lines)
Saved 1 msg to /u/hanna/mbox
```

If *mbox* already exists, Z-Mail displays this instead:

```
Appended 1 msg to /u/hanna/mbox
```

To save the message to a folder other than *mbox*, enter the folder name after the message number. For example, the next example saves the current message to the folder *cherry*:

```
Msg 1 of 5: s cherry
```

If the folder is located in a directory other than your current directory, specify the pathname with the **save** command. So, if *cherry* is located in the directory *pies*, type the following:

```
Msg 1 of 5: s pies/cherry
```

By default, when you quit from Z-Mail, any messages that you saved are removed from your mailbox.

If you get a lot of mail, you'll probably want to set up a system for organizing your messages. For example, some people organize their mail by author, some by subject, others by date. We'll explain more about using folders to organize messages in Chapter 3, *Reading and Managing Mail*, and Chapter 5, *Z-Mail Shortcuts, Bells, and Whistles*.

If you don't want to keep the headers when you save messages, use the **write (w)** command instead of **save**. Just remember that you won't be able to access these messages like those in the system mailbox.

Deleting a Message

By default, Z-Mail keeps messages that you've already read in your system mailbox until you remove them explicitly. To keep the size of your system mailbox manageable, you should remove messages that you don't want to save.

To delete a message (or messages), use the **delete (d)** command. If you don't specify a message number, Z-Mail deletes the current message. For example, to delete messages 1 through 3, enter:

```
Msg 1 of 5: d 1-3
```

If you want to delete messages 1 and 3 (but not 2), you would enter:

```
Msg 1 of 5: d 1,3
```

The **delete** command doesn't remove the message from the system mailbox immediately; this command marks the message for deletion. When you quit from Z-Mail or update the folder, the message is then deleted.

Recovering a Deleted Message

Until you quit from Z-Mail, you can recover deleted messages using the **undelete** (**u**) command. However, Z-Mail doesn't display header summaries for deleted messages. To display the deleted messages so that you can specify messages to recover, use the **headers** (**h**) command with the **:d** option:

```
Msg 1 of 5: h :d
```

Z-Mail displays the messages that you deleted, marked with an asterisk character (*):

```
> 1  *  Dale Cooper      Jul  7 11:22 (14) Cherry pie
  2  *  Dale Cooper      Jul  7 12:00 (29) Re: Z-Mail Chapters
  3  *  Harry Truman     Jul 13 10:12 (42) Chapter 2
```

You can recover message 2 by entering:

```
Msg 1 of 5: u 2
```

When you exit using **quit** (**q**), Z-Mail completely removes deleted messages from your system mailbox and you can no longer recover them with **undelete**.

If you always want Z-Mail to show deleted messages in the header summary display, you can set the **show_deleted** variable. This is described in Chapter 3.

Exiting Z-Mail

You can exit Z-Mail in one of two ways, depending on whether you want to save changes to your system mailbox. To exit without changing your mailbox, use **exit** (**x**). This leaves the system mailbox in exactly the same state as when you invoked Z-Mail. Any messages that you read, deleted, saved, or printed are untouched; newly arrived messages also remain as if you hadn't seen them yet.

To update the system mailbox with the changes you made during this session, use **quit** (**q**) to exit. When you use **quit**, all messages that you marked for deletion using **delete** and that you saved are removed from your system mailbox. The rest of the messages return to your system mailbox and are marked as "old."

For example, if I save message 1 and delete message 2, when I use **quit** to leave Z-Mail, I see a message like the following example:

```
Updating "/usr/spool/mail/hanna": saved 3 messages
```

The next time I invoke Z-Mail, the status indicator for messages 3 through 5 is **U** for "old and unread." The display now looks something like this:

```
Z-Mail (2.0.0 7/1/91): Type '?' for help.
"/usr/spool/mail/hanna": 4 messages, 1 new, 3 unread
    1  U  Harry Truman       Jul 13 10:12 (42) Chapter 2
    2  U  Lucie              Jul 21  9:50 (84) phone message
    3  U  Albert             Jul 24 11:41 (49) Re: Great Coffee!!
>   4  N  Dale Cooper        Aug  1 18:02 (14) Vacation.
```

Note that Z-Mail renumbers the old messages and places the new message (4) at the end of the list. By default, new messages are appended to the end of the spool folder as they arrive.

Getting Help with Z-Mail

As you'll see in this section, there are several ways to get help on Z-Mail commands.

To get general help about Z-Mail, use the **help** command:

```
Msg 1 of 5: help
```

To get more specific help information, enter the following command, where *topic* is one of the **help** topics in Table 2-2:

```
Msg 1 of 5: help topic
```

Table 2-2. Help Topics

Topic	Description
path	Help on specifying file and directory pathnames.
msg-list	Special characters for referring to messages.
prompt	Information on changing your Z-Mail prompt.
hdr_format	Options for changing the header summary display.
variables	Information on setting variables.

For example, let's display the help information on *path* by entering the following:

```
Msg 1 of 5: help path
```

You see these messages:

```
Whenever "path" is specified, the following syntax is legal
besides the normal path addressing scheme used by unix:
  ~[user]    -- the home directory of specified user (yours by default)
  %[user]    -- /usr/spool/mail/login_name [user_name] (yours by default)
  +file      -- the directory described by `set folder'; file is `file'
```

You can display a list of all the Z-Mail commands using the question mark (**?**) command:

```
Msg 1 of 5: ?
```

You see the following list:

?	echo	ignore	quit	unbind
about	edit	jobs	read	unbind-macro
alias	error	lpr	replyall	unbutton
alternates	eval	ls	replysender	uncmd
ask	exit	mail	resume	undelete
attach	expand	map	retain	undigest
await	filter	map!	save	unfilter
bind	flags	mark	saveopts	unfunction
bind-macro	folder	merge	search	unignore
button	folders	msg_list	set	unmap
cd	foreach	my_hdr	sh	unmap!
close	from	next	shift	unmark
cmd	fullscreen	open	sort	unpreserve
copy	function	pick	source	unretain
delete	functions	pipe	stop	unset
detach	headers	preserve	top	update
dialog	help	previous	type	version
display	history	print	un_hdr	write
each	iconify	pwd	unalias	

```
Type: `command -?' for help with most commands.
```

Appendix B, *Z-Mail Commands*, also contains a complete alphabetical list and brief description of these commands.

To get help on a specific command, use one of the following formats at the prompt:

```
command_name -?
? command_name
help command_name
```

For example, to display the help information on the **delete (d)** command, enter any of the following commands at the prompt:

```
Msg 1 of 5: d -?
Msg 1 of 5: ? delete
Msg 1 of 5: help delete
```

When you enter one of these commands, you see the help information for **delete**:

```
        delete [msg-list]
        undelete [msg-list]

The "delete" command marks the listed messages as deleted.  If
no message list is given, the current message is deleted.

In line mode, deleted messages are not shown in the header summary
display unless the variable show_deleted is set.  In fullscreen
and GUI modes, deleted messages are shown so they can be selected
for undelete or other operations.

Deleted messages are ignored by the "pipe" command and by those
commands that display messages, but most other commands include
all messages whether deleted or not.

Deleted messages are lost forever when the folder is updated (by
the "update" command, by changing folders without the "!" flag,
```

or by exiting with "quit"). Messages can be recovered by the "undelete" command at any time BEFORE the folder is updated.

See also the variable $show_deleted.

Common Errors

Z-Mail allows you to address, compose, and send a mail message without checking to see that the person's name is valid. Z-Mail passes off the message, as you addressed it, to the MTA. If the name doesn't exist (for example, the person might be on another system or you misspelled the name), the MTA can't deliver the message and sends an error message.

For example, if you try to send mail to *leland*, but you misspell his name, you might see a message like this:

```
$ zmail leeland
To: leeland
Subject: Glen Miller

Remember to bring those Glen Miller
records when you come down to the
office.
^D
$
Saved letter in ~/dead.letter.
```

Depending on your system, you might also see a message like the following:

```
can't send mail to leeland
```

When you try to send a message to an address that doesn't exist, the MTA might also send you a mail message telling you that it couldn't send your message and including a copy of your original mail. Mail that is returned to you with an error message is called *bounced mail*. Sometimes mail is bounced back to you immediately (for example, if you tried to send it to another person on your system). If you're sending mail to someone on another system, it might take a day or two for a bounced mail message to get back to you.

In either case, you'll probably have a copy of the message, so you don't have to retype the entire message when you want to resend it.

To resend a message saved in *dead.letter*, first edit the *dead.letter* folder and remove the message headers.

NOTE

Because Z-Mail appends (rather than overwrites) messages to the *dead.letter* folder, this folder might also include other messages. Depending on your system, this folder might also include characters, such as a series of CTRL-A characters, between messages.

Remove everything but the text of your message from the folder.

Now, resend the message using command-line redirection from the UNIX prompt:

```
$ zmail leland < /u/hanna/dead.letter
```

To resend bounced mail, start up Z-Mail and save the message to a file using the **write** command. For example, use this command to save message 6 to a file called *resend.me*:

```
Msg 1 of 6: w 6 resend.me
```

Now, edit the file and remove everything but the text from your original message. Finally, send the *resend.me* file with command-line redirection:

```
$ zmail leland < resend.me
```

In this chapter, we introduced you to the basics of sending and receiving electronic mail using Z-Mail. You learned how to invoke and exit Z-Mail, how to interpret header summaries, and how to reply to, save, and delete messages from your system mailbox. Finally, we showed you how to get help on Z-Mail commands and resend a bounced mail message.

Once you've learned these basic tasks, you can go on to Chapter 3, *Reading and Managing Mail*, and Chapter 4, *Sending Mail with Z-Mail*, where we'll show you features of Z-Mail that make performing these tasks easier.

3
Reading and Managing Mail

In Chapter 2, *Getting Started*, you learned the basics of sending and reading messages. In this chapter, we'll explain all the commands and describe the features of Z-Mail that you can use to read and manage your mail. For each task, we'll explain the different commands and the various ways you can customize Z-Mail to help you get your work done quickly.

You'll learn about:

- Entering Z-Mail commands and getting help.

- Modifying Z-Mail commands with variables.

- Reading messages and redisplaying header summaries.

- Sending messages directly to the printer from within Z-Mail.

- Using patterns to select and sort messages in the folder.

- Organizing messages into files and folders using the folder directory.

- Updating the folder and exiting Z-Mail.

- Customizing your Z-Mail display.

Although we cover a lot of information in this chapter, remember that you may not need it all immediately; however, with this information, you'll get a sense of how you can better use Z-Mail to read and manipulate the messages that you receive.

You should try to remember how to use the commands presented here, but keep in mind that it's not important to remember all of the customization information. Later, we'll show you how to make your customizations permanent so you don't have to remember how to specify them each time.

Z-Mail Command-line Syntax

When you invoke Z-Mail without specifying any addresses, you enter the Z-Mail program. Z-Mail reads in the messages from your system mailbox and displays the header summaries, followed by the Z-Mail prompt, on your screen. Here's the syntax for entering commands at the Z-Mail prompt:

    command_name [options] [message_list] [addresses or files]

The syntax for the **reply** command is slightly different; in this case, reverse the order of *options* and *message_list*. We'll explain more about **reply** in Chapter 4, *Sending Mail with Z-Mail*.

Many Z-Mail commands have abbreviations. As in previous chapters, the abbreviation is shown in parentheses following the first mention of each command; in subsequent examples, we'll use only the abbreviation.

Anything that appears in square brackets ([]) is optional. Most Z-Mail commands act on the current message unless you specify a *message_list*. A message list is a number, a list of numbers, or a combination of special characters that refer to messages in your mailbox. As an example, you can refer to messages 4 through 8 using **4-8**. We'll explain more about message lists in the next section "What is a Message List?"

Some commands accept *options* that you can use to modify the command's behavior. We call these *command-line options* because they are optional and you supply them at the Z-Mail prompt when you enter the command line. These options usually begin with the dash character (–). We'll describe any options that are available with a command as we show you how to use it.

You can execute more than one Z-Mail command in a sequence on the same command line. Use the semicolon character (;) to separate the commands.

Addresses are the mail addresses for people to whom you want to send mail. (Note that **mail** and **reply** are the only commands that accept an address.) Sometimes, you might hear people refer to the list of addresses as the *distribution list*.

What is a Message List?

A *message list* is a list of zero or more message numbers following a Z-Mail command. If you don't specify a message number, Z-Mail performs the command on the *current message*. For example, to delete more than one message, use the **delete (d)** command and specify the message list at the prompt, as shown below:

    Msg 3 of 10: d 4 6 7

You can use spaces or commas (,) to separate the message numbers. The following command works exactly like the last:

```
Msg 3 of 10: d 4 6,7
```

Some characters have special meanings when you use them in a message list. For instance, use the dash (–) to indicate a range of messages:

```
Msg 3 of 10: d 4-7, 9
```

This list deletes messages 4 through 7 inclusive, and message 9.

Message list special characters give you more control over messages in the header summary list. Use them to execute commands on the first or last message, or all the messages in the list. Table 3-1 lists the special characters that you can use when specifying message lists.

Table 3-1. Message List Special Characters

Character	Description
(blank)	The current message (default).
.	The current message.
*	All the messages in the folder.
^	The first message in the folder.
$	The last message in the folder.
+	The next message in the list.
x-z	A range of messages, in ascending order, between x and z, inclusive. x and z can be a message-list special character.

So, if you want to save all messages from message 6 through the last message in the folder to a file called *messages* in the current directory, you would type:

```
Msg 3 of 10: s 6-$ messages
```

If you want to save 1 through 6 instead, type:

```
Msg 3 of 10: s ^-6 messages
```

You can exclude some part of a message list using the curly brace characters ({}). For example, if you want to save messages 1 through 10, but not messages 6 and 8, enter the following command:

```
Msg 3 of 10: s 1-10 {6 8}
```

NOTE

You *must* specify a message list before excluding a second message list inside curly braces.

Message numbers inside the curly braces must be within the range specified by the first message list, otherwise Z-Mail ignores them. For example:

```
Msg 3 of 10: s 5-9 {3,10}
```

In this case, Z-Mail ignores the second message list and saves messages 5 through 9.

Z-Mail processes message numbers in ascending numeric order, regardless of the order in which you specify them. The following example shows you how to save these messages to the file *~/zmail.book*:

```
Msg 3 of 10: s 10 1 2 6-8 ~/zmail.book
```

When Z-Mail saves this list, you see:

```
Saving msg 1 ... (2 lines)
Saving msg 2 ... (4 lines)
Saving msg 6 ... (12 lines)
Saving msg 7 ... (14 lines)
Saving msg 8 ... (10 lines)
Saving msg 10 ... (16 lines)
Saved 6 msgs to /u/hanna/zmail.book
```

As you see here, Z-Mail uses message lists as input to various commands. Many Z-Mail commands also produce message lists as their output. We'll show you how to manipulate the output in the section, "Combining Z-Mail Commands," in Chapter 5.

Getting Help with Z-Mail Commands

Before we start discussing specific commands, you can display the list of the available Z-Mail commands by entering a question mark (?) at the Z-Mail prompt. If you know the command name, you can get help either by entering **help** *command*, **?** *command*, or *command* **–?** to get help on that specific *command*. For example, let's display help information on the **quit** command by typing:

```
Msg 3 of 10: ? quit
```

You'll see a screen like this:

```
Msg 3 of 10: ? quit
     quit
     exit

These commands end a Z-Mail session. The command "quit" updates
all open folders. If new mail has come in, you are notified and
asked whether to continue the program or quit anyway. If the
multivalued variable verify is set to contain the field "quit",
then then you are prompted to confirm update of any and all open
folders that have been modified.

The command "exit" terminates Z-Mail, neither updating the open
folders nor checking for new mail. However, this command has a
special meaning in scripts and user-defined functions, causing
the script or function to exit but the program to continue. To
cause the program to exit from within a script or function, use
"builtin exit" or simply "x".
```

If you use the **?** *command* format, note that the space between the **?** and **quit** is essential. Thus, if you enter the following command:

```
Msg 3 of 10: ?quit
```

you get this error:

```
?quit: command not found.
```

Z-Mail interprets the first word, up to a blank, as the name of a command. The space between **?** and **quit** tells Z-Mail to interpret **?** as the command name. Because there is no Z-Mail command called **?quit**, you get the error. With Z-Mail, you can create your own commands, called *command-line aliases*; we'll show you how in Chapter 5.

Z-Mail gets the help information for commands from the */usr/lib/Zmail/cmd_help* file. Z-Mail reads information from this file whenever you:

• Use the **help** command.

• Enter a question mark (**?**) to display a list of available commands in line mode.

• Enter *command_name* **–?** to get information on a specific command.

If you get a message like this when you try to get help on a command, Z-Mail couldn't find your *cmd_help* file:

```
Cannot open help file "cmd_help": No such file or directory
```

Normally, the system administrator sets the location of the help files for Z-Mail. However, if the location of a help file changes, or you want to tell Z-Mail to read an alternate help file, you can set the new location with the **cmd_help** variable. See Chapter 8 for more information.

Modifying Commands with Variables

As you read through this chapter, you'll learn how to perform tasks using Z-Mail commands. In the course of describing the default behavior of the commands, we'll show you how to use *variables* to change the default behavior.

Syntax for Setting Variables

To set variables, use the **set** command. The syntax for **set** looks like this:

```
set [ [?]variable [= value] ]
```

Using this syntax, you can set variables for the current Z-Mail session at the Z-Mail prompt, but you lose the settings when you quit the program. To make the settings permanent, put them in the *.zmailrc* initialization file in your home directory. (In MUSH, the initialization file is called *.mushrc*.) Z-Mail reads this file automatically when you start the program; we'll explain more about initialization files in Chapter 8.

For example, to specify that Z-Mail prompt you with the **Cc** line when you press CTRL-D to send a message, set the **askcc** variable like this:

```
Msg 3 of 10: set askcc
```

We'll show you how to set different kinds of variables in the upcoming sections.

Displaying Current Variable Settings

To display the current list of variable settings, use **set** with no arguments at the line-mode prompt. For example, when I enter **set**, I see:

```
ask
askcc
cmd_help        /usr/lib/zmail/cmd_help
cwd             /u/hanna
dead            ~/dead.letter
dot
escape          ~
folder          ~/Mail
hdr_format      %25f %7d (%l/%c)
history         24
home            /u/hanna
hostname        holycow
indent_str      >
mbox            ~/mbox
nonobang
pager           more
prompt          Msg %m of %t:
realname        Hanna Nelson
tmpdir          /tmp
```

We'll explain the different types of variables, what they do, and how to set them in upcoming chapters.

Displaying Available Z-Mail Variables

To get a list and brief description of all the known variables that Z-Mail uses, enter this command at the Z-Mail prompt:

```
Msg 3 of 10: set ?all
```

If you want, you can limit the display of information to one particular variable using this format:

```
set ?variable
```

For example, let's see the description for **realname**:

```
Msg 3 of 10: set ?realname
```

Z-Mail displays:

```
realname:
Your real name, which is used in the From: header of outgoing messages.
```

Z-Mail gets the help information for variables from the file */usr/lib/Zmail/variables*. If this file doesn't exist or Z-Mail can't find it, Z-Mail will not run.

Unsetting Variables

If you set a variable at the Z-Mail command line, all you need to do to remove the setting is exit the program. To unset this variable without quitting, use **unset** at the Z-Mail prompt. For example, let's remove the **askcc** setting:

```
Msg 3 of 10: unset askcc
```

Now, if I use **set** to display my current variable settings, **askcc** is no longer listed.

If **askcc** is set in the initialization file, **unset** removes the setting for the current Z-Mail session only; the next time you start up the program (and read ~/.zmailrc), Z-Mail sets the variable again.

If you want to unset a variable in your initialization file, edit the file to remove the variable setting line. Let's say you want to remove the **askcc** setting permanently. Remove this line in ~/.zmailrc or comment it out by putting a pound sign in front of it.

```
set askcc
```

Your changes are read in automatically the next time you start Z-Mail.

To remove all the variable settings for the current Z-Mail session, use this command:

```
Msg 3 of 10: unset *
```

Reading Messages

Chapter 2, *Getting Started*, showed you the basics of reading messages; now, you'll learn some other commands and variables you can use to display messages. To read messages, use the **print (p)** or **type (t)** commands (they are identical). To read specific messages, enter the command followed by a message list or simply enter the message numbers of the messages that you want to read. Thus, to read message 6, type:

```
Msg 3 of 10: p 6
```

(If you specify more than one message with **print**, Z-Mail displays them as one continuous message.) When you use these commands with a message list, the "current message" changes to each message in the list as it is displayed. Thus, in the example above, the prompt changes to this:

```
Msg 6 of 10: _
```

When you try to use **print** to read a message that's been deleted, Z-Mail prompts you to restore the message first. For example, if message 3 is deleted and you try to read it, you see this prompt:

```
Message 3 deleted. Undelete first? [y/n] [y] _
```

Press RETURN or enter **y** to restore and read the message. If you enter **n**, you return to the Z-Mail prompt and the message remains deleted.

Displaying the Next or Previous Message

To display the next or previous unread message in the current folder, use the **next (n)** or **previous** commands. You can also use the plus (**+**) and minus (**–**) keys to do the same thing. Note that **+** doesn't display the message headers with the message text. When you use these commands, Z-Mail changes the current message and displays its contents.

Deleting and Displaying Messages

It's a good idea to get into the habit of deleting messages when you no longer need them. By default, Z-Mail automatically keeps messages in the system mailbox until you remove them manually. If you don't clean out your system mailbox periodically, it can get very large; a large mailbox takes a long time to open when you start Z-Mail. Use the **dt** command to delete the current message and display the next message in the folder. This command acts as if you entered **delete;print**.

You can set up Z-Mail so that when you delete a message, it automatically prints the next undeleted message in the folder. Do this with the **autoprint** boolean variable:

```
Msg 3 of 10: set autoprint
```

With **autoprint** set, the **delete** command now acts like **dt**.

Note that **dt** is one command (not a combination of the **delete** and **type** commands).

Paging Through Messages

When you use **print**, Z-Mail checks the value of the **crt** variable to determine how many lines (24 by default) of the message to display before calling an external pager. If you want to change this, set **crt** to another number. For example:

```
Msg 3 of 10: set crt = 20
```

Now, if the message has more than 20 lines, Z-Mail invokes a program to page through the message.

 To determine which pager to use, Z-Mail checks the **pager** variable, if set, or the **PAGER** environment variable. You can tell Z-Mail to use a UNIX command such as *more*, *less*,[1] or *pg* when you page through messages by setting the **pager** variable. For example, to use *more*, set **pager** like this:

```
Msg 3 of 10: set pager = more
```

The system administrator might have set the default value for **pager**.

Z-Mail also has a built-in pager called *internal*. This pager program is very simple: press the space bar to display the next number of lines (specified by **crt**) in the message, press RETURN to print the next line, and press **q** to quit the pager. If you want to use the internal pager, enter the following:

```
Msg 3 of 10: set pager = internal
```

Displaying the Tops of Messages

Sometimes, when you use **print**, you'll find yourself scrolling through 10 or 12 header lines just to read a two-line message. You can skip all the header lines by displaying just the top few lines of the message with the **top** command. To specify the number of lines that **top** displays, set the **toplines** variable as shown in the following example:

```
Msg 3 of 10: set toplines = 10
```

Now, when you use **top**, Z-Mail displays the first ten lines of the message (excluding the headers). If you don't set **toplines**, **top** shows the number of lines set by the **crt** variable, which specifies the number of lines on your terminal's display screen. Otherwise, **top** scrolls through the entire message.

 Another way to reduce the time spent paging through messages is to tell Z-Mail to remove blank lines in messages. This is useful if you frequently receive messages that contain large numbers of blank lines. To do this, set the **squeeze** variable:

```
Msg 3 of 10: set squeeze
```

Now, whenever you read or save messages that contain two or more consecutive blank lines, Z-Mail condenses the multiple lines into one.

---

[1] If it is available on your system, you might want to set **pager** to *less*; *less* allows you to page backward, as well as forward, in the message (and it's faster than *more*).

Redisplaying Header Summaries

After reading a message, you can redisplay the list of header summaries using the **headers** (**h**) command.

If you have more messages than fit on the screen, display the next screenful of header summaries using the **h +** command:

```
Msg 1 of 50: h +
```

Note that you must include the space between **h** and the plus sign (**+**). In this case, **h** is the command and **+** is an argument to the command. (You can also press **z** to display the next screenful of header summaries.)

Display the previous screen with:

```
Msg 1 of 50: h —
```

If you specify a message number with **h**, Z-Mail displays a screenful of messages starting with that number. For example, if you have 50 messages in your folder and you enter:

```
Msg 1 of 50: h 20
```

Z-Mail displays the header summaries, beginning with message 20. If there aren't enough messages after the number you specify to fill an entire screen, Z-Mail backs up far enough to display the last entire screenful of header summaries.

 The value of the **screen** variable determines the number of header summaries that Z-Mail displays in a screenful. (This is different from the **crt** variable, which determines how many lines of message text to display at a time.)

Because the height of my Wyse 60 terminal is 24 lines, I usually like to set **screen** with the following command:

```
Msg 1 of 50: set screen = 22
```

With this setting, Z-Mail displays the last prompt (and the last command that I executed) on the first line, followed by 22 header summaries, and the current prompt at the bottom of the screen.

However, sometimes I read mail over a slow modem (1200 baud). To minimize the amount of time I spend watching Z-Mail redraw the screen, I set **screen** to a smaller number for the current session. For example, when I set **screen** to 10, Z-Mail displays only ten header summaries at a time.

Listing Specific Header Summaries

The **from** (**f**) command can display messages with a specific pattern in the `From` line. The **from** command is case-sensitive; enter the search pattern exactly as it appears in the `From` line. For example, I can display all the messages from George:

```
Msg 2 of 20: f George
    1     George H.  Jul 21 12:37  (20)    Z-Mail Chapters
```

```
 6  Sr George H.   Aug  4 11:01  (33)    advanced commands
13  N  George H.   Aug  6  9:20  (26)    Review this!
```

Z-Mail uses the information in the `From` line; this line usually displays the mail address and real name of the person who sent the message. Thus, you can use **from** to find all the messages from the mail address *george* or from *George*, as in the example above.

If you use a pattern that's not unique, **from** displays all the messages that include the pattern. For example, if you use the following command:

```
Msg 2 of 20: f ian
```

to find all the messages from *ian*, Z-Mail also finds the messages from *brian*, *adrian*, and *dianne*.

You can also display the summaries for a certain list of messages by specifying the message list with **from**. Here's an example of how to list the summaries for messages 6 through 14:

```
Msg 2 of 20: f 6-14
```

Combining these two functions, you can restrict the display to only those messages in the specified range from a particular person. To do this, use **from** followed by the message range and then the pattern. The following example shows how to display the summaries for the messages between 6 and 14 that contain *dale* in the `From` line:

```
Msg 2 of 20: f 6-14 dale
 7  S  Dale Cooper   Jul 21 12:44  (17)   Chapter 5
11     r Dale Cooper  Jul 24 18:00  (86)   Re: Chapter 5
```

If you just want to print the header summary for the current message (the one indicated by the current message pointer), use **from** with no arguments.

 Use **from** to move the current message pointer to a different message by specifying a single message number. You can also use **from** to move the message pointer down the list, looking at each header summary without using **headers** to display the whole list. To show the next header summary in the list, use the **f +** command; to move it back one header summary, use the **f −** command.

You can use + and − to move the current message pointer to the first or last message that fits the description that you specify with **from** (either a message list or pattern). I frequently use the + and − characters to move the message pointer to the first or last message in the list. In the following example, the command moves the message pointer to the first message in the list:

```
Msg 3 of 20: f + 1
Msg 1 of 20: _
```

Note that this also changes the current message in the prompt.

Displaying Header Summaries by Status

You can display a subset of the header summaries in your folder using the status indicator character. Here's the syntax:

```
headers -H:c
```

The **-H:** option tells **headers** to pick out messages with the status indicator character *c*. Table 3-2 describes these status indicator characters.

Table 3-2. Status Indicator Characters

Character	Description
a	All messages.
d	Deleted messages (*).
f	Forwarded messages (**f**).
m	Temporarily marked messages (+).
n	New messages (! and **N**).
o	Old messages (everything but **N**).
p	Preserved messages (**P**).
r	Replied-to messages (**r**).
s	Saved messages (**S**).
u	Unread messages (**U**, **N**, and !).

For example, if you have a lot of messages in your folder and you want to look at the header summaries for those you haven't yet read, you can display only the summaries with the "unread" status indicator (**U**) using the following command:

```
Msg 3 of 10: h -H:u
```

Note that you must include the colon character (:). However, when you display messages by status, you don't need to specify the **-H** option or even the **headers** command. These commands also display the unread messages:

```
h :u
:u
```

In all of these cases, Z-Mail displays the unread messages:

```
 6   U Dale Cooper   Jul  7 10:49  (20) Chapter 3
 9   N Albert        Jul 14 11:37  (28) Z-Mail chapters
10   ! Harry Truman  Jul 28 12:45  (66) review copies
```

In the previous example, message 6 is unread from a previous Z-Mail session, message 9 is new to this session, and message 10 is newly arrived.

Here's another example that finds all the messages that you've already replied to:

```
Msg 3 of 10: :r
```

In this case, you see a list like this:

```
7    r Dale Cooper Jul 21 10:49  (50) Coffee
8    r Eudora Moo  Jul 30 11:00  (17) Chapter 4
```

 The :d option is particularly useful for checking the deleted messages before updating the folder to make sure that you haven't deleted any that you really want to keep. In line mode, the **headers** command alone does not normally show deleted messages. To display only the deleted messages, type the following:

```
Msg 3 of 10: h :d
```

You see a display like this:

```
1   *   Andrei      Jul 15  8:00  (77) Romanian poets
5   *   Matt B.     Aug  5 23:46  (81) Chaos
```

Displaying Deleted Messages

In line mode, Z-Mail doesn't display deleted messages. In fullscreen and GUI mode, deleted messages appear in the message list, marked with an asterisk (*). If you want Z-Mail to always show the deleted messages when you display them with **headers** in line mode, set the **show_deleted** variable, as in the following example:

```
Msg 3 of 10: set show_deleted
```

Z-Mail displays all deleted messages along with the rest of the messages in the header summary display, marked with an asterisk. Now, you'll never have to use **h :d** to display deleted messages; they appear in the display by default. With **show_deleted** set, you can use the **print** and **type** commands to read deleted messages without restoring them first and the **pipe** command (discussed in Chapter 5), doesn't skip deleted messages. In GUI mode, Z-Mail allows you to read a deleted message regardless of whether you set **show_deleted** or not.

Note that you still can't use **next** or **dt** to display the next deleted message; these commands skip deleted messages, whether displayed or not.

Printing Messages

If you want to keep a hard copy of a message, you can send it directly to a printer from within Z-Mail using the **lpr** command. When you use **lpr**, Z-Mail passes the message off to the UNIX system print command (for example, *lpr* or *lp*). You can specify the print command to which to send your messages; we'll show you how in this section.

For example, use the **lpr** command to send message 1 to the printer:

```
Msg 3 of 10: lpr 1
```

Z-Mail displays the following message:

```
printing message 1 ... (30 lines)
```

Use a message list to print more than one message. For example, to print all the messages in your folder, type:

```
Msg 3 of 10: lpr *
```

This command sends each message, separated by a form feed, to the printer.

If you don't want to include the header information in the printed copy, use the **−n** option. For example, use the following command to print messages 3 and 4 without header information:

```
Msg 3 of 10: lpr −n 3,4
```

With the **−P** option, you can tell Z-Mail to send messages to a specific printer. For example, to send messages 4 through 6 to a printer called *apple7*, type the following command:

```
Msg 3 of 10: lpr −Papple7 4-6
```

 If you don't specify a printer, Z-Mail uses a default printer. If the **printer** variable is set, **lpr** sends messages to that printer, by default. For example, set the default printer to *apple7* like this:

```
Msg 3 of 10: set printer = apple7
```

Now, every time you use **lpr** during the current Z-Mail session, Z-Mail sends the messages to a printer named *apple7*; you don't need to specify the printer name with **−P**.

 You might want to use a command other than the default system command, **lpr**, to send messages to the printer. To do this, set the **print_cmd** variable. For example, to send your messages to a PostScript printer, you might use:

```
Msg 3 of 10: set print_cmd = 'lp −dps'
```

Now, when you print messages with **lpr**, Z-Mail uses the UNIX command **lp** with the option **−dps** to send the message to the PostScript printer.

Here's an example of how to use a device-independent *troff*-style program and pass arguments to it:

```
Msg 3 of 10: set print_cmd = 'eroff −dps −ms'
```

Now, when you print a list of messages with **lpr**, Z-Mail sends the messages through the *eroff* command and passes the **−dps** and **−ms** arguments to *eroff*. Note that if you send plain text messages (not *troff* source) to a *troff*-style program, the text might not look the way you want it to because *troff* turns on "fill mode."

On some systems, you can use a utility called *enscript* to converts plain text to PostScript. If your system includes this utility, you can set the print command to *enscript* so that you can print it on a PostScript printer:

```
Msg 3 of 10: set print_cmd = enscript
```

If you set **print_cmd**, Z-Mail ignores the value of **printer**, if set. If you use **−P** to specify a printer name for **lpr**, Z-Mail ignores this, too.

Picking Messages from the Display

Earlier in this chapter, we showed you how to display the header summaries for messages from a certain person or between a certain range of numbers using the **from** command. Other MUAs also provide this feature, but Z-Mail gives you even more control over which header summaries to display. One of the most useful features of Z-Mail is its ability to select all the messages in a folder that contain a specific pattern in a specific header using the **pick** command.

Let's say I kept a message in my system mailbox containing information about a project I'm working on and I want to go back and read the message. Unfortunately, I don't remember the message number. Instead of going through the folder, reading each message in hopes of finding that one message, I can use **pick** to display the header summaries for all the messages that contain the project name.

In addition, with the **pick** command, you can select messages from a particular person, sent on a specific date, or with a priority setting. I generally use **pick** instead of **from** because I like to select messages that contain a certain pattern in the headers, rather than simply on the basis of who sent them. (Note that **from** is useful for moving the current message pointer to a different message; you can't move the current message pointer with **pick**.)

Here's the syntax for **pick**:

```
pick [options] [pattern]
```

We describe the options to **pick** in Table 3-3.

Table 3-3. pick Options

Option	Description
+*n*	Specify the first *n* message numbers.
−*n*	Specify the last *n* numbers.
−ago *format*	Select messages relative to the current date.
−d [+ | −]*date*	Display messages sent on, after (**+**), or before (**−**) a specific *date*.
−e	Use all the following arguments as the pattern to match.
−f	Match the pattern in the **From** field.
−h *header*	Match the pattern in the specified *header* field.
−i	Ignore case when matching patterns.
−p *priority*	Select messages with the specified *priority* (**A–E**).
−r *message list*	Search only the specified message list.
−s	Match the pattern in the **Subject** field.
−t	Match the pattern in the **To** field.
−x	Display messages that *do not* match the specified pattern.

You can specify only one of the **−ago**, **−d**, **−f**, **−h**, **−p**, **−s**, or **−t** options in one **pick** command. Unless you specify one of these options, **pick** scans entire messages (both headers and body), including messages marked for deletion, for the *pattern*.

If you just want to display the last *n* messages that match a pattern, use the *–n* option; *+n* limits the display to the first *n* messages. For example, to display the last two messages, use:

```
Msg 3 of 10: pick -2
```

If your current folder has 10 messages, you see a display like the following:

```
Finding the last 2 messages
  9   Harry Truman   Aug 1 12:37  (20)  Coffee
 10   Albert         Aug 4 10:01  (8)   Review copies
```

Similarly, type this command to display the first five messages in the folder that contains the string "pick command":

```
Msg 3 of 10: pick +5 pick command
```

Z-Mail displays:

```
Finding the first 5 messages that contain "pick command"
```

followed by the messages that match the pattern.

Z-Mail interprets everything that follows the last option to **pick** as the string to search for. In other words, in the previous example, you don't need to put quotes around the string for Z-Mail to search for "pick command" (instead of "pick"). However, if you want to search for a string that begins with a dash character (–), you have to use the **–e** option to tell **pick** explicitly to interpret everything following the option as the string. So, if you wanted to pick messages that contain the string "-folder option", use this command:

```
Msg 3 of 10: pick -e -folder option
```

and you get this message:

```
Searching for messages that contain "-folder option"
```

Matching Patterns in Headers

Most of the time, I use **pick** to find all the messages from one person or with a specific word in the `Subject` header. Once you select these messages, you can then read them in sequence or manipulate them as a group.

As we explained earlier in this chapter, you can select all the messages from a particular person with the **from** command. For example, here's how to display messages from *george*:

```
Msg 3 of 10: from george
```

Another way to accomplish the same thing is to use **pick** with the **–f** option like this:

```
Msg 3 of 10: pick -f george
```

This finds all the messages with "george" in the `From` header.

Here's another example: a group of people have been discussing a certain topic over electronic mail and now your system mailbox contains these messages, as well as a bunch of others. You can use **pick** to select all the messages on that one topic so that you can read them in sequence, save them to a new folder, or delete them.

Use the –s option to select all the messages with the same pattern in the **Subject** header:

```
Msg 3 of 10: pick -s troff problems
```

This command searches and finds the messages with the string "troff problems" in the **Subject** header.

To save these messages to a folder called *troff_problems* to read later, type the following:

```
Msg 3 of 10: pick -s troff problems | save troff_problems
```

The pipe character (|) allows you to combine two or more Z-Mail commands (in this case, **pick** and **save**). We'll explain more about this in Chapter 5, *Z-Mail Shortcuts, Bells, and Whistles*. If you want to read the messages in the *troff_problems* file now, switch to the folder with this command:

```
Msg 3 of 10: folder troff_problems
```

We'll explain more about combining Z-Mail commands with pipes and switching folders in Chapter 5.

You can use the –i option to tell **pick** to ignore the case of letters when searching for the pattern. To find all the messages with "troff problems" as the **Subject** regardless of case (including strings like "Troff problems" and "TROFF PROBLEMS"), type the following:

```
Msg 3 of 10: pick -i -s troff problems
```

You're probably thinking that the command line looks like more than you'll ever want to type in just to find messages with a certain header. I didn't use this feature very much until I learned how to create command-line aliases with the **cmd** command. Command-line aliases are only available in the line mode. Briefly, a *command-line alias* is a short name that you can use to run a long command, a command with a lot of options (like the **pick** command in our example), or a series of commands.[2]

To create a command-line alias, enter **cmd**, followed by the short name, and finally the long command. So, to create a command-line alias to run the **pick** command and options in the previous example, enter a command like the following:

```
Msg 3 of 10: cmd pS 'pick -i -s'
```

 Now, to pick messages on a subject such as Z-Mail, I can use a command like the following:

```
Msg 3 of 10: pS Z-Mail
```

I chose the name "pS" for my command-line alias so that it did not get confused with the UNIX command **pS**, as described in this section "Using UNIX Commands from within Z-Mail," in Chapter 5. We'll explain **cmd** in more detail in Chapter 5.

Z-Mail also allows you to search other headers, such as **To** and **Cc**, for patterns. For example, sometimes messages in your folder aren't addressed specifically to you; rather they're sent to *mail aliases* which you belong to (see Chapter 4, *Sending Mail with Z-Mail*, for information on creating mail aliases). I like to pick out messages that are addressed to me personally and read them first. You can do this by searching for messages with particular patterns in the **To** line, using the –t option to **pick**. Note that **pick –t** also searches the **Cc** lines.

For example, to find the messages with my address listed specifically on the **To** or **Cc** lines, I use:

> Msg 3 of 10: `pick -t hanna`

To find all the messages in your folder that are addressed to the *docland* alias, use **-t**:

> Msg 3 of 10: `pick -t docland`

What if you're looking for a pattern that's not in the **From**, **To**, or **Subject** headers? Let's say, for example, that you want to pick the messages that have a specific name in the **Resent-From** line. Using the **-h** option, you can specify another header, like **Resent-From**, to search. Here's how to find all the resent from *karl* (messages that include "karl" in the **Resent-From** line):

> Msg 3 of 10: `pick -h resent-from karl`

You see the following message:

`Searching for messages that contain "karl" in the message header "resent-from:"`

The **pick** command ignores case in the header (thus **pick** finds the **Resent-From** header even though I indicated "resent-from") but case sensitivity still applies to the search string (unless you also include the **-i** option).

If you have a lot of messages in your folder, sometimes you'll want to search for the ones that *don't* explicitly contain your name in the **To** or **Cc** lines. Here's how to display all the messages that aren't addressed specifically to you by combining the **-x** with **-t**:

> Msg 3 of 12: `pick -x -t hanna`

and you see the following message:

`Searching for messages that do not contain "hanna" from the To: field`

Note that you can't use **-x** with the **+n** or **-n** options.

Here's a command-line alias I use to pick out all the messages that aren't addressed specifically to me:

> Msg 3 of 10: `cmd notme 'pick -x -t hanna'`

Now, simply enter **notme** at the Z-Mail command line to display these messages. Then, I can delete these messages with this command:

> Msg 3 of 10: `notme | delete`

Picking Messages by Date

You can also pick a message to display using the date the message was sent. This is useful for finding old messages that you want to remove. To do this, use the **-ago** and **-d** options. Note that if you use either of these options, you can't also specify a *pattern*.

The **–ago** (**–a**) option allows you to display messages by specific dates relative to the current date. Use this format:

```
pick —a n format
```

The *format* is either **days**, **weeks**, or **months**; *n* is a number. Z-Mail translates dates that you specify with **–ago** into days; thus, months are 30.5 days long. If you need a more precise date selection, use **–d** to specify exact dates. Note that you can abbreviate both the **–ago** option and the format specifiers to the first character of the word.

Here's one way to display all the messages that are one week old:

```
Msg 3 of 10: pick —ago 1 week
```

Another way to do this is with the *days* format:

```
Msg 3 of 10: pick —ago 7 days
```

Here's what this command looks like if you abbreviate the options:

```
Msg 3 of 10: pick —a 7d
```

You can also combine the format specifiers. For example, this command finds all the messages in the folder that are exactly one week and two days old:

```
Msg 3 of 10: pick —a 1w2d
```

To specify messages that were sent more than a number of days or weeks ago, use the **–** (before) and **+** (after) arguments with the format specifier. Thus, to pick out all the messages older than one week, use the command:

```
Msg 3 of 10: pick —a —1w
```

You might want to use this feature to clean out old messages in your *mbox* folder. For example, here's how to delete messages that are older than three months:

```
Msg 3 of 10: folder —N mbox ; pick —a —3m | delete
```

This switches to *mbox*, selects messages that are older than three months, and then deletes them.

Use **close** to update and close *mbox* and switch back to the system mailbox. (You can also use the **shut** command to close folders.) We'll explain more about this when we talk about switching and closing folders in Chapter 5, *Z-Mail Shortcuts, Bells, and Whistles*.

Specifying the Date Format

The **–d** option allows you to display messages sent on a particular *date*. The format for *date* looks like this:

```
[month] / [day] / [year]
```

You must include at least one slash character (/) in your date specification. Any pieces of the date (such as *month*) that you omit default to the current date. So, to specify June 1 of the current year, type the following:

```
6/1
```

The third of August (if the current month is August) looks like this:

```
/3/
```

Here's how to specify today's date in 1990:

```
//90
```

Use this command to display messages sent on October 17, 1989:

```
Msg 3 of 10: pick —d 10/17/89
```

To display messages sent before or after the specified date, use the — (before) and + (after) arguments. For example, use the following command to pick all the messages that were sent on or before November 26, 1990:

```
Msg 3 of 10: pick —d —11/26/90
```

If you want to display messages that were sent on or after a specific date in the current year, use the plus (+) argument. For example, this command selects the messages sent on or after November 26 of the current year:

```
Msg 3 of 10: pick —d +11/26
```

Here's how to display all the messages sent on or before the third day of the current month:

```
Msg 3 of 10: pick —d —/3
```

Use this command to display messages sent on or after the current date in 1990:

```
Msg 3 of 10: pick —d +//90
```

 If you want to read all the messages sent on the current date, use the slash (/) date format by itself. For example:

```
Msg 3 of 10: pick —d /
```

Here's a command-line alias that you can use to display today's messages:

```
Msg 3 of 10: cmd today 'pick —d /'
```

Now, simply enter **today** at the Z-Mail prompt.

Suppressing pick Descriptions

By default, **pick** displays a description of the search before performing the search unless you pipe the results of the **pick** operation to another Z-Mail command. For example, if you enter the following:

```
Msg 3 of 10: pick —s Chapter 2
```

Z-Mail displays this message:

```
Searching for messages that contain "Chapter 2" in the subject line.
```

However, if you use a pipe (|) to send the results of the **pick** command above to another Z-Mail command, Z-Mail does not display this message. For example, to forward the messages that contain "Chapter 2" in the Subject line to *dale*, you enter the following:

```
Msg 3 of 10: pick —s Chapter 2 | mail —f dale
```

In this case, Z-Mail doesn't give the description message.

You can specify that **pick** never display the description of the search operation. You'll find this useful when you use **pick** in scripts (see Chapter 8, *Customizing Z-Mail*, and Chapter 9, *Writing Scripts and Functions*, for information on creating scripts and functions). To suppress **pick** descriptions, include the word "pick" in the value of the **quiet** variable:

```
Msg 3 of 10: set quiet = pick
```

We'll explain **quiet** in more detail in Chapter 8.

Marking Messages

Now you know how to pick out messages based on certain patterns. What happens if you have a group of messages that you want to manipulate together, but they don't have a common pattern? For example, you might have five messages from different people on unrelated topics, all of which are very high priority. With Z-Mail, you can "mark" these messages with temporary tags or permanent priority marks and then display and manipulate them together using **pick**.

Temporary Marks

Let's say you have a message that requires some research before you can send a response. If you plan to respond during this Z-Mail session, you can create a temporary mark on the message to remind you to come back to it later. Use the **mark** command to mark the message with the plus character (+). The + is temporary; when you update the folder or quit Z-Mail, the mark isn't saved.

Here's how to create a temporary mark:

```
Msg 3 of 10: mark 10
```

The + character appears to the left of the status indicator (if any) for message 10 like this:

```
10 +U  Dale Cooper  Jul 21 10:49  (16)   zipcode for Seattle
```

 You can now display the header summaries for all the messages with temporary marks using the **–H:m** option to **headers**. For example:

```
Msg 3 of 10: headers —H:m
```

Remember, you can abbreviate this command as simply **:m**.

Marking a Message with a Priority

If you want to retain the mark when you quit Z-Mail, mark the message with a priority status letter (**A–E**, with **A** having the highest priority). Z-Mail saves these settings when you update the folder. Here's an example of how to assign top priority (**A**) to message 5:

```
Msg 3 of 10: mark —A 5
```

Now, when you list the header summaries, the **A** appears to the right of the message number like this:

```
5 A  Jimmy Chuck   Jul 14 11:37  (28)   README!
```

Messages may have both a temporary mark and a priority setting; however, if a message has both, the temporary mark character (**+**) takes precedence over the priority-setting character. Note that messages can have only one priority setting.

Picking Messages by Priority

 After marking messages with priority settings, you can select them using the **—p** option to **pick**. For example, let's say you marked messages 2, 4, and 7 with priority **C**; use this command to display them:

```
Msg 4 of 10: pick —p C
```

You can use multiple **—p** options to pick messages with several priorities. Here's an example of how to pick out all messages marked with either priority **A** or **C**:

```
Msg 4 of 10: pick —p A —p C
```

You see something like this (if you didn't set **quiet** to "pick"):

```
Searching for priority messages
   5 A  Jimmy Chuck   Jul 14 11:37  (28)   README!
   8 C  Dale Cooper   Jul 30  1:01  (40)   Important
```

Removing Marks

Because priority settings are saved when you update the folder, and even when you move messages to other folders, you'll probably want to strip the priority status mark when it loses its importance. To remove the priority, use this command:

```
Msg 3 of 10: mark —
```

Let's remove the setting for message 5:

```
Msg 3 of 10: mark — 5
```

Note that this command removes the priority setting, but does not *unmark* the message; the temporary mark + (if any) remains. To remove the temporary mark, use the **unmark** command:

```
Msg 3 of 10: unmark 5
```

Organizing Your Messages

In this section, we'll explain a little more about folders and how to use them to organize your messages. As we explained in Chapter 2, *Getting Started*, a folder is simply a file that contains messages with header information.[3] Regular files might contain messages, but not header information. This is an important distinction when you want to save messages to a folder that already exists or when switching folders.

In the next section, we'll show you how to use filename metacharacters to refer to special directories.

What Are Filename Metacharacters?

Filename metacharacters are special characters that are interpreted differently by Z-Mail. In Z-Mail, two metacharacters, the tilde (˜) and the plus sign (+), refer to special directories. As in the C shell and the Korn shell, the ˜ metacharacter refers to your home directory. When you refer to files in your home directory, you must include the slash (/) between the tilde and the filename, like this:

```
˜/chocolate
```

The reason for this is that you can refer to files in another person's home directory by specifying their name after the tilde, like this:

```
˜george/avocado
```

If you don't put the slash between the tilde and the filename, Z-Mail thinks *chocolate* is a person's name instead of a file in your home directory and gives you the following error:

```
˜chocolate: no such user: chocolate
```

The + character refers to your folder directory, *˜/Mail* by default. (We'll show you how to change the name of your folder directory later in this chapter.) When you refer to folders in your folder directory, the slash character (/) is optional; both of the following two examples reference the same file in the folder directory:

```
+conversation
+/conversation
```

---

[3] Some Mail Transport Agents (MTAs) also use special strings (for example, some versions of MMDF use four CTRL-A's) to separate messages stored in folders; if these strings are missing, Z-Mail won't recognize the file as a folder.

Saving Messages to Folders

Folders are files containing mail messages along with their header information. Files that contain message text without headers or a mixture of messages with and without their headers are not folders. You can read mail folders just like you read your system mailbox; we'll explain more about this in Chapter 5, *Z-Mail Shortcuts, Bells, and Whistles*.

You create new folders by saving messages from the system mailbox (or "spool folder") with the **save** (**s**) command. This command includes the header information with the saved message.

If you don't specify a folder name with **save**, Z-Mail saves messages to the *mbox* folder in your home directory. To save messages to a folder other than the default *mbox*, enter the folder name after the command. For example, to save the current message in the folder to *chapter.3* in the current directory, type the following:

```
Msg 3 of 10: s chapter.3
```

If the filename already exists, **save** appends the message to the folder; otherwise **save** creates a new file with the message.

If you use **save** to save a message to a file that isn't a folder (that is, it doesn't contain header information), Z-Mail displays this message:

```
"chapter.3": not a folder, save anyway? [n] _
```

Press RETURN to cancel the **save** command. To append the message (with its headers) to the file, enter **y**.

You can change the default folder that Z-Mail uses by setting the **mbox** variable. For example, here's how to tell Z-Mail to save messages to *saved.mail* in your home directory instead of the *mbox* folder:

```
Msg 3 of 10: set mbox = ~/saved.mail
```

Now, when use **save** without specifying a filename, Z-Mail saves the message to *~/saved.mail*.

Saving Messages to Files

Sometimes, you don't want to save the header information with the message. For example, let's say someone sends you the *troff* source to a document. If you saved the message with **save**, you'd have to edit the file to remove all the headers before you could print out the document. The **write** (**w**) command is identical to **save** except that it saves the body of the message without headers to a plain text file.

By default, if you specify an existing filename with **write**, Z-Mail appends the message to the file. If the file doesn't exist, **write** creates it.

If you use **write** to save a message to an existing file that contains header information (the file is a mail folder), you see a message like the following:

```
CAUTION: "zmail.spec" is a folder.  Write anyway? [n] _
```

You probably don't want to do things like this because Z-Mail appends the current message to the text of the last message in *zmail.spec*. You won't be able to read the message separately when you switch to that folder. Instead, enter **n** and either use **save** to save the message with its headers, or specify another filename. Use **write** to save messages to plain text files only.

By default, both **save** and **write** append messages to the file that you specify. (If you want to overwrite the contents of a file or folder with the message, use the **−f** (for "force") or **!** option). For example, use the following command to replace the contents of *chapter.3* with the text from message 5:

```
Msg 3 of 10: write −f 5 chapter.3
```

Changing and Listing Directories

When you're saving messages to files, it's handy to be able to switch to new directories and list the files. You can do this from within Z-Mail using the **cd**, **pwd**, and **ls** commands. These commands work exactly like the UNIX commands with the same names.

If you use **cd** with no arguments, Z-Mail changes the current directory to your home directory. By default, Z-Mail uses the directory specified by the **HOME** environment variable as your home directory.

Keeping Saved Messages

If the current folder is the system mailbox, the messages that you save with **save** and **write** are marked with an 3 in the status indicator field and then deleted when you update the folder or quit Z-Mail. If you use **dt** to delete the current message and display the next or when you use **next** (**n**), Z-Mail skips over these saved messages as if they were deleted. (You can still read saved messages using **print**, **type**, or by entering the message number.)

If you don't want Z-Mail to delete messages when you quit, use the **copy** (**c**) command to save them; **copy** is identical to **save** except that it doesn't mark the message as saved. If you don't want Z-Mail to delete *any* of the messages that you save, set the **keepsave** variable. With **keepsave** set, you have to remove saved messages from your system mailbox manually using the **delete** command.

Organizing Messages by Subject

People use different methods for organizing messages into files and folders. Some people like to use the name of the author as the folder name; others organize messages by the subject or the current month.

With Z-Mail, you can save a message to a file with the same name as the **Subject** line by using the **−s** option with **save**, **write**, or **copy**. When you use these options, Z-Mail converts spaces, apostrophes ('), and slash (**/**) characters in the **Subject** line to underscores (**_**) in the filename.

Say, for example, you have this message in your folder:

```
> 1   r Dale Cooper Aug 7  10:49  (20) Hanna's Chapters
```

If you enter the following command to save the message with its header information:

```
Msg 1 of 10: save -s 1
```

Z-Mail saves message 1 to a folder called *Hanna_s_Chapters*.[4]

If you specify more than one message to save, the -s option saves the messages to separate files, using the message `Subject` of each message as the filename. For example, if someone sent you several chapters of a book in separate mail messages, you could save them all to separate filenames by entering one command. Let's say your folder contains the following header summaries:

```
> 1   Dale Cooper  Jul 20 23:09  (864)  Chapter one
  2   Dale Cooper  Jul 21  1:37  (1238) Chapter two
  3 N Dale Cooper  Jul 21  1:45  (900)  Chapter three
```

Type the following command to save each message without header information to separate files:

```
Msg 1 of 10: write -s 1-3
```

This saves the messages to three files: *Chapter_one*, *Chapter_two*, and *Chapter_three*.

If you use -S instead of -s, Z-Mail saves all the messages to one filename, specified by the `Subject` line of the lowest message number in the list. In our example, if you type:

```
Msg 1 of 10: write -S 1-3
```

Z-Mail saves messages 1 through 3 (without headers) to a file called *Chapter_one*.

Organizing Messages by Author

If you're one of those people who likes to keep all the messages from one person together in one folder, you can use the -a or -A option with the **save**, **write**, or **copy** commands. These options save the message to a file with the same name as the author (the person you'd send a message to if you use **reply**). Let's say you have these messages in your folder:[5]

```
> 1   dan      Jul 21 10:49  (20)   Espresso bar
  2   bart     Jul 21 11:37  (709)  Chapter two
  3 N dale     Jul 21 11:48  (30)   Re: Z-Mail Chapters
  4   dale     Jul 29 23:00  (55)   review comments
  5   bart     Jul 29 23:32  (69)   Re: review comments
  6 N dan      Jul 29 23:59  (78)   Re: review comments
```

---

[4] On some UNIX System V systems, the filename is limited to the first 14 characters. Note that the character limit for filenames depends on your system.

[5] In this example, we modified the header summary format to show the login names of the authors (see the section "Customizing with Variables," later in this chapter for more information on how to do this).

Use the following command to save messages 1 through 3 to the filenames *dan*, *bart*, and *dale*, respectively:

```
Msg 1 of 10: save —a 1-3
```

In the example above, messages 4, 5, and 6 are about "review comments" and you want to save them all to a folder named *dale* (the person who originated the discussion of "review comments" by sending message 4). To do this, you type:

```
Msg 1 of 10: save —A 4,5,6
```

Organizing Folders

You can put mail folders anywhere you want—simply specify the UNIX pathname when you save messages. (You must have write permission to save messages to folders that aren't in your directory.) To help you organize your folders, Z-Mail uses a special directory in your home directory called the *Mail* folder directory.

Figure 3-1 demonstrates how you can organize messages in the folder directory.

Just as the tilde character (˜) refers to your home directory, the plus sign (**+**) is a special character that refers to the special folder directory. So, if you want to save message 4 to the folder called *project* in the folder directory, use this command:

```
Msg 3 of 10: s 4 +project
```

The slash character (/) is optional when referring to folders; both *+project* and *+/project* refer to the same file in the folder directory. The command in the previous example saves message 4 to */u/hanna/Mail/project*.

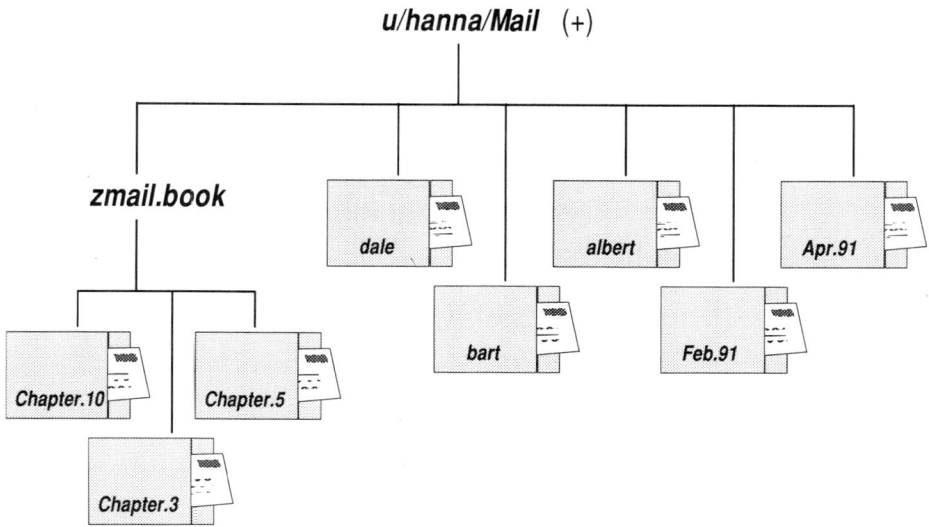

Figure 3-1. Organizing messages into folders

You'll probably want to create subdirectories in ˜/*Mail* so you can further organize messages by project or author. To do this, use *mkdir* from the UNIX prompt. For example, let's create a directory under ˜/*Mail* called *zmail.book*:

```
$ mkdir ~/Mail/zmail.book
```

Now, you can save messages to folders within this subdirectory using a command line like the following:

```
Msg 3 of 10: s 2-6 +zmail.book/from.dale
```

Listing the Folders in the Folder Directory

The next example demonstrates an easy way to list the names of all the folders in your folder directory:

```
Msg 3 of 10: folders
```

Z-Mail displays something like the following:

```
/u/hanna/Mail:
doc     fun      zmail.book

/u/hanna/Mail/fun:
bicycle      cookies      film

/u/hanna/Mail/zmail.book:
Chapter.10  Chapter.3  Chapter.5  Chapter.7  Chapter.9  review
Chapter.2   Chapter.4  Chapter.6  Chapter.8  from.dale
```

Note that **folders** doesn't list any hidden files; that is, files that begin with a dot character (.). This command also does not list any regular files (not folders) that might be in the folder directory. Remember that a folder must contain headers as well as message text.

Another way to list the contents of your folder directory is to use the **ls** command:

```
Msg 3 of 10: ls -FR $folder
```

The **ls** command in Z-Mail works almost exactly like the UNIX system command with the same name; it displays the directory listing in columns by default. The **–F** option puts the slash character after directory names and **–R** tells **ls** to list any subdirectories recursively. The dollar sign character ($) tells Z-Mail to substitute **folder** with the value of the **folders** variable. We'll explain more about referring to Z-Mail variables in Chapter 5, *Z-Mail Shortcuts, Bells, and Whistles*. In the next section, we'll show you how to change the value of **folder**.

The **ls** command doesn't list the name of the folder directory, so you get something like this:

```
doc     fun/      zmail.book/

/u/hanna/Mail/fun:
bicycle      cookies      film

/u/hanna/Mail/zmail.book:
Chapter.10  Chapter.3  Chapter.5  Chapter.7  Chapter.9  review
Chapter.2   Chapter.4  Chapter.6  Chapter.8  from.dale
```

The **ls** command can't distinguish between plain text files and folders, so if you have any plain text files in your folder directory, **ls** lists them along with the folders.

Changing the Name of the Folder Directory

If you don't want to use ~/*Mail* as your folder directory, you can change it by setting the **folder** variable as shown below:

```
Msg 3 of 10: set folder = ~/.Folders
```

Now, whenever you execute commands that recognize the plus character (**+**) as the folder directory, Z-Mail uses the ~/.*Folders* directory instead. For example, if you enter the following command:

```
Msg 3 of 10: s 10 +doc
```

you save message 10 to ~/.*Folders/doc*.

When you use the **folders** command, Z-Mail lists the folders in the directory specified by the **folder** variable. So now, with the **folder** variable set to ~/.*Folders*, when you use the **folders** command, you see a display such as:

```
/u/hanna/.Folders:
doc
```

Sorting Folders

Earlier in this chapter, we explained how to select messages from a folder based on certain criteria, such as the author, the subject, or the date the message was sent. In this section, we'll show you how to arrange all the messages in the folder by similar criteria using the **sort** command.

By default, the MTA delivers messages to your system mailbox, arranging messages in the order they were received; the most recently received message last. When you save messages to other folders, they are appended to the folder in the order in which you saved them. You might want to change the order in which the header summaries appear.

For example, because sometimes messages aren't received in the order they were sent, a response to a specific message might arrive before the original message. For this reason, you might want to sort the messages in your mailbox by the date they were sent rather than when you received them.

Another example is if you want to group together all the messages from the same person; you can sort the folder in alphabetical order by the name of the person who sent the message.

If you don't specify any options, **sort** arranges the messages by status (the character in the status indicator field). When sorting by status, Z-Mail places messages in the order described in Table 3-4.

Table 3-4. Sort Status Order

Order	Status	Status Indicator
1	New	N
2	Unread	U
3	Preserved	P
4	Replied-to	r
5	Printed	p
6	Marked	+
7	Read	(blank)
8	Deleted	*

If the messages in the folder have the same status, for example, unread (**U**), **sort** orders messages by priority marks (**A** through **E**). Use the **–r** option to reverse the status order.

The options to the **sort** command are listed in Table 3-5.

Table 3-5. Sort Options

Option	Description
–i	Ignore case when sorting alphabetically.
–r	Reverse the sort order of the option that follows.
–a	Sort alphabetically by author (**To** line).
–d	Sort by **Date** field (default).
–l	Sort by message length (smallest to largest).
–p	Sort by message priority (**A** to **E**).
–r	Reverses the sort order.
–R	Sort alphabetically by **Subject** line (including the **Re:** as part of the **Subject**).
–s	Sort alphabetically by **Subject** line (disregarding **Re:**).
–S	Sort by message status.

Z-Mail recognizes **sort** options even if you don't precede them with the dash character (–). If you use the – alone, Z-Mail interprets it as **–r**. You can use any combination of these options when you sort messages. If you use more than one option, **sort** applies the list of criteria from left to right.

To ignore the case of letters when you sort alphabetically (using the **–a**, **–s**, and **–R** options), specify the **–i** option. Thus, if you want to sort the **Subject** lines alphabetically, regardless of case, use this command:

```
Msg 3 of 10: sort –i –s
```

This example sorts the **To** lines alphabetically, ignoring case, then sorts the messages from each author alphabetically by **Subject**.

If you want to reverse the sort order, use **–r**. This option reverses the order of the first option that follows it. If you specify more than one **–r** option in succession, **sort** ignores all but the rightmost **–r**, only reversing the order of the option that follows it. Here's an example of how to sort messages by the `Subject` line in reverse alphabetical order (z to a):

```
Msg 3 of 10: sort -r -s
```

Z-Mail displays the `Subject` headers in header summary list in reverse alphabetical order, like the following:

```
    1  r Albert       Jul 17 10:01  ( 8)      zipcode for Seattle
 >  2    Dale Cooper  Jul 17 10:49  (16)      Re: zipcode for Seattle
    3  r Dale Cooper  Jul 20 16:17  (45)      coffee and donuts
    4  U Harry Truman Jul 20 12:37  (20)      Z-Mail testing
    5  N Jimmy Chuck  Jul 25 11:37  (28)      Thanks for the pie!
    6  N Lucie        Jul 25 11:48  (30)      Coffee
```

Let's say you want to group together all the messages that are responses to a previous message. In this case, use a command like the following:

```
Msg 3 of 10: sort -i -R
```

This command sorts the folder alphabetically by `Subject`, grouping together all the messages with `Re:` in the subject.

To sort the folder so that all the marked messages appear first, sort by priority using the **–p** option. Z-Mail places any marked messages first, followed by messages marked as priorities **A** through **E**, and lastly, the messages with neither a mark nor a priority setting.

To sort your folder by the date the messages were sent (sorted by date with the most recently sent message last), use the **–d** option. If you want **–d** to sort messages by the date that you received them instead, set the **date_received** variable:

```
Msg 3 of 10: set date_received
```

This example sorts the folder alphabetically by author and then sorts the messages for each author by reverse date, placing the most recent message first:

```
Msg 3 of 10: sort -a -r -d
```

Note that, in this example, the **–r** option applies only to the **–d** option. If you want to reverse the sort order of both author and date, you would enter:

```
Msg 3 of 10: sort -r -a -r -d
```

Group the **sort** options together if you prefer. The following three commands are identical:

```
sort -r -a -r -d
sort -ra -rd
sort -rard
```

When I don't have a lot of time to read my mail, sometimes I sort my messages by size, so that I can find the shortest messages and read them quickly. To sort the messages in your folder by size (number of characters, not number of lines), smallest to largest, use the **–l** option. To sort from largest to smallest, include the **–r** option immediately before **–l**.

Ordering Messages at Startup Time

By default, messages are arranged in folders by the date they were received (or saved) with the most recently received message last. If you want Z-Mail to sort your messages differently when you invoke Z-Mail, set the **sort** variable in your initialization file.

To sort the system mailbox by status at startup time, set the **sort** variable:

```
Msg 3 of 10: set sort
```

To sort messages by another criteria, for example, by author (**From** line), use the same options that you used with the **sort** command. See Table 3-5 for the list of options. Here's how to sort messages by author name using the **sort** command:

```
Msg 3 of 10: sort —a
```

And here's how you would do it by setting the **sort** variable:

```
Msg 3 of 10: set sort = —a
```

Note that setting **sort** in your initialization file only applies the sort order to the system mailbox at startup time. If you start Z-Mail reading a different folder or you switch to a new folder, the messages in that folder are arranged in the order in which they were saved.

If you ordinarily sort your system mailbox by the date the message was sent, you might want to change the sort order when you switch to different folders. For example, to switch to the **mbox** folder and sort the messages by date, use this command:

```
Msg 3 of 10: folder mbox ; sort —d
```

We'll cover the commands and shortcuts that you can use to switch folders in Chapter 5, *Z-Mail Shortcuts, Bells, and Whistles*.

Exiting Z-Mail

When you've finished selecting, reading, printing, deleting, saving, and otherwise manipulating your messages and you're ready to leave the Z-Mail program, use the **quit** (**q**) or **exit** (**x**) commands. To update all the open folders and quit Z-Mail, use **quit**; to exit immediately without making changes to any of the open folders, use **exit**.

When you use **quit**, Z-Mail automatically removes any messages that you delete or save with the **save** or **write** commands from all your open folders. If your current folder is the system mailbox when you quit, any messages that you've read (but not deleted) remain in your system mailbox, by default. For example, when I enter **q**, Z-Mail displays a message like this:

```
Updating "/usr/spool/mail/hanna" saved: 3 messages
```

If you want Z-Mail to move messages that you've read from your system mailbox to your *mbox* file automatically, unset the **hold** variable:

```
Msg 3 of 10: unset hold
```

In this case, Z-Mail doesn't retain read messages in your system mailbox. Now, if you want to hold specific messages, use the **preserve (pre)** command. When you preserve a message, the status indicator for the message changes to a **P**.

If you decide to remove that "preserve" status from a message so that Z-Mail moves it to your *mbox* file when you quit, use **unpreserve** (the **P** status indicator disappears).

I prefer to leave all the messages in my system mailbox unless I explicitly save or delete them, so I set the **hold** variable to keep Z-Mail from moving my messages to *mbox*. Note that this is the default behavior of Z-Mail. As you can see, "holding" and "preserving" are basically the same. You can make your life simpler (so that you don't have to remember two different terms for the same thing), by creating your own command-line alias with **cmd** like this:

```
Msg 3 of 10: cmd hold preserve
```

Now, **hold** keeps one message in your system mailbox and **set hold** keeps them all.

Note that, when you set **hold**, Z-Mail doesn't set the **P** status indicator for all your messages, but the messages still remain in the system mailbox when you quit.

By default, when you update your system mailbox folder, Z-Mail automatically deletes the messages that you saved with **save** or **write**. This behavior is specific to the system mailbox; saved messages remain in other folders until you explicitly delete them.

To prevent Z-Mail from removing a message that you've saved to another file or folder, use **preserve** on the messages to retain. If you don't want Z-Mail to remove *any* saved messages, set the **keepsave** variable:

```
Msg 3 of 10: set keepsave
```

Even if you've saved a message to another folder, Z-Mail retains a copy in your system mailbox.

If new mail arrives after you enter **quit**, but before Z-Mail updates the folder, you see the new mail message and the following prompt:

```
New mail -- Really Quit?  (y/n) [n]
```

Press RETURN to cancel the **quit** command or **y** to exit Z-Mail. The **exit** command doesn't check for new mail when you exit.

You might get the following message when you use the **exit** or **quit** commands:

```
Warning: Abort suspended compositions? (y/c) cancel _
```

If this happens, you've left an unfinished message in the background. To exit, you'll need to either select **y** to abort the compositions or press RETURN to cancel the **quit** command. Then, send the job (or cancel) the message. We'll explain how to suspend and restart messages in Chapter 4, *Sending Mail with Z-Mail*.

When you leave Z-Mail with **quit**, any "new and unread" (marked with **N** or **!**) messages that you didn't read during the current session return to your system mailbox. The next time you invoke Z-Mail, these messages appear as "old and unread" (marked with **U**). For example, let's say you have this message in your folder when you quit Z-Mail:

```
11  N Jimmy Chuck   Jul 14 12:45  (20) I HATE this game!
```

When you invoke Z-Mail again, the header summary looks something like the following:

```
 8  U Jimmy Chuck   Jul 14 12:45  (20)  I HATE this game!
```

Note that the **N** changes to **U** and the message number changes.

Ignoring the End-of-file Character

By default, if you press the end-of-file character (CTRL-D) at the line-mode prompt, you exit Z-Mail without updating the folder (as if you used **exit**). You can change this default behavior using the **ignoreeof** variable.

If you set **ignoreeof** as a boolean variable (with no value), when you press CTRL-D, Z-Mail does not exit and sounds the terminal bell.

You can also set **ignoreeof** to execute a Z-Mail command. For example, here's how to set **ignoreeof** to display an error message:

```
Msg 3 of 10: set ignoreeof="echo 'Use the quit command to quit Z-Mail.'"
```

We use the **echo** command to print out the arguments that you give it; you'll see more examples of **echo** in upcoming chapters. The **ignoreeof** setting prints the following message whenever you press CTRL-D at the line-mode prompt:

```
Use the quit command to quit Z-Mail.
```

Here's another example of an **ignoreeof** setting that tells Z-Mail to update the current folder (without exiting) when you press CTRL-D:

```
Msg 3 of 10: set ignoreeof = update
```

The next section explains what happens when you update the folder with the **update** command.

Updating the Current Folder

To update your current folder without exiting Z-Mail, use the **update** (**u**) command. When you use **update**, Z-Mail deletes and saves messages as if you used **quit**. Any messages with **N** in the status indicator field retain the "new and unread" status when you update the folder with **update**; if you use **quit**, the status indicator of these messages changes to **U** ("old and unread").

You can update the folder and prevent any further modifications by switching it to read-only mode using the **-r** option:

```
Msg 3 of 10: u -r
```

If you want to retain the **N** status of any messages that you didn't read during the current Z-Mail session when you exit, create this command-line alias with **cmd**:

```
Msg 3 of 10: cmd quit "update;exit"
```

We'll explain folders in more detail in Chapter 5.

Updating Folders Automatically Before Exiting

If you dial in over a phone line to read mail, and you unexpectedly lose the connection, then Z-Mail exits the current folder without updating. If you want Z-Mail to update the folder before exiting in this situation, set the **hangup** variable:

```
Msg 3 of 10: set hangup
```

Unless Z-Mail encounters a write error, the folder contains only those messages that were not deleted at the time the disconnect occurred. If Z-Mail encounters a write error, it preserves both the current temporary file and as much of the current folder as possible. However, if an error occurs when Z-Mail loads new mail before the update, you lose the new mail.

Customizing with Variables

In addition to the variables we've discussed in the context of using various commands in this chapter, there are several other Z-Mail variables you might find handy when reading and managing your messages. The following sections describe these variables.

Displaying Warning Messages

If your Z-Mail environment was set up by another user or the system administrator, you might want to set the **warning** variable:

```
Msg 3 of 10: set warning
```

You can use **warning** to notify you of any routines or assertions that fail, but aren't fatal enough to interrupt Z-Mail execution. With **warning** set, Z-Mail also warns you of any changes in the default environment in these situations:

- The date format of a message is unknown.

- You unset a variable without first setting it.

- A command-line alias (created with **cmd**) is identical to a Z-Mail command.

- Z-Mail can't find a header for a digest article.

If Z-Mail does not recognize the date format in the **Date** header of one of the messages in your folder, it searches other headers for a valid date. If none are found, Z-Mail displays a message like the following:

```
Unknown date format: Mon, 4 1991 20:56:06 PST
```

(This date might be the date you received the message rather than the date it was sent.)

Another situation where Z-Mail warns you is when you try to unset a variable before setting it. Let's say the **pager** variable hasn't been set and you enter this command:

```
Msg 3 of 10: unset pager
```

You get a warning like this:

```
unset: pager not set
```

The **warning** variable is particularly useful if you're new to Z-Mail or electronic mail in general.

Changing the Header Summary Format

By default, when you use the **headers** command in line mode, header summaries in your folder look something like this:

```
1    Dale Cooper <cooper@tp.go Jul 29, (6/701) "Re: Review Copies"
```

(Note that the address field is truncated in this example.)

You can change the format of the header summaries by setting the **hdr_format** variable to a different string. You can use special formatting characters that begin with the percent sign (%) in your **hdr_format** variable setting. For example, Z-Mail uses this **hdr_format** setting to display the header summary in the previous example:

```
set hdr_format ='%24f %M %-2N, (%l/%c) "%25s"'
```

The special formatting characters are listed in Table 3-6. If you're familiar with the C programming language, you'll recognize this type of format from the **printf** function. You can also use these special formatting characters in the **in_reply_to** and $[%fmt] variables, and in the three **indent_str** variable settings; we'll describe these variables in Chapter 4, *Sending Mail with Z-Mail*, and Chapter 9, *Writing Scripts and Functions*.

Table 3-6. hdr_format Special Formatting Characters

Character	Description
%a	Author's address.
%c	Number of characters (in bytes) in the message.
%d	Message date.*
%f	From field (author's name and address).
%i	Message-ID number (if present).
%l	Number of lines in the message.
%m	Month number of the message date.
%M	Month name of the message date.
%n	Name of the author.
%N	Day of the month (number).
%p	Priority of the message.
%s	Subject of the message.
%t	To field (recipients of the message).
%T	Message time.†

*The day the message was sent (by default). Change this to the day you received it by setting the **date_received** variable.
†Change the time format so that Z-Mail displays the time in 24-hour time by setting the **mil_time** variable.

Table 3-5. hdr_format Special Formatting Characters (continued)

Character	Description
%u	User name of the author (from %a).
%W	Day of the week (Sun, Mon, etc.).
%y	Year (the last 2 digits only).
%Y	Year of the message.
%Z	Time zone of the message.
\n	newline.
\t	TAB.

Note that the "24" in the **From** field (**%f**) in the previous example is a *field-width specifier*. Use field-width specifiers to print the first specified number of characters in the string.

Put the field-width specifier between the % and format characters. In this example, **%24f** tells Z-Mail to include only the first 24 characters of the name and address.

You can also display either the name or the address strings in your **hdr_format** using **%a** and **%n**. Z-Mail uses the **From** (or **Reply-To**) line in each message to determine the **%a** and **%n** strings. Z-Mail might display the name (**%n**) first in parentheses (( )) and the address (**%a**) as the rest of the **From** line like this:

    (Hanna Nelson) hanna@holycow.santa-cruz.ca.us

or Z-Mail might display the name first, followed by the address in angle brackets (**< >**), like this:

    Hanna Nelson <hanna@holycow.santa-cruz.ca.us>

(For more information about address formats and comments in mail headers, see Chapter 11, *Z-Mail Addressing*.)

If the address is the only thing on the **From** line, then the name and the address are the same.

Regardless of the **hdr_format** that you set, in line mode, Z-Mail always prints the message number for each message and the right angle bracket (**>**) to the left of the current message.

Here's another sample **hdr_format** setting:

    Msg 3 of 10: set hdr_format='%20n %6d %40s'

With this setting, your header summary display looks like this:

    15   N   Gary Larsen   Aug 12 Re: The Cows are Coming

The field-width specifiers in the **hdr_format** setting tell Z-Mail to display no more than 20 characters of the author's name, no more than 6 characters of the date, and no more than 40 characters of the **Subject** line.

If your **hdr_format** contains **%f**, **%a**, or **%n** fields and your folder contains messages from you (with your address in the **From** header), Z-Mail converts these fields to reflect who you sent the message to. Thus, messages that you keep copies of appear in the header summary display like this:

```
16   TO: gerard   Gerard Depardieu  Jul 14  Re: Bastille Day
```

This is useful for **record** files that keep copies of your outgoing mail (otherwise, this field for all the messages contains your address). We'll explain **record** files in Chapter 4, *Sending Mail with Z-Mail*.

If you don't want Z-Mail to replace your name with the **TO** construction, you can use the *%?hdr?* special format in your **hdr_format** setting. To do this, replace the *%f*, *%a*, or *%n* field with *%?from?*. Thus, if you have this **hdr_format** setting:

```
Msg 3 of 10: set hdr_format='%20%f   %6d   %40s'
```

you get this display:

```
12   TO: Spalding Gray   Aug 11  Re: "Swimming to Cambodia"
```

To remove the **TO** construction, use this **hdr_format**:

```
Msg 3 of 10: set hdr_format='%20?from?   %6d   %40s'
```

and you get this display instead:

```
12   hanna@holycow.santa-  Aug 11  Re: "Swimming to Cambodia"
```

There's a special format for displaying the contents of headers, such as personalized headers created with the **my_hdr** command, not listed in Table 3-5. (We explain how to create personalized headers using the **my_hdr** command in Chapter 4.) Here's the syntax for including personalized headers in the header summary display:

```
set hdr_format = "%?header_name?"
```

For example, here's how to include the address, name, and phone number (if the message contains a custom **Phone** header) of the author of the messages in your folder:

```
Msg 3 of 10: set hdr_format = "%10a   %20n   %?phone?"
```

Note that you must include both question marks (**?**). Z-Mail recognizes the header, regardless of case.

Now, the header summaries for messages that contain a **Phone** header look something like this:

```
16  N  garciam   Gabriel Garcia Marqu  800-333-9090
```

In this example, note that Z-Mail truncates the name (*%n*) to 20 characters. The "*%?phone?*" field in the header summary display is left blank for any messages that don't have a **Phone** header.

Setting Your Prompt

By default, the prompt for Z-Mail's line-mode interface looks like this:

```
(%T) %f: #%m of %t>
```

The **%T** gives the current time, **%f** specifies the folder name, **%m** is the number of current message, and **%t** is the total number of messages in the current folder. For example, the prompt might look like this:

```
(2:54) hanna: #3 of 10> _
```

The examples in this book use the following simplified prompt format:

```
Msg %m of %t:
```

In this case, the prompt looks like this:

```
Msg 3 of 10: _
```

If you want to include other types of information in the prompt, set the **prompt** variable to a string. The string can contain any of the formatting characters in Table 3-6.

Table 3-6. prompt Special Formatting Characters

Character	Description
%d	Number of deleted messages in the current folder.
%f	Name of the current folder.
%F	Full path of the current folder.
%m	Current message number.
%M	Month name of today's date (Jan, Feb, etc.).
%n	Number of new messages.
%N	Current day of the month (number).
%t	Total number of messages in the folder.
%T	Current time.
%u	Number of unread messages.
%W	Current day of the week (Sun, Mon, etc.).
%y	Current year (the last 2 digits only).
%Y	The current year (1991).
%$	Precedes variable name.
\n	newline.*
\t	TAB.

*If you use Z-Mail in fullscreen mode, it's generally not a good idea to put newlines in the **prompt** because of the **continue** prompt.

You can also use the special **prompt** formatting characters with the **$(%c)** and **title** variables. We'll describe the **title** variable in Chapter 6, *Using the Fullscreen Mode*; for more information on **$(%c)**, see Chapter 9, *Writing Scripts and Functions*.

If you want to include the value of a variable, such as **cwd** (to display the current directory) or **thisfolder** (to show the current folder name), use the special **%$** sequence. Let's set the prompt to include the current message and the current directory:

```
Msg 3 of 10: set prompt = '%m %$cwd> '
```

Note that we enclosed the variable sequence in single quotes (') to prevent Z-Mail from expanding the **cwd** variable while we set the **prompt** variable. Now (with the current message pointer on message 1 in the *chapters* folder), the prompt looks like this:

```
1 /u/hanna/Mail/chapters> _
```

Here's an example of two different ways to include the name of the current folder (the value of the **thisfolder** variable) in your prompt:

```
Msg 3 of 10: set prompt = '%F> '
Msg 3 of 10: set prompt = '%$thisfolder> '
```

The only difference between these two commands is that, if you invoke Z-Mail in read-only mode (by specifying the **–r** option with **zmail** from the command line or with **folder**), the **%F** prompt setting adds the string "[read-only]" to the end of the prompt. So, if you started Z-Mail like this:

```
$ zmail –r
```

your prompt might look similar to this:

```
/usr/spool/mail/hanna [read-only]> _
```

If you use Z-Mail on different computers, you might want to include the name of the host computer. To do this, use the **hostname** variable in your prompt as follows:

```
Msg 3 of 10: set prompt='%$hostname> '
```

In this example, if **hostname** is set to *espresso*, your prompt now looks like this:

```
espresso> _
```

If you forget the percent sign (%), Z-Mail interprets the string literally and your prompt is:

```
$hostname >_
```

Reviewing the Variables

We've covered a lot of variables in the previous sections; let's take a minute and review what they all do. Table 3-7 describes the variables presented in this chapter.

Table 3-7. Chapter 3 Variable Review

Variable	Description
cmd_help	Set an alternate location for the Z-Mail help file.
autoprint	Specify that the **d** command automatically print the next undeleted message.
crt	Specify the number of lines of message text Z-Mail displays before calling an external pager.
pager	Set the pager for Z-Mail to call.
toplines	Indicate the number of lines to display with **top**.
squeeze	Remove blank lines when reading messages.
screen	Set the number of header summaries to display in one screenful.
show_deleted	Display header summaries for deleted messages.
printer	Set the default printer to use with **lpr**.
print_cmd	Specify the UNIX print command for **lpr** to run.
quiet	Suppress messages in certain instances.
mbox	Set the location of the *mbox* folder.
folder	Indicate the location of the folder directory.
date_received	Display dates as when you received the message, not when the message was sent.
sort	Sort messages by certain criteria.
keepsave	Retain saved messages in the system mailbox.
ignoreeof	Specify that CTRL-D does not exit Z-Mail.
warning	Display warning messages in certain situations.
hdr_format	Change the format of the header summary display.
prompt	Change your Z-Mail prompt.

Test Your Z-Mail Skills

In this chapter, we covered the basics of entering Z-Mail commands, how to get help, and how to modify the behavior of commands by setting different variables. Then, we explained the Z-Mail commands that you use to read and manage your messages and how to update your folder and exit Z-Mail. Finally, we showed you some ways to customize the Z-Mail display.

We've covered so many commands and different ways to read and manage your mail, you're probably wondering how you're ever going to remember it all. So, to help you review what you've learned so far, here's a short quiz. Match the commands on the left with the tasks on the right. (Don't worry if you don't get all the answers right; we've included the answers below.)

1.	**from mattb**	a.	Select messages by `Subject`.
2.	**mark 2**	b.	Select messages with a priority.
3.	**print $**	c.	Sort the folder by date.
4.	**folders**	d.	Save all the messages from one person.
5.	**pick -ago 7 days**	e.	Display the messages from *mattb*.
6.	**h +**	f.	Display the deleted messages.
7.	**:d**	g.	Update the folder without quitting Z-Mail.
8.	**? mail**	h.	Create a temporary mark.
9.	**mark –B**	i.	Delete two messages.
10.	**lpr 8**	j.	Get help on the **mail** command.
11.	**pick –ago 1 week**	k.	Save the current message to a file with the same name as the `Subject` header.
12.	**update**	l.	Display the last message.
13.	**d 6-9**	m.	Send a message to the printer.
14.	**cd +**	n.	List the contents of the folder directory.
15.	**d 6,9**	o.	Delete four messages.
16.	**s –s**	p.	Select messages that are one week old.
17.	**pick –i –s Z-Mail**	q.	Change to the folder directory.
18.	**sort –d**	r.	Save the current message to a file in the folder directory.
19.	**s +from.mattb**	s.	Set a priority on a message.
20.	**pick –p B**	t.	Display the next screenful of header summaries.
21.	**pick -f harry | save from_harry**		

Review Quiz Answers

1.	e.	**2.**	h.	**3.**	l.	**4.**	n.	**5.**	p.	**6.**	t.	**7.**	f.
8.	j.	**9.**	s.	**10.**	m.	**11.**	p.	**12.**	g.	**13.**	o.	**14.**	q.
15.	i.	**16.**	k.	**17.**	a.	**18.**	c.	**19.**	r.	**20.**	b.	**21.**	d.

In the next chapter, we'll cover the features of Z-Mail to use when sending and replying to messages with Z-Mail.

4
Sending Mail

In Chapter 2, *Getting Started*, we covered the very basics of sending mail with Z-Mail; in this chapter, we'll cover the more advanced Z-Mail commands and the features you can use when sending mail.

We'll show you how to:

- Send and respond to messages.

- Change the message text and headers once you've started composing a message.

- Add other information to your message, such as files and other messages.

- Use tips for responding to and forwarding messages along to other people.

- Suspend message compositions.

- Send files and programs as "attachments."

- Create mail aliases.

- Customize your outgoing messages with commands and variables.

Sending and Replying to Mail

To send a message from within Z-Mail, use **mail (m)** command. Sending a message with **mail** is basically the same as using the **zmail** command from the UNIX system prompt. Enter the **mail** command followed by the addresses of the people to whom you want to send the message. For example, to send mail to *andreic* and *mattb*, use this command:

```
Msg 3 of 10: m andreic mattb
```

If you don't specify an address with **mail**, Z-Mail prompts you for the **To** line.

At this point, Z-Mail displays the **To** line and prompts you for the message subject:

```
To: andreic, mattb
Subject: _
```

You can choose to suppress the **Subject** prompt, so you might not see it. (See the section, "Changing the Subject," in this chapter for more information on setting the **Subject** prompt).

As described in Chapter 2, when you press RETURN at the **Subject** prompt, you enter *compose mode*. Enter your message from the keyboard and press CTRL-D on a line by itself to send it.

Z-Mail includes a number of options that you can use with the **mail** command; Table 4-1 describes these options.

Table 4-1. Mail Command Options

Option	Description
–A [*type*:]*file*	Attach a file to the message, optionally specifying the file's *type*.
–b *Bcc-list*	Specify people to receive blind carbon copies.
–c *Cc-list*	Specify people to receive carbon copies.
–e	Enter editor immediately.
–E	Edit outgoing headers with text.
–f [*msg-list*]	Forward the specified *msg-list* (unindented).
–F	Add a "fortune" to the end of the outgoing message.
–h	*file*
–H *file*	Read in *file* as a prepared text without headers.
–i [*msg-list*]	Include specified messages without headers in outgoing mail.
–I [*msg-list*]	Include messages with headers in outgoing mail.
–s [*Subject*]	Prompt for or optionally set the **Subject**.
–u	Don't append signatures and fortunes to the message.
–U	Send message draft immediately without editing (with **–h** or **–H**).

We describe each of these options in greater detail in the sections that follow.

Another way to send mail from within Z-Mail is to reply to a message in your folder using the **reply** (**r**) or **replyall** (**R**) commands. Use **reply** to send a message to the author of the message only; **replyall** includes all the original recipients in your response.

You can use the same **mail** options listed in Table 4-1 with **reply** and **replyall**. In general, these two commands work the same as **mail**. The difference is that, when replying to a message with **reply** or **replyall**, Z-Mail fills in the **To** (and **Subject**, if it exists) lines automatically and you enter compose mode immediately. With **mail**, you have to supply the address and subject yourself.

For example, suppose you receive a message with the following headers:

```
From: Dale Cooper <cooper>
To: Hanna Nelson <hanna>, Harry Truman <harry>
Subject: Great cherry pie!
Cc: albert
```

To reply to the author of the message (*cooper*), use **reply**:

```
Msg 3 of 10: r
```

Z-Mail constructs the following header lines and places you in compose mode:

```
To: Dale Cooper <cooper>
Subject: Re:  Great cherry pie!


—
```

If you use **replyall** instead, the headers look like this:

```
To: Dale Cooper <cooper>, Harry Truman <harry>
Subject: Re:  Great cherry pie!
Cc: albert


—
```

 Note that when you reply to everyone with **replyall**, Z-Mail removes your name from the list. If you want to keep your name on the **To** line, set the **metoo** variable:

```
Msg 3 of 10: set metoo
```

With **metoo** set, when you use **replyall**, the headers in our example look like the following:

```
To: Dale Cooper <cooper>, Hanna Nelson <hanna>, Harry Truman <harry>
Subject: Great cherry pie!
Cc: albert
```

See Chapter 11, *Z-Mail Addressing*, for more information about the other functions of **metoo**.

Compose-mode Escapes

Once you invoke Z-Mail to send or reply to a message, you enter *compose mode*. This section explains the syntax for entering special commands from within compose mode. These commands are called *tilde-escapes* (or *compose-mode escapes*) because they begin with the tilde character (˜) and they allow you to escape from the compose-mode line editor to run commands. Compose-mode commands don't work when you send a message from the GUI mode; however, the GUI mode includes options that perform most of the same functions.

To execute a tilde-escape, enter the tilde character as the first character on the line. The syntax looks like this:

```
˜escape_name [message_list] [filename] [program_name]
```

The *escape_name* is a single alphabetic character or metacharacter. Some tilde-escapes take a *message_list* (a list of message numbers, or special characters described in Table 3-1). If you specify more than one message, Z-Mail interprets them in ascending order. Other tilde-escapes also take a file (or folder) name, or even a program name.

 To display the valid tilde-escapes and a brief description, enter the following escape in compose mode:

    ˜?

Z-Mail displays a list like this:

```
--------------------------------------------------------------------
˜commands: [OPTIONAL argument]

˜˜                 Begin a line with a single ˜

Modify [set] headers:              ˜h            All headers
˜t [to list]    To                 ˜s [subject]  Subject
˜c [cc list]    Cc                 ˜b [bcc list] Bcc

View or edit message text:         ˜u            Edit previous line
˜e [editor]     Enter editor       ˜v [editor]   Visual editor
˜p [pager]      View message body and headers using pager
˜| cmd [args]   Pass the message body through the unix command "cmd"

˜E[!]           Erase message body after [not] saving to dead.letter

Include other text:
˜i [msg#'s]     Bodies of messages [msg#'s], indented by "indent_str"
˜I [msg#'s]     Bodies and headers of messages, indented
˜f [msg#'s]     Bodies and headers of messages, marked "forwarded"
˜r filename     Contents of file "filename" (not indented)

˜S[!]           Add [suppress] signature when sending letter
--more--
```

If you want to see the second screen of help information, press the space bar. To return to compose mode, press **q**. Note that Z-Mail doesn't insert this help information in your message.

After running ˜? (and most of the other tilde-escapes), you get a message like this:

    (continue editing letter)

    —

At this point, you are still in compose mode. Any more text that you enter is appended to the message. If you want, enter another tilde-escape or send the message in the usual way by pressing CTRL-D on a line by itself.

Z-Mail interprets any tilde character in the first column on a line as beginning a tilde-escape. So, if you want to begin a line with a single tilde, enter two tildes. Otherwise, Z-Mail interprets the single tilde as a tilde-escape and responds with this error message:

    `'`: unknown ˜ escape. Use ˜? for help.

The following sections discuss the tilde-escapes in detail.

Changing or Adding Recipients

Sometimes, when you respond to a message, you'll want to add more people to (or otherwise change) the distribution list. To add more people to the **To** line, specify them at the end of the **reply** or **replyall** command line. For example, if you receive a message with the following headers:

```
From: Dale Cooper <cooper>
To: Hanna Nelson <hanna>
Subject: Great cherry pie!
Cc: albert
```

To respond to the author of the message, everyone on the **To** and **Cc** lines, and add *ben* and *jerry* to the distribution list, use the **R** command:

```
Msg 3 of 10: R ben jerry
```

Z-Mail constructs a return address line like this:

```
To: Dale Cooper <cooper>, Harry Truman <harry>, ben, jerry
Subject: Re: Great cherry pie!
Cc: albert
```

You can use this method to reply to all the people on the original **To** line but not the ones on the **Cc** line. (We'll explain how to change the **Cc** line later in the section "Sending Copies to Other People.") So, in the example above, respond to *cooper* and *harry* (but not *albert*) with the **r** command:

```
Msg 3 of 10: r harry
```

When you use **mail** to send a message, Z-Mail does not require that you specify a distribution list when you start writing the letter, but you must supply one at some time before sending it. If you try to send a message without addressing it, you get this error message:

```
You must have a To: recipient to send mail.
(continue)
—
```

If you want to send the message, you have to add people to the **To** line. How can you do this if you're already in compose mode? The answer is to use a tilde-escape. In this case, use ˜t to add people to the **To** line. If you enter ˜t alone, Z-Mail prompts you with the current **To** line. In this case, there aren't any names on the **To** line so it looks like the following:

```
˜t
To: _
```

Enter the names at this prompt and press RETURN.

If there are already names on the distribution, Z-Mail displays them; you can add or erase names to change the current list. Use spaces or commas to separate the names.

If you include names on the ~t line, Z-Mail appends this list to the current **To** list (if any). For example, to append *suzzy* to the current list, type:

```
~t suzzy
(continue editing letter)
__
```

At any time when you're editing the message, you can look at the **To** line with ~t. If the distribution list is fine, simply press RETURN to leave it unchanged.

Changing the Subject

It's generally a good idea to give your message a **Subject**. That way, people can get a sense of what your message is about by glancing at the header summaries. If you're replying to a message, Z-Mail fills in the **Subject** line for you, but if you're sending a new message, you'll have to think one up yourself.

If Z-Mail doesn't automatically prompt you for the **Subject** when you send mail, then the **ask** variable isn't set. Use this command to set it:

```
Msg 3 of 10: set ask
```

You don't need to set **ask** to specify the **Subject**; you can set it from within Z-Mail using the −s option with **mail** and **reply** and from the UNIX prompt using **zmail −s**. However, if you set **ask**, you don't need to remember to set the **Subject** each time you send a message. Here's an example of how to set the **Subject** with −s:

```
Msg 3 of 10: m −s "Setting the Subject" cooper
```

You can also use this option to change the **Subject** when you reply to a message. This is useful when you reply to multiple messages because Z-Mail uses the **Subject** from the first message in the list as the **Subject** line of your response. Here's how to specify a different **Subject**:

```
Msg 3 of 10: R 4 7 10 −s "All the replies are in!"
```

Remember to put the **Subject** string in quotes if it contains spaces.

Let's say you're used to being prompted for a **Subject** line when you send mail (the **ask** variable is already set). What happens when you send a message from another machine and Z-Mail doesn't prompt you? Or what if you decide to change the **Subject** after you've started composing the message? You can set the **Subject** from within compose mode using the ~s tilde-escape.

When you use ~s without specifying a string, Z-Mail gives you the **Subject** prompt (and the current **Subject**, if any). Enter a **Subject** or use the compose-mode editing commands (such as CTRL-W and BACKSPACE) to back up and change the current **Subject**. Return to compose mode by pressing RETURN.

If you specify a string with ~s, Z-Mail *replaces* the current subject (if any) with the new one and returns you to compose mode. For example, type:

```
~s Lousy Coffee
(continue editing letter)

—
```

Now, if you use ~s, you see:

```
~s
Subject: Lousy Coffee_
```

Sending Copies to Other People

You can send copies of your message to other people in addition to those on the **To** line. For example, you might want to respond to a message and send a copy to your boss. There are two recipient lists—**Cc** (carbon copy) and **Bcc** (blind carbon copy)—for sending copies. When people read messages, addresses on the **To** and **Cc** lines appear in the message header; people listed on the **Bcc** line receive a copy of the message, but their addresses don't appear.

 By default, Z-Mail doesn't prompt for the **Cc** and **Bcc** lines. However, if you want Z-Mail to prompt you for the **Cc** list every time you send and respond to mail, set the **askcc** variable in your *.zmailrc* file, as shown below:

```
Msg 3 of 10: set askcc
```

Now, when you press CTRL-D to send the message, the **Cc** prompt appears. If you don't want to send copies to anyone, simply press RETURN.

Although I don't often include people on the **Cc** list, I like having Z-Mail prompt me for one because it gives me one last chance to cancel or return to editing the message before sending it.

With **askcc** set, you might find it annoying to get the **Cc** prompt every time you send a message. If you don't use this feature very often, you might want to unset **askcc** and set the **Cc** line only when you need it.

To create a **Cc** line and add people to it, use the ~c tilde-escape from compose mode. When you enter ~c, you see:

```
~c
Cc: _
```

Enter the addresses at the **Cc** prompt and press RETURN to return to compose mode.

You can also use ~c to add addresses to an existing **Cc** line. For example, if *george* and *ringo* are already listed on the **Cc** line and you type:

```
~c john,paul
```

The list of carbon-copy recipients now looks like this:

```
Cc: george, ringo, john, paul
```

Another way to set the **Cc** line is to use the **–c** option with **mail** and **reply**. You can also use this option when sending mail from the UNIX prompt with **zmail**.

For example, here's how to set the **Cc** list when you use **reply**. Enclose the addresses in double quote characters (") or separate the addresses with a comma character (,):

```
Msg 3 of 3: r –c "john paul"
```

Now, *john* and *paul* appear on the **Cc** list. If instead you use **replyall** to reply to a message that already had a **Cc** list, the **–c** option *adds* your addresses to the list.

If you are also specifying **To**-recipients on the command line, you must enclose the carbon-copy addresses in double quote characters ("), as shown in the following example:

```
Msg 3 of 10: m –c "john paul" george ringo
```

When you set the carbon-copy recipients like this, Z-Mail doesn't give you the **Cc** prompt when you send the message.

Creating Blind Carbon Copies

Blind carbon copies are similar to carbon copies; everyone on the list receives a copy of the message. However, when everyone reads the message, the **Bcc** line (and addresses) don't appear in the list of headers. Sometimes this is useful if you want to get someone's opinion on something you've written, but you don't necessarily want the other people to know who you've sent copies to.

I've seen this feature used in situations where people use **replyall** instead of **reply**. If you send blind copies, recipients can only reply to you, whether they use **replyall** or **reply**, and will not generate mail to others on the distribution list of the original message.

Blind copies are also useful if you want to send yourself a copy of your message without listing yourself on the **To** or **Cc** lines. You might think (as my friend Bart does) that sending blind copies to other people is sneaky and dishonest. But, the truth of the matter is that, if you keep a copy of your outgoing message (with **Bcc**, **Cc**, or by saving outgoing messages with the **record** variable), you can forward it to whomever you please, without anyone on the original distribution knowing about it.

One thing I should mention is that sometimes people don't notice they've been blind copied. If they send a response to everyone on the original distribution with **replyall**, they've blown your cover. For this reason, you should be careful about sending blind copies.

There are two ways to specify blind carbon copies: from the Z-Mail prompt and from within compose mode. To set the **Bcc** list at the prompt, use the **–b** option (this works exactly like **–c**), as shown in the following example:

```
Msg 3 of 10: m –b "bart lisa" maggie
```

If you're already in compose mode when you decide to send blind carbon copies, use the ˜**b** tilde-escape. Like ˜**c**, if you include addresses with ˜**b**, you add the addresses to the **Bcc** line, otherwise, Z-Mail prompts you for the blind carbon-copy recipients.

Editing All the Header Fields

If you want to look at or change all the headers, use ¯h. Z-Mail prompts you for each of the To, Subject, Cc, and Bcc lines. To leave any header line as it stands, simply press RETURN at the prompt.

Now that we've explained the different ways to specify and modify the different headers in your outgoing message, we'll go on to the commands and variables that give you more control while composing the actual message text.

Tips for Editing Your Message

As we showed you in Chapter 2, *Getting Started*, when you enter compose mode, Z-Mail starts up a simple line editor. Remember that this editor is very limited in what it allows you to do—it only lets you correct mistakes on the current line. We showed you that, with the simple editor, once you press RETURN, the mistake is there to stay.

In the next few sections, we'll cover the Z-Mail features that allow you to wrap lines automatically, change mistakes on the previous line, and edit the entire message using a full-featured text editor. Table 4-2 reviews the editing keys that you use on the current line.

Table 4-2. Line Editor Keys

Key	Description
BACKSPACE or CTRL-H	Erase the previous character.
CTRL-W	Erase the previous word.
CTRL-U	Erase the entire line.

Wrapping Lines Automatically

Because long lines are difficult to read in mail messages, you should try to keep your lines short. You can configure Z-Mail to wrap lines automatically at a specific column as you type using the **wrapcolumn** variable. Z-Mail wraps lines only at whitespace (spaces or tabs); if a line doesn't contain whitespace to the left of the specified column, Z-Mail does not wrap the line.

For example, to wrap lines at column 70, set **wrapcolumn**:

```
Msg 3 of 10: set wrapcolumn = 70
```

If you set **wrapcolumn** but don't specify a column number, Z-Mail automatically wraps the lines at column 78.

Disable line wrapping with either of the following commands:

```
Msg 3 of 10: unset wrapcolumn
Msg 3 of 10: set wrapcolumn = 0
```

Editing the Previous Line

With standard UNIX mail programs, once you press RETURN on a line, there's no way to correct any mistakes without starting up a full-blown text editor like *vi*. With Z-Mail, however, if you press RETURN and notice mistakes or missing information on the previous line, you can use the ~u tilde-escape to move up one line.

For example, if you type the following line and you want to edit it after pressing RETURN:

```
This is mighty fine cheeerry pie!
~u_
```

the ~u tilde-escape redisplays the previous line and places the cursor at the end of the line, as shown below:

```
This is mighty fine cheeerry pie!_
```

Now, you can erase and re-enter the line using the editing keys in Table 4-2. When you finish making changes to the line, press RETURN to continue.

Note that you can only move up one line with ~u. Also note that you can't use another tilde-escape on the line that you are editing with ~u. So, if you backspace to the beginning of the line and then enter another tilde-escape, Z-Mail displays the following error:

```
(Warning: ~ escapes ignored on ~u lines.)
```

Thus, you can't enter ~u repeatedly to edit previous lines. To edit the entire message, you must invoke an editor, such as *vi*. We'll show you how in the next section.

Starting Up a Text Editor

If you make a mistake on a line and notice it only after continuing down several lines (you pressed RETURN more than once so you can't use ~u to edit the line in question), you can still correct your mistake by starting up an editor on your message.

You can invoke an editor using the ~e tilde-escape. To specify the editor to use, include it on the tilde-escape line. For example, let's invoke *emacs* on the current message buffer:

```
~e emacs
```

 If you don't specify an editor, Z-Mail uses the editor specified by the **editor** variable or the **EDITOR** environment variable. If neither variable is set, ~e invokes the default visual editor, *vi*.

Use the ~v escape to enter the visual editor. With ~v, Z-Mail uses the editor specified by the **visual** variable or the **VISUAL** environment variable. If neither of these is set, ~v invokes *vi*, by default.

The rationale behind having two tilde-escapes is that you can set ~e to call up a line editor, such as *ed* or *ex*, and ~v to call a visual editor. Although most people use a visual editor like *vi*, you want to use *ed* sometimes because it's faster when you just want to make a few changes. Another situation where you might prefer to use a line editor is when you edit messages using Z-Mail over a modem. If you use *ed*, you won't have to wait for the editor to redraw the screen.

When you use either of these commands, Z-Mail invokes the editor on the message that you are composing. You can now edit your message just as you would a regular file. When you finish editing the message, exit the editor (in *vi*, press **ZZ** or **:wq** to exit; in GNU *emacs*, press CTRL-X CTRL-C) and you return to compose mode. For example, when I quit *vi*, I see the following:

```
~
~
"/u/hanna/.eda15566" 8 lines, 120 characters
(continue editing message)

—
```

The */u/hanna/.eda15566* file is a temporary file created by Z-Mail. When I send the message, Z-Mail removes this temporary file.

Let's say you always use *emacs* to edit your messages. To set up Z-Mail so that whenever you enter ˜e, you start up *emacs*, set the **editor** variable:

```
Msg 3 of 10: set editor = /usr/bin/emacs
```

The pathname of different text editors is somewhat system-dependent.

If you want to use the editor when sending mail from the UNIX prompt, you must either set **editor** or **visual** in your initialization file, or set the **EDITOR** or **VISUAL** environment variables in your *.profile* (for Bourne or Korn shell) or *.cshrc* (for C shell) files.

If you know ahead of time that you are going to need to call up a text editor, use the **–e** option with **mail** from the Z-Mail prompt:

```
Msg 3 of 10: m —e dan bart
```

You can do this with **reply**, too. For example, use this command to reply to message 3 and enter the editor immediately:

```
Msg 3 of 10: r 3 —e
```

You can even use **cmd** to create your own command-line alias for when you want to enter the editor automatically when you send mail. Remember, we introduced the **cmd** command in Chapter 3, *Reading and Managing Mail*. Here are a couple of examples:

```
Msg 3 of 10: cmd me 'mail —e'
Msg 3 of 10: cmd re 'reply —e'
```

If you enter these two commands, exactly as they appear here, you create two command-line aliases. The first is called **me** (for "mail-edit"). When you use **me** instead of **m** to send a message, Z-Mail invokes the editor automatically.

Use the second command, **re** ("reply-edit") to reply to the current message and invoke the editor automatically. Thus, if you use **re** to reply to the author of the current message and enter the editor, the command looks like this:

```
Msg 3 of 10: re
```

This command sends a reply to the author of message 3 and enters the editor automatically.

For more information on **cmd**, see Chapter 5, *Z-Mail Shortcuts, Bells, and Whistles*.

If you find yourself frequently entering the editor, you might want to set it up so that every time you enter compose mode, you enter the editor automatically. To do this, set the **autoedit** variable. With **autoedit** set, you'll never have to deal with Z-Mail's simple line editor again; you'll always use your favorite text editor to compose outgoing messages.

If you want to go into the editor only when you send a new message (with **mail**) or when you reply to messages (using **reply** or **replyall**), set **autoedit** to one or more keywords. For example, to use the editor only on new messages, set **autoedit** with this command:

```
Msg 3 of 10: set autoedit = new
```

If you'd rather enter the editor only when you send replies, use this setting instead:

```
Msg 3 of 10: set autoedit = reply
```

Setting **autoedit** to both **new** and **reply** is identical to setting **autoedit** to no value.

Editing Headers with the Message Text

Normally, when you use a text editor to edit outgoing messages, Z-Mail doesn't include the headers for you to edit. If you want to be able to change the headers with the text, use the **–E** option with **mail**. This option doesn't have any effect until you enter the editor. So, you might use a command like this to enter the editor and edit the headers when you enter compose mode:

```
Msg 3 of 10: m —eE cooper
```

For example, if **editor** is set to *vi*, the message headers appear with the text at the top of the file like this (note the position of the cursor in this example):

```
From: hanna (Hanna Nelson)
Date: Sun, 28 Jul 1991 11:49:00 PST
X-Mailer: Z-Mail (2.0.0 7/1/91)
To: albert
Subject: Re: Review Copies
```

Use this feature to edit the contents of the header fields; don't modify the headers (the text that precedes the colon character (:)) themselves.

Here's a command-line alias that you can use instead of **mail** to enter the editor and edit the headers automatically each time you send mail:

```
Msg 3 of 10: cmd eE 'mail —eE'
```

Now, use the **eE** command to send a message.

If you like to edit the headers with the text editor, you can set the **edit_hdrs** variable so that every time you enter the editor, you edit the headers:

```
Msg 3 of 10: set edit_hdrs
```

Now, when you enter the editor (either by using the ˜v or ˜e tilde-escapes from compose mode, or by setting the **autoedit** variable), Z-Mail allows you to edit the headers with the message text.

If you set the **edit_hdrs** variable, Z-Mail won't prompt you for `Cc`; instead, when you enter the editor to edit the message, the `Cc` line appears with the rest of the message headers. You can add people to the `Cc` line at that point.

You also can't use any of the tilde-escapes that let you add or set header lines or clear the message buffer. For example, you can't add a `Subject` header with ˜s; if you try, you get this error:

    You must use an editor to change your headers.

When editing headers, be careful not to remove the `To` line; without a `To` line, Z-Mail can't send the message. If you try to send a message without a `To` line, you get this error message:

    You must have a To: recipient to send mail.
    (continue)

    —

To send the message, re-enter the editor (using ˜v or ˜e) and add a `To` line with a valid recipient name.

You can change the `From` line as long as you don't specify an invalid address. If the address is not valid, Z-Mail (silently) replaces your line with the original `From` line. Nothing happens if you change or remove the `Date` line because Z-Mail always replaces this header with a more accurate time and date.

 With **edit_hdrs** set, you can add a header to save the message to a file. Z-Mail recognizes the `Fcc` (File Carbon Copy) header and sends a copy of the message to any file or folder that you specify on the `Fcc` line. To keep a copy of the message in a file called *Chapter.8* in your folder directory, use this `Fcc` line:

    Fcc: +/Chapter.8

Note that the `Fcc` line is like `Bcc`—Z-Mail doesn't include this line when it sends your message. The same goes for blank headers. For example, if you add a `Cc` line, but don't include any addresses on it, Z-Mail removes the entire `Cc` line before displaying the message.

Canceling the Message

If you're in the middle of editing a message and you decide not to send it, you can cancel it by pressing twice the interrupt character (typically ^C or DEL). Another way to cancel the message is to use the ˜q tilde-escape. This cancels the message, saving its contents to the ˜/dead.letter file. The ˜x tilde-escape works just like ˜q except that it cancels the message without saving it to ˜/dead.letter. If you don't want Z-Mail to save all your dead messages when you use ˜q, set the **nosave** variable:

    Msg 3 of 10: set nosave

Now, when you cancel messages (either by pressing CTRL-C or using ˜q), Z-Mail doesn't save them.

If the message headers are fine, but you just want to start the message body over, use ˜E to clear the message buffer. For example, use this tilde-escape:

```
˜E
Message buffer empty
(continue editing message)
—
```

Now, you can start the message over without re-entering the **To**, **Subject**, and **Cc** lines.

The ˜E tilde-escape saves the interrupted message buffer to *˜/dead.letter* (if **nosave** is not set). To clear the buffer without saving the contents, use the ˜E! tilde-escape.

Note that if you set the **edit_hdrs** variable, you can't use ˜E to clear the message buffer. If you try, you get this error message:

```
You must use an editor to empty the message buffer.
```

In this case, use ˜v or ˜e to edit the message and remove its contents.

Including a Message

Have you ever received a response from someone with your message included and wondered how they did that? Here's an example of how this looks:

```
From albert Thur Jul 14 11:37:01 1991
From: Albert <albert>
Date: Thur, 14 Jul 1991 11:49:01 PDT
X-Mailer: Z-Mail (2.0.0 7/1/91)
To: Hanna Nelson <hanna>
Subject: Re: Z-Mail chapters

> Thanks for the quick turnaround on the Z-Mail
> review.   Can you take a look at the new stuff?

No problem.  I should have it finished by Monday.

Al
```

The text indented with the right angle bracket character (**>**) was originally sent by me to *albert*. When *albert* responded to my message, he included my mail and added his response at the end.

You can include messages like this when you send and respond to messages with the **mail**, **reply**, and **replyall** commands from the Z-Mail prompt. If you're sending mail from the UNIX prompt, there's no way to include messages from your system mailbox.

To include the text of a message in an outgoing message, use the **–i** option from the Z-Mail prompt like this:

```
Msg 3 of 10: r —i
```

This includes the current message (without headers) in your response. You can see from the prompt that the current message in this case is message 3. Remember that the **>** character in the header summary display (and the prompt in this example) indicates the current message. When you enter compose mode, you see something like this:

```
including message 3 ...(22 lines)
```

Z-Mail includes the message but doesn't display it. You can use ˜v or ˜e to edit it.

When you use ˜i, Z-Mail includes the current message by default. So if you want to include a different message, specify the message you want to include:

```
Msg 3 of 10: r -i 6
```

To respond to and include another message, for example, message 6, use this command:

```
Msg 3 of 10: r 6 -i
```

This command sends a response to the author of message 6 and includes the contents of message 6.

However, if you want to reply to message 6 and include a different message:

```
Msg 3 of 10: r 6 -i 5
```

This replies to message 6 and includes message 5 in your response.

Note that, when you reply to multiple messages, Z-Mail sets the current message pointer to the first message in your message list. This is an important consideration if you plan to include a message. If you aren't sure which is the current message, you can always specify the message number to include.

In these examples, -i includes the message text only—no headers. If you want to include the headers too, use -I instead.

If you forget to use -i or -I at the prompt, you can include a message with the ˜i tilde-escape from compose mode (use ˜I, if you want to include the headers). For example, to include the current message, enter this tilde-escape at the beginning of a line:

```
˜i
```

As with -i, you can specify other messages by entering the message number after the escape. If you specify more than one message (using either the command-line option or a tilde-escape), Z-Mail includes them in ascending order. For example, if you enter the following:

```
˜i 6 12 1
```

Z-Mail displays:

```
Including message 1 ... (32 lines)
Including message 6 ... (16 lines)
Including message 12 ... (44 lines)
(continue editing letter)

—
```

If you want the messages included in a specific order (for example, 6, 12, and then 1), execute the tilde-escapes like this:

```
˜i 6 12
˜i 1
```

If you like the idea of including messages in your outgoing mail, you might consider setting up your environment so that whenever you reply to a message, Z-Mail includes the current message. Do this by setting the **autoinclude** variable. Note that this only applies when you reply to messages; when you send a message with **mail**, the current message isn't included.

As we mentioned before, when you use the include options and tilde-escapes, the included messages are indented with the right angle bracket character (**>**) by default; the included message looks something like the following:

```
>
> This is an included message.
>
> Mark
>
```

We'll show you how to change the character that Z-Mail uses to indent an included message later in this chapter.

Forwarding Messages to Other People

Let's say you receive a message that contains information on a project and you think it might be useful to another person working on the same project. You could include the message in another message by using the **–I** option with **mail** or the **˜I** tilde-escape from within compose mode. While both of these actions include the message with the original header information, neither clearly shows that the included message was originally sent by another person and "forwarded" by you.

 You can forward a message with Z-Mail using the **–f** option to **mail**. When you use this option, Z-Mail marks the forwarded message as "forwarded." So, let's say you want to forward message 6 to *linda*. Type the following:

```
Msg 3 of 10: m –f 6 linda
```

When you use this command, you see a message such as:

```
forwarding message 6 ...(14 lines)
_
```

At this point, Z-Mail pauses and waits for you to either enter more text or send the message. (When you use **–f** with MUSH, the message is sent immediately; use **–ef** to tell MUSH to edit the message before forwarding it.) Z-Mail constructs the introductory and closing string that surrounds the forwarded message using the information from the original **From** line. Here's an example of what *linda* sees in her mail:

```
From: hanna@holycow.santa-cruz.ca.us (Hanna Nelson)
Date: Mon, 29 Jul 1991 21:14:06 PDT
X-Mailer: Z-Mail (2.0.0 7/1/91)
To: linda
Subject: Re: Z-Mail

--- Forwarded mail from Mark the Shark <mark@doc.com>

From mark Mon Jul 22 10:01:44 1991
From: Mark the Shark <mark@doc.com>
```

```
Date: Mon, 22 Jul 1991 10:10:43 PDT
X-Mailer: Z-Mail (2.0.0 7/1/91)
To: Hanna Nelson <hanna@holycow.santa-cruz.ca.us>
Subject: Z-Mail

The book on Z-Mail is very useful.

Mark

--- End of forwarded message from Mark the Shark <mark>
```

If you specify more than one message, Z-Mail includes them in ascending order. So, if you enter the following:

```
Msg 3 of 10: m —f 5 2 1 linda
```

Z-Mail displays:

```
forwarding message 1 ... (12 lines)
forwarding message 2 ... (22 lines)
forwarding message 5 ... (72 lines)
—
```

When you forward more than one message, Z-Mail puts the opening and closing strings around each message.

I have a command-line alias in my ˜/.zmailrc file for forwarding messages to other people. The **cmd** looks like this:

```
Msg 3 of 10: cmd Fwd 'mail —f'
```

With this **cmd**, I can forward message 6 to *linda* from the Z-Mail prompt:

```
Msg 3 of 10: Fwd 6 linda
```

If you're already in compose mode and you want to forward a message, use the ˜**f** escape like this:

```
˜f 6
```

Functionally, forwarding the message from compose mode works exactly as it does from the Z-Mail prompt. The only difference is that when you use ˜**f**, you get the following message:

```
Including message 6 ...(14 lines)
(continue editing letter)
```

If you want to forward the current message from the prompt immediately, without entering compose mode, add the **−U** option:

```
Msg 3 of 10: m —U —f linda
```

Note that, if you want to specify a message (or messages) to forward, you must put the message number immediately after **−f**:

```
Msg 3 of 10: m —f 6 4 —U linda
```

When you forward a message immediately with **−U**, Z-Mail doesn't surround it with the opening and closing strings. Instead, the forwarded message includes special headers, such as `Resent-To` and `Resent-From`, with the regular headers. (This is also true when you omit the **−e** option when forwarding messages with MUSH.) Z-Mail also removes any `Return-Receipt-To` headers from the original message when you forward it.

For example, the headers of the forwarded message might look like this:

```
From hanna Mon Jul 29 10:01:44 1991
X-Mailer: Z-Mail (2.0.0 7/1/91)
Resent-To: linda
From: Mark the Shark <mark@doc.COM>
Date: Mon, 22 Jul 1991 10:10:43 PDT
X-Mailer: Z-Mail (2.0.0 7/1/91)
To: Hanna Nelson <hanna@holycow.santa-cruz.ca.us>
Subject: Z-Mail
```

As you can see, the message still has the name of the original author on the **From** line (in our example, *mark*). The message appears in *linda*'s mailbox as if it were sent directly from *mark*. For this reason, be careful using the **–U** option to forward mail. If *linda* uses **r** or **R** to respond to the message, her response goes to the original author (*mark*).

Including a File

Suppose you have a file that you want to send to someone. You can do this from the UNIX prompt using command-line redirection like this:

```
$ zmail dale < outline
```

CAUTION

Be very careful with command-line redirection! If you use a right angle bracket character (>) instead of the left angle bracket character (<), Z-Mail overwrites the contents of your file with a Z-Mail session.

If you're like me and you can't remember the difference between the right angle bracket (>) and the left angle bracket (<), you might prefer to include a file another way (besides command-line redirection) when you send mail from the UNIX prompt. In this case, you can use the **–draft** option:

```
$ zmail –draft outline
```

When you do this, Z-Mail displays this message:

```
778 lines
(continue editing or ^D to send)

–
```

Z-Mail puts you in compose mode and expects that *outline* contains a **To** header. If it doesn't, you can add the header with ˜t. You can also add information to the end of the message, use ˜e to enter the editor, or ˜s to add a **Subject** line.

You can't use redirection from within Z-Mail; however, you can use the **–draft** (or **–H**) option with **mail** instead. The **–draft** option works like **–draft** with **zmail** at the UNIX prompt except that you can use it to send a prepared draft without headers. If the draft doesn't include the **To** header, **mail** prompts you. You can also specify the **To** header at the prompt like this:

```
Msg 3 of 10: m –draft outline dale
```

What if you've already addressed and started editing your message and you remember that you want to include the *outline* file? To include the file in this situation, use the ˜r tilde-escape at the beginning of a line in compose mode:

```
˜r outline
```

Previewing the Message

Sometimes, you'll want to check the contents of the message before you send it, for example to make sure you've included the right message or file. To preview a message from compose mode, use the ˜p tilde-escape.

When you use ˜p, Z-Mail displays the header information as well as the body of your message. This is useful for double-checking the distribution list along with the message contents.

In this example, I used ˜i to include a message from *albert* and then previewed the buffer using ˜p:

```
˜p
To: albert
Subject: Lion Coffee
---------
Message contains:

> That coffee you sent from Hawaii is excellent.
> Do you have any more?
>
> Albert

(continue editing letter)

—
```

Saving the Outgoing Message to a File

Sometimes, when I'm in the middle of writing a message, I decide I want to keep a copy in a file for myself. In this case, use ˜w or ˜a to save the current buffer to a file.

To save a copy of the message to a file, use the ˜w tilde-escape with a filename. If you specify a filename that already exists, ˜w automatically overwrites the contents of the old file with the current message. For example, to save the current message to *chapter_4*, enter the following:

```
˜w chapter_4
```

Z-Mail displays this message:

```
chapter_4: 1963 lines
(continue editing letter)

—
```

This saves the contents of the message, without header information by default, to *chapter_4*.

Similarly, to append the contents of the current message to an existing filename, use `a followed by the filename:

```
~a chapters
```

and you see this message:

```
chapters: added 1963 lines
(continue editing letter)
_
```

The *chapters* file exists, so `a appends the current message to it; otherwise, it creates the *chapters* file and puts the message in it.

After you write or append the message to a file, you return to compose mode so that you can continue editing the message or cancel it.

 If you set **edit_hdrs** or used the –E option to edit the message headers with the text, `w and `a save the message with its headers to a *draft* file. We'll explain more about resending draft files later in this chapter.

Suspending a Message Composition

Suppose you're in the middle of composing a message and you decide for one reason or another that you're not ready to send it. In previous sections, we showed you how to save the message to a file and how to cancel it. Here's another solution.

Z-Mail allows you to compose more than one message at a time. This doesn't mean that you can edit them at the same time, but rather that you don't have to finish one before you start another. When you use Z-Mail in either line or fullscreen mode, you can use a function similar to the job-control feature in some shells to suspend messages. You don't need this feature in GUI mode because each message composition has its own input window. MUSH does not allow you to suspend composing a message.

To suspend the message that you're currently composing, enter the `z tilde-escape from compose mode. When you use `z, you see a message like this:

```
~z
[1]  Stopped.
Msg 3 of 10: _
```

You return to the Z-Mail prompt. The message that you were composing hasn't been canceled; it's just waiting in the background.

To list suspended message compositions, use the **jobs** command. If you enter **jobs**, you see:

```
[1] + To: andreic     Tourists and Terrorists
```

The message shows that you have one suspended message addressed to *andreic*. If you had more than one, the list might look something like this:

```
[1]   To: andreic     Tourists and Terrorists
[2]   To: ians         blue velvet
[3] + To: lyndab       Seattle
```

The number in square brackets ([]) is the job number ([1] is the first job that you suspended). The plus (+) indicates the last message that you worked on.

To bring a stopped job to the foreground and continue editing it, enter **resume** followed by the job number. If you don't specify the number, **resume** starts the most recently suspended job (in our example, job 3). Let's resume editing the message to *ians*:

    Msg 3 of 10: resume 2

This brings job number 2 to the foreground. Now, you're in compose mode; you see this familiar message:

    (continue editing letter)

You can add more text, enter another tilde-escape, or send the message with CTRL-D. (You can also use **fg** to resume compositions.)

If you forget that you've suspended messages and you try to exit Z-Mail (either with **quit** or **exit**), you get an error like this one:

    Warning: Abort suspended compositions? (y/c) [cancel] _

Before Z-Mail lets you quit, you must send (or abort) these messages. To abort the messages and return to the UNIX prompt, enter **y** at this prompt. If you want to finish the jobs before exiting Z-Mail, press RETURN and you return to the Z-Mail prompt. Now, you can bring the jobs to the foreground and then send them.

Use **jobs** to display the suspended jobs and **resume** to bring the jobs to the foreground. If you've forgotten what's in the message, use ˜**p** to look at the contents. If you decide not to send it, use ˜**x** or ˜**q**.

Running Z-Mail Commands from Within Compose Mode

Z-Mail includes a special tilde-escape, ˜:, that allows you to run line-mode commands from within compose mode. Using this command, you can run almost any command that you run from the line mode. If you set the **unix** variable, you can even run UNIX commands from compose mode. Briefly, when you set **unix**, Z-Mail interprets any commands that it does not recognize as UNIX commands. (We'll explain **unix** in Chapter 5, *Z-Mail Shortcuts, Bells, and Whistles*.)

For example, suppose you're composing a message from within Z-Mail and you want to include another message, but you aren't sure of the message number. You could suspend the message, run the **headers** command to display the list of header summaries, and then restart the message again. Another way to do this is to use the ˜: command to run **headers** from within compose mode. To do this, enter:

    ˜:h

Z-Mail displays the header summary list without modifying the message that you are composing (Z-Mail doesn't insert this list in your message composition):

    ˜:h
    > 1   Dale Cooper   Jul 21 10:49   (16)   Great cherry pie!
      2   Jimmy Chuck   Jul 21 11:37   (28)   Beta Test

```
    3   Lucie          Jul 21 11:48  (30)    phone message
    4 r Harry Truman   Jul 21 12:37  (20)    Coffee
    5   Albert         Jul 22 10:01   (8)    Status report
(continue editing letter)
__
```

Now, select a message and include it with ~i or ~I.

 Let's say you want to include a message from a particular person. To display all the messages from one person, use ~: with the Z-Mail command **from**:

```
    ~:from harry
```

If you want to display all the messages with a particular `Subject` header, use ~: with the Z-Mail command **pick**. For example, to display messages with "status" in the `Subject` header, enter the following:

```
    ~:pick —s status
```

If you want to include a file in your message, but you don't remember the name, use ~: with the Z-Mail **ls** command to list the files in the current directory:

```
    ~:ls
```

When you find the file, use ~r to include it.

Or, list the contents of your folder directory using this command:

```
    ~:folders
```

 You can even include a message from a folder other than the current one in the current message. For example, here's how to include message 6 from the folder *reviewers* in the current message:

```
    ~:folder —N +reviewers
    ~i 6
```

The **folder** command switches to the *reviewers* folder in the folder directory. When you exit compose mode (for example, by sending or canceling the message), the current folder is the folder that you switched to in compose mode. If you want to return to the current folder after including the message, use this command from compose mode:

```
    ~:folder —N #
```

We'll explain more about the **folder** command and how to switch folders in Chapter 5.

 You can also use ~: to set a Z-Mail variable for the current session from within compose mode. For example, I've used this feature to change the value of the **realname** variable after realizing (while composing the message) that my **realname** variable was inappropriate for my audience. To change this variable from within compose mode, enter the following:

```
    ~:set realname="Hanna Nelson"
```

The result of this ˜: command is that my outgoing message contains the new string as my **realname** variable.

You can even execute UNIX commands from within compose mode if you set the **unix** variable. (We'll cover **unix** in Chapter 5.)

Here's how to set **unix** from within compose mode:

```
˜:set unix
```

Now, you can execute UNIX commands.

For example, if you can't remember how to spell "precede," you can now use the UNIX command *look* to check the spelling:

```
˜:look prece
```

You see a display like this:

```
˜:look prece
precede
precedent
precept
precess
precession
(continue editing letter)

_
```

NOTE

Using ˜:, you cannot run any Z-Mail commands that send mail, such as **mail** or **reply**. If you want to start another message before completing the current one, suspend the current message using ˜z, as described in the section "Suspending a Message" earlier in this chapter.

Piping Message Compositions Through UNIX Commands

Let's say your message contains a list of names that you want to appear in alphabetical order. Using the ˜| tilde-escape, you can pipe the message buffer through a UNIX command, such as *sort*:

```
˜|sort
```

Now, the message contains the sorted list.

CAUTION

The output of the UNIX command *replaces* the contents of the message. For example, if you enter a command like ˜|**date**, the original contents of your message is erased and the output of the **date** command appears in its place.

Note that, if you have **edit_hdrs** set, the ˜| command pipes the message headers (as well as the message text) through the UNIX command. In many cases, it's probably better to use your text editor to pipe message text through a command. For example, with *vi* you can sort lines by escaping to UNIX from the *ex* command line (the colon (:) prompt). To do this, first use ˜v to invoke the editor on the message. Let's say your message has these headers:

```
From: hanna (Hanna Nelson)
Date: Mon Jul 15 17:36:36 PDT 1991
To: lyndab
Subject: address list
```

To sort the contents of the message, excluding these header lines (in other words, to sort lines 5 through the end of the message), use this command:

```
:5-$!sort
```

This sorts and replaces the text just as ˜|**sort** did.

Some UNIX systems include a *fmt* program that fills text to the left margin, creating easy-to-read formatted text. For example, you've created this message:

```
Will -

I just wanted to let you
know how much I enjoyed reading your play,
"Measure for Measure."  I do hope you'll be able to
attend the Shakespeare festival this summer in Santa Cruz.

Looking forward to seeing you,

Audrey
```

To format the text of your message text with *fmt*, use this command:

```
˜| fmt
```

This replaces the contents of your message buffer with the formatted message:

```
Will -

I just wanted to let you  know how much I enjoyed
reading  your play, "Measure for Measure."   I do
hope  you'll  be able to attend  the  Shakespeare
festival this summer in Santa Cruz.

Looking forward to seeing you,

Audrey
```

Sending the Message

When you are ready to send the message, press CTRL-D. Remember that once you press CTRL-D, Z-Mail sends your message and *you can't take it back*. Always make sure that you really want to send the message before sending it.

If you'd rather use the dot character (.) on a line by itself to send the message, set the *dot* variable:

Msg 3 of 10: **set dot**

With *dot* enabled, you can either enter the dot (.) or press CTRL-D on a line by itself to exit compose mode and send your message.

 If you want Z-Mail to give you one last chance to abort an outgoing message before actually sending it. By setting the **verify** variable, you can tell Z-Mail to prompt you before sending the message. Use either of these settings to do this:

Msg 3 of 10: **set verify**
Msg 3 of 10: **set verify = mail**

Now, when you press CTRL-D to exit compose mode and send your message, Z-Mail displays a prompt:

Send Message? (y/n/c) [y] _

To send the message, press RETURN (or **y**). If you want to return to compose mode to continue editing the message, select **n**. To cancel the message entirely (saving it to *~/dead.letter*), select **c**. In MUSH, the prompt is different, but you respond in exactly the same way.

Sending Files

Earlier in this chapter, we showed you how to send files from the UNIX prompt using command-line redirection and the –**draft** option to **zmail** and **mail**. In this section, we'll explain some different kinds of files and how to use Z-Mail to send them to other people.

Draft Files

Z-Mail recognizes files that contain headers as the first lines as *draft* files. For example, if you save a message using the ~w tilde-escape (and you have **edit_hdrs** set), you save the message with its headers as a draft file.

Because draft files already contain the header information needed to send the file, you can send the file using the –**draft** (or –**h** for "header-file") option from the UNIX prompt without specifying recipients. For example, this command will send the *send.later* draft file:

$ zmail –draft ~/send.later

Z-Mail includes the file and places you in compose mode; send the message with CTRL-D.

If you want to send the draft immediately without entering compose mode, add the –**send** (or –**U** for "unedited") option:

$ zmail –draft –send ~/send.later

You can only use the **-send** option in conjunction with **-draft**. Use **-send!** to tell Z-Mail not to append any signature or fortune to the message. Signatures and fortunes are discussed later in this chapter.

To send a draft file from within Z-Mail, use the **mail** command:

```
Msg 3 of 10: m -h ~/send.later
```

As with using **zmail** from the UNIX prompt, **mail** puts you in compose mode; add **-U** to send the draft immediately:

```
Msg 3 of 10: m -Uh ~/send.later
```

If you don't want signatures or fortunes, add **-u** like this:

```
Msg 3 of 10: m -uUh ~/send.later
```

When you send a draft file, Z-Mail updates the **Date** header in the file (if any) with the new date and time. If the file contains no **Date** or **From** headers, Z-Mail adds them. The only header that *must* appear in the draft file for Z-Mail to send it is the **To** header. If there is no **To** line, or the first line in the file is blank, Z-Mail displays this error when you try to send it:

```
You must have a To: recipient to send mail.
```

At this point, use ~t to add a **To** line.

If you want to send a file that doesn't include headers, use the **-H** option with **mail** from within Z-Mail. When you use **-H**, Z-Mail prompts you for a To line before including the message. To send a file without headers from the UNIX prompt, use command-line redirection.

Form Letters

Let's say you frequently send messages that are almost identical in form. For example, you send bug reports in which most of the information is the same (your name, address, and operating environment), and only specific details change. Another situation is if you send weekly status reports to your boss—the project you're working on remains the same; only the details of the project's status change. Or, let's say your job requires that you take phone messages for other people in the office; in this case, you can use a Z-Mail-equivalent to a "While You Were Out" form.

With Z-Mail, you don't have to re-enter all the static information each time you send the message; you can create *templates* (or *form letters*) to use instead. Templates are a new feature for Z-Mail, and not found in MUSH. For example, here's the phone message template included in your distribution (in the */usr/lib/Zmail/forms* directory, by default):

```
To:
Subject: Phone Message

Phone:
Caller:
Organization:

    [ ] Please Call
    [ ] Will Call Again
```

```
[ ] Wants to See You
[ ] Came to See You
[ ] Returned Your Call
```

Message:

To use this form as a template to send phone messages, specify the **–p** option to **mail** as shown in the following example:

```
Msg 3 of 10: m —p phone
```

This command loads the **phone** template automatically and you see:

```
16 lines
(continue editing or ^D to send)

—
```

Now, you'll want to enter the editor so that you can fill out the form. Use the ˜v or ˜e tilde-escapes to start the editor. It's probably more useful to start up the editor on the form automatically; use this command to do this:

```
Msg 3 of 10: m —e —p phone
```

 You can create a command-line alias for sending phone messages. Here's an example:

```
Msg 3 of 10: cmd phone 'mail —e —p phone'
```

Now, when you enter **phone**, Z-Mail includes the *phone* form letter and starts up the editor.

Changing the Templates Directory

By default, Z-Mail stores templates in the *forms* directory under the Z-Mail library directory (*/usr/lib/Zmail*). If you create your own forms, you might want to specify a new location for your templates directory. Use the **templates** variable to do this.

First, create a directory in which to store your template files. For example, I use *forms* in my *folder* directory. Then, set the **templates** variable to the name of that directory:

```
Msg 3 of 10: set templates = +forms
```

Then put your template files in your template directory.

Now, when you use the **–p** (for "prepared") option to **mail**, Z-Mail looks in the directory set by **templates** for the file that you specify. For example, to use the *+forms/report* template, enter the following:

```
Msg 3 of 10: m —p report
```

With this command, Z-Mail includes *+forms/report* and puts you in compose mode.

Sending Attachments

Mail Transport Agents (MTAs) can only process ASCII files. Generally, if a file contains CTRL characters or non-ASCII data, it's not considered an ASCII file. Before Z-Mail, if you wanted to send a non-ASCII file, such as a binary (program) or database file, you had to convert it to ASCII using a program like *uuencode* or *btoa* (binary to ASCII). When you converted the file to ASCII to send it to someone else, you had to include instructions for the recipient on how to convert the file back to its original form. This is, in fact, how you had to send binary files through the mail using MUSH or any other standard mailer.

With Z-Mail, you can "attach" both ASCII and non-ASCII files to mail messages. In other words, the file is not included as part of the message text but is considered a separate unit and appended to the message. These files are called *attachments*. If you attach a file that is not plain ASCII text, Z-Mail automatically encodes the file before sending it. If the file is plain text, Z-Mail prompts you for instructions on encoding the file. In either case, Z-Mail prompts you for a description of the attachment.

Including an attachment is different from sending a file with command-line redirection (using the left angle bracket character (<)). When the recipient reads your message, the attachment does not appear with the message text; to read the attachment, the recipient has to "detach" the file. If Z-Mail converted the file when you attached it, Z-Mail automatically converts it back to it's original format when it's detached.

 To attach a file to your message, use ˜A in compose mode. For example, let's send a message and attach a binary file (a program) called *cookie*. Here's the procedure:

1. First, enter this tilde-escape:

   ```
   ˜A ˜/bin/cookie
   ```

2. Z-Mail prompts you for the type of file that you're sending. For example, if the file is ASCII, Z-Mail prompts you with "text." In our example, the file is binary, so the prompt looks like the following:

   ```
   Attachment type (? for list): binary_
   ```

   At this prompt, you enter a keyword that represents the type of the attachment. To use the "binary" keyword, simply press RETURN. To display a list of attachment types, use CTRL-W to backspace over "binary," enter **?**, and then press RETURN. You see a list like this:

   ```
   Attachment type (? for list): ?
   text    tarmail    folder    bitmap    xpml    xwd    binary
   Attachment type (? for list): binary_
   ```

   For example, if you're attaching a mail folder, use the **folder** keyword to indicate the attachment type.

   The Z-Mail library file is **attach.types** found in */usr/lib/Zmail*. The location of the file can be set via the ZMLIB environment variable. This file contains the current list of keywords and the operations that are mapped to each keyword. You can tell Z-Mail to look in an alternate file by setting the **attach_types** variable to another location.

If you specified an alternate file, Z-Mail reads the *usr/lib/Zmail/attach.types* file and then that file. Z-Mail adds the entries from the alternate *attach.types* file to the system file; if you have more than one attachment definition with the same name, Z-Mail uses the first one it reads. We'll explain how to add attachment type entries to *attach.types* in Chapter 8, *Customizing Z-Mail*.

3. Now, Z-Mail prompts you for a description of the attachment:

```
Attachment description: _
```

Enter a short description of the attachment and press RETURN. Z-Mail displays this description when the recipient uses **detach** to list the attachments. In our example, we'll use "fortune cookie" as the attachment description.

4. Now, you see the prompt for encoding the file. If the attachment type is "text," the default encoding is "none," otherwise Z-Mail uses *compress*. In our example, we specified the type of the attachment as binary, so the prompt looks like this:

```
Encoding: (? for list) compress_
```

If you want to use *compress* to encode the file, simply press RETURN at this prompt.[1] If you don't want to use *compress*, you can specify another keyword (from *attach.types*) for Z-Mail to use to encode the file. To display a list of encoding keywords, enter CTRL-W to backspace over the default keyword and enter **?**:

```
Encoding: (? for list) ?
compress  btoa    uuencode
Encoding: (? for list) _
```

In our example, to use *btoa* (to convert binary to ASCII) instead of *compress*, use CTRL-W to backspace over "compress" and then enter **btoa**. Another common encoding and decoding keyword is **uuencode**; like *btoa*, the *uuencode* utility also converts a binary file to ASCII. (We'll get to decoding and detaching in a minute.)

5. Now, Z-Mail displays the **To** prompt; address, compose and send your message as usual. You can attach as many files as you like; simply use ~A and specify the new filename to attach.

You can also include attachments when sending messages from the Z-Mail prompt. Use the **−A** option to **mail**:

```
Msg 3 of 10: m −A ~/bin/cookie
```

Again, Z-Mail prompts you for the attachment type, a description of the attachment, and encoding information.

To include an attachment when sending a message from the UNIX prompt, use the **−attach** (**−A**) option with **zmail**:

```
$ zmail −attach ~/bin/cookie
```

You are prompted for the same information as with **mail −A**.

---

[1] You might be familiar with a UNIX command named *compress* whose output is binary; the Z-Mail **compress** keyword converts binary to ASCII (using the *btoa* utility).

If you're using command-line redirection to send the attachment, you can specify the file to attach and the attachment type at the UNIX prompt:

```
$ zmail —attach text:zmail.book dale < frame.text
```

This sends the file *frame.text* with the attachment *zmail.book* to *dale* and specifies the attachment type keyword "text").

Note that you can also specify the type like this when you use **–A** from the Z-Mail prompt to send an attachment.

Listing the Current Attachments

At any time when you're composing a message, you can use ˜**A** without a filename to list the current attachments. For example, you see a list like the following:

```
˜A
Part    Name         Type Key    Encoding    Size        Description
1       cookie       binary      compress    (pending)   fortune cookie
2       haiku        text        (none)      (pending)   haiku for you
(continue editing letter)

—
```

Note that Z-Mail doesn't fill in the "Size" field until you send the message. Also note that Z-Mail doesn't preserve the full pathname of the attachment. In our example, we attached ˜/*bin/cookie*; it appears in this attachment listing as *cookie*.

Removing Attachments

If you change your mind about attaching the file, you can "unattach" it using ˜**A!**. For example, enter ˜**A!**. Z-Mail displays the list of current attachments and prompts you for which one to remove:

```
˜A!
Part    Name         Type Key    Encoding    Size        Description
1       cookie       binary      compress    (pending)   fortune cookie
2       haiku        text        (none)      (pending)   haiku for you
Remove part (number or name): _
```

Enter the part number or name of the attachment at the prompt. For example, to remove the "cookie" attachment, enter **1** or **cookie**.

Now, when you list the current attachments, Z-Mail displays:

```
˜A
Part    Name         Type Key    Encoding    Size        Description
1       haiku        text        (none)      (pending)   haiku for you
(continue editing letter)

—
```

Detaching Attachments

When you receive a message with an attachment, use the **detach** command to save the attachment to a file. Here's the syntax for **detach**:

```
detach [options] [message_number] [filename]
```

The options to **detach** are listed in Table 4-3.

Table 4-3. Detach Options

Option	Description
–list	List the attachments to a message.
–part *number*	Detach the part with the given *number*.
–name *name*	Detach the part with the given *name*.
–all	Detach all the parts.
–encode *keyword*	Decode the attachment using the specified *keyword*.*
–use *type*	Use the specified *type* as the type for display.
–display	Display after detaching (**–use** does this automatically).
–rehash	Reread the files specified by the **attach_types** variable and *attach.type* so that **detach** recognizes new types and encodings.

*See the previous section, "Sending Attachments" in this chapter for information on the encoding keywords.

To list the attachments for a message, use this command:

```
Msg 3 of 10: detach -l
```

Here's what Z-Mail displays:

```
Part    Name            Type Key    Encoding    Size    Description
1  *    Msg112.A01      Text        (none)      106     (no description)
1       haiku           text        (none)       77     haiku for you
```

If the message has no attachments, you see the following:

```
Message 3 has no attachments.
```

If a person reads the message using an MUA other than Z-Mail, they see the special Z-Mail attachment headers in the message:

```
From hanna Sun Jul 14 16:21:43 1991
X-Mailer: Z-Mail (2.0.0 7/1/91)
To: cooper
Subject: Haiku
X-Zm-Content-Type: multipart
X-Zm-Content-Length: 11449
Date: Sun, 14 Jul 91 16:21:43 PST
From: Hanna Nelson <hanna@holycow.santa-cruz.ca.us>

X-Zm-Content-Type: Text
X-Zm-Content-Length: 101
X-Zm-Data-Type: Text
```

In this case, the recipient can save the message with **write** and perform any necessary converting by hand.

Sending Large Files

Normally, when you send messages and files, Z-Mail creates a temporary file in the directory specified by **tmpdir**. If you have a very large file to send and a very full file system, you might not want Z-Mail to do this.

To tell Z-Mail to pass the file directly to the MTA (Mail Transport Agent) without storing it in the temporary file, use the **–direct (–D)** option with **zmail** and command-line redirection. For example:

```
$ zmail —direct james < large.file
```

Z-Mail ignores the **–direct** option unless you redirect input from a file or a pipeline on the UNIX prompt.

WARNING

Some electronic mail hosts will not transmit extremely large files.

Mail Aliases

A *mail alias* is a shorthand name for a long mail address or a list of mail addresses. Aliases are particularly useful for sending mail to a large group of people; you type in the list of names once and then use the alias name each time you send mail. For example, I've created an alias called *unixdoc* to send mail to all the people in my group that are working on the UNIX documentation. When I want to send mail to everyone, I use the *unixdoc* alias like this:

```
$ zmail unixdoc
```

To use an alias from the UNIX prompt like this, you must make the alias permanent by adding it to the initialization file. We'll show you how to do this in Chapter 8, *Customizing Z-Mail*.

Creating Mail Aliases

To set up a mail alias, use the **alias** command:

```
alias [ name [expansion] ]
```

The *name* is the shorthand name for *expansion* (a list of one or more mail addresses). If the alias expansion includes special characters, such as single quotes ('), enclose the entire expansion in double quotes ("). When you want to send mail to *expansion*, use the alias *name* instead.

Let's set up the *unixdoc* alias. Enter the following command on one line at the **zmail** prompt:

```
Msg 3 of 10: alias unixdoc arthur, faith, stewart,\
        mattb@chaos.com, teresa@grafix.com
```

(The examples in this section use the backspace character (\) to break the **alias** definition lines so that they fit on the page; enter these commands as one line at the line-mode prompt.)

Note that some of the people in this example are on the same computer (or network) as I am; the others (*mattb* and *teresa*) are on different computers (*chaos.com* and *grafix.com*). You can also create separate aliases for the people on other computers if you don't want to enter the entire address each time you send them mail.

Now, send mail to those people on the *unixdoc* alias like this:

```
Msg 3 of 10: m unixdoc
```

Z-Mail *expands* the alias and sends your message to each person on the alias. When these people read the message, they see all the names on the **To** line:

```
To: arthur, faith, stewart, mattb@chaos.com, teresa@grafix.com
```

You can use the alias feature to create short names for people on your system. For example, I send mail to *alastair*, but I usually call him "Al." If I set up this alias:

```
Msg 3 of 10: alias al alastair
```

then, when I send mail to *al*, Z-Mail sends it to *alastair*.

Keep in mind that any aliases that you create in Z-Mail override the system-wide aliases or other mail addresses on your system. For example, if you create the *al* alias and there's another person on your system named *al*, when you send mail, it will always go to the person named in your alias. To avoid conflicts with other names on the system, you should try to use unusual alias names.

If you want the alias name (rather than the expansion) to appear on the **To** line, set the **no_expand** variable:

```
Msg 3 of 10: set no_expand
```

Now, for this Z-Mail session, aliases aren't expanded in your outgoing messages. The **To** line looks like this instead:

```
To: unixdoc
```

Setting **no_expand** is useful in situations where you are managing large mailing lists; it is not useful as a default setting.

If you set *edit_hdrs* and you enter the editor, Z-Mail expands any aliases that you use on the command line, even if you set *no_expand*. For example, let's say you set the *unixdoc* alias in our previous example and then send mail to it. When you enter the editor, Z-Mail expands the *unixdoc* alias:

```
From: hanna (Hanna Nelson)
Date: Sun, 26 Jul 1991 11:49:00 PST
X-Mailer: Z-Mail (2.0.0 7/1/91)
To: arthur, faith, stewart, mattb@chaos.com, teresa@grafix.com
Subject: Re: Review Copies
```

This is useful for checking the contents of an alias before sending the message. However, if you don't have **edit_hdrs** set, you can always check the definition of an alias from within compose mode using the ˜: tilde-escape. We'll show you how in the next section, "Displaying Mail Aliases."

You can include filenames in your aliases so that every time you send mail to the alias, you keep a copy in a file for yourself. To do this, you must specify the full pathname; the file must begin with a slash (/), plus (+), or tilde character (˜). (Note that the filename can't include the at character (@).) Let's include the file *ug.out* in my home directory in the *unixdoc* alias:

```
Msg 3 of 10: alias unixdoc arthur, faith, stewart, \
             mattb@chaos.com, teresa@grafix.com ˜/ug.out
```

Now, when I send a message to the *unixdoc* alias, a copy is automatically saved in ˜/ug.out.

Another way to keep copies of messages that you send to aliases is to include your own address in the alias. For example:

```
Msg 3 of 10: alias unixdoc arthur, faith, stewart, \
             mattb@chaos.com, teresa@grafix.com hanna
```

Now, when I send mail to *unixdoc*, Z-Mail sends me a copy, too.

Displaying Mail Aliases

You can display all your mail aliases and their expansions using **alias** with no arguments:

```
Msg 3 of 10: alias
```

Z-Mail displays a list like this:

```
al        alastair
unixdoc   arthur, faith, stewart, mattb@chaos.com, teresa@grafix.com
```

To print the expansion for one particular alias, enter **alias**, followed by the alias name. For example, when I enter this:

```
Msg 3 of 10: alias unixdoc
```

I see this:

```
arthur, faith, stewart, mattb@chaos.com, teresa@grafix.com
```

The *expansion* can contain other alias names and even filenames, in addition to mail addresses. For example, let's say you have aliases for *keith* and *paul* that look like this:

```
Msg 3 of 10: alias keith keith@bodega.com
Msg 3 of 10: alias paul paul@surf.edu
```

You can include the *keith* and *paul* aliases in another alias (*zbook*) like this:

```
Msg 3 of 10: alias zbook keith, paul, dale, george@vegan.edu
```

Now, if you enter this command:

```
Msg 3 of 10: alias zbook
```

you see the following:

```
keith, paul, dale, george@vegan.edu
```

If you want to see the actual addresses for the aliases within the *zbook* alias, use the **expand** command. For example, you type the following:

    Msg 3 of 10: expand zbook

and Z-Mail displays this list:

    zbook: keith@bodega.com, paul@surf.edu, dale, george@vegan.edu

Checking Aliases from Within Compose Mode

 To check the value of an alias from within compose mode, use the ~: tilde-escape to run a command like the following:

    ~:expand unixdoc

Z-Mail expands the alias, for example:

    arthur, faith, stewart, mattb@chaos.com, teresa@grafix.com
    (continue editing letter)
    _

(Note that Z-Mail doesn't insert the alias definition in your letter.)

If you can't remember the name of an alias, use this command to display all your aliases:

    ~:alias

In this case, if you have more than one page of alias definitions, Z-Mail pages through the list. To exit the list, press **q**.

Unsetting Mail Aliases

Unless you set up aliases in your initialization file, the definitions disappear automatically when you quit Z-Mail. If you want to use the alias name for another expansion during the current Z-Mail session, simply redefine the alias. To remove the alias definition completely without exiting Z-Mail, use the **unalias** command, like this:

    Msg 3 of 10: unalias unixdoc

Now, if you enter the following:

    Msg 3 of 10: alias unixdoc

Z-Mail responds like this:

    unixdoc is not set

If you try to send mail to *unixdoc*, the mail bounces.

If you set the alias in your initialization file, **unalias** only unsets the alias for the current Z-Mail session. The next time you start up the program (Z-Mail reads the initialization file at startup time), the aliases are active. To unset aliases permanently, remove the alias definition from your initialization file.

Customizing Your Outgoing Mail

In this section, we'll explain several other commands and variables that you can use to customize your outgoing mail messages and change the way Z-Mail behaves when you use it to send mail.

Setting Your Real Name

You can specify your real name (as opposed to your login name or full address) for Z-Mail to display on `From:` header lines when people read your message. To do this, set the **realname** variable to a string:

```
Msg 3 of 10: set realname="Hanna Nelson"
```

Now, Z-Mail uses this:

```
From: Hanna Nelson <hanna@holycow.santa-cruz.ca.us>
```

The string "Hanna Nelson" can appear in the header summary list when the recipient looks at their header summary. Whether or not this appears in the header display is dependent on the recipient's mailer and its settings.

If you don't set **realname**, Z-Mail uses the value of the **NAME** environment variable by default. For Bourne and Korn shell, set **NAME** in ˜/.profile; for C shell, set it in ˜/.cshrc. For example, I set **NAME** like this (in Korn shell):

```
NAME="Hanna Wacker Nelson"
export NAME
```

If neither **realname** nor **NAME** are set, Z-Mail uses information from the /etc/passwd file, if it's available. For example, Z-Mail uses the fifth field from my line in /etc/passwd:

```
hanna:*:1000:40:Hanna Baby Nelson:/u/hanna:/bin/ksh
```

If these variables and fields all contain something different, Z-Mail uses the value of **realname**.

Introducing the Included Message

Earlier in this chapter, we showed you different ways to include a message in your composition. We explained that Z-Mail indents the included text with the right angle bracket character (>) by default. Now, we'll show you how to tell Z-Mail to use a different indent string with the **indent_str** variable.

For example, let's change the indent string from > to "* ":

```
Msg 3 of 10: set indent_str = "* "
```

Now, when you include a message, Z-Mail uses the new string:

```
 *
 * This is an included message.
 *
 * Mark
 *
```

Note that we included a space in the **indent_str** setting so that when we include the message, there's a space between the indent character and the message text.

You can also set strings to precede and follow the included message. To add a string on the line preceding the first line of the included message in your outgoing message, set the **pre_indent_str** variable. The **post_indent_str** variable inserts a string after the last line of the included text. (By default, neither of these variables is set.)

You can use these variables together with **indent_str**. For example, if you're a C programmer, you might want to make the included message look like a comment in C code. Do this by using these settings together:

```
Msg 3 of 10: set pre_indent_str = "/*"
Msg 3 of 10: set indent_str = " * "
Msg 3 of 10: set post_indent_str = " */"
```

Now, when you include messages in your outgoing mail, Z-Mail uses these strings to set off the included text. In our example, the included message now looks like this:

```
/*
 * This is an included message.
 *
 * Mark
 *
 */
```

The **pre_indent_str** variable adds the "/*" before the included message, **post_indent_str** adds the " */" after the message and **indent_str** changes the default ">" to " * ".

You can also use special formatting characters to include information, such as the date, subject, or the author's address, in the **pre_indent_str**, **indent_str**, and **post_indent_str**. You can use the special formatting characters that are used with the **hdr_format** variable in all three of the **indent_str** variables. (If you're familiar with the C programming language, you'll recognize this type of format from the **printf** function.) See Table 3-6 for a list of these special characters.

For example, if you set *pre_indent_str* like this:

```
Msg 3 of 10: set pre_indent_str="On %M %N, %T, %n wrote:"
```

Z-Mail automatically places an introductory line like the following before the included message:

```
On Jul 26, 9:34pm, Mark the Shark wrote:
```

In this example, Z-Mail uses the information from the headers in the included message and makes the following substitutions:

%M   Month name (July) from **Date** header.
%N   Day of the month (26) from **Date** header.

%T   Time the message was sent (9:34pm) from `Date` header.

%n   The author's name from the `From` header.

Here's another **pre_indent_str** example:

```
'At %T on %7d in the message with the Subject\n  "%s", %f wrote:'
```

Now, when you include a message, you'll see an introduction as follows:

```
At 14:26 on Jul 29, in the message with the Subject
    "Re: Review Copies", albert@tp.com (Albert) wrote:
```

In this example, **mil_time** is set; if this variable is not set, the time (%T) appears as "12:26pm."

Remember that the number between the % and format characters is a *field-width specifier*; use it to print the first specified number of characters in the string. In this example, **%7d** tells Z-Mail to include only the first seven characters of the message date. If you use **%d** (with no "7"), Z-Mail displays all 14 characters in the date. It looks like this:

```
Jul 29,  14:26
```

Here's another sample **pre_indent_str**:

```
set pre_indent_str = 'On %7d %n sent me this %l-line message:
```

Now the introduction to your included message looks like this:

```
On Jul 23, D Neilson sent me this 675-line message:
```

Note that the comma (,) is included in the seven characters of the date specification. If you include a comma after "%7d" (as my instinct tells me to) in your **pre_indent_str** variable, your string has an extra comma:

```
On Jul 24,, Mel Gibson sent me this 27-line message:
```

To get around this, either leave off the comma in your **pre_indent_str** setting, or use **%6d** instead.

Setting the In-Reply-To Header

You can tell Z-Mail to include the special `In-Reply-To` header that specifies what the message is about in your responses. To do this, set the **in_reply_to** variable to a string. Use the same formatting characters in the string value that you used with the **indent_str** variables; see Table 3-6 for a list of these characters.

For example, let's set **in_reply_to** like this:

```
set in_reply_to = "%n's %l-line message dated %W %N %M %Y [%T]"
```

Now, when you respond to a message, Z-Mail adds a line like this to your message:

```
In-Reply-To: Alfred Hitchcock's 4-line message dated Wed 28 Jul 1991 [ 2:26pm]
```

Here's another example that includes the contents of the `Subject` line in the `In-Reply-To` header:

```
set in_reply_to = 'The message about "%s" \n   from %a dated %d'
```

Z-Mail adds this line to my response:

```
In-Reply-To: The message about "Strangers on a Train"
     from alfred@moocow.com dated Jul 26, 3:48pm
```

Note that if you use \n in the **in_reply_to** variable, you must follow it with whitespace or \n (TAB). Otherwise, the MTA might get confused.

Creating Message Headers

As you begin to use mail to communicate with people in different companies, you might want to include some information, such as the name of your company or your phone number, in every message that you send. With Z-Mail, you can use the **my_hdr** command to create your own personalized headers that appear along with the regular headers, like `To` and `Subject`. You'll probably want to make these personalized headers permanent by putting them in your *.zmailrc* initialization file so that they are defined automatically each time you start Z-Mail.

 For example, let's create a header called **Phone-Number** and set it to your phone number. Use a command like this:

```
Msg 3 of 10: my_hdr Phone-Number: (900) 860-0911
```

The header (the string immediately to the right of **my_hdr**) cannot contain spaces or tabs; as in the example, use the dash character (–) to separate words. The header must always end with a colon character (:); Z-Mail interprets anything following the colon as text to associate with the specified mail header.

 You could create an **Organization** header and set it to your company name like this:

```
Msg 3 of 10: my_hdr Organization: "O'Reilly & Associates, Inc."
```

Now, when people read your messages, they see this header along with the regular Z-Mail headers:

```
From hanna Thu Jul 4 20:19:49 1991
From: Hanna Nelson <hanna@holycow.santa-cruz.ca.us>
Date: Thu, 4 Jul 1991 20:19:47 PST
Phone-Number: (900) 860-0911
Organization: O'Reilly & Associates, Inc.
To: dan, bart
Subject: Z-Mail Chapters
```

In the previous example, the value is enclosed in double quotes because it includes a single quote. Otherwise, Z-Mail complains:

```
Unmatched '.
```

It's generally a good practice to enclose strings in double quotes. If you include other metacharacters, such as double quote (**"**), semicolon (**;**), or pipe (**|**), you must enclose the entire string in double quotes. Otherwise Z-Mail might interpret the character as a command-line modifier. If the string includes double quotes, enclose it in single quotes.

To list all of your personalized mail headers, enter **my_hdr** with no options. Thus, if you enter **my_hdr** after setting the headers in the examples above, Z-Mail displays this:

```
Phone-Number:       (900) 860-0911
Organization:       O'Reilly & Associates, Inc.
```

If you just want to display the value of a particular header, enter **my_hdr** followed by the header name (don't forget the colon). If you enter the following:

```
Msg 3 of 10: my_hdr Phone-Number:
```

Z-Mail displays:

```
(900) 860-0911
```

If you forget the colon, you see an error like this:

```
header labels must end with a ':' (Phone-Number)
```

If you mistype the header name, Z-Mail displays a message like this:

```
phone-number: is not set
```

You can also create your own versions of standard headers. If you set your own **From** header, Z-Mail tests it to determine whether the address that you specify is valid. If the address is valid, Z-Mail uses your **From** header; if not, Z-Mail generates a valid address and uses it instead.

NOTE

Some MTAs don't allow Z-Mail to supply a **From** header; in these cases, the MTA (silently) replaces your **From** header with the header that it generates.

You can't set the **Date** header; if you try to, the system overwrites your date when it sends your message.

Creating Reply-To Headers

Many MUAs use the special **Reply-To** header to construct a return path when people reply to messages. Generally, the MTA on the system that you're sending your message from adds this header to your outgoing messages. However, you can specify your own **Reply-To** header if you like. Let's say you're sending mail from one machine, but you want replies to your message to go to an account on another machine. In this case, you can use **my_hdr** to create a special **Reply-To** header:

```
Msg 3 of 10: my_hdr Reply-To: hanna@holycow.santa-cruz.ca.us
```

Now, if I send a message from my account on *espresso*, Z-Mail inserts this header in my message. Any responses to my message go to my *holycow* address.

When forwarding mail without editing it (using **mail –Uf**), Z-Mail does not add the `Reply-To` header.[2]

Requesting a Return-Receipt

With many MTAs, you can request a *return-receipt*, a message from the MTA telling you that your message was delivered to the recipient. This is the electronic mail equivalent to registered mail. Here's an example of a return-receipt message from MMDF:

```
From mmdf Thu Jul  4 14:14:02 1991
From: holycow MMDF Mail System <mmdf@holycow>
Date: Thu, 4 Jul 91 14:13:08 PST
To:  hanna
Subject: Re: testing return-receipt
Message-ID:  <9102031413.aa03530@holycow>

Your message (id <9102031413.aa03525@holycow>)
was delivered on holycow as follows:

james: Delivery to file '/usr/spool/mail/james' succeeded.
```

These MTA's recognize the `Return-Receipt-To` header as a request for a return-receipt. You can use **my_hdr** to create a personalized `Return-Receipt-To` header and set it to your own address using a command like the following:

`Msg 3 of 10:` **my_hdr Return-Receipt-To: hanna@holycow.santa-cruz.ca.us**

Z-Mail now puts the `Return-Receipt-To` header in every outgoing message and you'll get return-receipts when these messages reach their destinations.

If you don't want to get return-receipts for all your outgoing messages, you can use the ˜R tilde-escape to request a return-receipt for individual messages. For example, when you enter:

˜**R**

you see the following:

```
Requesting return receipt.
(continue editing letter)

_
```

Note that the ˜R escape uses the address from the `From:` line in your outgoing message. So, if your outgoing `From:` line contains:

`From: Hanna Nelson <hanna@holycow.santa-cruz.ca.us>`

the `Return-Receipt-To` line looks like this:

`Return-Receipt-To: hanna@holycow.santa-cruz.ca.us`

---

[2] MUSH always adds all of your personalized headers, even when forwarding. However, note that when forwarding, MUSH changes the `From` header to `Resent-From`.

If you create a personal **Return-Receipt-To** header with **my_hdr** to include return-receipts in all your outgoing messages, you can leave it off for specific messages using the ⁻**R!** tilde-escape.

Removing Personal Headers

You might want to disable a personalized header for specific messages. To do this, use the **un_hdr** command. For example, if you're testing a mail address, you might want to turn off return-receipts. Here's how to turn off the **Return-Receipt-To** header for the current session:

```
Msg 3 of 10: un_hdr Return-Receipt-To:
```

To remove *all* of the headers that you set with **my_hdr**, enter the following:

```
Msg 3 of 10: un_hdr *
```

To temporarily suppress your personalized headers, set the **no_hdrs** variable. If you don't want to include the **Return-Receipt-To** header from our example, use the **set** command:

```
Msg 3 of 10: set no_hdrs
```

Note that this turns off *all* of your personal headers, but does not unset them. To turn the headers back on, use the **unset** command:

```
Msg 3 of 10: unset no_hdrs
```

Another way to use return-receipts is to turn them on for specific messages using command-line aliases. For example, use these command-line aliases for turning return-receipts on and off:

```
cmd register "my_hdr Return-Receipt-To: hanna@holycow.santa-cruz.ca.us"
cmd noregister "un_hdr Return-Receipt-To:"
```

 You can even create command-line aliases for sending messages with **Return-Receipt-To** headers:

```
cmd mailreg "register;mail;noregister"
cmd replyreg "register;reply;noregister"
```

These commands turn on the return-receipts for the current message and then turn them back off again once you've sent the message.

You might also want to turn off personal headers when you send mail to specific users. We'll show you how to perform functions like this using **if** statements in initialization scripts and functions in Chapter 8, *Customizing Z-Mail*, and Chapter 9, *Writing Scripts and Functions*.

Signing Your Name

You can tell Z-Mail to append a prepared *signature* to your outgoing messages. The signature is useful for including some more information about yourself, such as your real name, company, electronic mail address, or telephone number. Some people include disclaimers (if they don't want their opinions connected with their employer) or favorite quotations. If you've read news on Usenet, you've probably seen signatures at the end of postings. Here's an example:

```
--
From the disk of Dale Cooper <cooper@fbi.gov>
The opinions expressed above are mine, not my employers.
    and still carry a tune.''  -- Woody Allen
```

To tell Z-Mail to append a signature to outgoing messages, create a file called *.signature* in your home directory. For example, here's what my signature file, */u/hanna/.signature*, looks like:

```
                Hanna Nelson
hanna@holycow.santa-cruz.ca.us  or  hannan@sco.com
```

To include the contents of *˜/.signature* in the current message, use the ˜S tilde-escape. When you use ˜S, Z-Mail displays this message:

```
Adding signature at end of message.
(continue editing letter)
—
```

Note that Z-Mail doesn't append anything until you actually send the message. For example, when I press CTRL-D, Z-Mail appends my signature to the message and displays this message:

```
Signing letter... 2 lines
```

When the person reads my message, my signature appears like this at the end:

```
--
                Hanna Nelson
hanna@holycow.santa-cruz.ca.us  or  hannan@sco.com
```

Z-Mail automatically inserts the two dashes (--) to separate the body of the message from the signature.

To tell Z-Mail to append the signature automatically to *all* outgoing messages, set the **autosign** variable:

```
Msg 3 of 10: set autosign
```

With **autosign** set, you can tell Z-Mail *not* to add the signature to the current message using the **-u** option from the Z-Mail prompt:

```
Msg 3 of 10: m -u cooper
```

If you're already in compose mode when you decide not to include the signature, use the ˜S! tilde-escape like this:

```
˜s!
```

You can also set **autosign** to include a file other than *˜/.signature* or even a literal string. If you set **autosign** to a string, Z-Mail interprets the string in one of three ways, depending upon the special character that precedes it. If you set **autosign** to a value, such as another filename, Z-Mail appends it to your outgoing messages. Use the tilde and plus special characters (~, +) to refer to your home and folder (~/*Mail*, by default) directories. For example, to sign your messages with the .*include_me* file in your home directory, set **autosign** like this:

```
Msg 3 of 10: set autosign = ~/.include_me
```

If you keep your signature file in the folder directory, use a command like this:

```
Msg 3 of 10: set autosign = +sign
```

In each of these situations, Z-Mail appends the contents of the file, separated from the message body text with two dash characters (--).

Instead of telling Z-Mail to include a file, you can specify a literal string to append to your messages. To do this, set **autosign** to a string that begins with the backslash special character (\):

```
Msg 3 of 10: set autosign = "\Hanna Nelson"
```

Another way to do this is to surround the string with square brackets ([]) as shown in the following example:

```
Msg 3 of 10: set autosign = "[Hanna Nelson]"
```

In either case, when I send the message, Z-Mail appends the string "Hanna Nelson" (without the backslash or square brackets) to my messages. When my message is read, the string appears like this:

```
Hanna Nelson
```

Note that the two dash characters don't appear above the string when you sign your messages with a literal string.

By default, when Z-Mail adds the signature to your outgoing message, you see a message like this:

```
Signing letter...
```

If you don't want Z-Mail to display this message when it appends the signature, set the **quiet** variable to include the string "autosign":

```
Msg 3 of 10:set quiet = autosign
```

When you set **quiet** to this string, Z-Mail suppresses all messages when appending signatures.

If you use command-line redirection to send your message, Z-Mail doesn't include any signature in your outgoing mail. Thus, if you use this command:

```
$ zmail -s "Chapter three" dale < ~/zmail/chapter.3
```

you're redirecting the file *chapter.3* as input to the **zmail** command; Z-Mail won't append the signature in this case.

Including an Alternate Signature File

In some cases, your signature file might be inappropriate for the audience of your message. For example, my signature file contains the full domain address for sending mail to me; this information isn't necessary for sending mail internally (on the same machine or network). Another example might be that your signature file is more familiar than you want it to be with people you don't know; for example, your signature might include a silly nickname that only your friends understand.

In these situations, you can specify an alternate signature to append using the **autosign2** variable. You can also use **autosign2** to tell Z-Mail not to append *any* signature to messages that you send to certain addresses.

Here's the syntax for **autosign2**:

```
set autosign2 = "[address_list]:value"
```

The *address_list* is the list of users' addresses that you want to get the specified signature, and *value* is the alternate signature. The colon character (:) separates the addresses from the signature. Any of the formats for setting **autosign** are valid with **autosign2**. So, let's set an alternate signature to use when sending mail to the president and vice president:

```
Msg 3 of 10: set autosign2 = "larry doug:\Hanna Nelson, x6266"
```

When I send mail to *doug* and *larry*, Z-Mail appends the string "Hanna Nelson, x6266" to the end of my message. Note that both *doug* and *larry* must be included or Z-Mail won't append the string. If one or more of the recipients is not specified in **autosign2**, Z-Mail signs the message using the file (or string) specified by **autosign**. For example, given these settings:

```
Msg 3 of 10: set autosign
Msg 3 of 10: set autosign2 = "dan bart dale george:~/.sign.me"
```

If you send mail to *dan* and *bart*, Z-Mail signs the message with ~/.sign.me. However, if you send mail to *dale*, *george*, and *lisa*, Z-Mail uses the file specified by **autosign** (~/.signature, by default) because *lisa* is not on the **autosign2** list. If **autosign** isn't set, no signature is added. If you set **autosign2** without also setting **autosign**, the only way to append the alternate signature is by using the ~S tilde-escape.

If you don't specify the *address_list* or you forget to include the colon, Z-Mail appends the alternate signature to every outgoing mail message.

Table 4-4 specifies the types of addresses that you can use in **address_list** when you set **autosign2**.

Table 4-4. autosign2 Address Types

Type	Description
address	Legal mailing addresses that don't contain comment fields.
*username	Any occurrence of *username* on the recipient list, regardless of whether the person resides at a remote site or locally.

Table 4-4. autosign2 Address Types (continued)

Type	Description
!hostname	Anyone on the specified *hostname*.
!host!host2 . . .	Anyone on the last host of the specified pathname.
@hostname.domain	A person that resides on any host within the specified *domain*.

For example, let's say you set **autosign2** like this:

```
set autosign2 = "*cooper albert !moocow !ucscc!espresso @tp.com:\Hanna"
```

In this case, Z-Mail appends the string "Hanna" to the end of outgoing messages as long as all the addresses on the **To** list meet one of the following criteria:

- *cooper* on any machine, local or remote.

- *albert* on the local machine only.

- Anyone on the machine *moocow*.

- Anyone on the machine *espresso*, as long as the mail is sent through *ucscc*.

- Anyone within the *tp.com* domain.

If any of the addresses on the **To** line do not meet this criteria, Z-Mail appends the **autosign** signature. If **autosign** isn't set, Z-Mail doesn't sign the message.

One way to use **autosign** and **autosign2** is to specify a signature for local mail and another for mail to remote sites. For example, when I send mail internally at SCO, I don't need to specify my mail address—people internally can send mail to just "hannan" and it gets to me. However, when I send mail to friends at SGI and Apple, I like to include my complete mail address (in case they've forgotten it). To set up the two different signatures, I use:

```
Msg 3 of 10: set autosign2 = "@sco.com:\-- Hanna"
Msg 3 of 10: set autosign = "\Hanna Nelson (hannan@sco.com)"
```

Now, when I send mail to people at SCO, Z-Mail appends "-- Hanna" to my messages. When I send messages to anyone outside of the *sco.com* domain, Z-Mail signs my messages with "Hanna Nelson (hannan@sco.com)." Remember that the backslash character (\) tells Z-Mail to include the string that follows it rather than include a file.

You can also set up **autosign2** to append one signature to messages to anyone on the same machine, and another signature to anyone *not* on that machine. For example, my local machine name is *holycow*. To set up the local machine and remote signatures, I enter the following:

```
Msg 3 of 10: set autosign = "~/remote.sig"
Msg 3 of 10: set autosign2 = "!holycow:~/local.sig"
```

Now, Z-Mail appends the file *~/remote.sig* to any messages not addressed to people on my local machine *holycow*.

In general, if you want to use **autosign2**, you must also set **autosign**. However, if you want to include a signature file (other than ˜/.*signature*) *only* when you use ˜S, set **autosign2** without setting **autosign**. For example:

```
Msg 3 of 10: unset autosign
Msg 3 of 10: set autosign2 = ":˜/.alternate"
```

Now, when you enter ˜S as the first character on a line in compose mode, Z-Mail appends the file ˜/.*alternate* to your current outgoing message. When you send the message, you see the following:

```
Using alternate signature... /u/hanna/.alternate: 1 line
```

NOTE

If you don't *unset* **autosign**, Z-Mail appends the ˜/.*alternate* file to *all* your outgoing messages, not just to the messages that you specify with ˜S.

As with **autosign**, if you use command-line redirection, Z-Mail does not include the **autosign2** signature in your outgoing mail.

Including a Fortune

For fun, you can tell Z-Mail to append a random fortune to your outgoing messages. When you set the **fortune** variable, Z-Mail runs the UNIX *fortune* command to generate the fortune and then appends it to your outgoing messages. Here's how to set **fortune**:

```
Msg 3 of 10: set fortune
```

When you send your messages, you see this line:

```
You may be fortunate... added 1 line
```

When the person reads your message, a fortune like this appears at the end:

```
The attention span of a computer is only as
long as its extension cord.
```

Because Z-Mail doesn't actually append the fortune until you send the message, there's no way to see the fortune before you send the message. For this reason, you probably won't want to include the fortune with every message you send. To tell Z-Mail *not* to include a fortune in the current message, use the **–u** option to **mail** like this:

```
Msg 3 of 10: m –u harry
```

Note that this option also suppresses signatures.

If you're already in compose mode, use this tilde-escape command to suppress *fortune* for the current message:

```
˜F!
```

If you'd prefer to include fortunes manually, use **–F** on the Z-Mail command line like this:

```
Msg 3 of 10: m -F cooper
```

From within compose mode, use this tilde-escape to include a fortune:

```
~F
```

These commands have the same effect as temporarily activating the *fortune* variable. Again, Z-Mail doesn't append the fortune until you actually send the message.

By default, Z-Mail runs **fortune** with the −s (short) option (to generate relatively short fortune messages). To tell Z-Mail to use a different option, (for example, −l, for long fortunes), set **fortune** to a value that begins with a dash character (−). For example, let's include long fortunes in our messages:

```
Msg 3 of 10: set fortune = -l
```

Now, when you send a message, Z-Mail appends long fortunes like this one:

```
To determine how long it takes to write and debug a program,
take your best estimate, multiply that by two, add one, and
convert to the next higher units.
```

To get more information about the options to *fortune*, enter this command at your UNIX prompt:

```
$ fortune -
```

Your system might not have the *fortune* command. If this is the case, when you send your message, Z-Mail displays an error like this:

```
sh: fortune: not found
```

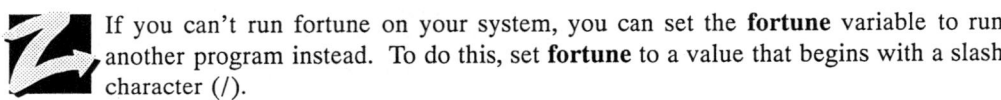 If you can't run fortune on your system, you can set the **fortune** variable to run another program instead. To do this, set **fortune** to a value that begins with a slash character (/).

For example, I use a public domain program called *enquirer* to generate random tabloid headlines and another program called *cookie* that my friend Karl wrote to retrieve my own fortune cookie quotes.

To use *enquirer* headlines instead of **fortune**, I set the fortune variable to run *enquirer* like this:

```
Msg 3 of 10: set fortune = "/u/hanna/bin/enquirer /u/hanna/lib/headline"
```

With this **fortune** setting, instead of a fortune, Z-Mail appends a tabloid headline like this to the end of my outgoing messages:

```
Feral Grapefruits Menace Nevada.
```

If I set **fortune** to run *cookie* instead, I get a quote from the *cookie* file:

```
To err is human, to moo, bovine.
```

Specifying Who Gets a Fortune

When you set **fortune**, Z-Mail appends the fortune (or alternate) message to *all* outgoing mail messages (except when you use ˜**F!** or **–u**). If you don't want everyone to get a fortune, you can specify a list of users that you do want to receive fortunes with the **fortunates** variable. Note that you must set **fortune** or use ˜**F** for **fortunates** to work. For example, set these commands:

```
Msg 3 of 10: set fortune
Msg 3 of 10: set fortunates = dan unixdoc bart
```

Now, when you send mail, if the **To** or **Cc** lines contain an address that is not on the **fortunates** list, Z-Mail won't add the fortune. So, if you send a message to the alias *unixdoc* and *dan*, Z-Mail includes a fortune. However, if you send mail to *bart* and *dale*, Z-Mail won't include a fortune because *dale* is not on the **fortunates** list. In this case, Z-Mail displays this message:

```
"fortunates" does not contain "dale".
No fortune added.
```

If you don't want Z-Mail to display messages like this, set **quiet** to include the string "fortune," as shown in the following example:

```
Msg 3 of 10: set quiet = fortune
```

When you set **quiet** like this, Z-Mail suppresses all messages when appending fortunes.

Note that you can't force Z-Mail (with ˜**F**) to add a fortune to a message addressed to someone that is not listed on the **fortunates** list. When you send the message, you see the error message above.

You can also use the **fortune** and **fortunates** variables to sign your name with another signature (in addition to the ones specified by **autosign** and **autosign2**). For example, these settings append the string "Hanna (Wacker) Nelson" to the end of all messages to people on the machine *fscott*:

```
Msg 3 of 10: set fortune = '/bin/echo "Hanna (Wacker) Nelson"'
Msg 3 of 10: set fortunates = !fscott
```

Saving Copies of Your Outgoing Messages

If you want to keep a copy of an outgoing message, you can include your name on the **Cc** line of the message. However, this can get tedious if you want to save copies of *all* your outgoing messages. In this case, set the **record** variable to a folder name where you want to save the messages. For example, enter the following:

```
Msg 3 of 10: set record = +.out.mail
```

Now Z-Mail saves a copy of all your outgoing messages to the folder *.out.mail* in your folder directory. Remember that you can use the special characters tilde (˜) and plus (+) at the beginning of the pathname to indicate your home and folder (˜/*Mail*, by default) directories.

You can also specify that Z-Mail save messages to specific people in separate folders by setting the **record_users** variable:

```
Msg 3 of 10: set record_users
```

With **record_users** set, Z-Mail checks addresses in your outgoing mail against folder names in your folder directory. If Z-Mail matches the person's name to a folder, it puts a copy of the message in that folder. (The file must exist *before* you send the message.) For example, if I have a folder ~/*Mail/dale*, whenever I send mail to *dale*, Z-Mail puts a copy of that message in the *dale* folder.

If you set both **record** and **record_users**, Z-Mail keeps copies of a message in both the folder specified by **record** and the folders in the folder directory. For example, if you set these two variables and create the folder ~/*Mail/james*, whenever you send messages to *james*, Z-Mail keeps a copy in the record folder *and* in ~/*Mail/james*.

Sometimes you don't want to save certain outgoing messages; for example, when you send a file to another person. In this case, you can use a conditional expression to unset **record** in specific instances. We'll explain how in Chapter 8, *Customizing Z-Mail*.

Creating a Message Header Log

Another way to keep track of outgoing mail is to save only the headers. To do this, set the **logfile** variable; **logfile** is identical to **record** except that it only records the headers. This is useful for verifying that you've sent messages without keeping copies of the text of each message. If you set both **logfile** and **record**, you can use the log folder to scan the contents of the record folder more quickly; the headers for these folders are identical.

To save the headers to the default folder, ~/*mail.log*, set **logfile** like this:

```
Msg 3 of 10: set logfile
```

If you want to use a different folder, specify the name, as shown below:

```
Msg 3 of 10: set logfile = +.headers
```

The header information from each outgoing message is saved in */u/hanna/Mail/.headers*. In this case, you can use the *.headers* file to verify that you sent a message, but you won't be able to see what the message was about. We'll explain more about looking at messages in other folders when we show you how to switch folders in Chapter 5, *Z-Mail Shortcuts, Bells, and Whistles*.

Specifying the Dead Letter Folder

While composing a message, you can cancel it by entering two interrupt characters (CTRL-C or DEL) or by using the ~q or ~E tilde-escapes. When you do this, Z-Mail saves the contents of the message to the ~/*dead.letter* folder, by default. You can tell Z-Mail to store dead letters in another folder by setting the **dead** variable:

```
Msg 3 of 10: set dead = +dead
```

Now, Z-Mail saves interrupted mail messages to the folder *dead* in the folder directory.

You can also specify that Z-Mail send the contents of interrupted letters to a UNIX command using the following syntax:

```
Msg 3 of 10: set dead = "|UNIX_command"
```

Note that you must enclose the *UNIX_command* value in single (') or double quotes (").

Changing the Tilde-escape Character

Another way to customize the behavior of Z-Mail when sending mail is to change the character that invokes tilde-escapes. For example, the tilde key might be in an awkward place on your keyboard and you find it difficult to invoke tilde-escapes. You can change the character that invokes tilde-escape by setting the **escape** variable to a different character.

Let's change the escape character from the tilde (˜) to to a single quote character ('):

```
Msg 3 of 10: set escape = '
```

Now (if you set the **warning** variable), when you enter compose mode, Z-Mail displays this reminder message:

```
(escape character is set to `'')
```

When you want to invoke a command from within compose mode, enter ' at the beginning of a line followed by the single-character escape command.

Note that, with this setting, you can't enter a line like this:

```
'Tis the season to be merry.
```

When you press RETURN at the end of the line, you get this error:

```
`T': unknown ' escape. Use `? for help.
```

Keep this in mind when changing the tilde-escape character.

Reviewing the Variables

This chapter covers a lot of variables in the context of how you use them to customize the way Z-Mail behaves when you send messages. As we did in Chapter 3, *Reading and Managing Mail*, let's review the variables we've explained so far. Table 4-5 gives a list of the variables in this chapter.

Table 4-5. Chapter 4 Variable Review

Variable	Description
metoo	Tell Z-Mail to preserve your address on replies.
ask	Prompt for `Subject` when sending mail.
askcc	Prompt for `Cc` line when sending mail.
wrapcolumn	Wrap lines automatically in compose mode.
editor	Set the default editor.
autoedit	Enter the editor automatically when composing messages.
edit_hdrs	Edit headers with the text when composing messages.
nosave	Don't save canceled mail in ⁻/*dead.letter*.
dot	Send messages with **.** on a line by itself.
verify	Prompt for confirmation in specific situations.
templates	Set the location of the template directory.
realname	Specify the way your name appears on outgoing `From` headers.
indent_str	Change the string that indents included messages.
pre_indent_str	Specify a line to precede included messages.
post_indent_str	Specify a line to follow included messages.
no_hdrs	Turn off personal headers (but don't unset them).
autosign	Append a signature to messages automatically.
autosign2	Specify an alternate signature.
fortune	Append a random fortune to messages.
fortunates	Specify people to get fortunes.
record	Save outgoing messages to a folder.
record_users	Save outgoing messages to specified users in separate folders.
logfile	Create a log of outgoing message headers.
dead	Change the location of the *dead.letter* file.
escape	Change the character that invokes tilde-escapes.

Reviewing the Commands

In this chapter, we covered the different ways you can send and reply to message using the Z-Mail program. In addition to showing you how to use **mail** and **reply**, we explained the different command-line options and tilde-escapes that you can use to access some of the more powerful features of Z-Mail. Finally, we covered the variables you can set to change the behavior of Z-Mail while sending mail.

Because this chapter, like Chapter 3, covers so many commands and features of Z-Mail, we've included a quiz that you can use to review the things you've learned. Again, the commands are on the left, so match them up with the tasks listed on the right.

1. **m –b larry,moe,curly**
2. **˜s "A New Subject"**
3. **˜z**
4. **resume 2**
5. **m –e**
6. **˜S**
7. **r 6-8 –i**
8. **set record=+.out.mail**
9. **zmail mattb < ˜/poems**
10. **˜?**

11. **˜i 6**
12. **m –f 7 mattb**
13. **detach -l**
14. **˜v emacs**
15. **˜A +outline**

16. **r –i 6-8**
17. **˜u**
18. **˜:alias project**
19. **˜h**
20. **m –p phone**
21. **˜E!**

a. Include a signature file.
b. List the detachments.
c. Edit the previous line.
d. Forward a message to *mattb*.
e. Copy the 3 Stooges blindly.
f. Reply to three messages, include one.
g. Send a file to *mattb*.
h. Edit all the message headers.
i. Edit the message using *emacs*.
j. List the people on an alias from compose mode.
k. Change the `Subject`.
l. Erase the message buffer.
m. Get help on tilde-escapes.
n. Save outgoing messages to a file.
o. Reply to the current message, including three messages.
p. Suspend a message composition.
q. Include a message in the current message.
q. Send a phone message.
r. Continue editing a message.
s. Include an attachment.
t. Send a message, entering the editor immediately.

Review Quiz Answers

1.	e.	2.	k.	3.	p.	4.	r.	5.	t.	6.	a.	7.	f.
8.	n.	9.	g.	10.	m.	11.	q.	12.	d.	13.	b.	14.	i.
15.	s.	16.	o.	17.	c.	18.	j.	19.	h.	20.	q.	21.	l.

In the next chapter, we'll show you how to use the tools that make Z-Mail more flexible and efficient; you'll see how these features really distinguish Z-Mail from other electronic mail programs.

5
Z-Mail Shortcuts, Bells, and Whistles

This chapter covers the many of the commands and variable settings that just don't fit easily into Chapter 3, *Reading and Managing Mail*, and Chapter 4, *Sending Mail with Z-Mail*. It's not that these commands are particularly difficult to use or esoteric; they just don't apply when discussing the tasks of reading and sending mail. In fact, I think that the tools discussed in this chapter are really what makes Z-Mail stand out in the crowd of mail programs available on UNIX systems. These are the features and shortcuts that allow you to use Z-Mail to manage your mail so much more efficiently than with other programs.

We'll begin the chapter by describing the different types of Z-Mail variables, including the read-only variables, and how to refer to them. Then, we'll explain how to:

- Combine Z-Mail commands using pipelines.

- Display, modify, and re-execute previous commands using command history.

- Create command-line aliases.

- Press a key to tell Z-Mail to complete a filename.

- Open and combine different folders.

- Tell Z-Mail to ignore message headers in specific situations.

- Escape to the shell and run UNIX commands from within Z-Mail.

Additional Z-Mail Command-line Syntax

In Chapter 3, we introduced you to the concept of modifying the behavior of Z-Mail by setting some common *variables*. In this section, we'll expand on the coverage in Chapter 3 and explain more about the Z-Mail command-line syntax. We'll cover the different variable types, including the special *read-only* variables, and explain how to refer and modify variable values. Finally, we'll show you how to use the output of one Z-Mail command as input to another by combining the commands with the pipe character (|).

Remember, if you set variables from the Z-Mail prompt, they are set for the current Z-Mail session only; you lose the settings when you exit the program. For this reason, you'll probably find it more practical to put variable settings in your initialization file (˜/.zmailrc, by default); .mushrc in MUSH.

We explain more about this in Chapter 8, *Customizing Z-Mail*.

Z-Mail Variable Types

There are four types of Z-Mail variables: *boolean, string, numeric,* and *multi-valued*. Boolean variables are variables that you turn on and off (that is, you toggle them); you don't set them to any value. String and numeric variables are set to a single value. Multi-valued variables are set to a list (separated by commas or spaces) of strings.

Let's say you have the following variable settings:

```
ask
dot
folder          ˜/Mail
history         24
mbox            ˜/mbox
pager           internal
alwaysignore    include printer
unix
```

Here are the types of the variables in this example:

Boolean	String	Numeric	Multi-valued
ask	folder	history	alwaysignore
dot	mbox		
unix	pager		

Here's the syntax for setting boolean variables:

```
set variable
```

For string or numeric variables:

```
set variable = string/number
```

For multivalued variables:

```
set variable = 'string string string ...'
```

Note that the whitespace surrounding the equal sign (=) is optional; however, if you include whitespace on one side of the equal sign, you must include it on the other. In other words, if you set a variable like this:

```
Msg 3 of 10: set editor =/usr/bin/vi
```

Z-Mail displays an error like the following:

```
=/usr/bin/vi: No variable specified.
```

Also note that Z-Mail only expands the tilde (˜) to **$HOME** if it is preceded by whitespace.

If you want to use double quotes (") or spaces in the string, enclose the entire string in single quotes ('). Likewise, if you use single quotes in the string, enclose it in double quotes. Thus, to set a multi-valued variable, such as **alwaysignore**, to more than one string, use single quotes like this:

```
Msg 3 of 10: set alwaysignore = 'include printer'
```

To include single quotes in the string, enclose the string in double quotes. For example:

```
Msg 3 of 10: set in_reply_to = "%n's message dated %W %N %M %Y"
```

Referring to Variables

To refer to variables, use the $*variable* format. So, to check the value of the **hdr_format** variable use this command:

```
Msg 3 of 10: echo $hdr_format
```

Z-Mail displays the value of the variable like this:

```
%20n %6d %40s
```

If the variable isn't set, you see:

```
hdr_format: undefined variable
```

You can refer to variables in other variable settings. For example, to include the current directory in your Z-Mail prompt, use a command like the following to refer to the **cwd** variable:

```
Msg 3 of 10: set prompt=$cwd>
```

If I'm in my home directory, the prompt looks like this:

```
/u/hanna> _
```

If you want to include spaces or other variables in your prompt, use the double quote characters (") to separate the reference to the variable from the other items. For example, to include the current message number:

```
Msg 3 of 10: set prompt="$cwd":"msg #%n">
```

Now, the prompt is:

```
/u/hanna:msg #8> _
```

As in C shell, use double quotes around references to variables if you want Z-Mail to expand the variable (in our example, **$cwd** is expanded to **/u/hanna**). Generally, unless the variable includes spaces or single-quote characters, you can leave off the double quotes.

If you want Z-Mail to interpret the special characters, such as **$**, literally, place the variable in single quote characters ('). In our example, if we use single quotes instead of double quotes, the prompt looks like the following:

```
$cwd:msg #8> _
```

Variable Substitution Modifiers

You can modify the information that is substituted for the variable when you use $*variable* using *variable substitution modifiers*. These are similar to the C shell variable substitution modifiers (also called *colon modifiers*) that allow you to select specified words (arguments) from a variable substitution. To select an argument from a referenced variable, append a colon character (:) and a variable modifier to the variable reference. Table 5-1 describes these modifiers.

Table 5-1. Variable Substitution Modifiers

Modifier	Description
:t	Treat the variable as a file pathname, substituting the name of the file for $*variable*; this modifier returns everything to the right of the last slash character (/).
:h	Treat the variable as a pathname, substituting the *head* of the pathname for the $*variable*. This modifier returns everything up to, but not including, the last /.
:l	Convert all alphabetic characters in the value of $*variable* to lowercase.
:u	Convert all alphabetic characters in the value of $*variable* to uppercase.
:*number*	Convert $*variable* to a list of space-separated words, numbered from one (1). This modifier selects and returns the word described by *number*. If *number* is greater than the actual number of words, this modifier returns an empty string.

You can only use one variable substitution modifier for each $ variable expansion.

Here's an example of how to reference and modify variable substitutions. Use this **my_hdr** command to create a `Reply-To` header and set it to your mail address:

`Msg 3 of 10: my_hdr Reply-To: "$home:t"@"$hostname ($realname:1)"`

This command uses the values of the **home** (the **:t** indicates everything to the right of the last slash character), **hostname**, and **realname** (the **:1** specifies the first word) variables. Thus, if the value of $**home** is */u/hanna*, the value of $**hostname** is *holycow.santa-cruz.ca.us,* and the value of $**realname** is *Hanna Nelson*, then this command sets `Reply-To` like this:

`Reply-To: hanna@holycow.santa-cruz.ca.us (Hanna)`

Note that, because **realname** contains a space, the **:1** uses the first word of the value.

Read-only Variables

A *read-only* variable is a Z-Mail variable whose value you can reference, but not modify. These variables, listed in Table 5-2, are mostly used in Z-Mail scripts and functions. See Chapter 8, *Customizing Z-Mail*, and Chapter 9, *Writing Scripts and Functions*, for examples of how to use these variables.

Table 5-2. Read-only Variables

Variable	Description
cwd	The current working directory.
output	The output of the last successful command.
status	The status of the last command (0 for success; a negative number for failure).
thisfolder	The current folder.
version	The version of the software.

With the exception of **version**, Z-Mail changes the values of these variables when you perform some action, such as switching folders or changing directories; you won't ever need to set them manually.

If you attempt to set a read-only variable, Z-Mail displays an error. For example, try to set **version** with this command:

```
Msg 3 of 10: set version
```

and you get this error:

```
You can't change version with "set".
```

Current Working Directory

Z-Mail automatically sets the *current working directory* string at setup time and stores this information in the **cwd** string variable. Each time you use the **cd** or **pwd** commands, Z-Mail resets **cwd** to reflect the new directory. So, if you **cd** to */u/hanna/food/chocolate* and then enter the following:

```
Msg 3 of 10: echo $cwd
```

you see:

```
/u/hanna/food/chocolate
```

Output of the Last Command

Each time you execute a command successfully, Z-Mail stores the output of the command (a message list) in the **output** variable. You can use this variable to capture and use (without affecting) the output of a Z-Mail command.

For example, let's say you use this command to find all the messages send by Dale:

```
Msg 3 of 10: pick -f -i dale
```

Z-Mail displays something like this:

```
Searching for messages that contain "dale" from author names
2    Dale Cooper    Jul 21 10:49    (631)    RISKS DIGEST 11.21
4    dale           Aug 10 12:37    (20)     Review copies
7    Dale D.        Aug 15  2:30    (66)     online doc
```

and then stores the output of the command in **$output**. So, to display the value of **output**, enter the following:

```
Msg 3 of 10: echo $output
```

and you get this message:

```
2,4,7
```

The **output** variable contains the output of the **pick** command, "2," "4," and "7" (the message list).

Each time you execute a command, Z-Mail replaces the contents of **output** with the output of the most recent successful command. Commands that return an error status don't change the value of **output**.[1] However, if a command that doesn't return a message list, such as the *history* command which returns a listing of previous commands, $output is cleared. Thus, in the example above where we displayed the contents of $output, the output of the **echo** command resets $output to an empty string.

Once you select messages that meet your criteria, you can manipulate the message list in a number of ways using the pipe character (|). We'll show you how in the section on combining Z-Mail commands later in this chapter.

Status of the Last Command

To check the status of the last command you executed, use the **status** variable. Let's say you enter the following:

```
Msg 3 of 10: echo $status
```

If the last command succeeded, Z-Mail prints 0 (zero) for success; if it failed, you see a negative value.

For example, if the message pointer currently points to the last message in the folder and you use the **next** command to display the next message, Z-Mail displays this error:

```
No more messages.
```

In this case, the **next** command failed. Display the status by entering this command:

```
Msg 3 of 10: echo $status
```

Z-Mail displays —1 to indicate that the last command failed.

---

[1] Many fullscreen-mode commands return an error status indicating that you altered the display, even though no error actually occurred. For this reason, the **output** variable is more useful when you use Z-Mail in line mode, and in scripts and functions.

The **status** variable is most useful in scripts and functions to test the success of an operation before proceeding. See Chapter 9 for examples of how to use **status**.

Current Folder Name

Z-Mail automatically sets the full pathname of the current folder at startup time and stores this information in the **thisfolder** variable. Each time you use the **folder** command to switch to a new folder, Z-Mail changes the value of **thisfolder**.

To display the value of **thisfolder**, enter the following:

```
Msg 3 of 10: echo $thisfolder
```

For example, when I first invoke Z-Mail, **thisfolder** might be set to:

```
/usr/spool/mail/hanna
```

If I use the **folder** (or **open**) command to switch to my outgoing mail file, **thisfolder** changes to:

```
/u/hanna/mail/outgoing
```

When Z-Mail sources the ˜/.zmailrc initialization file at startup time, **thisfolder** isn't set. This is because Z-Mail has not yet read the current folder. However, if you use the **–source** (**–F**) and **–folder** (**–f**) options like this:

```
$ zmail —source ˜/.zmailrc —folder ˜/.out.mail
```

Z-Mail scans the folder (˜/.out.mail) before reading the initialization file ˜/.zmailrc and sets **thisfolder** to /u/hanna/.out.mail.

If you want to refer to **$thisfolder** in an initialization script, you'll probably want to test the value of the variable first. So, you'd refer to **thisfolder** inside an **if** expression like this:

```
if $?thisfolder == /u/hanna/mail/outgoing
    pick —ago —1 month | delete
endif
```

Initialization scripts and how to use conditional statements to test the value of a variable are covered in Chapter 8.

Current Version Number

The **version** string variable contains the string that tells you which version of the software you're running. Z-Mail displays this string at startup time and includes it in the `X—Mailer` header in your outgoing messages. If you want to see what the value of **$version** is, enter the following:

```
Msg 3 of 10: echo $version
```

You can also get this information using the **version** command.

For an example of how to use **$version** to test for the version of your Z-Mail software in a script, see Chapter 8. Note that Z-Mail displays the version string at startup time as long as the **quiet** variable does not include the string "startup."

Combining Z-Mail Commands

With the Z-Mail line mode, you can use the output of one command (a list of messages) as input to another by creating command *pipelines*. These pipelines are similar to pipelines in the C shell (*csh*), Bourne shell (*sh*), and Korn shell (*ksh*) except that in Z-Mail, commands return a list of messages instead of text. To "pipe" commands together, separate them on the Z-Mail command line with the pipe character (|) like this:

```
command1 | command2
```

When you pipe one command to another, the second command acts only on the message list that the first command outputs. If a command produces text output, Z-Mail suppresses it in most cases.

Using pipes is a particularly effective way to manipulate messages selected with **pick**. Let's look at a number of different examples. The first example, shows how to pick out all the messages from a particular person and then save those messages to a folder:

```
Msg 3 of 10: pick -f harry | save from_harry
```

These commands find all messages from *harry* and then save them to a folder called *from_harry*. Z-Mail stores the output from the first command (**pick**) in **$output** and then uses this as the input to the second command (**save**).

Similarly, you can select messages with the same **Subject** line and then send them to the printer:

```
Msg 3 of 10: pick -s Z-Mail | lpr
```

This sends the result of the **pick** command—a message list—to the **lpr** command.

Here's another example. Let's say someone new just joined your group and you want to send them all the messages from the project lead. Use the following command to forward all the messages from one person (*dan*) to another (*bart*):

```
Msg 3 of 10: pick -f dan | m -f bart
```

This selects all the messages from *dan* and then forwards them to *bart*.

If you have a lot of old messages in your system mailbox or your *mbox* file, you can use this command to find all the messages that were sent more than a month ago and save them in a folder called *old.mail*:

```
Msg 3 of 10: pick -ago -1m | save +old.mail
```

(The *old.mail* folder is located in the folder directory.)

You can specify more than one criteria for **pick** to search by combining **pick** commands. Let's say you want to find all the messages with the same **Subject** from a particular person. Use a command like the following:

```
Msg 3 of 10: pick -f dave | pick -s -i Z-Mail
```

The first **pick** finds all the messages from *dave*. Those messages are used as input to the second **pick** command which finds all the messages with "Z-Mail" in the **Subject**. The output is the list of header summaries for all the messages from *dave* about "Z-Mail" (either case).

You can also pipe multiple commands on a command line. For example, to find all the messages sent between October 31, 1989 and October 31, 1990 that contain the string "Halloween Party" in the `Subject` line, use the following:

```
pick -d 10/31/89 | pick -d -10/31/90 | pick -s "Halloween Party"
```

You can run the **pick** command to determine which messages to manipulate before actually piping them to the next command. It's easy to do with command-history referencing. For example, by running the previous **pick** command line, you can examine the header summaries to make sure that you really want to delete them. Then, use the exclamation mark (!) to run the previous command beginning with **pick** and pipe those messages to **delete**:

```
Msg 3 of 10: !pick | delete
```

Another way to do this is with **$output**. Remember, when you execute a command successfully, Z-Mail stores the output in the **output** variable.

For example, let's say you want to run **pick** and look at the messages before deleting them. To do this, first, run the **pick** command. Now, delete the messages in **$output**, like this:

```
Msg 3 of 10: $output | delete
```

Remember that **$output** contains the results of the *last* command only.

You can also pipe the results of another command to **pick**. For example, this command switches to the folder *old.mail* and then finds all the messages from *albert*:

```
Msg 3 of 10: folder +old.mail | pick -f albert
```

Here's an example that limits the results of **$output** to messages from *harry* only:

```
Msg 3 of 10: $output | pick -f harry
```

Use other commands to specify a subset of messages to pipe to a command. For example:

```
Msg 3 of 10: headers :r | delete
```

This command finds all messages that I've already sent a reply to (the messages with **r** status indicator) and then deletes them.

You can also specify a message list for both commands to act on. For example, the following example demonstrates how to sort an exact list of messages by specifying that message list on the command line and then piping the results to **sort**:

```
Msg 3 of 10: 3-12 | sort -d
```

Here's another example that shows how to print messages 3 through 8 and then delete them:

```
Msg 3 of 10: lpr 3-8 | delete
```

This command sends messages 3 through 8 to the printer and then deletes them. Note that **sort** only works on consecutive message numbers.

Using Command History

Command history is a list of previous commands that you entered in the current Z-Mail. The Z-Mail line mode includes a command-history referencing function similar to that in the C shell session. Using command history, you can display, re-execute, and otherwise reference previous commands and arguments.

 By default, Z-Mail saves only the most recent previous command that you entered. Like C shell, you can tell Z-Mail to remember more commands by setting the **history** variable. For example, set **history** to store the previous 100 commands:

```
Msg 3 of 10: set history = 100
```

Now, you can display, reference, and re-execute the last hundred commands in the current Z-Mail session. We'll show you how in the next sections.

Displaying Command-line History

As in C shell, to display your command history, use the **history** command. Here's the syntax for Z-Mail's **history**:

```
history [ -r ] [ n ]
```

With no arguments, **history** displays the number of commands saved in command history, numbered with the most recent command last. For example, if you enter **history** at the command line, you might see a list like this:

```
1  p
2  R
3  dt
4  h
5  history
```

The last command, **history**, produced the output.

If you set **history** to a number greater than the number of lines on your screen and you execute more than that number of commands during the Z-Mail session, Z-Mail displays the more prompt when you use the **history** command. Press RETURN to display the next command in the history list; press the space bar to display the next screenful. For this reason, you might want to set **history** to the number of lines that fit on the screen at one time; for example, the same value as the **screen** variable.

To display the commands in reverse order, use the **-r** option. Note that the number of each command doesn't change, just the display order.

You can also specify the number (*n*) of previous commands to display. For example, to display only the last four commands in the command history, use **history 4.**

Re-executing Previous Commands

As in the C shell, you re-execute previous commands using the exclamation mark (!). Table 5-3 describes the history reference commands available with Z-Mail.

Table 5-3. History Reference Commands

Command	Description
!!	Execute the last command (identical to !-1).
!*pattern*	Execute the most recent command beginning with *pattern*.
!?*pattern*?	Execute the most recent previous command containing *pattern*.
!*n*	Execute command number *n* from the history list.
!-*n*	Execute command *n* previous to the current one.
!$	Refer to the last word of the last command.
!*	Refer to all arguments of the last command.

For example, you enter **history** and see the following list:

```
1  headers
2  reply
3  dt
5  ls ~/books
6  history 4
7  print
8  history
9  pick -f hanna
```

The following commands are possible with the history list above:

Use:	To Do:
!!	Execute the last command in the history list (9).
!d	Execute the last command beginning with the pattern "d" (3).
!?int	Execute the last command containing the pattern "int" (7).
!2	Execute command number 2 from the history list.
!-2	Execute the second command previous to the current command (8).
mail !$	Use the last word ("hanna") of the last command (9) in the current command.
mail !*	Use the arguments ("-f hanna") from the last command (9) in the current command.

You can re-execute a previous command and append a string to it by adding the string to the end of the history reference. Let's re-execute the second command (**reply**) and give "3" as an argument:

```
Msg 3 of 10: !2 3
```

In this example, you send a reply to message number 3. Note the space that separates the history reference from the appended string. If you forget the space, Z-Mail tries to re-execute command number 23.

You can also use curly braces ({}) as separators. Here's an example:

```
Msg 3 of 10: !{1}*
```

This executes the first command, **headers**, and appends the *, displaying all the header summaries in the current folder. If you didn't use the curly braces and entered:

```
Msg 3 of 10: !1*
```

Z-Mail tries to execute all the arguments to the first command. In this case, there aren't any arguments to execute, so Z-Mail doesn't do anything. If you entered this command instead:

```
Msg 3 of 10: !5*
```

Z-Mail tries to execute "~/books" as a command and displays an error message like the following:

```
/u/hanna/books: command not found
```

In addition, you can select specified words (arguments) from previous command lines in the history list using a subset of C shell history modifiers. The first word (usually a command) is argument 0 of the referenced command line, the second word (the first argument) is 1, and so on.

To select an argument from a referenced command, append a colon character (:) and an argument selector to one of the following history reference formats:

!pattern
!?pattern?
!n
!-n

The argument-selector characters available with Z-Mail are listed in Table 5-4; these characters function in the same manner as they do in C shell.

Table 5-4. Argument Selectors

Character	Description
:$	Select the last word of the referenced command.
:*	Specify all arguments of the referenced command (identical to **:1-$**).
:*n*	Use word *n* of the referenced command.
:*n–x*	Use words *n* through *x* of the specified command.
:*–n*	Use word 0 (command name) through *n* of the referenced command.
:*n–*	Use word *n* through the next-to-last word in the command.
:p	Display, but don't execute, the referenced command.

You cannot combine the **:p** modifier with any other modifier.

The *n* and *x* arguments can either be the argument number (beginning with 0) or **$** (the last word in the command).

For example, you enter **history** and see this list:

```
1  headers
2  reply
3  dt
4  ls
5  ls ~/books fiction
6  history 4
7  print 12 14 6
8  history -r 4
9  pick -f hanna
```

The following arguments are possible with the history list above:

Use:	To Do:
print !h:$	Find the last command beginning with "h" (8) and use the last argument ("4") as the argument for **print**. Z-Mail executes **print 4**.
delete !7:2	Use the second argument ("14") of the seventh command in the history list as the argument to **delete**. Z-Mail executes **delete 14**.
reply !-3:3-4	Use words 3 and 4 ("14" and "6") of the third command previous to the current command (7) as the arguments to **reply**. Z-Mail executes **reply 14 16**.
!!:p	Display the last command, but don't execute it.

Turning Off History Referencing

Regardless of whether you set the **history** variable, Z-Mail recognizes the exclamation mark (! or "bang") as a history reference. You may find this behavior frustrating when you try to send mail to UUCP-style addresses that use the ! character to separate the login name from the hostname. Here's an example:

```
Msg 3 of 10: m holycow!hanna
```

Normally, if you want to send mail like this from the Z-Mail command line, you have to "escape" the ! character by putting the backslash character (\) in front of it like this:

```
Msg 3 of 10: m holycow\!hanna
```

You don't need to escape ! characters in the initialization file because history referencing is not in effect when Z-Mail reads these files (either at startup time or when you use the **source** command), explained in Chapter 8, *Customizing Z-Mail*. However, if your initialization file contains command-line aliases (created with **cmd**) that reference command-line arguments, it's good practice to escape any ! characters. We'll explain **cmd** in detail later in this chapter.

To turn off Z-Mail's interpretation of the ! as a history reference completely, set the **ignore_bang** variable, like this:

```
Msg 3 of 10: set ignore_bang
```

With this set, Z-Mail no longer recognizes the ! as the history-referencing character.

NOTE

With **ignore_bang** set, you also won't be able to use history references for argument substitutions with **cmd** command-line aliases.

Now, if you try to execute a previous command in your history list, you get an error stating that the command wasn't found.

Ignoring History-reference Errors

Let's say you want to use command history to re-execute previous commands and your command-line aliases depend on argument substitutions, so you don't want to turn off history referencing by setting **ignore_bang**. But what if you also send a lot of messages to UUCP-style (!) addresses? In this situation, you could escape each individual ! on the command line (no fun) or you can set the **nonobang** variable.

By default, if a history reference doesn't match, Z-Mail generates an error message. For example, in this command:

```
Msg 3 of 10: m ucscc!help
```

Z-Mail attempts to match "help" as a reference to a previous command and you get this error:

```
help: event not found
```

 To tell Z-Mail to suppress error messages from unsuccessful history references, set the **nonobang** variable:

```
Msg 3 of 10: set nonobang
```

Now if a history reference fails, Z-Mail doesn't try to expand it and doesn't generate an error message. In the example:

```
Msg 3 of 10: m ucscc!help
```

If Z-Mail can't match the string "help" in the history list, it ignores the reference. However, if Z-Mail finds a match in the history list, it substitutes the text of the command for "!help." Thus, if "help" appears in the history list because you previously entered a command such as **help hdr_format**, and then if you ran the **mail** command above, Z-Mail will replace the "!help" with "help hdr_format". You'll get the following results:

```
m ucscchelp hdr_format
To: ucscchelp, hdr_format
Subject: _
```

This is a pretty unlikely scenario, but be aware that it could happen when you send mail to addresses with the same names as Z-Mail commands.

Creating Command-line Aliases

The Z-Mail line mode includes a *command-line alias* feature similar to that in the C shell. Command-line aliases are similar to mail aliases except that the short name is a substitute for a Z-Mail command or series of commands, rather than a long mail address or a list of addresses. (We describe mail aliases in Chapter 4, *Sending Mail with Z-Mail*.)

However, to create command-line aliases in C shell, you use the *alias* command. In Z-Mail, this command is used for creating mail aliases; to create command-line aliases, use the **cmd** command. (To maintain backwards-compatibility with BSD UNIX *Mail*, **alias** is used to create mail aliases.)

After you set up the command-line alias, you can use the short name to execute commands.

Setting Up Command-line Aliases

To set up a command-line alias, use **cmd** like this:

```
cmd [ [ name ] command ]
```

The *name* is the shorthand name you're giving to your new command and *command* is the Z-Mail line-mode command (or commands) that you want to execute when you enter *name*. If the **cmd** expansion contains pipes (|), semicolons (;), or other metacharacters, enclose it in single or double quotes.

Command-line aliases that you enter at the Z-Mail prompt are not permanent. You can use them in the current Z-Mail session only; when you exit, you lose the alias definitions. We'll show you how to make the definitions permanent by including them in your initialization file (~/.zmailrc) in Chapter 8.

It's a good idea to test out the command-line aliases that you create with **cmd** to make sure they work before making them permanent. The examples in this section show you how to create the aliases by entering them from the Z-Mail command line.

Let's create a simple command-line alias to display the next screenful of header summaries in the current folder:

```
Msg 3 of 10: cmd H 'headers +'
```

Now, instead of having to type **headers +** every time you want to see the next screen in Z-Mail, enter **H** instead. Use this syntax to create your own aliases for other long (or hard-to-remember) Z-Mail commands.

You can also use **cmd** to modify the behavior of a Z-Mail command. Let's say you always pass certain command-line flags to the **mail (m)** command. Using a command-line alias, you can modify **m** to do this automatically. For example, to specify that the **m** command always enter the editor and include the outgoing mail headers, use this command:

```
Msg 3 of 10: cmd m 'mail —eE'
```

Or, let's say you want to keep a copy of only the messages you send with **m**. Use an alias like this:

    Msg 3 of 10: cmd m 'mail -b hanna'

Now, when you use **m** to send messages, Z-Mail includes this header:

    Bcc: hanna

(See Chapter 4 for more information on blind carbon copies.)

Here are a couple of useful command-line aliases for forwarding mail:

    Msg 3 of 10: cmd Fwd 'mail —U —f'
    Msg 3 of 10: cmd fwd 'mail —U —e —f'

In MUSH, you don't need to include the **—U** option to forward the message immediately. The **Fwd** alias forwards a message immediately, without entering the editor; **fwd** forwards a message, but starts the editor so you can edit the forwarded message. As an example, this command sends the last message in the folder to *erin*:

    Msg 3 of 10: Fwd $ erin

Three command-line aliases that I use pretty regularly are:

    Msg 3 of 10: cmd pf 'pick —i —f'
    Msg 3 of 10: cmd pt 'pick —i —t'
    Msg 3 of 10: cmd pS 'pick —i —s'

The first command finds all the messages from a particular person (or people). For example, to find all the messages from *David*, enter the following:

    Msg 3 of 10: pf David

The **—i** option tells **pick** to ignore the case. So, if I have any mail with **David** in the **From** header anywhere, **pick** finds it. This is particularly useful if you get mail from people whose addresses don't contain their names, but whose real names appear in the **From** header. For example, if you get a message with this header:

    From: James Joyce <writer@dublin.edu>

you can use **pf** to find messages from *james* (or *joyce*), as well as *writer*.

The **pt** and **pS** command line aliases are similar, except that they find the messages with a specified pattern in the **To** or **Subject** lines. I use the alias **pS** (with an uppercase "S") instead of "ps" because otherwise, I wouldn't be able to run the UNIX command *ps* from the line-mode prompt (with the **unix** variable set). The aliases that you create with **cmd** override any UNIX command names that you might want to run from Z-Mail.

In line mode, you can execute more than one command on a command line using the semicolon character (;). For example, you might use this combination of commands to delete the current message and display the header summary for the next message in the list:

    Msg 3 of 10: d ; f

If you find yourself executing these two commands together, create an alias for the whole command line:

    Msg 3 of 10: cmd df 'delete ; from'

Although it's possible to use abbreviations for commands in command-line aliases, I prefer to spell out commands to make it easier to tell at a glance exactly what each alias does. In this example, I use **delete** instead of **d** in the alias definition.

Now, when you enter:

```
Msg 3 of 10: df
```

Z-Mail deletes the current message and displays the next header summary.

As long as you enclose the commands in single (') or double (") quotes, you can use the command-separator characters, semicolon (;) and pipe (|) in your command-line aliases.

Using **cmd**, you can even set variables when you execute certain commands. For example, these commands change the behavior of Z-Mail depending on whether you're sending a message or replying to one:

```
Msg 3 of 10: cmd mail 'set fortune; \mail'
Msg 3 of 10: cmd reply 'unset fortune; \reply'
```

The first command sets the **fortune** variable (and appends a fortune) whenever you use **mail** to send a message. The second command unsets **fortune** before you reply to messages.

Note that if you set the **warning** variable and you create a command-line alias with the same name as a Z-Mail command (as in our example above), Z-Mail warns you whenever you use the alias. In this case, when you send a message using **mail**, Z-Mail displays this message before displaying the **To** line:

```
(real-command: "mail" aliased to "set fortune; \mail")
```

The warning message doesn't affect the behavior of the command-line alias.

As we saw earlier, with the pipe character (|) you can use the output of one command as input to another. You might use | to pick out messages that meet a certain criteria and then send them to another command. For example, these commands select all the messages with "Z-Mail" in the **Subject** and then save them to the file *book.info* in my folder directory:

```
Msg 3 of 10: pick -s Z-Mail | save +book.info
```

You can use a pipe character (|) in your alias definitions, too. Create an alias so you can do all this in one command:

```
Msg 3 of 10: cmd pZ 'pick -s Z-Mail | save +book.info'
```

Now, enter **pZ** to save the messages about "Z-Mail."

In addition, you can use other command-line alias definitions within **cmd**s. For example, we've already got the **pS** command to execute **pick -s**. So, we can change the **cmd** above to use **pS** like this:

```
Msg 3 of 10: cmd pZ 'pS Z-Mail | save +book.info'
```

 Here's another example of piping messages in alias definitions:

```
Msg 3 of 10: cmd cleanup 'pick -ago -30 days | delete'
```

Now, enter the following command to find and delete all the messages in your folder that are 30 days old or older:

    Msg 3 of 10: **cleanup**

If you want to create commands that take arguments from the command line, use the **!***
history-referencing construction in your alias. (Remember that **!*** refers to all arguments of
the command.) When you use this construction in a **cmd** at the line-mode prompt, you must
escape the exclamation mark character (**!**) with a backslash (\ ). Although the backslash
isn't required inside the initialization file, it's a good idea to include it. As an example, this
command-line alias takes arguments, such as a list of messages, from the command line:

    Msg 3 of 10: **cmd R 'reply \!* —eI'**

Using this alias, you can enter **R** followed by a message list and Z-Mail executes **reply** with
the **–I** (to incorporate the original message and headers) and **–e** (to start the editor) options.
If you don't specify a message number, **R** sends your message to the author of the current
message.

You can use other history references, such as \!:1 (to execute the first word of the last
command) and \!$ (to execute the last word of the last command). See the previous section
on using command history.

 Here's another command-line alias you might find useful. You can use this alias to
make your mail and command-line aliases permanent by adding them to your
initialization file (¯/.zmailrc) and then reading in your changes (note that you must
have **unix** set for this alias to work):

    Msg 3 of 10: **cmd mod "vi ¯/.zmailrc; source ¯/.zmailrc"**

Now, enter **mod** to change ¯/.zmailrc. When you leave vi, Z-Mail sources the ¯/.zmailrc file.

Displaying Command-line Aliases

Use **cmd** by itself to get a list of the current command-line aliases:

    Msg 3 of 10: **cmd**

Z-Mail displays a list like this:

    Fwd   mail —f
    R   r \!* —e —I
    df   delete ; from
    H   headers +
    fwd   mail —ef
    m   mail —eE
    mod   vi /.zmailrc; source ¯/.zmailrc
    pf   pick —i —f
    pt   pick —i —t
    pS   pick —i —s

If you just want to see the expansion for a particular alias, enter **cmd** followed by the name of the alias. For example, to see what **fwd** does, enter the following:

```
Msg 3 of 10: cmd fwd
```

and Z-Mail displays:

```
mail —ef
```

Unsetting Command-line Aliases

If you create the command-line alias from the Z-Mail prompt, the alias definitions are good for the current session only. When you quit, the aliases disappear. To remove an alias without quitting, use **uncmd**:

```
Msg 3 of 10: uncmd fwd
```

Note that, if you set up **fwd** in your initialization file, this command removes the setting for the current Z-Mail session only. The next time you start up Z-Mail, the **fwd** alias is active.

To unset all of your aliases, type the following:

```
Msg 3 of 10: uncmd *
```

Using Filename Completion

Filename completion is a handy way to avoid entering long filenames and pathnames; it's similar to using wildcards in the UNIX system shell. The asterisk character (*) doesn't mean the same thing in Z-Mail as it does in the UNIX shell, however, so you must use filename completion to specify patterns in filenames. You enter the prefix for a word and then press a key to tell Z-Mail to complete the word.

When you enable filename completion in Z-Mail, you press a *completion character* at the end of a filename prefix and Z-Mail interactively completes the word. By default, the completion character is the ESCAPE key (^[). If the prefix isn't unique when you press the completion character, Z-Mail completes the word as far as possible and then beeps the terminal bell. At this point, you can use the *completion-listing* character (CTRL-D, by default) to display all the possible completions for the prefix.

To enable filename completion, set **complete** as a boolean variable:

```
Msg 3 of 10: set complete
```

With **complete** set, you can use filename completion whenever you enter filenames. Here are a few possible uses:

- From line mode, use **ls** with filename completion to list specific files in a directory.

- From compose mode, use filename completion with ˜**r** to include a file in the current message.

- From fullscreen mode, when you use **save**, press the filename completion character at the save prompt.

- In the GUI mode, use filename completion in the Filename and Command fields. Note that you can't use the default ESCAPE character to complete filenames in GUI mode. If you want to use filename completion, set **complete** to another string, such as @; we'll explain how to do this later in this section.

I find filename completion handy for manipulating files because of the method I use to name my files. When I'm working on a book, I keep each chapter in a separate file. The filename consists of the chapter number, followed by the dot character (.) and a word that describes its contents, ending with the suffix "s" (for source). For example, the filename for this chapter is *5.bells.s.*

With this naming scheme, it's easy to pick out a particular file using wildcards at the UNIX command line and file completion from Z-Mail. For example, here's how I list *4.advan.s* at the UNIX prompt:

```
$ ls 5*.s
```

In this case, the shell matches all the files that begin with "5" and end with the ".s" suffix. To do this from the Z-Mail prompt, press the ESCAPE key at the end of this command line:

```
Msg 3 of 10: ls 5
```

Z-Mail expands "5" to "5.bells.s" leaving the cursor at the end of the word.

If there's more than one word beginning with "5," Z-Mail completes the word as far as it's unique and then sounds the terminal's bell. Use the completion-listing character (CTRL-D) to display all the possible choices. For example, when you press CTRL-D after entering **ls 5** at the line-mode prompt, you might see the following:

```
Msg 3 of 10: ls 5
5.bells.err  5.bells.s  5.err  5cats  5cookies  5corners 5dogs
Msg 3 of 10: ls 5_
```

Note that Z-Mail redisplays the prefix that you entered, leaving the cursor in the same position.

What if you want to use more than one filename, for example, you want to look for a pattern in all the chapter files in a directory (files with the ".s" suffix)? In this case, you can use the filename metacharacters from C shell to complete all possible matches. You'll find a list of these metacharacters in Table 5-5.

Table 5-5. Filename Metacharacters

Character	Description
*	Match any string (or zero) of characters.
?	Match any one character.
[]	Match any one of the characters inside the brackets.
{,}	Match each string inside the curly braces.

Z-Mail treats these metacharacters slightly different from the way the shell treats them. For example, when you use the metacharacters to expand filenames on the Z-Mail command line, you must press the filename completion character after entering the string. Then, Z-Mail expands the list of filenames on the Z-Mail command line and waits for you to press RETURN. On the UNIX command line, you don't need to press any special keys before pressing RETURN.

In the following examples, I'll explain how to use these filename metacharacters to match patterns in filenames at the UNIX prompt, and then I'll show you the Z-Mail equivalent. (Many of the Z-Mail examples depend on the **unix** variable being set in order to run UNIX commands from within Z-Mail. We'll explain this variable in detail later in this chapter.)

For example, I use a command like the following from the UNIX command line to look for the pattern "complete" in all the files with the ".s" suffix:

```
$ grep complete *.s
```

To do this from the Z-Mail command line, enter the pattern followed by ESCAPE. Thus, to use the UNIX *grep* command on all the chapter files, use this command, and press ESCAPE at the end of the command line:

```
Msg 3 of 10: grep complete *.s
```

In this case, Z-Mail replaces "*.s" with all the filenames that end in ".s" and you see:

```
Msg 3 of 10: grep complete 1.intro.s 2.start.s 3.read.s 4.send.s 5.bells.s_
```

At this point, simply press RETURN to execute the command.

Note that if the list overflows the command-line buffer (256 characters), Z-Mail truncates the list and you get the following error:

```
Warning: string too long.  Truncated at 256 characters.
```

What if the files that you want to match have different suffixes? For example, I often name my temporary files *tmp1*, *tmp2*, *tmp3*, and so on. As in C shell, use the question mark (?) to match a single character. Thus, to remove all my temporary files from the UNIX command line, I enter the following:

```
$ rm tmp?
```

To do this from Z-Mail, enter the UNIX *rm* command, and press ESCAPE:

```
Msg 3 of 10: rm tmp?
```

Z-Mail replaces "tmp?" with the filenames that match and you see:

```
Msg 3 of 10: rm tmp1 tmp2 tmp3_
```

Again, press RETURN to execute the *rm* command.

Use the square bracket characters ([]) to match one of the characters in the brackets. I use it for listing files such as:

```
$ ls [Mm]ake
```

This lists all the files *Make* and *make*. As before, to use this command from Z-Mail, press ESCAPE at the end of the pattern:

```
Msg 3 of 10: ls [Mm]ake
```

When you press ESCAPE, you see:

```
Msg 3 of 10: ls [Mm]ake
Make   make
Msg 3 of 10: _
```

This construction is also useful for listing files that match a range of characters. For example, our source control system adds an "r" to files checked out for reading and an "e" to files that you can edit. I use the [] construction to list specific files:

```
$ ls e.[4-6]*.s
```

This command displays a list like the following:

```
e.4.send.s e.5.bells.s e.6.full.s
```

Again, to do this from Z-Mail, press ESCAPE at the end of the pattern:

```
Msg 3 of 10: ls e.[4-6]*.s
```

In the C shell, the curly braces ({}) allow you to match the strings inside. For example, if you have files that begin and end with the same characters, you can list them on the UNIX command line (% is the C shell prompt):

```
% ls 3.{old,new,latest}.s
```

This gives you the following:

```
% ls 3.old.s 3.new.s 3.latest.s
```

From Z-Mail, press ESCAPE after entering the following:

```
Msg 3 of 10: ls 3.{old,new,latest}.s
```


Excluding Patterns from Completions

You can exclude specific filename patterns from filename completions using the **fignore** variable. To do this, set **fignore** to a list of filename extensions (*.c*, *.o*, and *.s*), a list of filename patterns that contain the filename metacharacters listed in Table 5-5, or a mixture of both. You must use spaces to separate each element in the list.

Then, when you use filename completion, Z-Mail tests **fignore** and omits any filenames containing the extensions that you set with **fignore**.

For example, let's say you use this **fignore** setting:

```
Msg 3 of 10: set fignore = ".o .s [Mm]ake*"
```

Z-Mail now excludes any filenames from filename completions that end in *.o* or *.s* and any filenames that begin with *Make* or *make*. In other words, if the current directory contains these files:

```
5.bells.err 5.bells.s 5doggies 5kitties makefile
```

when you enter the following command (and press the filename completion character) to display all the files that begin with "5":

> Msg 3 of 10: ls 5*

Z-Mail checks **fignore**, finds ".s" and "[Mm]ake*" in the value and ignores *5.bells.s* and *makefile*. You see:

> Msg 3 of 10: ls 5.bells.err   5doggies   5kitties

Note that, if all the files in the current directory match the **fignore** values, Z-Mail disables **fignore** and enables filename completion. For this reason, you probably won't want to include "*" in your **fignore** setting.

Changing the Completion Character

If you don't like using the ESCAPE key to complete words, you can change the completion character to another character by setting **complete** to a value. For example, if you want to use the asterisk character (*) for filename completion, set **complete** with the following command:

> Msg 3 of 10: set complete = *

Note that if you use the * character as a filename completion character, you can no longer use it to refer to all the messages in the current folder. If you try, for example, to use this command to delete all the messages:

> Msg 3 of 10: delete *

Z-Mail sounds the bell and doesn't display the * character.

If you set **complete** to a single character, Z-Mail disables the completion-listing functionality. (Remember, with **complete** set as a boolean variable, you could use CTRL-D to list the possible completions where the prefix wasn't unique.) To re-enable the completion listing character, set **complete** to two characters: the completion character followed by the completion-listing character. For example:

> Msg 3 of 10: set complete = ()

Now, you can use the (character to complete a word. If the prefix isn't unique, Z-Mail sounds the bell and you type the) character to display the possible completions.

You can also use control-key sequences as either your completion or completion-listing characters. For example, if you want to change the completion-listing character to something other than CTRL-D, but you want to keep ESCAPE as the completion character, use a command like the following:

> Msg 3 of 10: set complete=\E^L

Now, ESCAPE still completes the filename, but you use CTRL-L instead of CTRL-D to list the possible completions. Z-Mail uses "\E" to refer to the ESCAPE control character and ^L to refer to CTRL-L. See Table 6-11 for a list of the other special control sequences.

Currently, Z-Mail supports completion for filenames only. Word completion is not available when you invoke Z-Mail with the **–echo** option (which tells Z-Mail to process input only after you press RETURN).

 If you don't want Z-Mail to sound the terminal's bell with filename completion, set the **quiet** variable to include the word "complete":

```
Msg 3 of 10: set quiet = complete
```

More About Folders

In Chapter 3, *Reading and Managing Mail*, we showed you how to organize your messages by saving them to folders in the folder directory. Here, we'll explain how to read folders other than your system mailbox when you start up Z-Mail, open new folders and switch between them. We'll also show you how to streamline your folders by editing messages and combining folders.

Reading Folders at Startup Time

When you invoke Z-Mail to read mail, Z-Mail reads the messages stored in your system mailbox. If you prefer, you can tell Z-Mail to read another folder instead. You can use any folder, as long as it contains headers. Even though the **logfile** doesn't contain message text, you can still read it because it does contain headers.

These are the three command-line options for reading a different folder at startup time:

–folder [*folder_name*]	(**–f**)	Read the specified *folder_name* or the file specified by the **mbox** variable, if set (*mbox* in your home directory, by default). If you don't specify a *folder_name*, make sure the **–folder** or **–user** option comes last on the command line.
–mailbox *mailbox_path*	(**–m**)	Use the specified pathname instead of the system mailbox.
–user [*user*]	(**–u**)	Read the system mailbox for the specified *user* (or *root*'s system mailbox, if not specified).

 If you want to read the system mailbox for another user, for example, *erin*, use the **–user** (**–u**) option like this:

```
$ zmail –u erin
```

Of course, you must have appropriate permissions to read another user's mailbox. If you don't, you get an error like this one:

```
Unable to open /usr/spool/mail/erin: Permission denied
```

With the **–folder** (**–f**) option, you can start up Z-Mail reading any folder in which you've saved messages, such as your *mbox* folder or your outgoing message folder (set with the **record** variable).

In an earlier example in Chapter 4, we set the **record** variable so that all your outgoing mail is saved to the folder *.out.mail* in your folder directory. To tell Z-Mail to read this file on startup, type the following:

```
$ zmail -f +.out.mail
```

Now *+.out.mail* is the current folder when you start Z-Mail.

Switching Folders

If you're already in the system mailbox and you want to read messages in a different folder, you don't have to quit Z-Mail and start up again to read the new folder. You can switch to a new folder using the **folder (fo)** command. Z-Mail lets you have more than one folder "open" at a time, although only one folder is currently "active" (that is, you can only read messages in one folder at any given time). Note that MUSH supports only one open folder at a time; you must close the active folder to open a new one. Table 5-6 contains a list of the options to **folder**.

Table 5-6. folder Options

Option	Description
&	Switch to *mbox*.
%	Switch back to your system mailbox.
% [*user*]	Switch to *user*'s mailbox.
#	Switch to previous folder.
#*n*	Switch to folder number *n*.*
−a	Open a new folder, adding it to the list of open folders (don't update the current folder).*
−d	Close (delete from the open list) the named folder.*
−f	Run filters when opening the folder.*
−F	Don't filter messages when opening the folder.*
−l	List the open folders.*
−N	Don't display header summaries when switching to the new folder.
−n	Don't update current folder before switching or closing.
−r	Switch to new folder in read-only mode.

*These options are not available with MUSH.

Z-Mail interprets the pathname as relative to the current directory when you specify a folder name that doesn't begin with one of the following characters: the slash (/), plus (+) or tilde (˜).

Let's say you're in *+.out.mail* and you want to switch and read messages in your *+recipes* folder. Use the following command to close the current folder and open the new one:

```
Msg 3 of 5: fo +recipes
```

Z-Mail updates +.*out.mail*, switches to +*recipes*, and displays the new folder name at the top of the message list:

```
[1]+ "+recipes": 4 messages, 0 new, 0 unread, 0 deleted
```

If you *don't* want to update the current folder before switching to the new one, use the **−n** option:

```
Msg 3 of 5: fo −n +recipes
```

Because Z-Mail supports multiple open folders, you don't have to close a folder to open another one. This also means that you don't have to update or abandon any changes that you made to the current folder if you just want to read messages in a new one. Simply add the new folder using the **−a** (add) option; when you return to the previous folder, it's in the same state you left it.

Use the **fo −a** command instead of **fo** to open and add the +*recipes* folder to the list of open folders:

```
Msg 3 of 5: fo −a +recipes
```

Note that if the current folder is the system mailbox, you don't have to specify the **−a** option; Z-Mail automatically adds the new folder to the list of open folders. Likewise, if you're adding the system folder, the current folder remains open regardless of whether you use the **−a** option or not.

Suppose that while you're working with +*recipes*, new mail arrives in your system mailbox. Z-Mail displays a message like this at the line-mode prompt:

```
You have new mail in your system mailbox.
```

You might want to open and switch to your system mailbox to read the new mail. Z-Mail provides a shorthand name for referring to your system mailbox when you switch folders with **folder**—the percent character (%). For example, to switch back to your system mailbox, enter:

```
Msg 3 of 5: fo %
```

Z-Mail displays the system mailbox name at the top of the message list:

```
[0]+ "/usr/spool/mail/hanna": 14 messages, 4 new, 4 unread, 0 deleted
```

Another way to open new folders without updating or closing the current folder is by using the **open** command; **open** is equivalent to **fo −a** and is not available in MUSH. For example, use this command to open the system mailbox:

```
Msg 3 of 5: open %
```

You can use all the **folder** options except **−d** (delete), **−a** (add), and **−n** (don't update the current folder) with **open**. If you use these options, Z-Mail simply ignores them.

If you're just switching to a folder to check something and you don't intend to modify it, it's a good idea to open the folder in read-only mode using the **−r** (read only) option. Here's how to switch to the *commentary* folder in your home directory and set it to read-only mode:

```
Msg 3 of 5: open −r ~/commentary
```

The folder name line at the top of the header summary list shows you that the folder is in read-only mode. Here's what this looks like:

```
[2]+ "~/commentary" [read only]: 30 messages, 0 new, 0 unread, 0 deleted
```

 In addition to using % to refer to the system mailbox, Z-Mail also recognizes the ampersand character (&) as the shorthand name for your *mbox* folder (as specified by the **mbox** variable). For example, let's switch to the *mbox* folder:

```
Msg 3 of 5: open &
```

 Now, let's use the **–l** (list) option to display a list of the folders that are currently open (you can also use **open –l**):

```
Msg 3 of 5: fo -1
```

Z-Mail displays a list like this:

```
[0]  "/usr/spool/mail/hanna": 14 messages, 4 new, 4 unread, 0 deleted
[1]  "+recipes": 4 messages, 0 new, 0 unread, 0 deleted
[2]- "~/commentary" [read only]: 30 messages, 0 new, 0 unread, 0 deleted
[3]+ "~/mbox": 5 messages, 0 new, 0 unread, 0 deleted
```

From this list, you can see that there are four open folders. Z-Mail numbers the open folders beginning with **0**; the folder number appears in square brackets ([]) before the folder name. Note that, although we started Z-Mail reading +*.out.mail*, the folder is not listed (it's not open) because we switched from +*.out.mail* to +*recipes* without using **–a**.

The system mailbox is always **0**. Even though we opened +*recipes* before opening the system mailbox, the system mailbox is still considered **0**. The plus character (+) indicates the currently active folder. The last folder that was active is marked with a dash character (–).

Because you can have more than one folder open at a time and you don't have to update the current folder to switch to a new one, switching to open folders is almost instantaneous. Z-Mail doesn't have to create the temporary folder and read in the messages each time you switch folders—the temporary folder already exists. The number of folders that you can have open at one time is limited only by the resources of your operating system.

 Z-Mail recognizes the pound character (#) as shorthand for the last folder that was previously active. For example, here's how to switch back to the previously active (in this case, ~/*commentary*) folder:

```
Msg 3 of 5: fo #
```

You can also use the folder numbers to switch to open folders. For example, let's switch to +*recipes* (folder 1):

```
Msg 3 of 5: fo #1
```

If you've been switching around, and you've lost track of the current folder, display the name of the current folder using **fo** (or the **open** command) with no options:

```
Msg 1 of 4: fo
```

You see this message:

```
[1]  "+recipes": 4 messages, 0 new, 0 unread, 0 deleted
```

Editing Messages in Folders

When you're saving messages and manipulating folders, you'll probably notice a lot of extraneous information in the saved messages. For example, let's say you've got a message that contains important information about a project you're working on. Unfortunately, the message also includes some dated (and trivial) information about going out for pizza three weeks ago. To save the message without the "garlic versus onion" discussion to another folder, edit the message in the folder using the **edit** (**e** or **v**) command. (Note that the ability to edit messages in the folder is not currently available in GUI mode.)

To determine which editor to use when you enter **e**, Z-Mail checks the **editor** variable, the environment variable **EDITOR**, the **visual** variable, and finally, the environment variable **VISUAL**. If none of these is set, Z-Mail uses the default visual editor (set up by the system administrator). If you use **v** instead, Z-Mail checks the **visual** and **VISUAL** variables only. See Chapter 4, for a discussion of setting the **editor** and **visual** variables.

To remove the pizza discussion, edit message 6 with the following command (if you don't specify a list of messages, you edit the current message):

    Msg 4 of 10: e 6

This calls up the default editor on message 6.

NOTE

When you finish editing the message, make sure that you update the folder, otherwise your changes will be lost!

When editing messages with **edit**, make sure you don't remove message headers such as `Date` or `From`. In most cases, if you remove an important header, like `From`, Z-Mail displays the following error when you leave the editor:

    File not left in correct message format.

If your MTA is MMDF, Z-Mail doesn't display this error. However, the next time you look at the header summary display (using **headers**), Z-Mail refuses to read the message and displays an error like this one:

    Warning: unable to find who msg 6 is from!

and the header summary display won't show the author of the message. In this case, if you leave the folder without updating (using **exit**), the message returns to its original state.

Combining Folders

At some point, you might find that you don't need to maintain separate folders for messages. For example, you're working on a complex project where you keep messages from different people in separate folders. Once you finish the project, you might want to combine the folders into one folder. To read messages from another folder into the current folder, use the **merge** command.

For example, to merge the contents of the current folder *questions* with another folder (in the folder directory) *answers*, type the following:

```
Msg 1 of 6: merge +answers
```

You can tell Z-Mail not to display the header summaries of the folders as the messages are merged by using the **−N** option, like this:

```
Msg 1 of 6: merge −N +answers
```

To remove the *+answers* folder, switch to the folder, and delete all the messages:

```
Msg 1 of 6: open −N +answers; delete *; close −N
```

You see:

```
Updating "/u/hanna/Mail/answers": removed
```

If **save_empty** is set, Z-Mail doesn't remove the folder. In this case, use the following command to remove *+answers*:

```
Msg 1 of 6: sh rm +answers
```

The **sh** command allows you to "escape" to the UNIX shell to run the UNIX command *rm*. We'll explain this further later in this chapter.

If the folder that you are merging with the current folder has been modified, you must manually update it (using **update** and specifying the folder number) before using **merge**. If you don't update prior to combining the folders, the modifications to the folder aren't reflected when you combine the two folders.

What if you want to move several (not all) messages from one folder to another? To do this, use the **save** or **copy** commands. For example, to move messages 4, 6, and 8 from the current folder (either the system mailbox or another folder) to *zmail.book/Chapter.5* in my folder directory, I use this command:

```
Msg 3 of 10: s 4 6 8 +zmail.book/Chapter.5
```

Now I can delete the messages from the current folder.

Note that when you update (or quit) the system mailbox, messages that you've saved are automatically deleted from the system mailbox. If you save messages from other folders, Z-Mail leaves the original message in that folder when you update it. You can tell Z-Mail to delete saved messages from folders other than the system mailbox by setting the **deletesave** variable:

```
Msg 3 of 10: set deletesave
```

(The **deletesave** variable is not available in MUSH.) If you don't want Z-Mail to delete any of your saved messages (in your system mailbox and other folders), set the **keepsave** variable.

Closing Open Folders

When you exit the program, Z-Mail closes all the open folders automatically. If you use **quit**, Z-Mail updates all the open folders; with **exit**, none of the folders are modified.

What if you want to update some of the folders and leave others unchanged? In this case, you can close each folder individually using the **close** command. (The **close** command isn't available with MUSH; use **fo -d** instead.) For example, let's say the following folders are open:

```
[0]  "/usr/spool/mail/hanna": 14 messages, 4 new, 4 unread, 1 deleted
[1]  "+recipes": 4 messages, 0 new, 0 unread, 0 deleted
[2]- "~/commentary" [read only]: 30 messages, 0 new, 0 unread, 0 deleted
[3]+ "~/mbox": 5 messages, 0 new, 0 unread, 0 deleted
```

You've made changes to all of them, but you only want to save changes to your system mailbox. To do this, use the **close** command with the **-n folder** option (don't update the folder before closing):

```
Msg 3 of 5: close -n #1 #2 #3
```

This closes folders 1, 2, and 3 without updating them. Now, if you enter **open -l**, you see the following message:

```
[0]+ "/usr/spool/mail/hanna": 14 messages, 4 new, 4 unread, 1 deleted
```

Now, use **quit** to update the system mailbox (folder 0) and exit Z-Mail.

Another way to do this is to close each folder individually with the **-d** (delete from open folders list) option:

```
Msg 3 of 5: fo -d %
```

The **-d** option updates the system mailbox and removes it from the open folders list. If you use the **-l** (list) option now, you see these messages:

```
[1]  "+recipes": 4 messages, 0 new, 0 unread, 0 deleted
[2]- "~/commentary" [read only]: 30 messages, 0 new, 0 unread, 0 deleted
[3]+ "~/mbox": 5 messages, 0 new, 0 unread, 0 deleted
```

Now, you can use **exit** to leave Z-Mail without updating these last folders.

If you plan to use the pound character (**#**) to refer to specific folder numbers in functions or scripts, be aware that Z-Mail interprets this character as a comment in these situations. To prevent this from happening, surround the **#** character with double quotes ("). For example, to refer to folder 3 in a script file, use this format:

```
folder "#3"
```

We'll explain more about initialization files and comments in Chapter 8, *Customizing Z-Mail*. For more information about functions, see Chapter 9, *Writing Scripts and Functions*.

Saving Empty Folders

Normally, when you delete all the messages from any folder except the system mailbox, Z-Mail automatically removes the empty folder when you close the folder with **close** or exit Z-Mail with **quit**. (Z-Mail never removes the system mailbox when it's empty.) You can tell Z-Mail not to remove any empty folders by setting the **save_empty** variable as shown below:

```
Msg 3 of 10: set save_empty
```

Now, Z-Mail retains zero-length folders instead of removing them. When you exit Z-Mail from an empty folder, you'll see a message like this:

```
Updating "/u/hanna/Mail/February": empty
```

Z-Mail does not remove empty folders when you use **update**. Therefore, an alternate method for preserving empty folders is to use this command to exit Z-Mail:

```
Msg 3 of 10: update;exit
```

Suppressing Message Header Display

When you read messages, Z-Mail displays all the message headers with the text body of the message by default. The full header display looks something like this:

```
From ora!scribe!dale Sat Aug  3 06:30:49 1991
Received: from sco by holycow.santa-cruz.ca.us
        id aa01931; Sat, 3 Aug 91 6:30:48 PST
Received: from altos by sco.sco.COM id aa28289; Sat, 3 Aug 91 4:48:53 PST
Received: by altos.Altos.COM (5.52/smail2.5)
        id AA17041; Sat, 3 Aug 91 04:01:47 PST
Received: from ora.UUCP by uunet.uu.net with UUCP
        (5.61/UUNET-primary-gateway) id AB23993; Fri, 2 Aug 91 19:41:44 -0500
Received: by ora.ora.com (/=-/ Smail3.1.18.1 #18.76)
        id <m0jErhZ-00005aC@ora.ora.com>; Fri, 2 Aug 91 19:22 EST
Received: by scribe.ora.com (smail2.5)
        id AA00542; 2 Aug 91 16:27:20 PST (Fri)
From: Dale <dale@scribe.ora.com>
Date: Fri, 2 Aug 1991 16:27:19 PST
X-Mailer: Z-Mail (2.0.0 7/1/91)
To: hanna@holycow.santa-cruz.ca.us
Subject: Draft
Message-Id: <9103090027.AA00540@scribe.ora.com>
Status: ORr
```

Many of these message identifier fields are cumbersome and uninteresting. To filter unnecessary fields when you read messages, use the **ignore** command.

For example, use this command to specify that Z-Mail suppress the `Received`, `Message-Id`, and `Status` fields when displaying the text of the message:

```
Msg 3 of 10: ignore Received Status Message-Id
```

Now, when I display the message above, the header list looks like this (much better):

```
From ora!scribe!dale Sat Aug  3 06:30:49 1991
From: Dale <dale@scribe.ora.com>
X-Mailer: Z-Mail (2.0.0 7/1/91)
To: hanna@holycow.santa-cruz.ca.us
Subject: Draft
```

Each additional **ignore** command that you issue is cumulative. If you enter the command in the previous example, and then this command:

```
Msg 3 of 10: ignore In-Reply-To
```

Z-Mail adds **In-Reply-To** to the current list of ignored headers. To see which headers Z-Mail currently ignores, type the following:

```
Msg 3 of 10: ignore
```

Z-Mail displays:

```
In-Reply-To
Message-Id
Received
Status
```

If you just want to see the text and not the headers when you view messages, use **ignore** to suppress all the headers:

```
Msg 3 of 10: ignore *
```

To restore all the headers, use **unignore**:

```
Msg 3 of 10: unignore *
```

The asterisk (*) can also be used as a wildcard to ignore headers that match a pattern. For example, let's ignore all the headers that start with the string "Resent-":

```
Msg 3 of 10: ignore Resent-*
```

With this setting, Z-Mail matches headers beginning with the string "Resent-", such as:

```
Resent-Date
Resent-From
Resent-Message-Id
Resent-To
```

Specifying Message Headers to Display

Another way to control the message header display is to specify a list of headers that you *do* want to display using the **retain** command.

For example, let's say you want to display only the **From**, **Date**, **Subject**, **To**, and **Cc** headers. You can either use **ignore** to filter out all the headers except these, or you can use **retain** like this:

```
Msg 3 of 10: retain From Date Subject To Cc
```

Now, when you display messages, Z-Mail displays only the headers that you specify:

```
From cooper Fri Aug 2 10:49:01 1991
From: Dale Cooper <cooper@fbi.com>
Date: Fri, 2 Aug 1991 10:49:01 PDT
To: Hanna Nelson <hanna>
Subject: Z-Mail Chapters
Cc: albert
```

If you use **ignore** to filter out a list of headers, you can use **retain** to disable them. Thus, if you enter this command:

```
Msg 3 of 10: ignore To Subject Via
```

and you also use **retain** like this:

```
Msg 3 of 10: retain From Date Subject To Cc
```

then Z-Mail *only* displays the headers specified by **retain**. In other words, **retain** overrides **ignore**.

As with **ignore**, you can use the asterisk (*) with **retain**. Thus, **retain Resent-*** keeps all the messages beginning with "Resent-".

If you want to reverse the effects of **ignore** to tell Z-Mail to display a particular header, such as `Status` again, enter a command like this:

```
Msg 3 of 10: unignore Status
```

To remove messages from the "retained" list, use **unretain**. For example:

```
Msg 3 of 10: unretain Cc
```

Suppressing Headers in Other Situations

When you use **ignore**, Z-Mail filters out the specified headers *only* while displaying messages. To tell Z-Mail to ignore headers in other situations (such as when you send a message to the printer or include a message in a reply), set the **alwaysignore** variable. Here's the syntax for **alwaysignore**:

```
set alwaysignore [ = keywords ]
```

If you set **alwaysignore** like this:

```
Msg 3 of 10: set alwaysignore
```

in addition to when you read your mail, Z-Mail ignores those headers that you specify with **ignore** in these situations:

- When you send the message to the printer with **lpr**.

- When you include the message in an outgoing message using the ˜f or ˜I tilde-escapes.

- When you include the message using the **–f** or **–I** command-line options with the **mail** and **reply** commands.

- When you display the contents of messages using the **Print (P)** or **Type (T)** commands.

For example, if you use **ignore** to filter out the `Received, Message-Id, Via,` and `X-Mailer` headers, and you set **alwaysignore**, Z-Mail ignores these headers in each of the four situations in the list above.

You can also set **alwaysignore** to *keywords* that describe specific situations for Z-Mail to ignore headers. If you use more than one keyword, use commas or spaces to separate them and enclose the entire list in double quotes. We describe these keywords in Table 5-7.

Table 5-7. alwaysignore Keywords

Keyword	Description
forward	Ignore headers when forwarding messages with ˜f.
include	Ignore headers when including messages with ˜I or –I.
pipe	Tell the **pipe** command to ignore headers.*
printer	Ignore headers when you print messages with **lpr**.

*We explain **pipe** later in this chapter.

Thus, in our example, use this command to filter out the ignored headers when you send messages to the printer and when you include messages:

    Msg 3 of 10: set alwaysignore = "printer include"

Note that when you update the folder (with **quit** or **update**) and when you save a message to a file (with **save**), Z-Mail doesn't ignore headers. The reason for this is that you might set **alwaysignore** so that Z-Mail ignores a header that it requires to read folders.

Reading Mail Digests

A *mail digest* is a group of mail messages (a folder) compiled by a moderator who then mails them to other people on a mailing list. Let's say you're on a mailing list and you receive a mail digest from the moderator. With Z-Mail, you can "burst" the digest into separate messages for reading. Use the **undigest** command to do this; here's the syntax for **undigest**:

    undigest [–m] [–p pattern] [msg_list] [filename]

For example, to separate the current digest into messages, enter **undigest** at the prompt. If you don't specify a *filename*, Z-Mail creates a temporary file using the first word in the `Subject` header of the original message. Let's say message 6 is a digest:

    6   Dale Cooper Aug 3 10:49 (631)   RISKS DIGEST 11.21

If you enter **undigest**, Z-Mail bursts the messages into a folder and you see this message:

```
undigesting message 6
Added 19 messages to "./RISKS".
```

Now, to read the messages in the *RISKS* folder, enter the following:

```
Msg 3 of 10: open RISKS
```

Z-Mail opens the folder and displays each header summary. Here's what the folder title for this digest looks like:

```
[1]+ "/u/hanna/RISKS": 19 messages, 19 new, 19 unread, 0 deleted
```

Now, you can read and manipulate each article as a message in a folder. You can merge the messages into the current folder instead, using the **–m** option:

```
Msg 3 of 10: undigest —m 6
```

To specify a folder in which to put the messages, use **undigest** like this:

```
Msg 3 of 10: undigest 6 +risks.digest
```

This puts the messages in the file *+risks.digest*, instead of *./RISKS*.

The default mail digest article separator is eight hyphens:

Most USENET moderators use this as the article separator. If your moderator uses a different pattern, you can specify the alternate pattern using the **–p** option. Note that the pattern must match literally at the beginning of the line. If your moderator uses this string to separate articles:

```
**********
```

use this command to burst the messages to *risks.digest* in the folder directory:

```
Msg 3 of 10: undigest —p ********** 6 +risks.digest
```

 You can also use the **–p** option to separate forwarded messages from the current message. In Z-Mail, forwarded messages are introduced with the "Forwarded mail" string:

```
--- Forwarded mail from "Homer J. Simpson" <homer@springfield.com>
```

Here's how to separate the forwarded message and merge it with the current folder:

```
Msg 3 of 10: undigest —m —p "--- Forward"
```

Note that if you set the **warning** variable, if Z-Mail can't find the header for a digest article when you use **undigest**, it displays a message. This warning occurs when Z-Mail finds an article separator (generally eight dash characters) but can't find the **From** or **Date** headers in the text that follows.

Accessing the Shell from Z-Mail

In addition to providing the built-in commands that work like UNIX system commands, such as **ls**, **pwd**, and **cd**, Z-Mail includes the **sh** command for running commands at the shell. This command invokes the shell specified by the **SHELL** environment variable or the Z-Mail **shell** variable, if either is set. If neither are set, **sh** invokes the default shell, defined by the system administrator.

 I like to use the Korn shell (*ksh*), so I set the **shell** variable as shown in the following example:

    Msg 3 of 10: set shell = /usr/bin/ksh

When I enter **sh**, Z-Mail starts an interactive *ksh* shell and displays my shell prompt. To exit the shell, enter **exit** or CTRL-D.

If you include the optional *command* argument, the **sh** command executes the specified command under the Bourne shell and then returns you to the Z-Mail command line. For example, if you enter this command:

    Msg 3 of 10: sh date

Z-Mail returns the output of the UNIX command **date** like this:

    Sun Aug 04 17:28:58 PDT 1991

To run the *command* in the background, include the ampersand character (**&**) at the end of the **sh** command. For example:

    Msg 3 of 10: sh lps pie.file&

This command runs the UNIX command, **lps**, in the background.

In the next section, we'll show you how to run UNIX system commands from within Z-Mail so you won't have to use the **sh** command. However, you'll still need to use **sh** to escape to the UNIX shell to redirect and pipe output from UNIX commands and for running noninteractive commands in scripts (see Chapter 9).

If your system has job control, you'll rarely need **sh** because you can temporarily suspend Z-Mail while you run UNIX commands. We'll explain how to do this in the section "Suspending the Z-Mail Process," later in this chapter.

Using UNIX Commands from Within Z-Mail

If you find yourself frequently executing shell escapes to run UNIX commands, you can set the **unix** variable to allow you to run UNIX commands from the Z-Mail line-mode prompt. With **unix** set, Z-Mail interprets any commands that it doesn't recognize as Z-Mail commands as UNIX commands. Set **unix** like this:

    Msg 3 of 10: set unix

You can now run UNIX commands from line mode; if you want to run UNIX commands from fullscreen mode, you must first escape temporarily to line mode using the **line-mode** (:)

command. In GUI mode, Z-Mail ignores the **unix** variable because there might not be a window available for Z-Mail to display input and output from the UNIX command. However, you can run UNIX commands from GUI mode by using **sh** in the Command field of the main Z-Mail window.

When you set **unix**, you can run simple UNIX commands. For example, run the UNIX command *ps* and you see something like this:

```
Msg 3 of 10: ps
   PID TTY       TIME COMMAND
   663  p5      0:02  ksh
  2678  p5      0:00  zmail
  2691  p5      0:00  ps
Msg 3 of 10: _
```

If **unix** isn't set, you see this error:

```
ps: command not found.
```

In this case, if you want to run *ps*, you must either set **unix** or escape to your UNIX shell prompt using this command:

```
Msg 3 of 10: sh ps
```

When you set **unix**, you may have a problem when you want to run a UNIX command that has the same name as a Z-Mail command. For example, if you want to run the BSD UNIX command *w* to see who is logged into the system, Z-Mail interprets this command as the Z-Mail **write** command. Z-Mail attempts to save the current message and displays an error:

```
Must specify filename for 'w'
```

To run the UNIX *w* command, you can either use **sh** to escape to the UNIX shell before executing the command or you can specify the full pathname of the UNIX command like this:

```
Msg 3 of 10: /usr/bin/w
```

When creating command-line aliases, keep in mind potential name conflicts between UNIX and Z-Mail commands. For example, earlier in this chapter, I created a command-line alias to pick messages with a specific `Subject`:

```
Msg 3 of 10: cmd ps 'pick —i —s'
```

With this **cmd**, when I try to run the UNIX *ps* command, Z-Mail interprets this as my command-line alias instead and displays this error:

```
No pattern specified
```

I have three choices if I want to run the UNIX *ps* command: change the name of the Z-Mail command-line alias, escape to the UNIX shell before executing *ps* (**sh ps**), or specify the full UNIX pathname (**/bin/ps**). (I changed the name of my command-line alias to **pS**.)

Because UNIX commands don't affect messages, you can't use pipes (|) and other metacharacters when running UNIX commands from the Z-Mail command line. Z-Mail pipelines use message lists, *not* text. Thus, you can't use the Z-Mail piping mechanism to pipe the output of one UNIX command to or from a Z-Mail command, or to or from another UNIX command (unless you also use the **sh** command). However, you can pipe Z-Mail commands to a final UNIX command.

For example, if you set the **unix** variable, you could use this command to find all occurrences of the string "donuts" in messages from *cooper*:

```
Msg 3 of 10: from cooper | grep donuts
```

This gives you a list of all the lines with "donuts" in messages from *cooper*. Note that this is different from using **pick** to find the messages that contain the string. For example, if you pipe two **pick** commands together like this:

```
Msg 3 of 10: pick –f cooper | pick donuts
```

you get a list of the header summaries for messages that contain "donuts," not the actual lines in the text.

If you want to pipe the output of UNIX commands to other UNIX commands (or use any command-line redirection), first escape to the UNIX shell using **sh**.

If you want to execute UNIX commands in the Z-Mail pipeline, use the **pipe** command. We explain how to do this in the next section.

Sending Messages to UNIX Commands

To send a message directly to a UNIX command, use the **pipe** command. The UNIX command that **pipe** sends messages to is executed under the Bourne shell (*/bin/sh*), so note that you can't use any C shell (*/bin/csh*) aliases.

Here's the syntax for **pipe**:

```
pipe [ –p pattern ] [ message list ] [ UNIX_command ] [ options ]
```

By default, **pipe** sends the entire message, including headers to the specified command. To send only the body of the message to the UNIX command, use **Pipe** instead of **pipe**. In this case, none of the message headers are sent to the UNIX command.

To suppress any ignored headers (that you set with **ignore**), set the value of **alwaysignore** to include the word "pipe." For example, your **alwaysignore** setting might look like this:

```
Msg 3 of 10: set alwaysignore = "include pipe"
```

See the section earlier in this chapter, "Suppressing Message Header Display," for more information on ignored headers.

If you specify **pipe** with no arguments, Z-Mail searches the current message for a line beginning with the **#!** characters. These characters are used as the first line in a shell script to specify the program to use when running the script.[2] For example, if you use the C shell and you want to execute a Bourne shell script, you would put a line like this at the top of the shell script file:

```
#! /bin/sh
```

---

[2] BSD UNIX systems recognize this syntax, but it is generally not supported on System V UNIX systems earlier than Release 4.

Then, you can run the shell script as an executable file under the Bourne shell. We'll explain more about this in Chapter 9.

If the message contains these characters, Z-Mail sends the message, beginning with that line, to */bin/sh*, treating the message as a Bourne shell script.

Z-Mail sends all messages listed as arguments to **pipe** or **Pipe** to the standard input of the *same* process as a continuous stream. This might not be desirable when extracting shell scripts from messages. However, you can pipe each message separately using the **each** command. See Chapter 9 for examples of how to use **each**.

 Suppose someone sends you the source for a chapter and you want to send it directly to the *troff* command. To send the current message to a UNIX command like *troff*, specify it on the Z-Mail prompt, like this:

```
Msg 3 of 10: Pipe troff
```

This sends the current message without headers to *troff*.

You can specify a message or list of messages to send to the shell or to a specified UNIX command. For example:

```
Msg 3 of 10: Pipe 3 5 7 sh
```

This command sends the text of messages 3, 5, and 7 to the UNIX utility *sh*. Because **pipe** and **Pipe** send messages to the Bourne shell by default, this command is equivalent to:

```
Msg 3 of 10: Pipe 3 5 7
```

To send each message separately to *sh* enter:

```
Msg 3 of 10: each 3 5 7 Pipe
```

 Here's another example of sending a message list to **pipe**:

```
Msg 3 of 10: Pipe . uudecode
```

This command sends the text of the current message (.) to the UNIX command *uudecode*.

What if the message contains information that you *don't* want to send to **pipe**? If you specify a *pattern* with the **–p** option, Z-Mail searches for the line beginning with the specified pattern and then sends the message, beginning with that line, to */bin/sh*. If you want to specify a beginning and end pattern for Z-Mail to search, use this syntax:

```
pipe –p /pattern1/,/pattern2/ UNIX_command
```

In this case, Z-Mail searches the current message for the lines that begin with *pattern1* and *pattern2* and then sends the two lines and all lines between them to the specified *UNIX_command*.

 For example, if the current message contains PostScript code, use **–p** to search for the PostScript begin and end characters, and then send the code in between them to a PostScript printer:

```
Msg 3 of 10: pipe –p /%!/,/showpage/ lpr
```

This command sends the contents of the message between the lines that begin with "%!" and "showpage" to the default PostScript printer.

If *pattern2* is the end of the message, you don't need to specify it. If "showpage" is at the end of the message, you can use this command instead:

```
Msg 3 of 10: pipe —p %! lpr
```

Let's say you just want to strip off some information at the end of the message. You can specify a null pattern (//) at the beginning and specify just the ending pattern. (In MUSH, the **pipe** command does not understand the null pattern.) For example, a typical ending pattern in mail messages is two dash characters (--) on a line by themselves; this USENET convention specifies that a signature follows. Here's an example:

```
--
              Hanna Nelson
hanna@holycow.santa—cruz.ca.us  or  hannan@sco.com
```

Use a command like this to send everything up to and including the two dashes before the signature to the UNIX *lpr* command:

```
Msg 3 of 10: Pipe —p //,/--/ lpr
```

Another use for **Pipe** is resending mail bounced by a *mailer-daemon*, a mail delivery program running in the background on your system. Here's an example of a bounced mail message:

```
From mmdf Sun Aug  4 19:22:06 1991
From: MMDF Mail System <mmdf@holycow.santa—cruz.ca.us>
To: hanna@holycow.santa—cruz.ca.us
Subject: Failed mail
Date: Sun, 4 Aug 91 19:15:56 PST
Message-ID:  <9103031915.aa07657@holycow.santa—cruz.ca.us>
Status: OR

Trouble sending mail on holycow.santa—cruz.ca.us:

============ Transcript follows ============

(USER) Unknown user name in "melg"

============= Message follows =============
From: hanna@holycow.santa—cruz.ca.us (Hanna Nelson)
Date: Sun, 4 Aug 1991 19:20:31 PST
X-Mailer: Z-Mail (2.0.0 7/1/91)
To: melg
Subject: Australian Film
```

In this case, the mail bounced because I gave a nonexistent mail address. Ordinarily, you might resend the bounced-mail message by giving the correct address with a command like this:

```
Msg 3 of 10: m —Uf mel
```

The —U and —f options tell **mail** to forward the current message to *mel* immediately. However, if you do this, the forwarded message includes all the stuff from the mailer-daemon at the top of the message. In this case, when the recipient reads the message, it appears as if it was sent from the mailer-daemon.

If you want to resend just the message text instead, you can use **Pipe** to strip off everything at the beginning of the message and put the message text in a file. For example:

    Msg 3 of 10: Pipe -p From: "cat > ~/resend.msg"

This command tells Z-Mail to search for the pattern "From:" and then sends the text of the message, beginning with that line to the UNIX command *cat* which writes the input to the *~/resend.msg* file. In our example, *resend.msg* now contains the following header lines (in addition to the text of the message):

    From: hanna@holycow.santa-cruz.ca.us (Hanna Nelson)
    Date: Sun, 4 Aug 1991 19:20:31 PST
    X-Mailer: Z-Mail (2.0.0 7/1/91)
    To: melg
    Subject: Australian Film

Now, to resend the message, use the **–draft** (or **–h**) to read the *resend.msg* file as a prepared draft with headers:

    Msg 3 of 10: m —euh ~/resend.msg

This command reads in *~/resend.msg* as a message draft and starts up the editor (with the **–e** option) so that you can edit the headers if they were the reason the message bounced. The **–u** option specifies not to append signatures or fortunes (because the **Pipe** command didn't remove them if they were already included at the bottom of the message text).

 Here's a command-line alias that you can use to do the same thing. First, it removes everything up to the **From** line, places the rest of the message in the *~/resend.msg* file, and then sends the file as a prepared draft:

    cmd bounce 'Pipe -p From: "cat > ~/resend.msg" ; m —euh ~/resend.msg'

Put this command-line alias in your initialization file and resend bounced mail with **bounce** like this:

    Msg 3 of 10: bounce

This command starts up the editor on the message. When you exit the editor, press CTRL-D to resend the message.

You can also specify that **pipe** use the output of a Z-Mail pipeline as the message list. We explained how to do this in the section "Combining Z-Mail Commands" earlier in this chapter.

If you set the **unix** variable, you can use UNIX commands anywhere except as the first command in a Z-Mail pipeline without explicitly using the **pipe** command.

To send messages to **pipe** or **Pipe** instead of specifying a message list, you can use the pipe character (|). For example:

    Msg 3 of 10: 4 | Pipe nroff

This command sends the body of message 4 to *nroff*.

Suspending the Z-Mail Process

If your system has job control, you can suspend the Z-Mail process using the **stop** command. Using **stop** is equivalent to using a job-control stop character such as ^Z. This is useful if you need to exit to your UNIX command line (to use command-line redirection or pipe UNIX commands to each other) without updating the current folder or exiting Z-Mail.

When you enter **stop**, you might see a message like the following (this example is from Korn shell):

```
[1]  + Stopped                    zmail
```

To bring the Z-Mail job back to the foreground, use your job control command (**fg** for Korn shell and C shell).

Because you never need to exit Z-Mail, you can use **stop** and **await** to suspend the process until you get new mail, rather than exiting and restarting Z-Mail. The **await** command tells Z-Mail to wait, checking every 30 seconds, for new mail to arrive. Z-Mail waits until new mail arrives or until you press the the interrupt character (CTRL-C or DEL, depending on your system). You can specify a time interval other than 30 seconds by using the **–T** option with **await**.

Let's say you want Z-Mail to stop and wait for new mail. You can use the following command to change the behavior of the **q** command:

```
Msg 3 of 10: cmd q 'stop;await'
```

Now, when you use **q**, the Z-Mail process is suspended until new mail arrives. When you use **fg**, **await** reads in the new mail and sounds the terminal bell. (If you don't want **await** to beep when new mail arrives, set the **quiet** variable to include the string "newmail.") At this point, bring Z-Mail to the foreground again using the shell's job control commands: **fg** or **%zmail**.

If you use **await** in a pipeline, its output includes the list of new messages. If you want **await** to display the new header summaries and set the current message pointer to the first new message when new mail arrives, use this command:

```
Msg 3 of 10: await | from –
```

Reviewing the Shortcuts, Bells, and Whistles

Let's briefly review the variables and commands in Table 5-8 that make up the "shortcuts, bells, and whistles" in this chapter.

Table 5-8. Chapter 5 Variable Review

Variable	Description
history	Specify the number of previous commands to save.
ignore_bang	Turn off the ! character as a history reference.
nonobang	Ignore history reference errors.
complete	Enable filename completion.
fignore	Exclude specific filename patterns from filename completions.
deletesave	Delete saved messages from all folders automatically.
save_empty	Retain folders when you delete all the messages.
alwaysignore	Suppress message headers in different situations.
shell	Specify the UNIX shell to use for shell escapes.
unix	Tell Z-Mail to interpret unrecognized commands as UNIX commands.

Review Quiz

Here's a quiz you can use to review the commands we covered in this chapter. The commands that you use to perform the tasks appear on the left; match them up with the tasks listed on the right.

1. **set shell = /usr/bin/ksh**
2. **fo –l**
3. **zmail –folder ˜/mbox**
4. **close &**
5. **open %**
6. **!!**
7. **history**
8. **ignore Resent-***
9. **my_hdr Return-Receipt-To: hanna@holycow**
10. **set complete=\E˜L**
11. **echo $output**
12. **echo $version**

13. **pick –f harry | save from_harry**
14. **headers :r | delete**
15. **cmd Fwd 'mail –U –f'**
16. **fo #**
17. **set alwaysignore = printer**
18. **sh date**
19. **set unix**
20. **Pipe troff**
21. **stop**

a. Open the system mailbox.
b. Display previous commands.
c. Display the current date.
d. Suppress message headers.
e. Display the output of the last successful command.
f. Request a return-receipt.
g. Suspend Z-Mail.
h. Create a command for forwarding messages.
i. Switch to the previous folder.
j. Save all the messages from one person to a folder.
k. Close the *mbox* folder.
l. Display the current version of the Z-Mail software.
m. Suppress headers when printing messages.
n. Run UNIX commands from Z-Mail.
o. Send message text to *troff*.
p. Run the last command again.
q. Specify the UNIX shell.
r. Open the *mbox* folder.
s. List open folders.
t. Enable filename completion.
u. Delete replied-to messages.

Review Quiz Answers

1.	q.	**2.**	s.	**3.**	r.	**4.**	k.	**5.**	a.	**6.**	p.	**7.**	b.
8	d.	**9.**	f.	**10**	t.	**11.**	e.	**12.**	l.	**13.**	j.	**14.**	u.
15.	h.	**16.**	i.	**17.**	m.	**18.**	c.	**19.**	n.	**20.**	o.	**21.**	g.

At this point, you'll probably want to learn some more about how to customize the behavior of Z-Mail. A good place to start is Chapter 8, *Customizing Z-Mail*; this chapter explains the format of Z-Mail initialization files and the options you can use when starting up Z-Mail.

6
Using the Fullscreen Mode

The fullscreen mode is *screen-oriented* rather than command-line oriented like the line mode. Because fullscreen mode uses routines that are available on most but not all UNIX systems, you might not be able to use this mode on your system. In MUSH, this mode is called "curses."

This interface doesn't require that your computer or terminal have any special graphics capabilities. However, to run Z-Mail in the fullscreen mode, your terminal must have the minimum capabilities required by any fullscreen editor like *vi*.

The fullscreen mode is generally faster than line mode. The fullscreen-mode display allows you to access commands and messages more quickly—instead of typing in a command name followed by the message list, you press a key or key sequence to position the cursor on a message and then press another key to execute a command. However, keep in mind that with the gain in speed, you give up such features as command history, the ability to combine commands with the pipe character (|), and some line-mode commands such as **pick**.

By default, the keys and key sequences that you use to run fullscreen-mode commands are similar to those in the the *vi* visual editor; you can configure the fullscreen mode to emulate another editor, such as *emacs*, if you want.

In this chapter, we'll explain how to run Z-Mail using the fullscreen-mode commands. For details on the functionality of these commands, we'll refer you back to Chapter 3, *Reading and Managing Mail*, Chapter 4, *Sending Mail with Z-Mail*, and Chapter 5, *Z-Mail Shortcuts, Bells, and Whistles*.

Starting Fullscreen Mode

To start Z-Mail in fullscreen mode from the UNIX prompt, use the **−fullscreen** (**−V**) command-line option to **zmail**. (To start MUSH in curses mode, use the **−curses** (**−C**) command-line option.) For example, enter the following:

```
$ zmail −fullscreen
```

If you are using line mode and you want to switch to fullscreen mode, enter **fullscreen** at the line-mode prompt. (With MUSH, use the **curses** command.) For example:

```
Msg 3 of 10: fullscreen
```

If you want to enter fullscreen mode every time you start Z-Mail from the UNIX prompt, put the **fullscreen** command in your Z-Mail initialization file.

 Another way to do this is to create an alias in your login shell so that you always invoke Z-Mail with the **–fullscreen** option. For example, if you use the C shell, enter this command in your ˜/.cshrc file:

```
alias zmail 'zmail —fullscreen'
```

If you use the Korn shell, add this line to your ˜/.kshrc:

```
alias —x zmail="zmail —fullscreen"
```

For Bourne shell users, add the following commands to your ˜/.profile file:[1]

```
zmail() {
        /usr/bin/zmail —fullscreen $*
        }
```

These aliases don't affect the behavior of Z-Mail when you send mail from the UNIX prompt. Thus, the following command still sends mail as expected to *naomi* and *steve*:

```
$ zmail naomi steve
```

As with line mode, if you don't specify recipients and you have mail in your system mailbox, you start up Z-Mail in fullscreen mode.

Fullscreen-mode Display

When you have mail and you enter Z-Mail in fullscreen mode, you see a list of header summaries:

```
1 [0]+ "/usr/spool/mail/hanna": 5 messages, 5 new, 5 unread, 0 deleted
   1  N  Dale Cooper       Jul  8 12:00 (12) Continue Model
   2  N  Harry Truman      Jul 10  2:42 (21) Chapter Eight
   3  N  Lucie             Jul 24 11:41 (48) Phone Message
   4  N  Harry Truman      Jul 25 19:59 (12) Using Fullscreen Mode
   5  N  Albert            Jul 26 12:00 (11) Re: Great Coffee
```

This is the *top-level* header summary display. In fullscreen mode, this display looks exactly as it does from line mode except that there's no line-mode prompt and the current message appears in reverse video. (If you set **no_reverse**, Z-Mail marks the current message with a cursor to the left of the message number.)

Z-Mail determines the number of header summaries to display using the **screen** variable. If you don't have **screen** set, Z-Mail checks the baud rate of the terminal and automatically sets the size of the screen to the optimal refresh time.

Generally, if the baud rate is 300, Z-Mail displays 7 message header summaries; at 1200 baud, Z-Mail displays 14 summaries; and at 2400 baud, Z-Mail displays 22 summaries. At all higher baud rates, Z-Mail displays the number of messages that fit on the screen

---

[1] Note that not all BSD systems understand these commands.

(depending on the size of the screen). Z-Mail reserves the top line for status information and the bottom line for interaction with you, when required.

If you want to override Z-Mail's settings, set the **screen** variable. For example, to tell Z-Mail to display 15 header summaries at a time, regardless of the baud rate, set **screen** to 15. We'll show you how to set variables in fullscreen mode later in this chapter.

Entering Commands in Fullscreen Mode

When you use Z-Mail in fullscreen mode, you can't use the regular line-mode commands; Z-Mail understands only special fullscreen-mode commands. In fullscreen mode, Z-Mail "binds" each command to a specific key or key-combination. To use a fullscreen-mode command, press the key associated with that command and Z-Mail immediately executes the command.

Table 6-1 gives a complete list of the fullscreen-mode commands and default key bindings.

Table 6-1. Fullscreen-mode Commands

Command	Default Binding	Command	Default Binding	Command	Default Binding
alias	a	last-msg	$	saveopts	)
back-msg	k	line-mode	:	screen-back	Z
bind	b	lpr	|	screen-next	z
bind-macro	&&	mail	m	search-again	N
bottom-page	{	mail-flags	M	search-back	^
chdir	%	map	&:	search-next	/
copy	c	map!	&!	shell-escape	!
copy-list	C	mark	*	sort	o
delete	d	my-hdrs	h	sort-reverse	O
delete-list	D	next-msg	j	source	(
first-msg	^	reply	r	undelete-list	U
display	p	preserve	^P	top	T
display-next	n	quit	q	top-page	{
exit	x	quit!	Q	unbind	B
exit!	X	redraw	^L	undelete	U
folder	f	reply-menu*	^R	update	^U
folder-menu*	F	retain*	I	user-button*	\
goto-msg	g	reverse-video	~	variable	v
help	?	save	s	write	w
ignore	i	save-list	S	write-list	W
jobs-menu*	J				

*These fullscreen-mode commands are only available in Z-Mail not MUSH. In MUSH, the default binding for reverse-video is ^R.

When we discuss how to use these commands in the following sections, we'll give the default binding in parentheses after the first mention.

Note that when you use fullscreen mode, Z-Mail turns off your terminal's echo function so that the characters that you enter at the keyboard don't echo on the screen. After you enter certain commands, (for example when you send or reply to mail) the terminal's echo function returns so that the information you type at the keyboard appears on the screen.

Moving the Cursor

Z-Mail includes special commands for moving the cursor around the message list. Table 6-2 lists these cursor-movement commands.

Table 6-2. Cursor-movement Commands

Command	Default Binding	Description
next-msg	+, j, RETURN	Move to the next message.*
back-msg	-, K, k, ˆK	Move to the previous message.
goto-msg	g, *n*	Move to the specified message number.
first-msg	ˆ	Move to the first message in the list.
last-msg	$	Move to the last message.
top-page	{	Move to the message at the top of the screen.
bottom-page	}	Move to the message at the bottom of the screen.
screen-next	z	Display the next screenful of header summaries.
screen-back	Z	Display the previous screenful of header summaries.

*In MUSH, **J** is also one of the default bindings for **next-msg**; however **J** is bound to **jobs-menu** in Z-Mail.

Most of the cursor-movement commands simply move the cursor to the new header summary. For example, use **last-msg ($)** to move the cursor to the last message in the list:

```
    1      Dale Cooper          Jul  8 12:00 (12) Continue Mode
    2   N  Harry Truman         Jul 10  2:42 (21) Chapter Eight
    3      Lucie                Jul 24 11:41 (48) Phone Message
    4   N  Harry Truman         Jul 25 19:59 (12) Using Fullscreen Mode
    5   N  Albert               Jul 26 12:00 (11) Re: Great Coffee
```

However, when you use **goto-msg**, Z-Mail displays this prompt at the bottom of the screen:

```
goto msg: _
```

Enter a message number (or use one of the special message list characters) and press RETURN. To refresh your memory on message lists, refer back to the section "What is a Message List?" in Chapter 3, *Reading and Managing Mail*.

Because Z-Mail commands output a message list, you can also use any Z-Mail command at the **goto-msg** prompt. Simply enclose the string in backquotes (`` ` ``). To go to the first message from *cooper* use this **pick** command:[2]

```
goto msg: `pick -f cooper`
```

Instead of using **goto-msg** and then specifying a message number, you can simply enter the message number at either the top level or continue mode. When you enter a number, Z-Mail automatically shows the **goto** prompt. For example, to move the cursor to message 4, enter **4** and you see:

```
goto msg: 4_
```

When you press RETURN, Z-Mail moves the cursor to message 4. If you are in continue mode, you see:

```
    4  N  Harry Truman          Jul 25 19:59 (12) Using Fullscreen Mode
Msg 4 of 5: ...continue... _
```

Some of the message-list characters are bound to other fullscreen-mode commands. So, when you use $ to go to the last message in the list, Z-Mail executes the **last-msg** command and displays the header summary for the last message, but you don't see the `goto msg` prompt.

Use the **screen-next** (z) and **screen-back** (Z) commands to move the cursor forward and back one screenful of header summaries.

Continue Mode

After you read a message, Z-Mail enters *continue mode*. In continue mode, you see the line-mode prompt, followed by "`...continue...`." For example, after you use **display** (p) to read message 1, you see something like this:

```
Msg #1 (12 lines)
From cooper Fri Jul 12 12:00:11 1991
From: Dale Cooper <cooper>
Date: Fri, 12 Jul 1991 12:00:37 -0800
To: Hanna Nelson <hanna>
Subject: Continue mode

How do I redisplay the header summaries
when I'm in "continue mode?"

- The Coop

    1   Dale Cooper          Jul 12  12:00 (12) Continue mode
Msg 1 of 5: ...continue... _
```

---

[2] Note that **pick** is a line-mode command; for more information, see Chapter 3.

When you see the `continue` prompt, you are still in fullscreen mode. You can still enter another command or move the cursor up and down the list of messages using cursor-movement commands like **next-msg** and **back-msg**. With continue mode, Z-Mail saves you time by not redrawing the screen after each command.

NOTE

In continue mode, the Z-Mail prompt always includes the header summary for the current message immediately above the `continue` prompt.

Note that the cursor-movement commands work even if you are in continue mode. However, in continue mode, Z-Mail doesn't move the cursor but rather displays the header summary for the new message immediately above the `continue` prompt.

For example, you see this header summary for the last message you read:

```
    1    Dale Cooper        Jul 12  12:00 (12) Continue mode
    Msg 1 of 5: ...continue... _
```

When you use **next-msg (+)** at the `continue` prompt, you see the next header summary like this:

```
    1    Dale Cooper        Jul 12 12:00 (12) Continue mode
    2 N  Harry Truman       Aug 10  2:42 (21) Chapter Eight
    Msg 2 of 5: ...continue... _
```

Note that the prompt changes to reflect the new current message.

If you want to see the entire message list when you move the cursor, press the space bar to return to the top level first.

To return to the top-level display from continue mode, use either the **quit (q)** or **exit (x)** commands or press the RETURN or space bar keys. Note that this might be a little confusing if you're used to the line-mode commands. For example, to redisplay the header summaries in line mode, you use the **headers (h)** command; however, in fullscreen mode, the **h** key is bound to the **my-hdrs** command.

Z-Mail redraws the header summary list on your screen, placing the cursor on the message that you just read. (As in line mode, when you read a message, that message becomes the current message.)

Changing the Screen Display

Z-Mail includes two commands, **redraw (^L)** and **reverse-video (˜)**, that change the appearance of the screen display. If the display becomes scrambled, use **redraw** to refresh the screen.

By default, Z-Mail puts the current message in reverse video; to turn it off, use the **reverse-video** (˜) command. When you use **reverse-video**, the cursor appears to the left of the current message:

```
_   5  N   Albert          Jul 26 12:00 (11) Re: Great Coffee
```

You can also turn off reverse video by setting the **no_reverse** variable.

Getting Help in Fullscreen Mode

To get general help about fullscreen mode, use the **help** (?) command. Z-Mail displays this screen:

```
fullscreen

The fullscreen interface of Z-Mail does not require a graphics
display, but does requires a terminal which can handle upline
cursor movement capabilities.  All commands are one or two
keystroke commands and are executed as soon as the key is typed.

For a list of current key-to-command bindings, use the "bind"
command (defaults to 'b' in fullscreen mode).

See also the variable $fullscreen_help.
```

It's more likely that you'll want to display the current list of key-to-command bindings. To do this, use the **bind** (**b**) command:

```
bind [<CR>=all, -?=help]: _
```

Whenever Z-Mail displays a prompt like this in fullscreen mode, you can cancel the command by pressing the BACKSPACE key or the interrupt character (CTRL-C or DEL).

Press RETURN to display the current list of bindings. To display the next screen of binding settings, press the space bar at the **more** prompt. If you just want to display the next line, press RETURN. To quit the display and return to continue mode, enter **q**.

If you want to display help on the **bind** command, select **bind** and enter **-?** at the following prompt:

```
bind [<CR>=all, -?=help]: -?
```

We'll discuss how to bind different keystrokes to the fullscreen-mode commands in the section "Binding Keystrokes to Commands" later in this chapter.

Setting Variables in Fullscreen Mode

Variables allow you to change the behavior of Z-Mail. For example, to change the number of header summaries that Z-Mail displays at one time, set the **screen** variable. It differs from the **crt** variable that determines how many lines of message *text* to display at one time.)

To set variables in fullscreen mode, use the **variable** (**v**) command. When you use **variable**, you see the following menu:

```
Variables: set unset all help
```

Whenever you see a menu like this in fullscreen mode, select an option by moving the highlight or by pressing the first letter of the option.[3] (If you set **no_reverse**, Z-Mail replaces the highlight with a cursor below the first character of the selected option.) To cancel the command, press the ESCAPE key.

To set **screen**, choose the **set** option from the Variables menu. When you see this prompt, set the variable exactly as you did in line mode:

```
set: screen = 15
```

With this setting, Z-Mail displays 15 header summaries at a time.

Removing Variable Settings

To remove the variable setting, use the **unset** option from the Variables menu. This accomplishes the same thing as using the **unset** command in line mode. For example, to change **screen** back to the default, select **unset** and then enter the following:

```
unset: screen
```

Listing Current Variable Settings

If you're not sure what the current variable settings are, select **all** from the Variables menu. When you do this, you see a display like the following:

```
dot
editor          /usr/bin/vi
hold
home            /u/hanna
hostname        holycow
keepsave
mbox            /u/hanna/Mail/save.me
screen          15
```

Getting Help on Variables

For help on setting variables, select **help** from the Variable menu. When you see this prompt, press RETURN:

```
which variable? [all <var>]: _
```

To get help on just one variable, enter the variable name at the prompt. If you enter **keepsave** at the prompt above, Z-Mail displays this message:

```
If "keepsave" is set, 'saved' messages are not deleted in this way.  In
other folders, 'saved' messages are not deleted unless "deletesave" is
set.  Setting "keepsave" protects 'saved' messages from deletion in any
folder, even if "deletesave" is also set.  See also "hold".
```

Any variables that you set with **variable** are in effect for the current Z-Mail session only.

---

[3] MUSH doesn't have menus; however, you can still access options by selecting the first letter of the option.

When you leave the Z-Mail program, you lose these settings. To make variable settings permanent, include them in your initialization file. Each time you start up Z-Mail, the initialization file is read; Z-Mail sets any variables and runs any commands in this file.

Displaying a Menu of Key Bindings on the Screen

Because many of the key-to-command bindings in fullscreen mode are not mnemonic, I have a hard time remembering the key that executes a command. For this reason, Z-Mail provides a way to display some of the key bindings on your screen when you're at the top-level header summary display (in other words, not in continue mode). Here's what the default list looks like:

```
1 [0]+ "/usr/spool/mail/hanna": 5 messages, 5 new, 5 unread, 0 deleted
   1  N  Dale Cooper          Jul  8 12:00 (12) Continue Mode
   2  N  Harry Truman         Jul 10  2:42 (21) Chapter Eight
   3  N  Lucie                Jul 24 11:41 (48) Phone Message
   4  N  Harry Truman         Jul 25 19:59 (12) Using Fullscreen Mode
   5  N  Albert               Jul 26 12:00 (11) Re: Great Coffee

(RET) display  (s) save      (m) mail        (r) reply
(j) next-msg   (k) back-msg  (z) screen-next (Z) screen-back
```

To get this display, set the **fullscreen_help** variable. Use the **variable** command, select **set** and enter **fullscreen_help** at the prompt.

Most of the default commands in this display are pretty intuitive. If you want to specify different fullscreen-mode commands to display, set **fullscreen_help** to a list of fullscreen-mode commands. For example, let's say you want to list the default bindings for the **top-page**, **bottom-page**, **update**, **bind-macro**, **map!**, **source**, and **mark** commands. Use the following **fullscreen_help** setting (enter the entire command on one line):

```
set: fullscreen_help = "top_page bottom_page update bind-macro \
    map! source mark"
```

Use spaces to separate the command names and enclose the list in double quotes (").

Now, the help display at the bottom of your screen looks like this:

```
({) top-page    (^U) update     (&:) map    (() source
(}) bottom-page (&&) bind-macro (&!) map!   (*) mark
```

Note that the help list shortens the list of header summaries that Z-Mail displays at one time. If you want to see the header summaries at the bottom of the screen, move the cursor down past the last header summary. To redisplay the help information, use the **redraw** (^L) command.

Sending Mail

To send mail from fullscreen mode, use the **mail** and **mail-flags** commands. Table 6-3 lists these commands.

Table 6-3. Mail Commands

Command	Default Binding	Description
mail	m	Send a message.
mail-flags	M	Send a message using command-line options.

When you use **mail**, Z-Mail drops the cursor to the bottom line of the screen and displays the To prompt. At this point, you can address, compose, and send your message exactly as you did from line mode.

You can change the behavior of the **mail** command by specifying *command-line options*. For example, use command-line options to tell **mail** to forward the current message and enter the editor automatically. To do this from fullscreen mode, use the **mail-flags** (**M**) command and enter options at the prompt:

```
flags [-?]: -ef
```

These options tell Z-Mail to include the current message, mark it as "forwarded mail," and start up the editor.

If you don't remember **mail**'s command-line options, press RETURN when you see this prompt:

```
flags [-?]: _
```

Z-Mail displays the options that you can use with **mail**:

```
      mail [mail-flags] [recipients]

Compose and send a mail message.  The possible flags are:
  -A [type:]file   attach file, treating file as type "type"
  -b bcc-addrs     set blind-carbon-copy recipients
  -c cc-addrs      set carbon-copy recipients
  -e               immediately enter editor (autoedit)
  -E               edit outgoing headers
  -f [msg-list]    forward msg-list (not indented)
  -F               add fortune to the end of message
  -h file          read file as prepared draft (with headers)
  -H file          read file as prepared text (without headers)
  -i [msg-list]    include msg-list in letter
  -I [msg-list]    include msg-list with headers in letter
  -s [subject]     prompt for or set subject
  -u               do not append signatures and fortunes
  -U               send draft immediately (use with -h or -H)
  -v               verbose (not available on some systems)
```

We explained how to use these options with **mail** in Chapter 4, *Sending Mail with Z-Mail*.

Suspending and Resuming a Message Composition

As we explained in Chapter 4, you can suspend a message from within compose mode using the ~z command. (MUSH doesn't include this feature.) When you suspend a composition in fullscreen mode, Z-Mail displays a message like the following and returns you to continue mode:

```
[1] Stopped.
    8  N  Dale Cooper              Jul 18  9:50 (84) stopped jobs
```

When you want to continue composing the message, you first have to bring it to the foreground. To do this, use the **jobs-menu (J)** command. This command produces the Job Control menu:

```
Job Control: resume select list
```

To list the jobs that are currently suspended, select **list**. You see a display like this:

```
[1]     To: george        vegetarian lasgne
[2]   + To: dan           Technical Review
```

To select a message to continue editing, choose **select** from the Job Control menu. Z-Mail displays the current jobs and prompts you for a job number:

```
[1]     To: george        vegetarian lasgne
[2]   + To: dan           Technical Review
Job Number: _
```

Enter the number and press RETURN. For example, to continue editing the message to *george*, enter **1**. You return to continue mode, editing that message.

To resume editing the last message that you suspended (the one marked with a plus character (+)), select **resume** from the Job Control menu.

Note that if you try to exit Z-Mail without finishing your suspended jobs, you see the following message:

```
Warning: Abort suspended compositions? (y/c) [cancel] _
```

If you don't want to finish the messages, select **y** to exit Z-Mail. If you press RETURN, you return to Z-Mail in continue mode. You can then use the **resume** option from the Job Control menu to finish editing the messages and send them, or cancel them with ~x or ~q.

If you select **jobs-menu** when you don't have any messages in the background, you see this message:

```
No compositions.
```

Setting Mail Aliases

If you frequently send mail to a group of people or to someone with a long mail address, you can create a shorter *mail alias* to use instead. For example, I've created an alias to send mail to the people in my department at work. Now, instead of typing all 40 addresses when I want to send mail to everyone in the department, I just send mail to the *docland* alias. I also have a mail alias for my friend in Edinburgh, Scotland; I use the short name and Z-Mail expands it to the long address for mail to get to him.

In this section, we'll show you how to use the **alias** command from fullscreen mode to create mail aliases. For more detail on mail aliases, see Chapter 4, *Sending Mail with Z-Mail*.

To set up a mail alias, use the **alias (a)** command:

```
Aliases: set unset all help
```

To create a mail alias, select **set**. For example, to create an alias for my Scottish friend, I use the following:

```
set: neilson davidn@castle.edinburgh.ac.uk
```

To remove an alias, select **unset** from the Aliases menu. Enter the alias to remove when you see this prompt:

```
unset: neilson
```

To display the current list of aliases, select **all** at the Aliases menu:

```
bart       bart@zip.com
dan        dan@zip.com
neilson    davidn@castle.edinburgh.ac.uk
project    faith, james, kelly, martin, marty, stewart, teresa
zmail      dan, bart, dale, george@vegan.edu
```

In this example, note that if I want to send mail to *dan*, *bart*, *dale*, and *george*, I can send all of them mail by specifying the alias *zmail*:

```
To: zmail
```

To get help on setting mail aliases, select help from the Aliases menu.

Creating Your Own Message Headers

As we showed you in Chapter 4, *Sending Mail with Z-Mail*, you can create your own message headers to include in your outgoing mail messages. To create these message headers from fullscreen mode, use the **my-hdrs (h)** command. Here's how to create a header and set it to the name of your company. When you select **my-hdrs**, Z-Mail prompts you:

```
Custom Headers: set unset all help
```

Select **set** and then enter the new header:

```
set: Organization: "O'Reilly and Associates, Inc.
```

Remember, if the value includes metacharacters (such as the single quote character (') in the example above), enclose the whole string in double quotes ("). (Of course, if it includes double quotes, you should enclose the string in single quotes.) You must include the colon character (:) after the header name.

Suppose you get a new job and you want to change the **my-hdrs** setting. To do this, enter **my-hdrs** and select **set** again. At the prompt, enter the header with the new value:

```
set: Organization: "Z-Code Software Corp."
```

What if you go to work for yourself and you want to remove the "Organization" header altogether? Select **unset** and enter the header to remove:

```
unset: Organization
```

To list all your headers, select **all** from the the Custom Headers menu. In our example, you see the following list:

```
Organization:     O'Reilly and Associates, Inc.
Phone-Number:     (900) 860-0911
```

To get help on **my-hdrs**, select the **help** option. If you want more information on creating your own message headers, see Chapter 4.

Reading Messages

To read a message, move the cursor over the message you want and use the **display** and **top** commands. Table 6-4 lists commands you can use while reading messages.

Table 6-4. Display Commands

Command	Default Binding	Description
display	., p, t	Display the current message.
top	T	Display the top few lines of a message.
ignore	i	Tell Z-Mail to ignore headers when displaying messages.
retain	I	Specify headers to display.

To read message 5, move the cursor to the message and press **p**:

```
Msg #5 (11 lines)
From albert@fbi.gov Tue Jul 22 12:11:12 1991
In-Reply-To: Hanna Nelson's <hanna@holycow.santa-cruz.ca.us>
            message (Jul 21, 12:10pm)
References: <9103091210.aa02230@holycow.santa-cruz.ca.us>
X-Mailer: Z-Mail (2.0.0 7/1/91)
To: Hanna Nelson <hanna>
Subject: Re: Great Coffee!!
Date: Tue, 22 Jul 91 12:11:11 PST
From: Albert <albert@fbi.gov>
Message-ID: <9012201701.aa26961@fbi.gov>
```

```
                It's from an espresso bar in Seattle.

            Al
                5     Albert   Jul  22 12:11 (11)   Re: Great Coffee!!
            Msg 5 of 6: ...continue... _
```

As you can see, this message has more header information than message text. You can display just the top few lines of the message text (without the headers) using the **top** (**T**) command. For example, if you use **top** instead of **display** to read that last message, you see the following:

```
            Top of Message #5 (11 lines)
            It's from an espresso bar in Seattle.

            Al
                5     Albert          Jul 22 12:00 (11) Re: Great Coffee
            Msg 5 of 6: ...continue... _
```

By default, **top** displays the number of lines specified by the **crt** variable unless another value is specified by the **toplines** variable. So, if you want **top** to display five lines of message text at a time, set **toplines** to 5.

If you don't want to see all the headers when you read mail with **display**, you can tell Z-Mail not to display certain headers using the **ignore** (**i**) command. In the section, "Suppressing Message Header Display" in Chapter 5, we discuss the line-mode commands, **ignore** and **retain**, at greater length. These commands function identically in fullscreen mode.

When you enter **ignore** in fullscreen mode, Z-Mail displays this menu:

```
            Ignored Headers: set unset all help
```

So, let's say you want to ignore the `In-Reply-To`, `References`, `Message-Id`, `Date`, and `X-Mailer` headers. To do this, select **set** and then enter the following:

```
            set: In-Reply-To References Message-Id Date X-Mailer
```

Now, when you read message 5 with **display**, you see this:

```
            Msg #5 (11 lines)
            From: Albert <albert@fbi.gov>
            Subject: Re: Great Coffee!!
            To: Hanna Nelson <hanna>

            It's from an espresso bar in Seattle.

            Al
                5     Albert          Jul 22 12:00 (11) Re: Great Coffee
            Msg 5 of 6: ...continue... _
```

If you change your mind and decide that you want to see the `Date` header, use **unset** and enter the following:

```
            unset: Date
```

To get a list of the message headers that you're currently ignoring, select **all** from the Ignored Headers menu. In our example, when you use **all**, you see this list:

```
            In-Reply-To
            Message-Id
            References
            X-Mailer
```

To get help on **ignore**, select help at the Ignored Headers menu.

Another way to suppress headers is to specify just the headers that you want to see; use **retain (I)** to do this:[4]

> Retained Headers: ▮set▮ unset all help

Select **set** and enter the names of the headers that you want to keep at the prompt.

For more detail about **ignore** and **retain**, see Chapter 5, *Z-Mail Shortcuts, Bells, and Whistles*.

When New Mail Arrives

Z-Mail checks for new mail each time you enter a command. If you are in Z-Mail when new mail arrives, Z-Mail adds the new message to the list of header summaries; you might see a message like the following in the bottom line of the screen:

> New mail: (#6) Harry Truman   Jul 22 19:59 (12) Coffee

Move the cursor to the new message $. This moves the cursor to the last message (the newest in the list). Then use **display** to read it.

Replying to Messages

With Z-Mail, you can reply to all the recipients, or just the author, of the original message. Table 6-5 lists the commands you can use to reply to messages.

Table 6-5. Reply Commands

Command	Default Binding	Description
reply	r	Send a reply to the original author only.
reply-all	R	Reply to everyone on the distribution.
reply-menu*	^R	Display the Reply menu.

*This fullscreen-mode command is not available in MUSH. In addition, in MUSH, the ^R key is bound to **reverse-video** by default.

To send a response to the author of a message, use the **reply (r)** command; **reply** automatically fills in the To and Subject lines (adding the "Re:" to indicate that this message is a response to a previous message) and then places you in compose mode. If you want *all* the recipients of the original message to get your message, use **reply-all (R)**.

---

[4] Z-Mail 2.0.0 does not support the **retain (I)** command.

Another way to send a reply with Z-Mail is to select **reply-menu** (^R). Here's what the Reply menu looks like:

```
Reply: sender all Sender/include All/include
```

The **sender** option is equivalent to **reply**; **all** is the same as **reply-all**. As you can see, with the last two options on the Reply menu, you can tell Z-Mail to include the current message automatically. For more information about including messages, see Chapter 4, *Sending Mail with Z-Mail*.

There isn't any way to reply to more than one message (or to specify command-line options) in fullscreen mode. But you can do these things in line mode. We'll show you how to use line-mode commands from fullscreen mode later in this chapter.

Manipulating Messages

In this section, we'll show you the different ways you can manage the messages in your folder using fullscreen-mode commands. If you want more information and tips on using the functions described in this section, refer back to Chapter 3, *Reading and Managing Mail*.

Saving Messages to Folders and Files

You can organize messages that you want to keep by saving them to folders with the **save** (s) command. You can then access these messages, as you do the messages in your system mailbox, by switching folders. We'll explain how to do this later in this chapter. Table 6-6 lists the commands for saving messages to folders.

Table 6-6. Save Commands

Command	Default Binding	Description
save	s	Save the current message to a folder.
save-list	S	Save a list of messages.
write	w	Save the current message without headers to a file.
write-list	W	Save a list of messages.
copy	c	Copy the current message to a folder (don't mark it for deletion).
copy-list	C	Copy a list of messages.

Like their line-mode counterparts, **save** and **copy** save messages to folders; **write** saves messages without headers to ordinary text files. Chapter 3 explains more about saving messages to folders and files. For information on manipulating folders, see Chapter 5.

When you use the fullscreen-mode **save**, **write**, and **copy** commands, you see a prompt like this:

```
folder to save [~/mbox]: _
```

Enter the name of the folder at this prompt. If the folder already exists, **save** appends the message to it. If you decide not to save the message, press the BACKSPACE key to return to continue mode.

Press RETURN to save the current message to the folder specified by the **mbox** variable (in this case the *mbox* folder in your home directory). You can change the default folder by setting the **mbox** variable. For example, if you set **mbox** so that Z-Mail uses *~/saved.mail* instead of *mbox*, when you use **save**, you see this message:

```
folder to save [~/saved.mail]:  _
```

To save a group of messages, use **save-list (S)**, **write-list (W)**, or **copy-list (C)**. Suppose you want to save messages 3, 4, and 8 to a folder. To do this, use **save-list** and enter:

```
save msg list: 3 4 8
```

When you press RETURN, you see this prompt:

```
folder to save [~/mbox]: _
```

Enter the name of the folder (or press RETURN to save the messages to *~/mbox*).

Changing Directories

I often find myself saving messages to a file in one particular directory. For example, when I'm working on a project and people send me information, I like to keep all that mail in one place. When this happens, I change to that directory so that I don't have to enter the complete pathname of the file each time I save a message.

To change directories, use the **chdir (%)** command. You see this prompt:

```
chdir to [~]: _
```

Enter the directory name and press RETURN. For example, to change to the directory *zmail.book* in my folder directory, I use the following:

```
chdir to [~]: +zmail.book
```

and Z-Mail displays:

```
Working dir: /u/hanna/Mail/zmail.book
```

Now, when I save messages to files in the *zmail.book* directory, I don't have to specify the entire path (*/u/hanna/Mail/zmail.book*) or even the folder shorthand *+zmail.book*. Instead, I just specify the filename.

To change to the directory that is one level above the current directory, enter the following:

```
chdir to [~]: ..
```

Now, Z-Mail displays this message:

```
Working dir: /u/hanna/Mail
```

To return to your home directory (˜) quickly, simply press RETURN at the **chdir** prompt.

Deleting Messages

When you read messages, it's a good idea to delete the ones that you don't want to keep; otherwise, they remain in your system mailbox forever. To delete a message, move the cursor to the message that you want to get rid of, and use the **delete** (**d**) command. When you delete messages in fullscreen mode, Z-Mail marks the deleted message with an asterisk character (*). If you delete a message from continue mode, you see the following:

```
    10    Richard Robinson    Jul 31 23:55 (780) Meaning of Life
deleted
    10 *  Richard Robinson    Jul 31 23:55 (780) Meaning of Life
Msg 10 of 20: ...continue... _
```

Unlike deleting mail in line mode, Z-Mail doesn't remove the message from the header summary display; you can still see the header summary. In the example below, messages 2, 4, and 6 have been deleted:

```
    1      Harry Truman   Jul 21 12:37  (16)  $$
    2  *r  Albert         Jul 22 10:01  ( 8)  Re: Great Coffee!!
    3      Leo J.         Jul 25 23:03  ( 6)  New shoes
    4  *    Albert         Jul 25 18:31  (10)  Z-Mail
    5  U   Harry Truman   Jul 24 10:01  ( 3)  Re: party
    6  *    Dale Cooper    Jul 22 18:11  (12)  Z-Mail Chapters
```

As in line mode, when you try to use **display** to read a deleted message, you see this message:

```
Message 2 deleted; type 'u' to undelete.
```

The **display-next** (**n**) command simply skips over any deleted messages.

To delete more than one message at a time, use **delete-list** (**D**). Z-Mail displays this prompt:

```
delete msg list: _
```

Use any of the special message-list characters to delete the list. Let's say you want to delete messages 1 through 4:

```
delete msg list: 1-4
```

Restoring Deleted Messages

To restore a message that you deleted (any message marked with an asterisk), move the cursor to the message and use **undelete** (**u**). To restore more than one message at a time, use **undelete-list** (**U**):

```
undelete msg_list: _
```

Specify the messages to restore. For example, restore messages 3, 5, and 6 by entering the following:

```
undelete msg_list: 3,5-6
```

Preserving Messages

By default, when you update your system mailbox, Z-Mail keeps messages that you've read until you explicitly delete them. If you want Z-Mail to move messages that you've already read to the ~/*mbox* file automatically, unset the **hold** variable. When you unset **hold**, you can still prevent Z-Mail from moving specific messages to ~/*mbox* using the **preserve** (^P) command. This command marks messages with the **P** status indicator:

```
 6  P  Dale Cooper    Jul 22 18:11   (12)   Z-Mail Chapters
```

When you exit Z-Mail, preserved messages remain in your system mailbox.

To "unpreserve" a message, enter **preserve** again. This toggles off the **P** status indicator; Z-Mail then removes the message when you update the mailbox.

We discuss the effects of **preserve** and **hold** in more detail in Chapter 3.

Sending Messages to the Printer

If you'd rather keep a hard copy of your message instead of saving it to a file, use **lpr** (|) to send the message to the printer. When you use **lpr**, Z-Mail displays a message like this:

```
printing message 6...(16 lines)
```

The **lpr** command marks printed messages with a (lowercase) **p**:

```
 6  p  Dale Cooper    Jul 22 18:11   (12)   Z-Mail Chapters
```

If you want to use a different print command (other than **lpr**) or change the default printer, see the section "Printing Messages" in Chapter 3.

Marking Messages

We discussed how to mark special messages in line mode in Chapter 3; in this section, we'll cover how to do it in fullscreen mode.

Sometimes, when you read a message, you want to wait until you have more time before responding. Use the **mark** (*) command to mark messages that you want to come back to later. To do this, select the message and use **mark**; this marks the message with a temporary mark, the plus character (**+**):

```
   6 +   Dale Cooper   Jul 22 18:11   (12)   Z-Mail Chapters
```

To remove the + mark, enter **mark** again.

Note that Z-Mail doesn't save these marks when you update the folder. However, you can set permanent priority marks on messages using the line-mode **mark** command. We'll show you how to do this from fullscreen mode later in this chapter.

Searching for Patterns

If you want to read all the messages on a particular subject or from the same person, you can do this by searching for a pattern in the header summary list. This is similar to using **pick** in the line mode. For example, to read all the messages from *richardr*, search for the pattern "richardr." Table 6-7 lists the commands for searching in fullscreen mode.

Table 6-7. Search Commands

Command	Default Binding	Description
search-next	/	Search forward in the message list.
search-back	^_	Search backward in the message list.
search-again	^N	Repeat the last search pattern (forward or backward in the message list).

Because some terminals use ^/ (CTRL-slash) for ^_ (CTRL-underscore), you might want to rebind this key. We explain how to bind different keys to commands later in this chapter.

When you use **search-next** or **search-back**, Z-Mail displays a prompt like the following:

```
forward search: _
```

Enter the pattern to search for and press RETURN. Z-Mail searches for the next message with the specified pattern. If Z-Mail finds a header summary with the pattern, it moves the cursor to that message. For example, let's say your message list looks like this:

```
   1  N  Dale Cooper        Jul  8 12:00 (12) Continue Mode
   2     Harry Truman       Jul 10  2:42 (21) Chapter Eight
   3     Lucie              Jul 24 11:41 (48) Phone Message
   4  N  Harry Truman       Jul 25 19:59 (12) Using Fullscreen Mode
```

```
    5  N  Albert              Jul 26 12:00 (11) Re: Great Coffee
    6     Dale Cooper         Jul 30  7:05 (17) Z-Mail Chapters
```

and you use the **search-next** command to find the next header summary with "Chapter":

>   forward search: **Chapter**

Z-Mail moves the cursor to message 2. If Z-Mail doesn't locate the pattern, the cursor doesn't move, and you see this message:

>   Pattern not found.

Use **search-again** to display the next header summary with the pattern. In our example, you see this:

```
      continue forward search...
        6     Dale Cooper         Jul 30  7:05 (17) Z-Mail Chapters
      Msg 6 of 6: ...continue... _
```

If Z-Mail finds another occurrence of the pattern, it moves the cursor to that header summary. If it doesn't, the cursor remains on the message containing the pattern.

Z-Mail automatically wraps the message list when searching. If you use **search-again** at this point, Z-Mail wraps to the beginning of the message list automatically and moves the cursor to the next message with the pattern, message 2.

Sorting Folders

In Chapter 3, we discussed how to use the **sort** command in line mode to change the order in which messages appear in folders. Here, we'll cover how to do the same thing from fullscreen mode.

Let's say that you want to read all the messages on a particular subject in sequence and you don't want to use **search-next**. You can group together all these messages by sorting your message list alphabetically by `Subject` line. To do this, use the **sort** and **sort-reverse** commands. Table 6-8 lists these commands and their default bindings.

Table 6-8. Sort Commands

Command	Default Binding	Description
sort	o	Sort messages by author, date, length, status, subject, or priority.
sort-reverse	O	Reverse the sort order.

For example, suppose your message list looks like this (note that the messages are sorted by date):

```
    1 p  Lucie            Aug 21 11:48  (30)  phone message
    2 +  Harry Truman     Aug 21 12:37  (16)  $$
    3 r  Albert           Aug 21 10:01  ( 8)  Re: Great Coffee!!
    4 *  Dale Cooper      Aug 22 18:11  (12)  Z-Mail Chapters
    5 P  Tom C.           Aug 23 12:37  (20)  electronic mail
```

```
6   U   Harry Truman   Aug 24 10:01   ( 3)   Re: party
7   N   Albert         Aug 25 18:31   (10)   Z-Mail
8       Leo J.         Aug 25 23:03   ( 6)   New shoes
9       Harry Truman   Aug 30 14:00   ( 8)   Z-Mail
```

When you use **sort**, Z-Mail displays this menu:[5]

```
Order messages by: author date length priority subject Re:subject Status
```

Select **subject**. Z-Mail reorders your messages and now they look like this:

```
1 +   Harry Truman   Aug 21 12:37   (16)   $$
2   r   Albert         Aug 22 10:01   ( 8)   Re: Great Coffee!!
3       Leo J.         Aug 25 23:03   ( 6)   New shoes
4   *   Dale Cooper    Aug 22 18:11   (12)   Z-Mail Chapters
5   N   Albert         Aug 25 18:31   (10)   Z-Mail
6       Harry Truman   Aug 30 14:00   ( 8)   Z-Mail
7   P   Tom C.         Aug 23 12:37   (20)   electronic mail
8   U   Harry Truman   Aug 24 10:01   ( 3)   Re: party
9   p   Lucie          Aug 21 11:48   (30)   phone message
```

Z-Mail sorts the `Subject` lines alphabetically, putting special characters first, followed by uppercase letters (ignoring the "Re:"), with lowercase last.

If you don't want Z-Mail to ignore "Re:" when sorting by `Subject`, select **Re:subject** from the menu.

Sorting by Date

After you read all the messages on one subject, return your mailbox to its presorted state (sorted by date) using **sort** again, but this time select **date** at the **sort** menu. Now, Z-Mail orders your messages by the date that they were sent, most recent first.

If you want **sort** to display your messages by the date you received them, set the **date_received** variable.

Sorting by Author

To read all the messages from the same person, sort the list alphabetically by author. Enter **author** at the menu. Now, your message list looks like this:

```
1   r   Albert         Aug 22 10:01   ( 8)   Re: Great Coffee!!
2   N   Albert         Aug 25 18:31   (10)   Z-Mail
3   *   Dale Cooper    Aug 22 18:11   (12)   Z-Mail Chapters
4   +   Harry Truman   Aug 21 12:37   (16)   $$[6]
5       Harry Truman   Aug 30 14:00   ( 8)   Z-Mail
6   U   Harry Truman   Aug 24 10:01   ( 3)   Re: party
7       Leo J.         Aug 25 23:03   ( 6)   New shoes
8   p   Lucie          Aug 21 11:48   (30)   phone message
9   P   Tom C.         Aug 23 12:37   (20)   electronic mail
```

---

[5] MUSH displays a similar menu, but does not include the "Re:subject" menu option; to select an option from the MUSH **sort** menu, enter the first character of the option.

Sorting by Status

Use **sort** to sort messages by status (such as read, replied-to, or deleted) or by priority. If I have a lot of messages, I find this option useful to see which messages I haven't read yet (the new and unread messages appear first in the list when you sort by status).

When sorting by status, Z-Mail puts messages in the order described in Table 6-9.

Table 6-9. Sort Status Order

Order	Status	Status Indicator
1	New	N
2	Unread	U
3	Preserved	P
4	Replied-to	r
5	Printed	p
6	Marked	+
7	Read	(blank)
8	Deleted	*

Let's say you use **sort** and then select **Status**. Z-Mail orders your messages like this:

```
1  N  Albert        Aug 25 18:31  (10)  Z-Mail
2  U  Harry Truman  Aug 24 10:01  ( 3)  Re: party
3  P  Tom C.        Aug 23 12:37  (20)  electronic mail
4  r  Albert        Aug 22 10:01  ( 8)  Re: Great Coffee!!
5  p  Lucie         Aug 21 11:48  (30)  phone message
6  +  Harry Truman  Aug 21 12:37  (16)  $$
7     Leo J.        Aug 25 23:03  ( 6)  New shoes
8     Harry Truman  Aug 30 14:00  ( 8)  Z-Mail
9  *  Dale Cooper   Aug 22 18:11  (12)  Z-Mail Chapters
```

If you have marked messages with priority settings, you can sort messages by priority. (For information on how to set priorities, see Chapter 3, *Reading and Managing Mail.*) When you sort by priority, Z-Mail puts any marked messages first, followed by messages marked as priorities A through E, and lastly, the messages with neither a mark nor a priority setting. For example, when you select **sort** and then **priority**, the list looks like the following:

```
1  +   Harry Truman  Aug 21 12:37  (16)  $$
2  A r Albert        Aug 22 10:01  ( 8)  Re: Great Coffee!!
3  A   Leo J.        Aug 25 23:03  ( 6)  New shoes
4  Cp  Lucie         Aug 21 11:48  (30)  phone message
5  EP  Tom C.        Aug 23 12:37  (20)  electronic mail
6  N   Albert        Aug 25 18:31  (10)  Z-Mail
7  U   Harry Truman  Aug 24 10:01  ( 3)  Re: party
8  *   Dale Cooper   Aug 22 18:11  (12)  Z-Mail Chapters
9      Harry Truman  Aug 30 14:00  ( 8)  Z-Mail
```

To reverse the sort order, use **sort-reverse** (**O**) instead of **sort**.

Using Folders

In this section, we'll show you how to switch between and update folders when using Z-Mail in fullscreen mode. For details on manipulating folders, see the section, "More About Folders," in Chapter 5.

Switching Between Folders

After organizing messages by saving them to a folder, you can switch to the new folder and manipulate these messages just like the ones in your system mailbox. Use the **folder-menu** (**F**) command. Here's what the Folder Operation menu looks like:

```
Folder Operation: change add Close list directory help
```

Let's say you want to display the contents of your folder directory (*~/Mail*) before you switch. To do this, select **directory** and you see a listing like the following:

```
/u/hanna/Mail:
zmail.book

/u/hanna/Mail/zmail.book:
Chapter.5    Chapter.6    Chapter.7    Chapter.8
```

To close the current folder and switch to a new folder, use the **change** option from the Folder Operation menu. This is identical to using the **folder** (**f**) command; Z-Mail prompts you for the folder name and switches to the new folder. If you set the **verify** variable to include the keyword "update" and the current folder has been modified, Z-Mail prompts you to update the current folder except when switching from the system mailbox (%) to another folder. Here's the update prompt:

```
Update ~/Mail/zmail.book?
yes no cancel
```

Press RETURN to update the current folder.

If you select **no**, you see this message before switching to the new folder:

```
Change anyway? yes  no
```

If you select **yes**, you switch to the new folder without updating the current folder. In this case, none of the changes to the old folder are retained. Selecting **no** cancels the folder switch operation.

When you switch to a new folder, Z-Mail displays the name of the current folder at the top of the message list:

```
30 [1]+ "~/commentary": 30 messages, 0 new, 0 unread, 0 deleted
```

This line is known as the *title* of the folder. By default, the title includes information about the state of the current folder (the number and status of the messages in the folder). You can change the information displayed in the title by setting the **title** variable and using any of the **prompt** formatting characters. (The **title** variable is not available in MUSH. Setting the **title** variable also changes the title bar at the top of the Z-Mail window in GUI mode.) For example, you might want to include the current time in the title. To do this, include **%T** in your **title** setting. For more information about setting variables and using formatting characters, see Chapter 3, *Reading and Managing Mail*, and Chapter 8, *Customizing Z-Mail*.

Z-Mail allows you to have more than one folder open at a time. To open a new folder without closing the current one, select **add**. When you see this prompt, enter the name of the folder that you want to add:

```
New folder: +zmail.book/Chapter.8
```

Listing Open Folders

Let's say that in the course of switching around, you've opened a few folders and you're not sure which ones are open. To see a list of open folders, use the **list** option on the Folder Operation menu. When you select **list**, you get a display like this one:

```
[0]- "/usr/spool/mail/hanna": 10 messages, 9 new, 9 unread, 0 deleted
[1]+ "~/Mail/zmail.book/Chapter.8": 3 messages, 0 new, 0 unread, 0 deleted
```

For more information about this display, see the section, "More about Folders," in Chapter 5.

Closing Open Folders

It's a good idea to update and close folders when you finish using them. Use the **Close** option to close the currently active folder. Select **Close** from the Folder Operation menu. If you modified the current folder, Z-Mail prompts you to update it. Then, Z-Mail closes the active folder, making the last active folder current. In this case, the only other open folder is the system mailbox, so Z-Mail switches to this folder.

When you close the last open folder, you see this message:

```
0 [0] <System Mailbox, closed>
```

If you use **list** now, Z-Mail doesn't list any open folders. You can open new folders at this point using the **change** and **add** options.

Unless you use **exit** or **exit!** when you quit, Z-Mail updates and closes each open folder before quitting.

Updating the Folder

In fullscreen mode, when you delete messages you can still see them in the message list. If your folder contains a lot of deleted messages or messages that you saved to other files using **save** and **write**, you can remove them from the display without exiting Z-Mail. Do this by updating the folder with the **update** (^U) command. This also moves messages that you've already read to your ~/*mbox* file.

If you set **verify** to include the word "update" and you've modified your folder, you see this prompt when you use **update**:

```
Update /usr/spool/mail/hanna? yes no cancel
```

Press RETURN to update the folder and redraw the screen. Select **n** to cancel the **update** command and leave the folder unchanged.

If you haven't modified the folder, **update** simply redraws the screen.

Using Line-mode Commands from Fullscreen Mode

The line mode has more features and more flexibility than fullscreen mode. For example, you can create a command-line alias in line mode that allows you to execute a series of commands with a few keystrokes. Another example is the line-mode **mark** command that allows you to mark messages with a priority setting; you can't set priorities on messages with the fullscreen-mode **mark** command.

Before you give up on the fullscreen mode and switch to line mode, let's see how you can escape temporarily to the line mode to run commands. To do this, use the **line-mode** (:) command. When you enter the **line-mode** command, Z-Mail drops the cursor to the bottom line of the screen and displays the colon (:) prompt (regardless of the current binding for **line-mode**). Here's what this looks like:

```
1 [0]+ "/usr/spool/mail/hanna": 5 messages, 5 new, 5 unread, 0 deleted
    1    Dale Cooper          Jul  8 12:00 (12) Continue Mode
    2    Harry Truman         Jul 10  2:42 (21) Chapter Eight
    3    Lucie                Jul 24 11:41 (48) Phone Message
    4  N Harry Truman         Jul 25 19:59 (12) Using Fullscreen Mode
    5  N Albert               Jul 26 12:00 (11) Re: Great Coffee
:_
```

Enter a line-mode command at the colon (:) prompt.

For example, if you set the **unix** variable, you can run UNIX commands from the Z-Mail line-mode prompt. In this case, to run the UNIX command *cal* from fullscreen mode, enter the following:

```
:cal 7 1991
```

and you get a display like this:

```
     July 1991
 S  M Tu  W Th  F  S
    1  2  3  4  5  6
 7  8  9 10 11 12 13
14 15 16 17 18 19 20
21 22 23 24 25 26 27
28 29 30 31
    6  p  Dale Cooper   Jul 22 18:11  (12)  Z-Mail Chapters
Msg 6 of 6: ...continue... _
```

Let's say you don't have **unix** set, but you want to run some UNIX commands. You can do this by running the line-mode command **sh** to escape to the UNIX prompt and then entering the UNIX commands:

```
:sh
```

When you see your UNIX prompt, enter the commands to run. To return to Z-Mail in fullscreen mode, simply enter **exit** (or whatever command you normally use to escape from a shell) at the UNIX prompt and you return to continue mode.

 In fullscreen mode, you can only use **mark** to mark messages temporarily with the + status indicator. When you exit Z-Mail, you lose these mark settings. The line-mode **mark** command allows you to mark messages permanently with a priority setting. To do this from fullscreen mode, enter a command like:

```
:mark —C 2-5
```

This marks messages 2 through 5 with the priority **C** and then returns to continue mode. Now, you can sort your messages by priority as we explained earlier in this chapter.

Another example is to escape to the line mode temporarily to run the **pick** command. I like to use **pick** instead of **search-next**. They're similar except that **search-next** simply finds the next message that contains a given pattern in the header summary. With **pick**, you can specify a particular date, author, or subject and display only those header summaries that match your criteria. You can also combine **pick** commands with the pipe character (|) to limit your search even further.

 Let's say I just want to read the messages that *dale* sent to me on November 26, 1990 with "Donuts" in the `Subject` line:

```
:pick —f dale | pick —d 11/26/90 | pick —s Donuts
```

Z-Mail displays something like the following:

```
Searching for messages that contain "dale".
  6    Dale Cooper   Nov 26 12:00  (12)  Donuts
  3    Lucie         Nov 24 11:41  (48)  Phone Message
Msg 3 of 6: ...continue... _
```

(Remember that the Z-Mail prompt always includes the header summary for the current message, in this case message 3, immediately above the `continue` prompt.) Note that **pick** doesn't move the current message pointer like **search-next**; the prompt shows you that the current message is still 3, even though **pick** displays the header summary for message 6.

 You might find that you frequently escape to the UNIX prompt to edit your initialization file. After modifying the file, you want to read in your changes. To do this using fullscreen-mode commands, you would have to use **shell-escape** (!), edit the file, and then run **source**. (The (character is the default binding for **source**.) You can do this with one command-line alias from the line mode, but fullscreen mode doesn't support command-line aliases. However, if you put the command-line alias in your initialization file, you can then run it from fullscreen mode by escaping to the line mode. First, put this command in your initialization file:

```
cmd mod "vi ~/.zmailrc; source ~/.zmailrc"
```

Now, start Z-Mail and use the command-line alias **mod** from fullscreen mode:

```
:mod
```

This command starts up *vi* on your initialization file. When you quit *vi* (using **:wq** or **ZZ**), Z-Mail sources your initialization file (so that your changes take effect immediately), and then returns you to continue mode.

You can create command-line aliases for other line-mode commands; simply put the **cmd** definitions in your initialization file and then run them from fullscreen mode using the **line-mode** command.

Accessing the UNIX Shell

Have you ever wanted to run a UNIX command while reading mail? Let's say you want to run *date* or *cal* to check the current date, or *ls* to list the files in a directory. As we showed you in Chapter 5, you can run UNIX commands from within Z-Mail by setting the **unix** variable. In fullscreen mode, you can "escape" to the UNIX command line to run one command using the **shell-escape** (!) command. When you use **shell-escape**, you see this message:

```
Shell command: _
```

Enter the UNIX command at the prompt and press RETURN. For example, to display a calendar for July of 1991, type the following:

```
Shell command: cal 7 1991
```

Z-Mail displays something like this:

```
    July 1991
 S  M Tu  W Th  F  S
    1  2  3  4  5  6
 7  8  9 10 11 12 13
14 15 16 17 18 19 20
21 22 23 24 25 26 27
28 29 30 31

    6  p  Dale Cooper   Jul 22 18:11  (12)   Z-Mail Chapters
Msg 6 of 6: ...continue... _
```

The **shell-escape** command is useful for changing your initialization file from within Z-Mail (for example, to make a variable setting permanent). Use **shell-escape** to run *vi*:

```
Shell command: vi ~/.zmailrc
```

Remember that these changes won't take effect during the current session unless you source the initialization file. We'll explain the **source** command later in this chapter.

Let's say you want to list the files in the directory *~/zmail/Chapters*. From line mode, you can use the **ls** command. To do this from fullscreen mode, use **shell-escape** and then enter this command:

```
Shell command: ls -C ~/zmail/Chapters
```

Z-Mail displays this list:

```
Chapter.1   Chapter.3   Chapter.5
Chapter.2   Chapter.4   Chapter.6
```

If you set the **unix** variable, you can use the **line-mode** command (we explain how in the next section) to escape to line mode to run a UNIX command. For information about the **unix** variable, refer to Chapter 5, *Z-Mail Shortcuts, Bells, and Whistles*.

Even if you don't set **unix**, you can escape to line mode and run the line-mode command **sh** to execute commands at the UNIX prompt. Chapter 5 explains more about using **sh**.

Exiting Fullscreen Mode

In this section, we describe the three ways to leave fullscreen mode: turn off fullscreen mode and return to line mode, exit to the UNIX prompt from the top level, or exit to UNIX from continue mode.

Turning off Fullscreen Mode

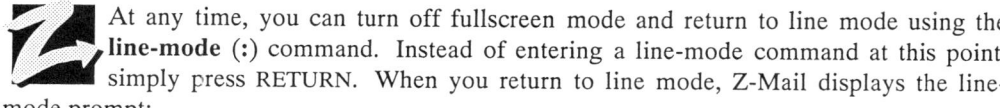 At any time, you can turn off fullscreen mode and return to line mode using the **line-mode** (:) command. Instead of entering a line-mode command at this point, simply press RETURN. When you return to line mode, Z-Mail displays the line-mode prompt:

```
Msg 3 of 6: _
```

Z-Mail doesn't redisplay the header summary list. (Note that some terminals don't clear the screen when you leave fullscreen mode.) If you want to see the header summary list, enter the line-mode **headers** (**h**) command at this prompt:

```
Msg 3 of 6: h
```

You can also turn off fullscreen mode using the **off** option to the **fullscreen** command in initialization files only. You can use **fullscreen off** in files that you read with the **–init** (**–I**) option from the UNIX command line. In all other instances, Z-Mail ignores the **fullscreen** command's **off** option.

For example, you can create a script that tests the terminal type before turning **fullscreen** on or off. For example, put this script in a file that you read in with **–init**:

```
if TERM == adm3a
      fullscreen off
else
      fullscreen
endif
```

This function turns off fullscreen mode if you're using an **adm3a** terminal. We'll explain more about creating scripts and using **if** expressions in Chapter 8, *Customizing Z-Mail*, and Chapter 9, *Writing Scripts and Functions*.

Exiting Z-Mail from the Top Level

If you are at the top level in fullscreen mode, you can exit Z-Mail and return to the login shell in one of two ways. The **quit (q)** command updates the current folder before exiting and **exit (x)** quits the current folder without modifying it. For information on what happens when you use **quit** and **exit**, see the section "Exiting Z-Mail" in Chapter 3, *Reading and Managing Mail*.

Remember, you can always return to line mode at any time by entering the **line-mode (:)** command and pressing RETURN.

Exiting from Continue Mode

If you are in continue mode, the **exit** and **quit** commands return you only to the top level. To return to your login shell directly from continue mode, use **quit! (Q)** or **exit! (X)**. The **quit!** command updates the current folder; **exit!** returns you to the UNIX prompt without modifying the folder.

If you get a message like this when you try to exit or quit, it means that you still have suspended messages running in the background:

```
Warning: Abort suspended compositions? (y/c) [cancel] _
```

See the section "Suspending and Restarting a Message" earlier in this chapter for information on finishing the messages before you quit.

Binding Keystrokes to Fullscreen Commands

In this chapter, you've been executing the special fullscreen-mode commands by pressing the keys *bound* to these commands. Now, we'll show you how to customize the behavior of the Z-Mail fullscreen mode by *binding* new commands to these key sequences. Use the **bind (b)** command to show the current key-to-command bindings and to change these bindings.

Displaying Current Bindings

Let's look at the current (default) bindings. When you use **bind**, you see the following:

```
bind [<CR>=all, -?=help]: _
```

Press RETURN to get the current list of bindings:

```
bind [<CR>=all, -?=help]:
Current key to command bindings:

t    top
\    display
n    display-next
p    display
```

```
T    top
.    display
m    mail
M    mail-flags
r    reply
J    jobs-menu
j    next-msg
k    back-msg
K    back-msg
+    next-msg
-    back-msg
^K    back-msg
^    first-msg
$    last-msg
{    top-page
}    bottom-page
g    goto-msg
c    copy
--more--
```

Page through the list by pressing the space bar at the **more** prompt. Press RETURN to display the next line or press **q** to return to continue mode.

Appendix E, *Fullscreen-Mode Commands and Bindings*, contains a complete list and a brief description of all the fullscreen-mode commands and the default bindings.

You can find out which command a key is currently bound to by entering that key at the **bind** prompt. For example, to display the command for **z**, enter the following:

```
bind [<CR>=all, -?=help]: z
```

Z-Mail displays this:

```
"z" = <screen-next>: New binding [<CR> for list]: _
```

If you don't want to rebind **z**, press BACKSPACE or the interrupt character.

Changing a Key Binding

Let's say you want to change the default binding so that when you press **z**, you execute the **line-mode** command. To do this, use the **bind** command and enter the key that you want to rebind:

```
bind [<CR>=all, -?=help]: z
```

At this prompt, enter the new command:

```
"z" = <screen-next>: New binding [<CR> for list]: line-mode
```

Now, if you use **bind** to see which command is bound to **z**, Z-Mail displays the following:

```
"z" = <line-mode>: New binding [<CR> for list]: _
```

Note that this new binding is effective for the current Z-Mail session only. To make this binding permanent, you must include it in your initialization file. We'll discuss how to do this in Chapter 8, *Customizing Z-Mail*.

Instead of a single key, some commands are bound to a *key-sequence*. A key-sequence is one or two characters, control characters, or a sequence of control characters. Note that key-sequences can *never* begin with a digit. You also cannot bind such keyboard-generated signals as CTRL-C and CTRL-\. In addition, if your system supports job control, don't bind the suspend characters (usually CTRL-Z and CTRL-Y). Table 6-10 lists special key-sequences that you shouldn't bind, and explains what each means to the system. Note that **bind** only lets you bind a key (or sequence of keys) to a single fullscreen-mode command.

Table 6-10. Special Key-sequences

Key	Description
CTRL-C or DEL	Frequently used as the interrupt character.
CTRL-D	Usually used as EOF.
CTRL-I	TAB.
CTRL-J	Same as \n.
CTRL-M	Same as \n.
CTRL-Q	XON (in flow control).
CTRL-R	Reprint line.
CTRL-S	XOFF (in flow control).
CTRL-V	Literal next (on BSD systems).
CTRL-Y	Delayed suspend (on systems with job control).
CTRL-Z	Suspend and sometimes EOF (on systems with job control).
CTRL-\	Quit.

If you have *function keys* on your terminal, you can bind commands to the characters they send. For example, the F10 key on my Wyse 60 terminal sends this control-key-sequence:

    ^AI

Z-Mail provides a special syntax for referring to control characters and other nonprinting characters in key-to-command bindings. Table 6-11 shows the format for referring to these special keys. Use the caret character (^) to represent the CTRL key. If you're using MUSH or an older terminal that has no ^ character, use \C to represent the CTRL key instead.

Table 6-11. Z-Mail Control Character Syntax

Key	Syntax
CTRL-*X*	^*X*
ESCAPE	\E
RETURN	\n
TAB	\t

So, to refer to the control-key-sequence that my F10 key sends, I would simultaneously press the CTRL and A keys, followed by I. As another example, the default binding for **search-again** is ^N; to execute this command, press the CTRL and N keys simultaneously. Let's say you want to run another command when you press CTRL-N. To do this, use the format in Table 6-12 to refer to the control-key-sequence. To refer to CTRL-N, enter the following:

```
^N
```

Thus, to display the default binding for CTRL-N, enter this at the prompt:

```
bind [<CR>=all, -?=help]: ^N
```

and Z-Mail displays the default binding:

```
"^N" = <search_again>: New binding [<CR> for list]: _
```

At this point, enter the new fullscreen-mode command (or press the interrupt character to leave the binding unchanged). To change the binding to run **display-next**, enter this at the `New binding` prompt:

```
display-next
```

Now, when you press CTRL-N, Z-Mail displays the next message in the list. If you use **bind** again and enter ^N at the prompt, you see the new binding:

```
"^N" = <display-next>: New binding [<CR> for list]: _
```

You can list all the fullscreen-mode commands by pressing RETURN at this prompt. When you do this, Z-Mail displays the whole list:

```
alias             back-msg          bind
bind-macro        bottom-page       chdir            copy
copy-list         delete            delete-list      display
display-next      exit              exit!            first-msg
folder            folder-menu       goto-msg         ignore
jobs-menu         last-msg          line-mode        lpr
macro             mail              mail-flags       map
map!              mark              my-hdrs          next-msg
preserve          quit              quit!            redraw
reply             reply-all         reply-menu       retain
reverse-video     save              save-list        saveopts
screen-back       screen-next       search-again     search-back
search-next       shell-escape      sort             sort-reverse
source            top               top-page         unbind
undelete          undelete-list     update           user-button
variable          version           write            write-list
help
"^N" = <display-next>: New binding [<CR> for list]: _
```

Enter a new fullscreen-mode command or press the interrupt character to leave the binding as is.

Unsetting a Key Binding

Sometimes, you might find that a particular key binding gets in the way. For example, because I use *vi* all day (every day), it's almost a reflex for me to use CTRL-U to move up one screen. In fullscreen mode however, the default binding for CTRL-U executes the **update** command. Because of this, I've updated my folder unintentionally when I just wanted to move the cursor up one screen. To get around this problem, I can either rebind the CTRL-U key (for example, to **screen-back**) or I can unset the CTRL-U binding.

To unset the binding, use the **unbind (B)** command. For example, let's unset CTRL-U. First, enter **unbind**. At this prompt, enter ^U:

    unbind what? ^U

Now, when I press CTRL-U, nothing happens except that Z-Mail sounds the terminal bell.

Check the current binding for CTRL-U by entering **bind** and then ^U. Now, Z-Mail displays the following:

    "^U" = <unset>: New binding [<CR> for list]: _

Leave it unset by pressing the BACKSPACE or interrupt character.

Making Key Bindings Permanent

When you use **bind** from fullscreen mode, you change or unset the key binding for the current Z-Mail session only. To make these changes permanent, you must enter your changes in your initialization file, *.zmailrc* (or *.mushrc* in MUSH). We'll explain how to do this in Chapter 8, *Customizing Z-Mail*.

Other Fullscreen Commands

This section goes over the fullscreen-mode commands that we haven't already covered in this chapter. In general, the functionality these commands provide is covered in greater detail elsewhere in the book. In this section, we'll briefly describe the commands and then point you to other chapters for more information.

Creating Macros in Fullscreen-mode

One of the most useful functions in fullscreen mode is the ability to create and use *macros* to execute Z-Mail commands. A macro is a shorthand definition for a longer series of commands. Macros are available in fullscreen, line, and compose mode.

Z-Mail provides the three fullscreen-mode commands listed in Table 6-12 for creating macros that work in each mode.

Table 6-12. Fullscreen-mode Macro Commands

Command	Default Binding	Description
bind-macro	&&	Create fullscreen-mode macros from fullscreen mode.
map	&:	Create line-mode macros from fullscreen mode.
map!	&!	Create compose-mode macros from fullscreen mode.

In addition to explaining these commands in more detail, Chapter 10, *Creating and Using Macros*, shows you how to create macros from line mode and compose mode.

Reading and Saving to the Initialization File

If you change your initialization file while you are still in Z-Mail (for example, you used the **shell-escape** command and then modified the ˜/.*zmailrc* file using an editor), you can read in your changes immediately with the **source** command. The default binding for **source** is the right parenthesis character. When you use **source**, Z-Mail prompts you for the filename to read:

```
Source filename [default]: _
```

Press RETURN to read the default file (˜/.*zmailrc*), or enter the name of an alternate file at the prompt. Z-Mail reads the file and returns you to continue mode.

Z-Mail also includes a command, **saveopts**, that allows you to save your current settings. The default binding for the **saveopts** command is the left parenthesis character. When you use **saveopts**, Z-Mail prompts you:

```
Save options to filename [default]: _
```

The default file is ˜/.*zmailrc*; press RETURN to save the current settings to that file. The first time you use **saveopts**, Z-Mail displays this message:

```
This action is necessary only if you want to save
these settings permanently.  The current settings
are already in effect for this session.
```

If the file that you specify already exists, Z-Mail displays this confirmation message:

```
Overwrite "˜/.zmailrc"?  yes no cancel
```

Select **yes** to overwrite the current file with the current settings. If you don't want to do this, press RETURN and you return to continue mode.

Chapter 8, *Writing Scripts and Functions*, explains the **source** and **saveopts** commands in more detail.

Executing Functions in Fullscreen Mode

One of the powerful features of Z-Mail is that you can create your own functions to run Z-Mail commands and bind them to "buttons." To learn how to do this, see Chapter 9, *Writing Scripts and Functions*. Then, to run a function from fullscreen mode, use the **user-button** (\) command. This command sets up a menu of user-defined functions.

For example, when I use **user-button**, Z-Mail displays:

```
Bounce Compose Forward Reply
```

To execute the function in fullscreen mode, enter the first character of the button name or move the highlight to the button and press RETURN. To exit the menu without selecting a function, press ESCAPE.

What is the Version Number?

If you're not sure what version of the Z-Mail software you're running, you can use the **version** (**V**) command to display it. For example, when I use **version**, Z-Mail displays:

```
Z-Mail (2.0.0 7/1/91)
Copyright 1990, 1991 Z-Code Software Corp.  All Rights Reserved
```

This command comes in handy when you write scripts that depend on the commands included in a specific version of the software. See Chapter 8 for more information.

Reviewing Fullscreen Mode

In this chapter, we explained how to use Z-Mail in the screen-oriented fullscreen mode. If you haven't done so already, you might want to read Chapter 3, *Reading and Managing Mail*, Chapter 4, *Sending Mail with Z-Mail*, and Chapter 5, *Z-Mail Shortcuts, Bells, and Whistles*. These chapters cover the Z-Mail commands that you can use from the line mode. Now that you know how to run line-mode commands from within fullscreen mode, you might want to go back and see what you can do from the line mode.

If you want to further customize your fullscreen-mode environment, read Chapter 8.

7

Using the Graphical User Interface

In this chapter, we'll show you how to use Z-Mail in the X-based Graphical User Interface (GUI) mode. (This mode is not available in MUSH.)

In the GUI mode, you use a mouse to move a pointer in a window and then press the mouse button to select messages, commands, and options. If you're a novice e-mail user, the GUI mode provides an easy way to access most of the features of Z-Mail through a windowing environment while also providing context-sensitive help in each window. Each window in the GUI mode is like a form that you use to perform a set of mail management tasks. To perform a task, select the proper form and fill it out.

In this chapter, you'll learn how to:

- Start Z-Mail in GUI mode.

- Manipulate messages and folders.

- Send, reply to, and forward messages to other people.

- Customize Z-Mail by setting variables, ignored headers, Z-Mail window buttons, and mail aliases.

- Move and resize windows.

Remember that Z-Mail's GUI mode runs on both the Motif and Open Look window managers and looks and behaves differently. For example, when you edit messages in GUI mode, Z-Mail uses the editing style defined by your window manager. We created the examples in this chapter running Z-Mail on the Motif window manager. If you're running Open Look, your screen will look slightly different from the examples, but should not affect the functionality of Z-Mail.

Starting the GUI

To start Z-Mail in the GUI mode, use the **–gui** option to the **zmail** command.[1] For example, enter the following command at the UNIX prompt:

```
$ zmail —gui
```

The main Z-Mail window opens. From this window, you can access all the GUI-mode features and forms for performing mail management tasks. Figure 7-1 gives an example of the main Z-Mail window.

 If you always want to enter GUI mode when you start Z-Mail, create an alias in your login shell (if you use the C shell or Korn shell) so that you always invoke Z-Mail with the **–gui** option. For example, use this alias in your ˜/.cshrc file (for C shell):

```
alias zmail '/usr/bin/zmail —gui'
```

Or, add this line to ˜/.kshrc (for Korn shell):

```
alias —x zmail="/usr/bin/zmail —gui"
```

For Bourne shell users, add the following commands to your ˜/.profile file:

```
zmail( ) {
     /usr/bin/zmail —gui $*
     }
```

Now, every time you enter **zmail** at the UNIX prompt, you start up Z-Mail in GUI mode. Note that the **zmail** program might be installed in another directory on your system.

The Main Z-Mail Window

The main Z-Mail window displays "Z-Mail" in the title bar. At the top of the main Z-Mail window, you see the Menu Bar. The Menu Bar includes seven menus: File, Edit, View, Options, Compose, Sort, and Help. Table 7-1 gives a brief description of the tasks that you perform using the options on these menus.

Table 7-1. Z-Mail Menu Bar Options

Menu	Description
File	Use folders, save and print messages, update, and exit Z-Mail.
Edit	Delete, restore, preserve, mark and set priorities on messages, and pick messages by pattern or date.
View	Display or "pin up" selected messages.

---

[1] Note that you can't send a message and enter Z-Mail in GUI mode (using **zmail** with the **–gui** option) on the same command line.

Table 7-1. Z-Mail Menu Bar Options (continued)

Menu	Description
Options	Set variables; ignore, retain, or customize headers, aliases, and buttons; or access the Toolbox.
Compose	Create new messages, send replies, forward current messages, or create and use templates.
Sort	Sort message list by subject, author, date, status, message length, or priority.
Help	Get general help with Z-Mail, message lists, and header summary format, or access the Help Index.

Using Menus

To pull down a menu, move the pointer to the menu and hold down the mouse button. (Unless we specify otherwise, always use the left mouse button.)[2]

When the menu appears, select an option by moving the pointer down the list (while still holding down the mouse button). The pointer highlights each option. To select an option, release the mouse button and the menu disappears. If you decide not to select an option, simply move the pointer from the menu area (you may have to click the mouse button after moving away) and the menu disappears.

Ellipses (...) following a menu option mean that Z-Mail opens a new window, also known as a *dialog box*. Each dialog box performs a different set of mail management tasks. We'll explain the dialog boxes as we discuss each task in this chapter. You can also access dialog boxes from the Toolbox window; we'll explain more about this later in the section "Using the Toolbox."

A right arrow character ($\rightarrow$) follows menu options that have an associated *pull-right submenu*. For an example of how this works, pull down the Compose menu and, while holding down the mouse button, select Reply. As long as you hold down the mouse button, Z-Mail displays the Reply submenu. Move the pointer and release the mouse button to select an option from the menu. As with regular menus, to quit from a pull-right menu without selecting an option, move the pointer from the menu area and release the mouse button.

We'll talk more about the options on these menus later. For now, let's continue looking at the Z-Mail window.

Below the Menu Bar is information about the Folder and Messages list. The Folder list displays the name of the current folder (in Figure 7-1, the current folder is my system mailbox, */usr/spool/mail/hanna*). The Messages field displays the message number for the currently selected message (message 1 in our example).

---

[2] In the Open Look version (not just the Open Look window manager), you use the right mouse button to pull down menus.

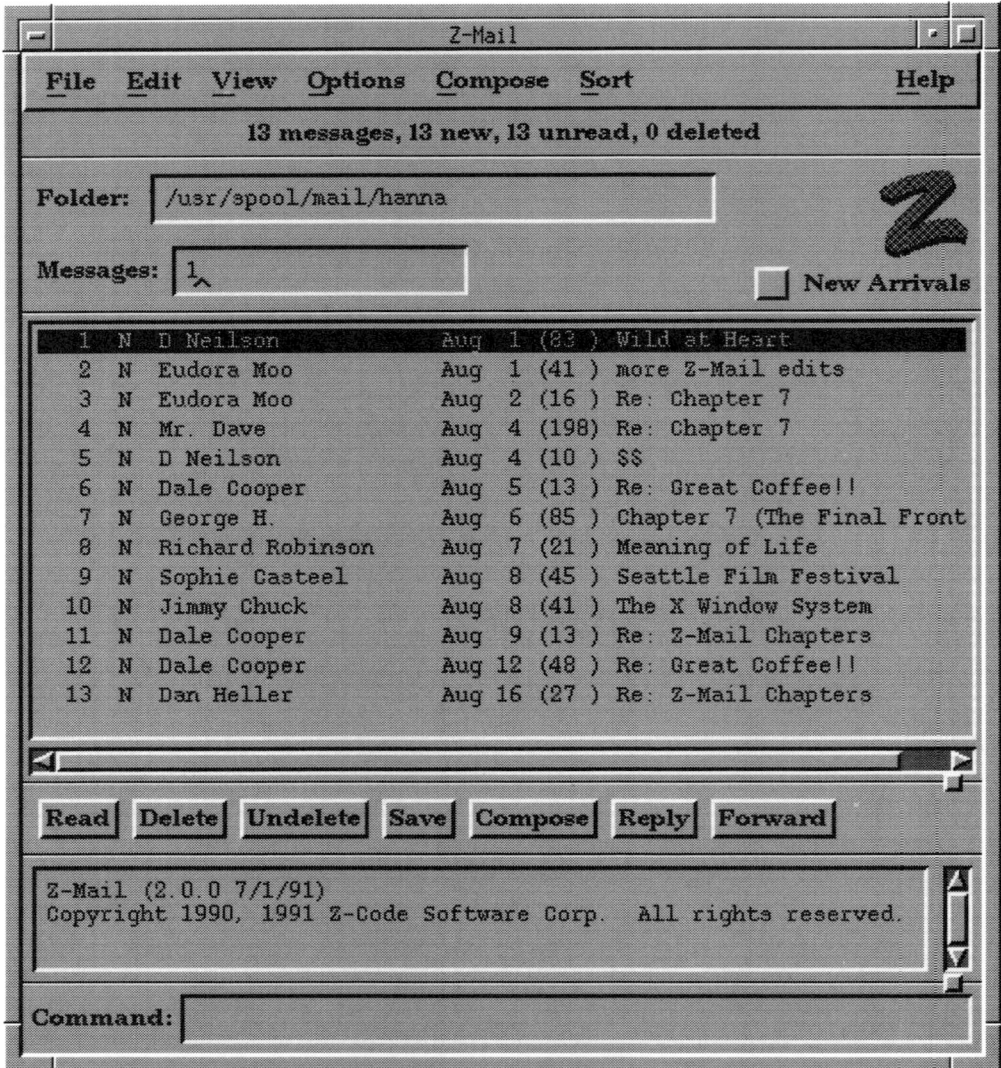

Figure 7-1. Main Z-Mail window

Below the Messages field is the Header Summary list, a scrollable display of header summaries. (We discussed the format of these header summaries earlier in Chapter 2, *Getting Started*.) Note that the currently selected message is displayed in reverse video. Let's review the status indicator characters in Table 7-2 you'll be seeing more of these characters as you read this chapter.

Table 7-2. Status Indicators

Character	Description
(blank)	Read
+	Marked
*	Deleted
!	Newly arrived
A-E	Marked with a priority setting
N	New and unread
P	Preserved in the system mailbox
S	Saved
U	Old and unread
p	Printed
r	Replied to
f	Forwarded

Using Scrollbars

By default, Z-Mail displays six header summaries in the Header Summary list. (You can change this by setting the **screen_win** variable to the number of header summaries to display.) If you have more than six messages in your folder, you get a *scrollbar* to the right of this list. Within the scrollbar (between the up and down arrows) is the *thumb*. The size of the thumb indicates the percentage of the list that you are viewing. If the thumb is tiny, the list is large (and vice versa). The position of the thumb in the scrollbar indicates which section of the entire list you are viewing. So, if the thumb is at the bottom of the scrollbar, you are viewing the bottom section of the list.

Use the thumb to scroll through the header summaries. Grab the thumb by putting your pointer on the thumb. Now, press down on the mouse button and *drag* the thumb down the scrollbar. You can also position the pointer on the up or down arrow and click the mouse button to move the list up or down one line at a time. Another way to scroll the header summary list is to position the pointer in the scrollbar and click the mouse button (thus, moving the thumb). Click the middle mouse button to move the thumb to the pointer position; click the left mouse button to scroll the list one full screen in the direction of the pointer.

Experiment with moving the thumb in different ways to scroll through the header summary list. Note that when you move the thumb to the bottom of the scrollbar, the currently selected message (still message 1) scrolls off the top of the list.

Z-Mail uses both horizontal and vertical scrollbars. The horizontal scrollbar works exactly like the vertical one in the Header Summary list.

The Action Area

Below the Header list is the *Action area* for displaying the buttons that you define. Depending on how Z-Mail is set up on your system, there may already be buttons in this area. In Chapter 8, *Customizing Z-Mail*, and Chapter 9, *Writing Scripts and Functions*, we'll explain how to customize your GUI interface by building your own commands and functions and attaching buttons to them.

In each Z-Mail window, the Action area contains buttons that affect messages in the list above. The Action area shown in Figure 7-1 contains seven buttons that you can use to manipulate the messages in the Header Summary list above. Table 7-3 gives a brief introduction to these buttons.

Table 7-3. Z-Mail Window Buttons

Button	Description
Read	Read the currently selected message.
Delete	Delete selected messages.
Undelete	Restore deleted messages.
Save	Save selected messages to a file or folder.
Compose	Compose and send mail messages.
Reply	Send a response to selected messages.
Forward	Forward selected messages to another person.

We'll explain how to use each of these buttons in the next few sections.

Below the Action area on the Z-Mail window is the Output area, a scrollable window for command output. Z-Mail uses this window to display error messages, warnings and other output from commands. For example, if you save a message, Z-Mail displays information about the **save** operation in this window.

Below the Output area is the Command field; use this field to enter line-mode commands. For example, to delete message 1, enter **d 1** in this field and press RETURN.

Using the Toolbox

You can access Z-Mail dialog boxes from the Toolbox window. (The exception is the Message Display window because you must first select a message to read.) To display the Toolbox window, pull down the Options menu and select Toolbox. You see the window displayed in Figure 7-2.

Each of the icons in the Toolbox window represents a Z-Mail dialog box. Each icon corresponds to an icon in the upper-right corner of the Z-Mail dialog box it represents. These dialog boxes are listed in Table 7-4.

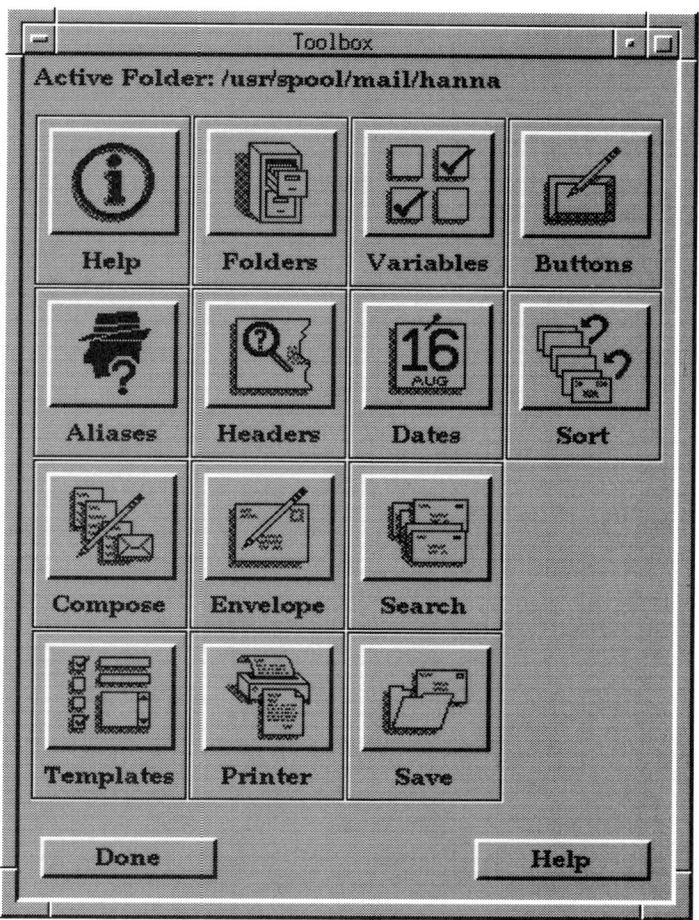

Figure 7-2. Toolbox window

Table 7-4. Toolbox Dialog Boxes

Dialog	Description
Help	Get help about Z-Mail.
Folders	Open, switch to, and list folders.
Variables	Set and remove variables.
Buttons	Create functions and attach buttons.
Aliases	Create mail aliases.
Headers	Ignore and retain Z-Mail headers.
Dates	Search for messages by date.
Sort	Sort messages in the folder.
Compose	Create and send a new message.
Envelope	Create and use personal headers.
Search	Select messages by patterns.

Table 7-4. Toolbox Dialog Boxes (continued)

Dialog	Description
Templates	Create and use form letters.
Printer	Send messages to the printer.
Save	Organize messages in files and folders.

Each of these functions are described in more detail in this chapter; the Toolbox option provides one way to access these tools. In Chapter 9, we'll explain how to create your own functions that call these dialog boxes.

Getting Help

The GUI mode provides context-sensitive help information in every window. The Help menu in the main Z-Mail window provides general information on Z-Mail and the GUI help system. In addition, this menu provides help on how to specify message lists and change the format of the header summary display. This menu also includes an option for accessing the Help Index, a complete list of help topics and text. Table 7-5 describes the Help menu options.

Table 7-5. Help Menu Options

Option	Description
General	Get general information on GUI-mode help.
Message Lists	Display help on specifying message lists.
Header Format	Get help on changing the header summary format.
On Context	Display context-sensitive help for items on the currently displayed Z-Mail window.
About	Get information about the Z-Mail program.
Index	Display an index of all the Z-Mail help topics and text.

The Help Index Window

The General, Message Lists, Header Format, and Index options all pop up the Help Index window, each with a different help topic selected and associated text displayed. Figure 7-3 shows the Help Index window.

To get help, move the pointer to a topic in the Help Index list on the left and click the mouse button to select it. The Help Text frame changes to display the text for the new help topic.

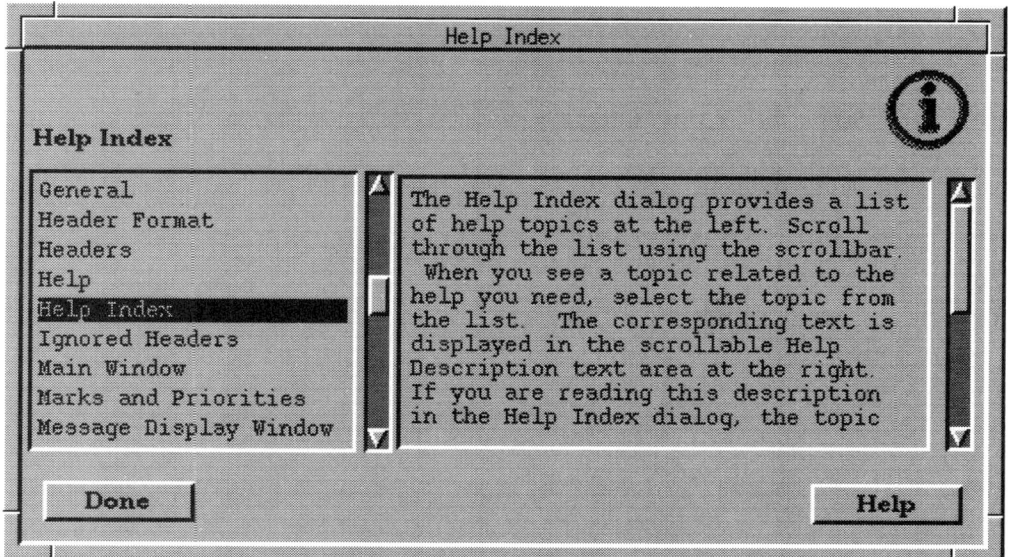

Figure 7-3. Help Index window

There are more topics than fit in the Help Index list and sometimes there is more text for a topic than fits in the Help Text frame. To see the rest of the information, drag the thumb at the right of each frame down the scrollbar frame.

When you finish with the help index, click the Done button.

About. Select this option from the Help menu to display the Help Index window with information about the authors of the software displayed in the Help Text frame. When you finish reading, click Done to close the window.

On Context. This option is useful for displaying information about any Z-Mail window currently displayed on the screen. When you select this option, the pointer changes to look like a little pointing hand. Use the pointer to select the item on the window that you want to display help for. For example, if you click the Save button with the On Context pointer, Z-Mail displays a pop-up box describing the Save button.

As you can see in Figure 7-4, Save is a button attached to a *user-defined function*. We'll explain more about buttons and functions in the section "Creating a Z-Mail Function." See Chapter 9 for more information on defining your own functions.

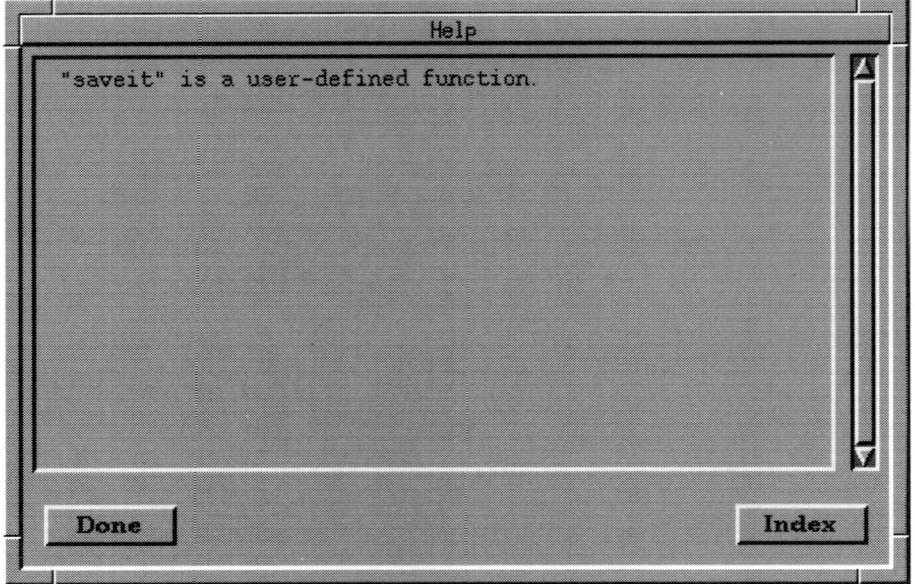

Figure 7-4. On Context Help

Selecting a Message

Before you can do anything to a message (such as read or delete it), select it by moving the pointer to the message and clicking the mouse button. This moves the highlight to the new message and changes the message number in the Messages field. The message is now *selected*. To select a different message, simply move the pointer to the new message and click the mouse button again.

Selecting Multiple Messages

To select more than one consecutive message, hold down the mouse button and drag the pointer over several messages. To select nonconsecutive messages, press the CTRL key while clicking the mouse button. Another way to select nonconsecutive messages is to enter the message numbers (or the special message list characters) in the Messages field. Use the following steps to do this:

1. Move the pointer to the Messages field at the top of the window.

2. Click the mouse button and the cursor appears.

3. Use the BACKSPACE key to clear the field and enter the new message numbers from the keyboard. As always, separate the message number with spaces, commas (,) or both.

You can also refer to messages using the special message list characters. For example, use a caret (^) to select the first message in the list and a dollar sign ($) to select the last message in the list. See Chapter 3, *Reading and Managing Mail*, for more information about these special characters; Table 3-1 lists them.

Reading a Message

The easiest way to read a message is to *double-click* (in rapid succession) the mouse button on a message in the list. Two other ways you can read the selected message are to click the Read button or pull down the View menu and select the Show Message option. In all cases, Z-Mail opens another window, the Message Display window, and displays the contents of the message. Figure 7-5 shows what the Message Display window looks like.

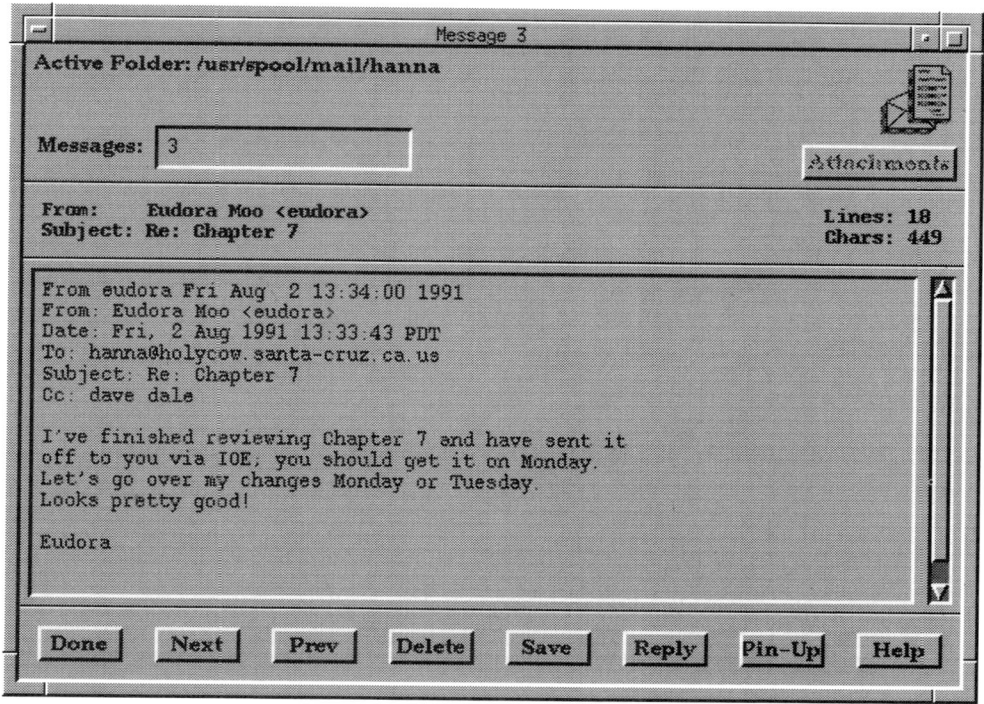

Figure 7-5. Message Display window

With the Pin-Up Message option on the View menu (and the Pin-Up button in the Message Display window), you can also open a fixed window to display—or "pin up"—the message. In this case, the Message Display window remains displayed until you delete it or until its folder is updated or closed.

The Message Display window displays the current active folder and message number at the top. Below this is the Header area and the Text area. By default, Z-Mail displays 12 lines of text in the Text area; if your message has more than 12 lines, a scrollbar appears at the right of the window. As you did with the Header Summary list in the Z-Mail window, move the thumb in the scrollbar to view more of the message. In Figure 7-5, you can see from the position of the scrollbar and from the number of lines displayed in the Header area that almost the entire message fits in the window. If the message were longer, you could scroll through the text by moving the scrollbar down.

 You can change the size of the Text area by setting the **crt_win** variable to the number of lines you want to display. For example, to display 24 lines, put this command in your ~/.zmailrc initialization file:

```
set crt_win = 24
```

Below the Text area is the Message Display window's Action area. Table 7-6 briefly describes each of the buttons in this Action area; we'll cover them in more detail in the following sections.

Note that almost all Z-Mail windows include the Done and Help buttons; these buttons function identically as they do in the Message Display window. For this reason, we'll mention them in the later sections, but we won't go into detail explaining them.

Table 7-6. Message Display Window Buttons

Button	Description
Done	Close the current window.
Next	Display the next message in the message list.
Prev	Display the previous message.
Delete	Delete the current message.
Save	Save the current message to a file or folder.
Reply	Send a response to the author of the current message.
Pin-Up	Keep the Message Display window pinned up for the current session.
Help	Get help about the Message Display window buttons.

Activating Another Window

You don't have to close the Message Display window to select a new message to read. You can make any window active simply by moving the pointer to the window. Depending on your window manager settings, you might also have to click the mouse button. To select a new message to read, activate the main Z-Mail window, select a new message, and then click the Read button again.

Viewing the Next Message

If you want to read the next or previous messages in the list, you don't have to activate the main Z-Mail window to select it. To read it, simply click the Next or Prev buttons.

If the message is the last or first message in the list, when you click Next or Prev, Z-Mail displays a Warning pop-up box. Simply click the OK button to make the pop-up box go away. You can tell Z-Mail to "wrap" the message pointer back to the top of the list by setting the **wrap** variable.

If the current message is not the last message in the list, Next replaces the current message in the Message Display window with the next message in the list. Note that the Message Display window title bar and Messages field change to reflect the new message.

Also note that, as in the line and fullscreen modes, Z-Mail skips all deleted messages when you read the next and previous messages.

Reading a Message with an Attachment

Attachments are special files (text, binary, or otherwise) that Z-Mail appends to the outgoing message. When a message that you're reading includes an attachment, the Attachments option on the Message Display window is available. To detach the attachment, select the Attachment option, and the Attachments window, shown in Figure 7-6, pops up.

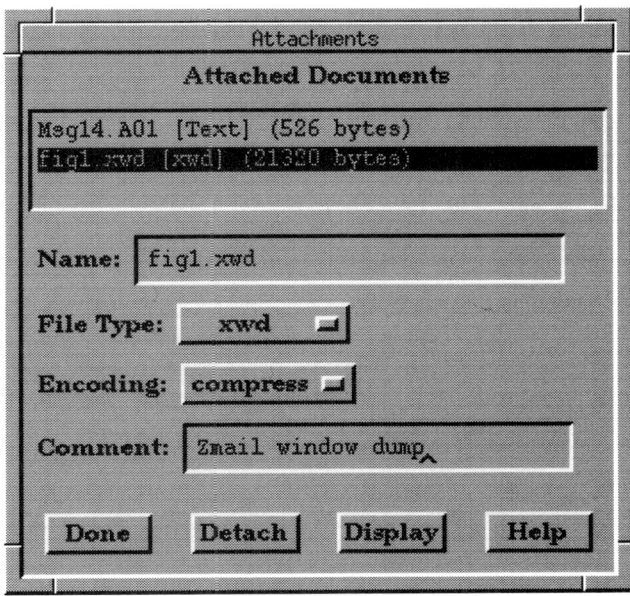

Figure 7-6. Attachments window

Note that the Attached Documents list contains information about the message text as well as the attachment. The Name, File Type, Encoding, and Comment fields contain the information (if available) for the selected attachment. If you select a different attachment (or the message text) from the Attached Documents list, the information in these fields changes. For information about these fields, see the section "Sending an Attachment," later in this chapter. Table 7-7 briefly describes the buttons in the Attachments window.

Table 7-7. Attachments Window Buttons

Button	Description
Done	Return to the Compose Message window.
Detach	Save an attachment to a separate file.
Display	Read the contents of an attachment.
Help	Get help about attaching files.

In the GUI mode, Z-Mail allows you to display the contents of an attachment without detaching it to a file first. To do this, select the attachment from the Attached Documents list and then click the Display button. Z-Mail opens a new window to display the attachment.

To detach an attachment, select the attachment and then click the Detach button. Z-Mail puts the attachment in the file specified in the Name field. If there's already a file by that name, Z-Mail displays a Warning pop-up box, prompting you to overwrite the file with the current attachment. To overwrite the file, select the OK button; to cancel the Detach operation, click Cancel. You can put the attachment in a different file by entering the new filename in the Name field *before* clicking Detach.

Deleting Messages

Once you read a message, it's a good idea to delete it unless you want to save it for future reference. As you know, the default behavior of Z-Mail is to keep messages that you've already read in your system mailbox folder when you quit, so it's a good idea to delete messages when you're through with them.

To delete the message currently displayed in the Message Display window, click the Delete button. Note that, as expected, Z-Mail changes the status indicator character for the message to an asterisk (*). Deleted messages still appear in the Header Summary display by default.

You might prefer to delete messages all at once after you've read them. Use these steps to delete more than one message at a time:

1. Activate the Z-Mail window.

2. Select the messages to delete from the Header Summary list.

3. Finally, click the Delete button, or pull down the Edit menu and select Delete.

Restoring Deleted Messages

The deleted messages remain in your mailbox until you quit Z-Mail. Until then, you can restore ("undelete") the selected messages by clicking the Undelete button on the main Z-Mail window, or by pulling down the Edit menu and selecting Undelete. Now, when you quit Z-Mail, the messages aren't removed.

If you want to read a message that you deleted, you can restore and read the message all at once. To do this, select the deleted message and then click the Read button. When you select Read to read a deleted message, a dialog box pops up, as shown in Figure 7-7. If you set the **show_deleted** variable, you don't have to restore deleted messages before reading them.

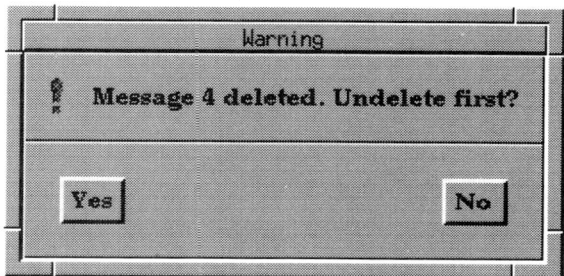

Figure 7-7. Reading a deleted message

Now, click the Yes button to restore the message and then display it. If you select No, Z-Mail returns you to the main Z-Mail window and does not restore the message.

Saving the Message

To save the message that you're reading to a file, click the Save button in the Message Display window. The Save Messages window, shown in Figure 7-8, pops up.

At the top of the window, you see the general information about the current folder and message number. Below this is the Folder list, a scrollable window that contains a listing of all the folders in your folder directory (~/*Mail*, the default setting of the *folder* variable).

Folder. Use this field to enter the name of a folder that you want to save the message to or select the name of the folder from the Folder list to display the name in this field. If the folder isn't located in the current directory, specify the full pathname. Click Save to save the currently selected message to the folder.

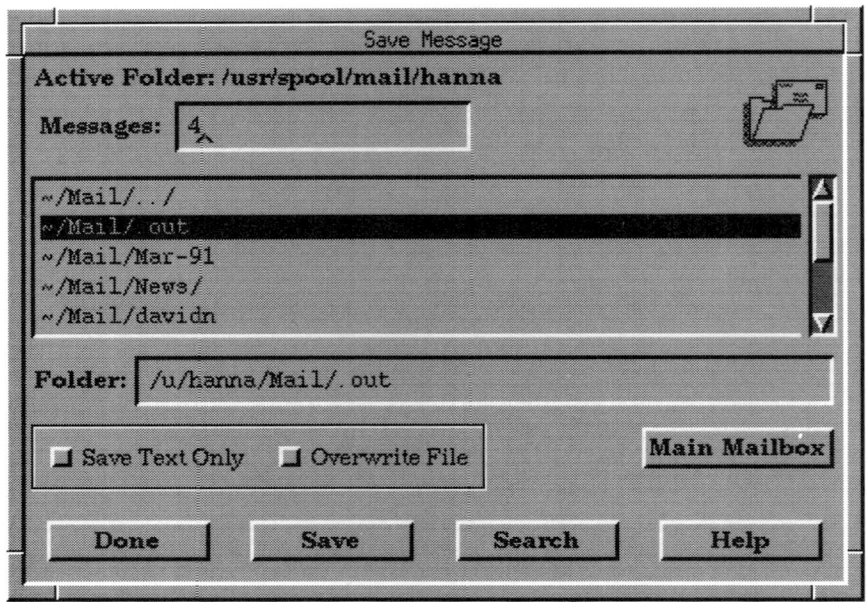

Figure 7-8. Save Messages window

Save Text Only. Use this option to tell Z-Mail to save the message text (not the headers) to the specified file; in other words, save the message to a plain text file rather than a folder. This is equivalent to the **write** command in line and fullscreen modes.

As with the other modes, when you save a message to a file that isn't a folder, or when you try to use the Save Text Only option to save a message to a folder, Z-Mail displays a warning. In GUI mode, this warning appears in a pop-up box.

Overwrite File. By default, Z-Mail *appends* messages to the existing file or folder. Use this option to tell Z-Mail to replace an existing file with the selected messages instead.

If you change your mind about any of the options like Save Text Only or Overwrite File, you can "unselect" the option by clicking the button on the option box again.

Main Mailbox. Use this option to save the selected messages to the folder specified by the **mbox** variable (`~/mbox` by default). Z-Mail puts the name of the main mailbox in the Folder list and saves the message to *mbox* when you click Save. This action is equivalent to the **save** command in the line and fullscreen modes without specifying or selecting a filename.

The Z-Mail Handbook

At the bottom of the Save Message window is the Action area that contains the buttons for this window.

To search for a particular folder, enter (or select from the Folder list) a directory name in the Folder list and click the Search button. This displays the contents of the directory in the Folder list. Now, you can select a folder and click the Save button. To save the message to a folder that doesn't already exist, simply enter the folder name (including the full pathname, if you don't want it in the current directory) in the Folder list. Once you specify a folder name, click Save to create the new folder and save the message to it.

Nothing happens in the Save Messages window when you click Save. In the main Z-Mail window, however, the status indicator character for the current message changes to S (for saved) and the Output area contains information about the save operation.

Canceling the Save Request

If you decide that you don't want to save the message after the Save Messages window pops up, click the Done button to close this window.

You can use the Done button at any time to close the current window. If you've already saved messages, using Done won't affect their status.

Printing the Message

You might want to keep a hard copy of messages. You can do this by sending messages directly to the printer from Z-Mail. To print, select the messages from the Header Summary list, pull down the File menu and select Print Message. Z-Mail opens the Printer window displayed in Figure 7-9.

Messages. This field contains the numbers of the currently selected messages. To print a different message, manually change the number in this field or select a different message in the main Z-Mail window.

Standard Message Headers. Use this option to specify that Z-Mail not print any headers suppressed by the **ignore** command. If you specified headers to display (using **retain**), Z-Mail displays only those headers. This is the default behavior if you set the **alwaysignore** variable, and is equivalent to using the **lpr –h** command from line mode.

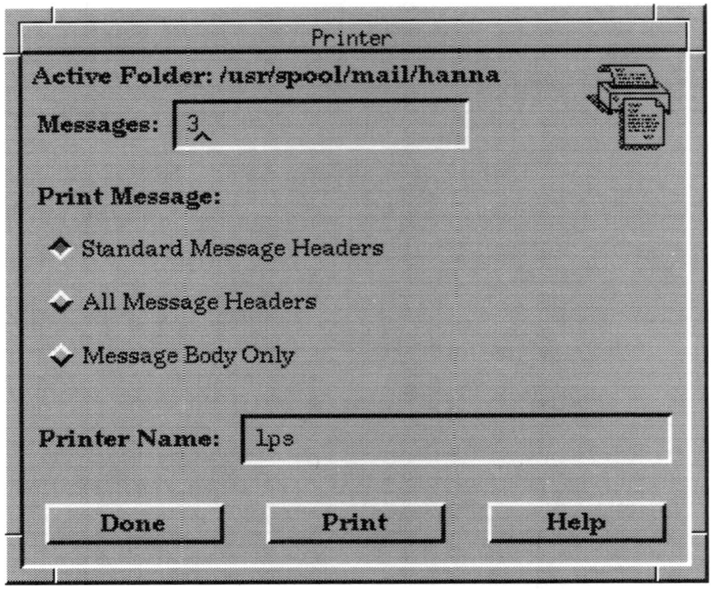

Figure 7-9. Printer window

All Message Headers. This option tells Z-Mail to print all the message headers along with the text, regardless of the value of **ignore** or **retain**. This is equivalent to the default action of **lpr**.

Message Body Only. Use this option to print only the message text, no headers. This is equivalent to using the **−n** option to **lpr**.

Printer Name. This field contains the name of the current printer; change this by manually entering the new printer name in this field. This is equivalent to specifying the printer name with the **lpr −P**.

To print the selected message to the current printer, simply click the Print button. Note that Z-Mail changes the status indicator character for the selected messages to **p** (for printed) and the Output area shows the output from the print operation.

Replying to the Message

To send a response to the author of the message that you're reading, click the Reply button in the Message Display window.

Another way to reply to a message is to select the message from Header Summary list in the main Z-Mail window. Then pull down the Compose menu and select an option from the Reply pull-right menu. (We discussed the Reply options at length in Chapter 4, *Sending Mail with Z-Mail*.)

Reply. The Reply menu describes the following options:

Option	Description	Line-mode Equivalent
Reply to Sender	Send a reply to only the author of the message.	r
Reply to All	Reply to everyone on the original distribution.	R
ReplySender/IncludeMessage	Reply to the author and include the current message.	r −i
ReplyAll/IncludeMessage	Reply to everyone and include the message.	R −i

Either way you reply, Z-Mail pops up the Compose Message window and fills in the **To** and **Subject** lines as shown in Figure 7-10.

Composing a Message

The procedure for composing a new message is identical to replying to a message; Z-Mail opens the Compose Message window for both and all the options apply. The only difference between the two actions is that, for replies, Z-Mail automatically fills in the lines for **To**, **Subject**, and **Cc**, if applicable.

At the top of the window is a Menu Bar containing six menus: File, Edit, Include, Compose, Deliver, and Headers. The following sections briefly describe each of the options on these menus and any fullscreen, compose, or line-mode command equivalent.

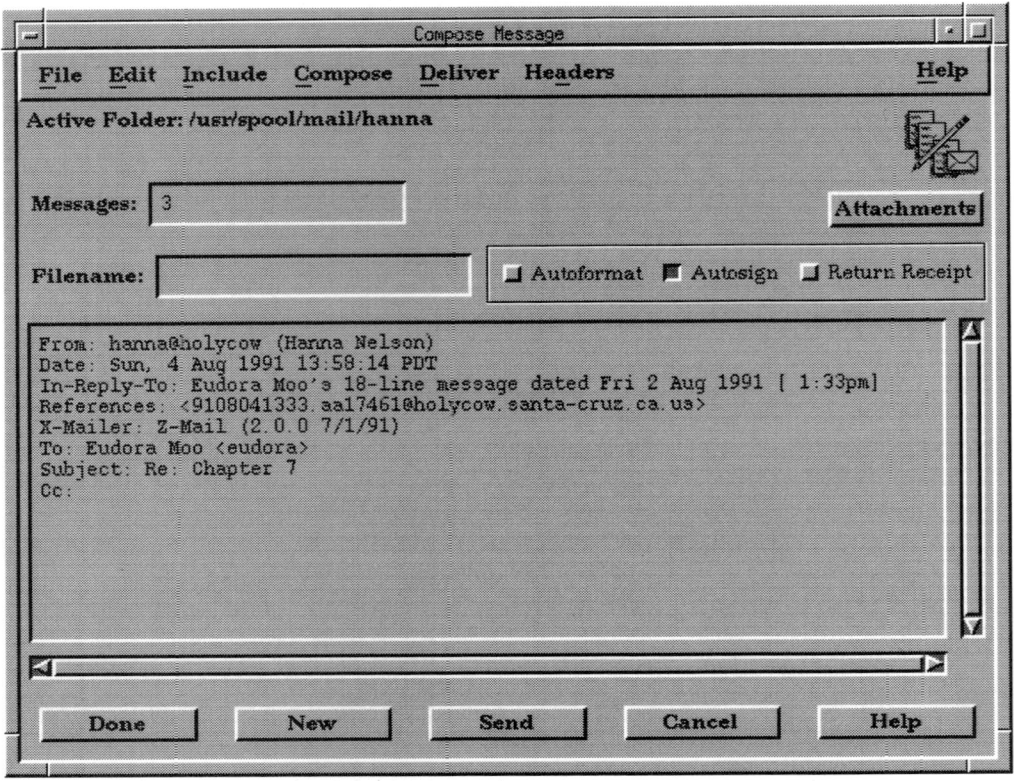

Figure 7-10. Compose Message window

File. The File menu includes the following options:

Option	Description	Compose-mode Equivalent
Open	Include a file in the current message.	~r
Save	Save the current message to a file.	~a
Done	Close the Compose Message Window.	(None)

Edit. The Edit menu includes the following options:

Option	Description
Cut	Select text to move.
Copy	Select text to copy.
Paste	Copy or move text.
Select All	Select entire message to manipulate.
Clear	Clear selected text.
Format	Format selected text into paragraphs.
Search	Pop up the Search and Replace window.
Editor	Invoke the default editor on message text (equivalent to ~v or ~e).

Include. The Include menu includes the following options:

Option	Description	Compose-mode Equivalent
Include Msg	Include a message in your outgoing message.	~i
Forward Msg	Include a message, marking it as "forwarded mail."	~f

Compose. The Compose menu includes the following options:

Option	Description	Compose-mode Equivalent
New	Compose a new message.**mail**	
Reply	Send a reply to a message.	**reply**
Forward	Forward a message.	**mail –f**
Templates	Open the Templates window.	**mail –p**

Deliver. The Deliver menu includes the following options:

Option	Description	Compose-mode Equivalent
Send	Send the current message.	CTRL-D
Send + Close	Send the message and close the Compose Message window.	(None)
Cancel	Cancel the current message.	˜x

Headers. The Headers menu includes the following options:

Option	Description	Compose-mode Equivalent
All	Edit all the headers.	˜h
To	Edit the **To** line.	˜t
Subject	Edit the **Subject**.	˜s
Cc	Change or add a **Cc** line.	˜c
Bcc	Change or add a **Bc** line.	˜b

Messages. This field displays the numbers for the currently selected messages. Z-Mail includes these messages when you select one of the options on the Include menu. If you want to include a different message, enter it in this field.

Filename. Use this field to specify the filename to save the current message to *or* the name of the file to include. Below the Menu Bar, you see general information about the current folder and message.

Autoformat. Use this option to wrap the text in the Compose area automatically at the right (without pressing RETURN). This option uses the value of **wrapcolumn** (78 by default).

Autosign. Use this option to append a signature to your outgoing message. This is the default action if you set the **autosign** variable. For more information, see the section "Signing Your Name," in Chapter 4, *Sending Mail with Z-Mail*.

Return Receipt. Select this option to request a *return receipt* from the MTA on the recipient's machine.

In the middle of the Compose Message window is the Compose area, a scrollable window that contains the message headers and text of the current message. Remember that, with replies, Z-Mail automatically addresses the message and constructs a `Subject` line beginning with "Re:" to indicate that this message is a response to a previous message.

The Action area for the Compose Message window contains five buttons. Table 7-8 briefly describes their functions; we'll cover them in greater detail in the sections that follow.

Table 7-8. Compose Message Window Buttons

Button	Description
Done	Close the current window.
New	Compose a new message.
Send	Send the current message.
Cancel	Cancel the current message.
Help	Get help about sending and replying to mail.

At this point, you can move the pointer to the Compose area, click the mouse button, and begin composing your response. Table 7-9 lists a subset of the editing commands and their default keyboard mappings that you use in the Compose area.[3] Note that these commands might be different if you're using the Open Look version.

Table 7-9. Compose Frame Text-editing Commands

Command	Description
CTRL-H	Delete the previous character.
BACKSPACE	Delete the previous character.
DEL*	Delete the previous character.
CTRL-W*	Delete the previous word.
CTRL-U*	Delete to the beginning of the line.
Up and down cursor (arrow) keys	Move cursor up and down one line.
Left and right cursor keys	Move cursor left and right one character.
CTRL left and right cursor keys	Move cursor by words.
CTRL up and down cursor keys	Move cursor by paragraphs.
SHIFT cursor keys	Move cursor and select text.

*These commands depend on setting Motif translations and thus might not work on some machines.

---

[3] For information on changing the default keyboard mappings, see the *X Window System User's Guide* (Volume 3), by Valerie Quercia and Tim O'Reilly.

 If you want to change the height (the number of lines) of the Compose area at startup time, set the **msg_win** variable in your ~/.zmailrc initialization file. For example, to set the height of the Compose area to 35 lines, include this line in ~/.zmailrc:

```
set msg_win = 35
```

To change the height of this window while running Z-Mail, you must resize the window manually (for more information, see the section "Moving and Resizing Windows," later in this chapter.)

In the following sections, we'll explain the menus at the top of the Compose Message window.

Including a Message

In Chapter 4, *Sending Mail with Z-Mail*, we showed you how to include a copy of the current message from compose mode using ~i. To include a message when sending mail in GUI mode, pull down the Include menu and select the Include Msg option. Specify the message number in the Messages field or accept the current message by default. If you want to include a different message (or a list of messages), enter the message number in the Messages field before selecting Include.

Chapter 4 has more information on customizing the way Z-Mail includes messages (for example, you can change the string that indents each line of the message).

Forwarding the Message to Another Person

To send a message from your mailbox to another person and mark it as "forwarded mail," pull down the Include menu from the Compose message window and select the Forward Msg option (or click the Forward button on the main Z-Mail window). You can also forward a message by pulling down the Compose menu on the main Z-Mail window and then selecting the Forward option.

This is equivalent to using the ~f tilde-escape command from compose mode or the −f command-line option with the **mail** (in line mode) and **mail-flags** (in fullscreen mode) commands. We covered this in Chapter 4, *Sending Mail with Z-Mail*, and Chapter 6, *Using the Fullscreen Mode*.

Including a File

In Chapter 4, we showed you how to send a file along with your message using ~r from compose mode. To include the file from the Compose Message window in GUI mode, enter the name of the file in the Filename field. Then, pull down the File menu, select the Open submenu, and then the Insert Text option. This inserts the text of the specified file in the message at the current cursor position.

To replace the current contents of the message with the specified file, select Replace Text from the Open submenu. Generally, the only time you would use the Replace Text option is when including prepared drafts or templates.

If you select an option from the File menu without specifying a filename in the Filename field, the message in Figure 7-11 pops up. Click OK to continue.

Figure 7-11. No filename specified

You might mistype a filename or forget to specify the full pathname (if the file isn't in the current directory). If this happens you see the pop-up box in Figure 7-12. Click OK to continue.

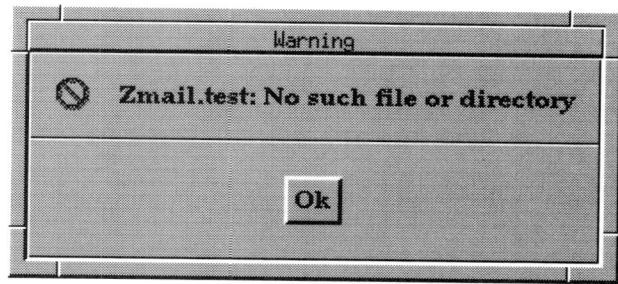

Figure 7-12. No such file

Saving the Current Message

If you compose the message, but decide that you don't want to send it right away, you can save the message buffer to a filename and then send the file later. To do this:

1. Enter the filename in the Filename field (don't forget to include the pathname).

2. Pull down the File menu and select Save.

This appends the text of the current message to the filename you specify.

Editing the Message Headers

If you want to add headers to the message, use the options on the Headers menu. Note that the **ask** and **askcc** variables are set by default; and you are prompted to enter the Subject and Cc, respectively. For example, you might want to create a Subject line. To do this, select the Subject option from the Headers menu. This inserts the Subject line, putting the cursor at the end; you can then use the editing commands in Table 7-9 to edit the subject.

If you just want to change information in the current headers, for example, you want to add people to the To line, simply move the cursor to the header and edit the contents.

We explain more about the headers and how to change them in Chapter 4.

Using Templates

As we explained in Chapter 4, *templates* are form letters that you can use to send multiple messages, like phone messages and status reports, which contain a lot of common information.[4]

To use a template, pull down the Compose menu and select the Templates option. Z-Mail displays the Templates window as shown in Figure 7-13. Select a template, for example *phone*, from the Form Templates list and then click the Use button. Z-Mail starts a new composition.

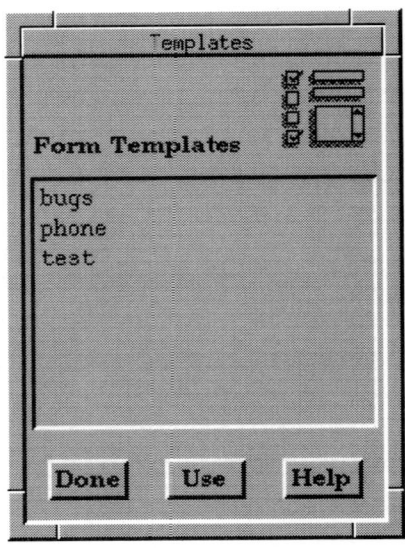

Figure 7-13. Templates window

---

[4] The directory where these templates are kept is specified by the **templates** variable. The default location is */usr/lib/Zmail/forms* or *$ZMLIB/forms*.

Figure 7-14 shows the contents of the *phone* template in the Compose Message window. Fill out the fields in the template and then click Send to send the message.

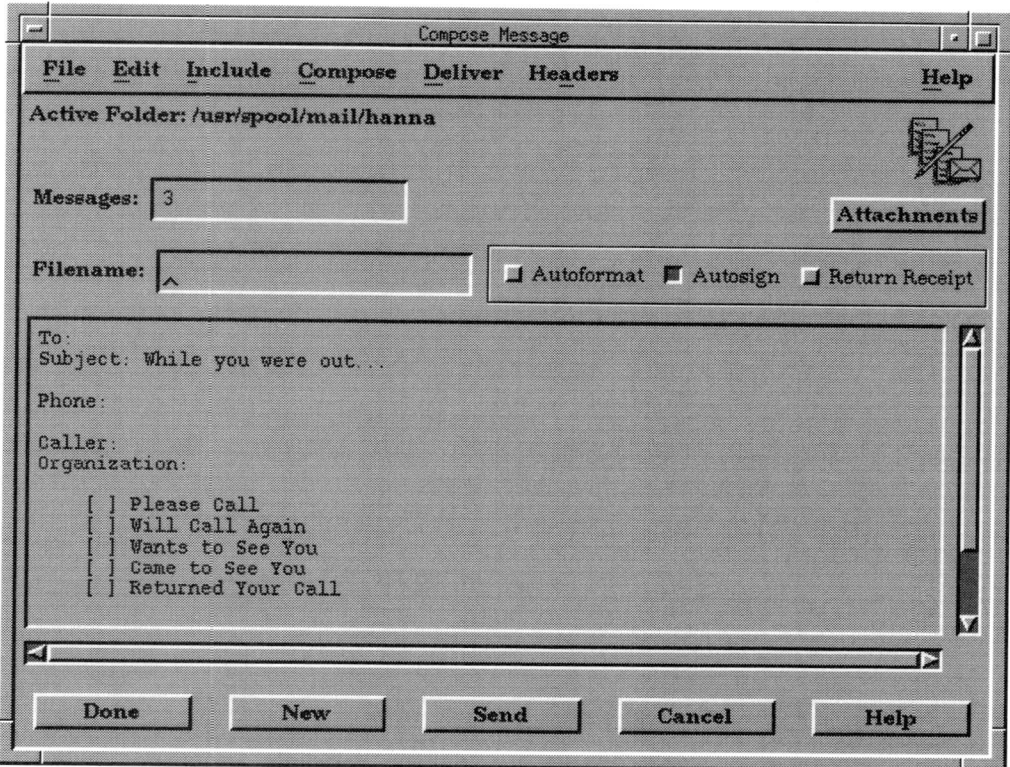

Figure 7-14. Phone template

Cutting and Pasting Text

Z-Mail allows you to cut sections of text and paste them elsewhere in the message. To do this, select some text in the message (the same way you select messages from the Header Summary list), pull down the Edit menu, and select the Cut option. Cut removes the selected text from the message. If you want to *copy* the text rather than *move* it, select Copy instead of Cut.

To paste this text to another place in the message, move the pointer to the selected place, press the mouse button, and the cursor appears. Now, pull down the Edit menu and select Paste. This puts the selected text in the new place in the message.

To clear the selected text from the buffer, select Clear from the Edit menu.

If you want to select the entire message (including headers) to copy or cut, pull down the Edit menu and choose Select All.

Searching and Replacing Text

Z-Mail allows you to search for a specific string in the letter that you're composing and replace it with another. To perform the search-and-replace operation, pull down the Edit menu on the Compose Message window and select Search. The Search and Replace window, shown in Figure 7-15, allows you to specify the strings to search for and its replacement. Only a search string is required.

Search. Enter the pattern that you want to search for in this field.

Replace. Enter the pattern that you want to replace the Search string with; this field is optional.

Next Occurrence. Use this option to find the next occurrence of the pattern in the Search field. You must select either this option or All Occurrences.

All Occurrences. Select this option to find and highlight all the occurrences of the pattern specified in the Search field.

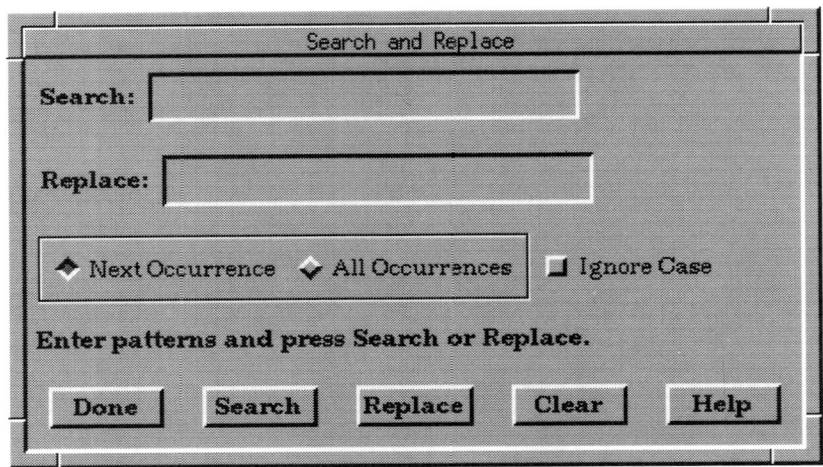

Figure 7-15. Search and Replace window

Ignore Case. Use this option to find the pattern in the Search field, regardless of case.

Click the Search button to highlight the string in your text; then click Replace to replace them with the new string.

Note that you don't have to search for the strings before replacing them; I just prefer to check the strings that Z-Mail finds before doing anything drastic.

Use the Clear button to remove the strings from the text fields before entering a new search pattern.

Using an Editor to Compose the Message

As we mentioned before, Z-Mail uses Motif-style editing commands in the Compose area. If you're not used to using these commands, you can edit your messages with another editor (I prefer *vi*). To bring up another editor to compose your message, select Editor from the Edit menu. (Z-Mail uses the editor specified by your **visual** variable in your initialization file (*vi*, by default)). Z-Mail iconifies the Compose Message window and replaces it with a window running your editor.

You can also specify the program that Z-Mail uses when it starts a *tty* window to run the editor by setting the **window_shell** variable. The default value of **window_shell** is "xterm –e." If you're using an X Window based editor that doesn't require a *tty* (for example, *gnuemacs* opens its own window), you should set **window_shell** to an empty string.

When you finish editing the message, exit the editor (for example, to exit *vi*, enter **:wq** or **ZZ**) and you return to the Compose Message window.

Sending the Message

When you've finished composing your message, send it by clicking the Send button in the Action area at the bottom of the Compose Window. You can also send the message by pulling down the Deliver menu and selecting Send. To send the message and close the Compose Message window in one action, select Send+Close from the Deliver menu.

When you activate the Z-Mail window, you see that the message that you replied to now has an **r** status indicator character.

Wrapping Text Automatically

When you select the Autoformat option, the text that you've entered (and will enter) in the Compose area wraps at the right automatically (without pressing RETURN). This is like using **wrapcolumn** when editing messages in line and fullscreen mode. The column at which Z-Mail wraps the text depends on the current size of the Compose area (in other words, if you change the size of the window, the Compose area might be bigger or smaller). Note that the text might not wrap at the same position when the message is sent.

When you send the message, all the text in the message body is wrapped at the leftmost of the column set in **wrapcolumn**. If you set **wrapcolumn**, Autoformat is always selected (you can turn it off by selecting the Autoformat button). If you don't have **wrapcolumn** set and you select the Autoformat option, Z-Mail inserts carriage returns at column 78, by default.

CAUTION

> Autoformat does *not* join lines, it only adds carriage returns. In other words, Autoformat splits long lines but does not combine short ones. If you type short lines, you can tell Z-Mail to format your message using the Format option on the Edit menu.

Signing Your Message

To append your signature file (˜/.*signature*, the default setting of the **autosign** variable), select the Autosign option. Note that Z-Mail appends the signature *after* you click the Send button to send the message; you can't preview your signature before you send the message.

Requesting a Return Receipt

In Chapter 4, we explained about "return receipts" and how to request them by including a special header in your outgoing mail messages. In the GUI mode, you can request a return receipt simply by selecting the Return Receipt option in the Compose Message window.

When you select Return Receipt, Z-Mail adds the special `Return-Receipt-To` header to your outgoing message. When the message arrives at its destination, the Mail Transport Agent (MTA) on the other system sends you a message to let you know it arrived. Remember that not all MTAs support return receipts. (For more information on return receipts, refer to Chapter 4.)

Sending an Attachment

To attach a file in GUI mode, select the Attachments option from the top right of the Compose area. You see a window like the one in Figure 7-16.

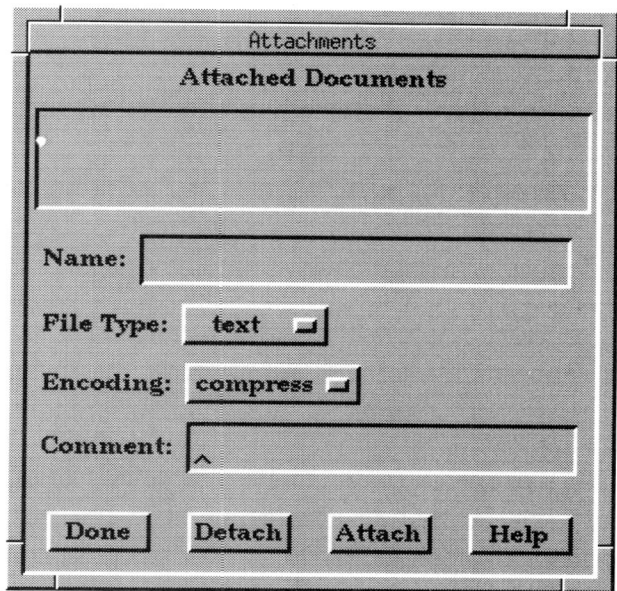

Figure 7-16. Attachments

Name. Enter the name of the file that you want to attach in this field. If the file is not in the current directory, remember to enter the full pathname.

File Type. Use this option to specify the type of file that you are attaching. Click the button in the File Type field to pull down a menu containing the following selections:

File Type	Description
text	Plain text (this is the default file type).
folder	File containing message and headers.
bitmap	ASCII text file created by the X program *bitmap*.
xpm1	Open Look pixmap.
binary	Non-ASCII or text with CTRL characters.

When you select any of the non-ASCII file types, Z-Mail automatically encodes the attachment using *btoa*.

Encoding. Specify the type of encoding you want to use with the file. Use the button in the Encoding field to display a menu with the following selections:

Encoding	Description
compress	Use *compress* to make the file smaller (this also converts ASCII to binary).
btoa	Convert from binary to ASCII.
none	Do not perform any encoding.

The default Encoding is *compress*. Because *compress* output is non-ASCII, if you use *compress*, Z-Mail automatically converts it to ASCII with *btoa*.

Comment. Use this field to enter a comment describing the file that you're attaching; this field is optional.

The information in each of these fields appears in the Attached Documents list at the top of the window when you attach the file and when the recipient displays the attachments.

There are several buttons in the Attachments window; Table 7-10 briefly describes them.

Table 7-10. Attachments Window Buttons

Button	Description
Done	Return to the Compose Message window.
Detach	Remove the attachment from the message.
Attach	Attach a file to the current message.
Help	Get help about attaching files.

To attach a file, fill out the form in the Attachments window. Enter the name of the file, the file type, the encoding information, and any comments that you want to include in the fields in the Attachments window. The File Type and Encoding fields have special buttons that display the available options. (For information on attachment types and encoding information, see the section on sending attachments in Chapter 4, *Sending Mail with Z-Mail*.)

When you finish adding information to the Attachments window fields, select Attach to attach the file. Z-Mail displays a description of the attachment in the Attached Documents list at the top of the window. You can attach more than one file to a message. If you decide that you don't want to send a particular attachment, click Detach.

When you're finished attaching files, click the Done button to return to the Compose Message window. When you send your message, Z-Mail attaches the file to it. For more information on attachments, see the section "Reading a Message with an Attachment," earlier in this chapter.

Composing a New Message

Z-Mail allows you to have more than one message composition in progress at any given time. In line and fullscreen mode, you use the ˜z tilde-escape command to suspend the current message composition so that you can start a new composition. From the GUI mode, you can simply open a new Compose Message window and start a new message without closing the current Message Display window. So, if you're currently composing a reply to a message, simply start up a new window (and a new message) by clicking the New button.

New is similar to Reply except that Z-Mail opens a new Compose Message window without filling in the To and Subject lines. The Compose Message window looks like the one in Figure 7-10, except that Z-Mail hasn't filled in the To and Subject lines for you.

Enter your message as you did with Reply and send it by clicking Send. Remember that you must specify a recipient on the To line before you can send your message. If you don't, Z-Mail displays a Warning message.

You don't have to read a message to compose a reply; you can also compose new messages using the Compose button from the Z-Mail window.

Canceling the Message

You can cancel the message at any time before sending it by clicking the Cancel button. The message that you were composing is still displayed in the Compose area, but you can't send it with Send. At this point, you can either click New to start a new message or click Done to return to the Message Display window.

Note that clicking Cancel *after* clicking Send to send the message *does not* prevent the outgoing message from being sent! Once you click Send, the message is sent and you can't take it back.

Closing the Compose Message Window

At any time, you can close the Compose Message window by clicking the Done button. If you haven't already sent the message and you click Done, a Warning message like the one in Figure 7-17 appears.

Figure 7-17. Closing before sending

To cancel the message and return to the Message Display window, click the Yes button. To return to the Compose Message window without canceling the message, click Cancel.

Replying to Multiple Messages

If you want to send a reply to the authors of more than one message, do this from the main Z-Mail window. First, select the messages from the Header Summary list that you want to respond to. Then, click the Reply button. Remember, you can also use the Reply pull-right menu from the Compose menu on the main Z-Mail window.

Z-Mail opens up a Compose Message window and fills in the To line with the addresses of each of the original authors like the example in Figure 7-18. If the **in_reply_to** variable is set, Z-Mail also inserts **In-Reply-To** headers to indicate exactly which messages you are replying to. Note that the **Subject** line contains the **Subject** header of the first selected message. You can change this by selecting Subject from the Headers menu. If you include the current message, Z-Mail includes all the selected messages by default. You can specify different messages to include by entering the message numbers in the Messages field before selecting Include Msg.

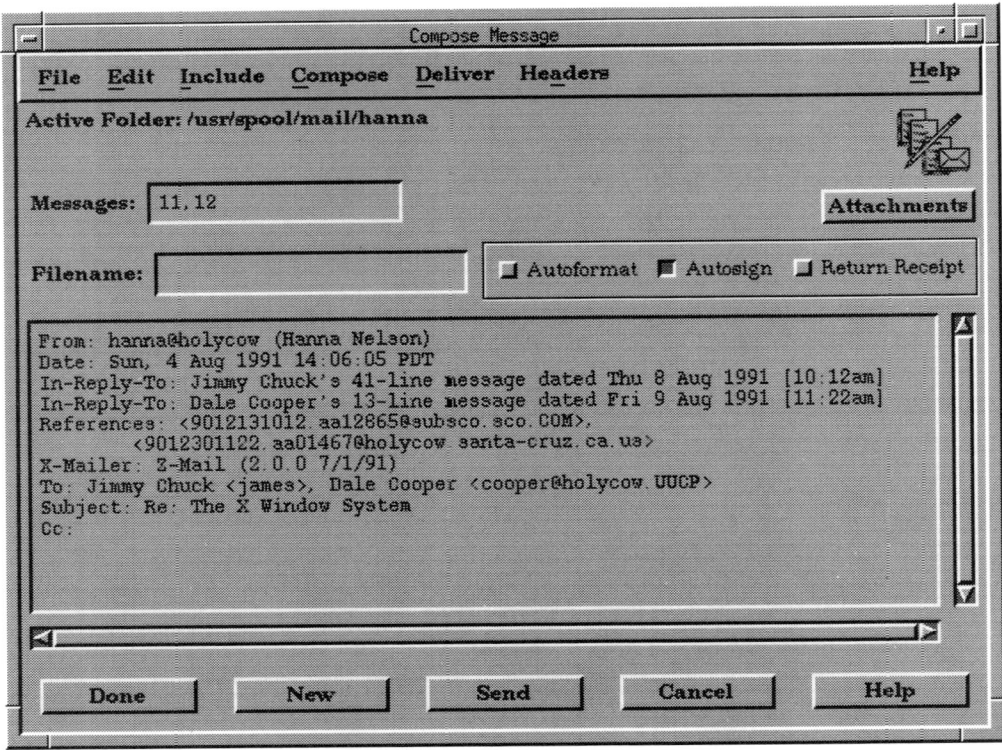

Figure 7-18. Replying to more than one message

When New Mail Arrives

New mail might arrive at any time. If you're using Z-Mail and new mail arrives, the main
Z-Mail window displays a check in the New Arrivals box and the header summary information for the new mail appears in the Output area. Figure 7-19 shows an example. The exclamation mark (!) indicates that the message has just arrived.

Figure 7-19. When new mail arrives

To read the new mail, move the scrollbar down so that the header summary appears and select it with the pointer. Or enter the new message number (usually, it's the last message in the list, so you can enter $ to select it) in the Messages field. Then, click the Read button.

When you're not using Z-Mail, but the Z-Mail window is iconified on the desktop, Z-Mail changes the icon to reverse video when new mail arrives. You can change the icons to display by setting the **mail_icon** and **newmail_icon** variables; see Chapter 8, *Customizing Z-Mail*.

Using Folders

You've already learned how to save messages to folders; now we'll show you how to create, switch, update, and exit folders using the Folders option in the File menu.

Switching Folders

A folder is a file that contains mail messages—message text and headers. You can switch to any folder by selecting Folders from the File menu.[5] When you select this option, Z-Mail opens the Find Folders window shown in Figure 7-20.

At the top of the Find Folders window is the name of the active folder. In our example, the active folder is my system mailbox, */usr/spool/mail/hanna*. Below this is the scrollable Folder list that contains a listing of all the messages in your folder directory. (This list is identical to the Folder list in the Save Messages window.) The Folder list can either contain the list of folder names in a directory or the list of folders that are currently open, depending on whether you select Find Folders or Show Open Folders.

Folder. By default, this field contains the name of the currently selected folder (or directory to search). You can also use this field to select or enter manually the name of the folder or directory that you want to switch to.

Find Folders. Select this option to display the names of all the folders in the currently selected directory (in the Folder list). This is roughly equivalent to using the **folders** command in line mode.

---

[5] Some MTAs require additional information to delimit messages in folders. For example, MMDF commonly uses four CTRL-A's.

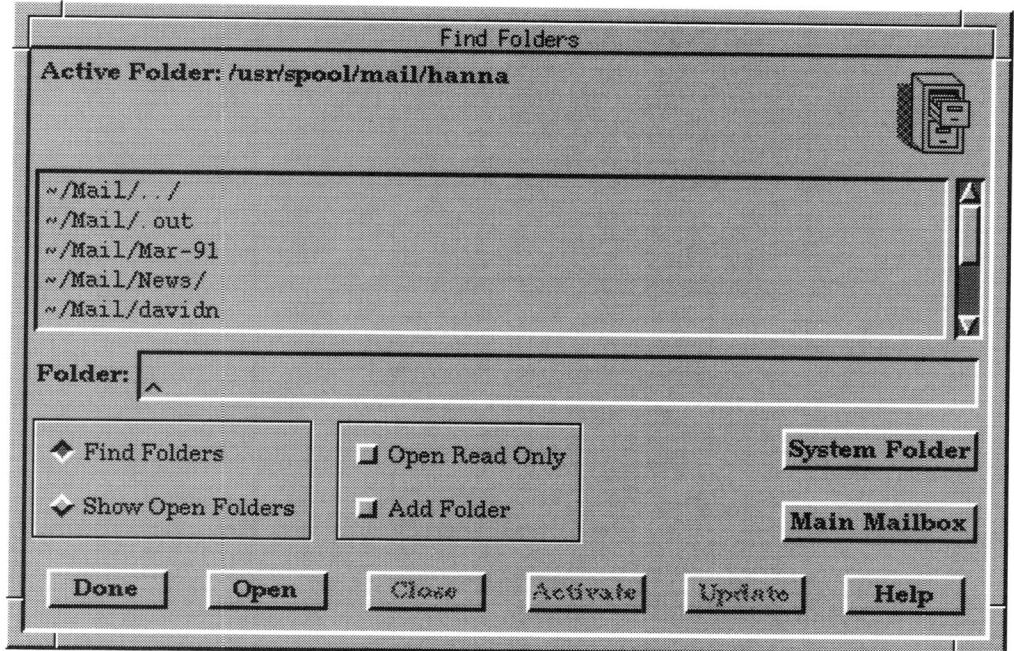

Figure 7-20. Find Folders window

Show Open Folders. Use this option to display a list of the currently open folders (replacing the folder names in the Folder list). This performs the same action as **open –l** in line mode.

Open Read Only. Select this option to open the selected folder in read-only mode, thus preventing you from making any modifications to the folder. This is identical to using the **open –r** command.

Add Folder. This option adds the new folder to the list of open folders (rather than replacing the currently open folder with the new folder). This is equivalent to **open –a**.

System Folder. To open and switch to the system mailbox, select this option. This is the same as entering **open %**.

Main Mailbox. Select this option to open the folder specified by the **mbox** variable, ˜/*mbox* by default; this is equivalent to **open &**.

The Find Folders option in Figure 7-20 is selected. To open and switch to a new folder, select the name from the Folder frame and click the Open button. You can select either the System Folder (your system mailbox; for example, */usr/spool/mail/hanna*) or the Main Mailbox (your ˜/*mbox* folder, which is set via the **mbox** variable) buttons and Z-Mail automatically puts the folder name in the Folder list. To open that folder, click Open.

For now, let's look in the *zmail.book* directory. First, select */u/hanna/Mail/zmail.book* and select the Find Folders option. The Folder list now contains a list of folders in */u/hanna/Mail/zmail.book*.

NOTE

> The Folders frame lists *only* the folders that contain messages with their header information intact. If the *zmail.book* directory includes files containing messages with no header information, Z-Mail does not display these files in the Folders frame. You cannot switch to files and access messages that you saved as text only.

To switch to a new folder, select the folder from the Folders directory. For example, earlier we saved a message to *review*. Now, we can switch to the folder and manipulate the message. To do this, select *review* and then click the Open button. The Active Folder changes to ˜/*Mail/zmail.book/review*. Note that you remain in the Find Folders window. (If you set the **autodismiss** variable to include the *folder* keyword, Z-Mail closes the Find Folders window when you switch folders. We'll explain **autodismiss** in Chapter 8, *Customizing Z-Mail*.)

To read the messages in the new folder, activate the Z-Mail window. Figure 7-21 shows the new Z-Mail window. Note that ˜/*Mail/zmail.book/review* contains only one message.

Opening a Folder in Read-only Mode

If you want to switch to the new folder just to look at the messages and you don't want to modify the folder in any way, open the folder in read-only mode. To do this, select the Open Read Only option before opening the folder. Now, if you accidentally make any changes to the folder, Z-Mail ignores them when you quit.

Opening More than One Folder at a Time

Z-Mail allows you to have more than one folder open at a time. Z-Mail doesn't open a new window for each folder, but once folders are open, you can switch between them quickly. To open another folder without closing the current folder, click the Add Folder button in the Mail Folders window before opening the folder with Open.

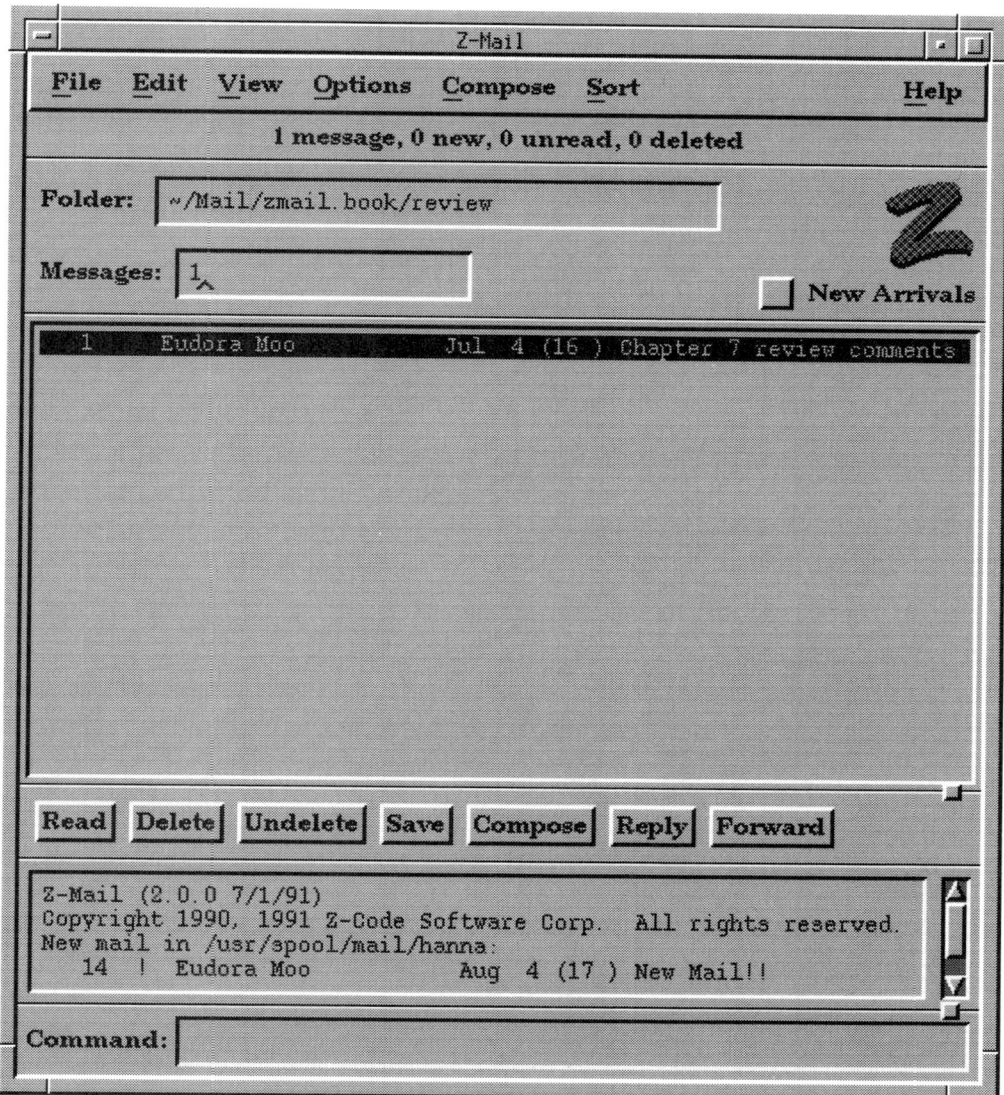

Figure 7-21. Switching to another folder

By default, if the current folder is the system mailbox, Z-Mail automatically adds the new folder. Also, if you're adding the system folder, the current folder remains open regardless of whether you use the Add Folder option or not. For more information about adding folders, see Chapter 5, *Z-Mail Shortcuts, Bells, and Whistles*.

Displaying the List of Open Folders

If you've opened more than one folder (using the Add Folder option), the folders are open but they aren't all displayed at once. To look at the list of open folders, select the Show Open Folders option from the Find Folders window. Z-Mail replaces the list of folders in the Folder list with the list of currently open folders. Now, the Find Folders window looks like Figure 7-22.

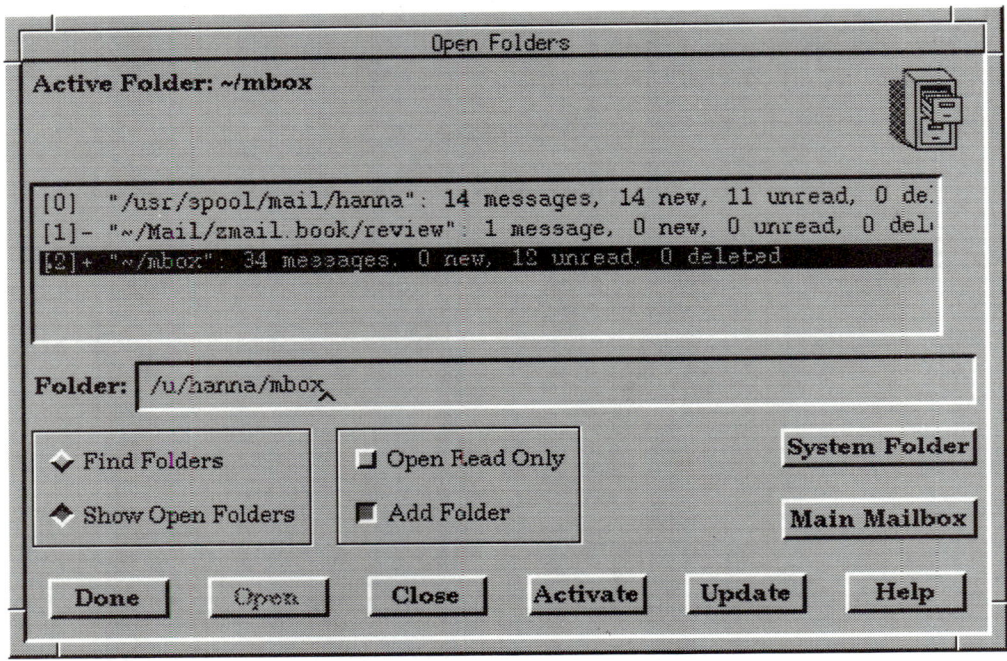

Figure 7-22. Open folders

In our example, you can see that */usr/spool/mail/hanna*, *˜/Mail/zmail.book/review*, and *˜/mbox* are open. The folders are numbered, beginning with **0** for the system mailbox. The plus (+) indicates the currently active folder and the minus (−) shows which folder was previously active.

Activating a Different Folder

To activate another folder in the Open Folders list, select it with the pointer and click the Activate button. The Active Folder at the top of the Open Folders window changes to indicate the folder that is currently active. When you activate the Z-Mail window, you now see the messages from the new folder in the Header Summary list.

Closing the Find Folders Window

At any time, you can close the Find Folders window by clicking the Done button. If you've already switched to the new folder by clicking Open, Z-Mail displays the header summaries for the new folder in the Z-Mail window. If you didn't click Open before clicking Done, you remain in the same folder you were in when you first selected Folders from the File pull-down menu.

Closing an Open Folder

If you're finished with a folder for the current Z-Mail session, you can close it using the Close button in the Open Folders window. To do this, select the folder to close from the Open Folders list. Then, click the Close button.

For example, when we close the ~/Mail/zmail.book/review folder, the Folders list now looks like the one in Figure 7-23. Z-Mail displays "<Closed>" in place of the review folder.

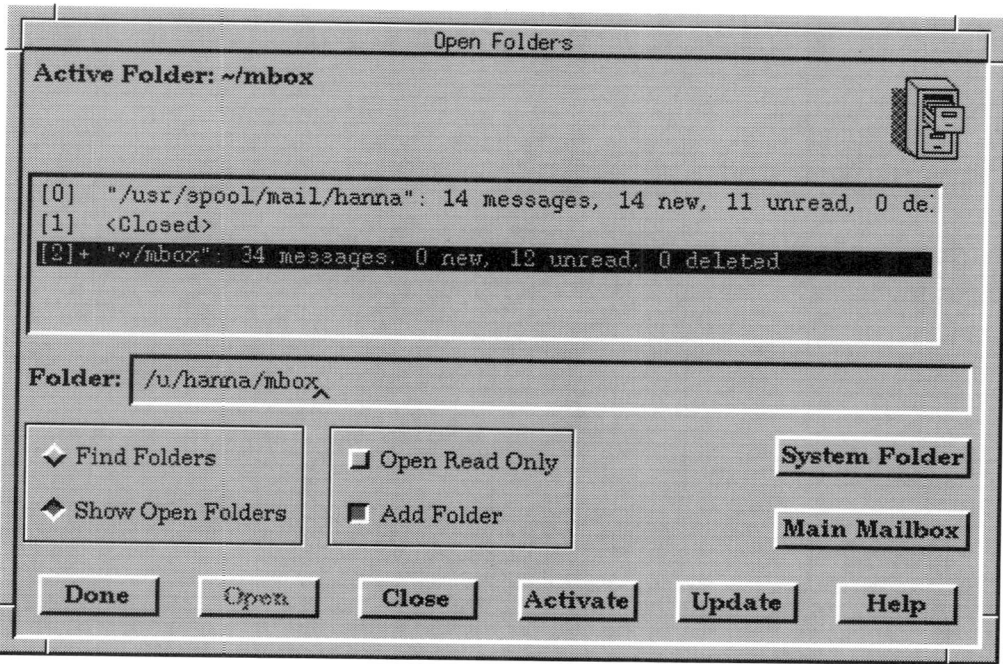

Figure 7-23. Closing a folder

By default, when you close a folder, Z-Mail updates it. If you want Z-Mail to prompt you before performing the update, set the **verify** variable to include the string "update." For example, include the following line in your initialization file:

```
set verify = update
```

(We'll show you how to set variables from within Z-Mail in the section "Setting Z-Mail Variables," later in this chapter.)

If you want to save your changes to the folder without closing the folder, click the Update button.

Updating the Current Folder

When you read, delete, or save messages, they aren't removed from the Header Summary list until you quit Z-Mail. If you have a lot of messages in your Header Summary list, these messages can get in the way. To get rid of them without exiting Z-Mail, update the folder.

To do this, pull down the File menu and select Update Folder. Z-Mail sounds a bell and updates the folder. The deleted messages are removed from the display. If the folder is your system mailbox, saved messages are also deleted; and any messages that you've already read remain in your system mailbox.

Exiting Z-Mail

To exit Z-Mail, pull down the File menu and select the Quit option. If you've modified the folder, you see a confirmation pop-up window like the one in Figure 7-24.

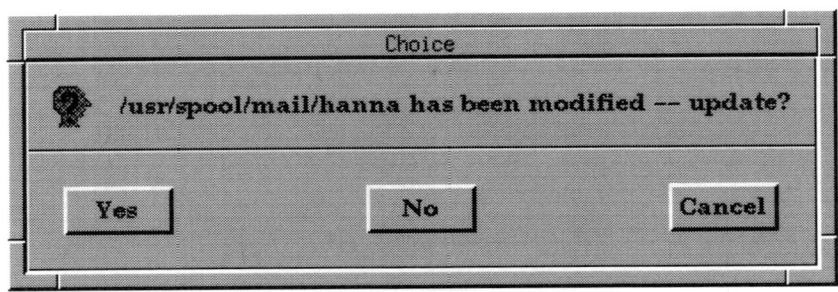

Figure 7-24. Updating the folder

Click Yes to update the folder and return to your system prompt. If you click No, you exit Z-Mail without updating the folder. To cancel the Exit request and return to the Z-Mail window, click the Cancel button.

For each folder that you have open at the time that you quit, you might see the pop-up window in Figure 7-24. If you want to quit without being prompted to confirm each update, remove the string "quit" from the **verify** variable setting.

Manipulating Messages

You can manipulate messages using certain status indicators, such as priority letters, with options on the Edit pull-down menu. The Edit menu options are listed in Table 7-20.

Table 7-20. Edit Menu Options

Option	Description
Delete	Delete messages.
Undelete	Restore deleted messages.
Preserve	Preserve messages in the system mailbox.
Unpreserve	Unset the preserve status for messages.
Mark	Mark messages temporarily with a plus character (+).
Unmark	Unset temporary marks.
Priority	Specify a priority for messages (pull-right menu).
Clear Priorities	Remove priority settings.
Pattern Search	Select messages by patterns.
Date Search	Select messages by date.

We've already covered the Delete and Undelete options; see the sections "Deleting Messages" and "Restoring Deleted Messages" earlier in this chapter. We'll cover the rest of these tasks in the coming sections.

Preserving Messages

If you don't set the **hold** variable, when you quit (or update) the system mailbox, Z-Mail moves the messages that you read to your ~/mbox folder. If the **hold** variable is set, which is the default, all messages are held in your mailbox, unless you explicitly delete them. In this case, if you want to keep messages in the system mailbox to come back to later, you can mark the messages as "preserved." To do this, select the messages from the Header window to preserve. Then, pull down the Edit menu and select the Preserve option.

Z-Mail changes the status indicator character for the selected messages to **P**. Now, when you quit Z-Mail, these messages remain in the system mailbox.

This action is identical to using the **preserve** command in the line and fullscreen modes. We show you how to do this in Chapter 3, *Reading and Managing Mail*.

Unpreserving Messages

To change the status of a preserved message to "unpreserved," first select the message. Then, pull down the Edit menu and select Unpreserve. This removes the P status indicator from the message. When you quit, Z-Mail moves the message to the ˜/mbox file. If the message has been saved, it is deleted from the system mailbox when you quit.

Marking Messages

To mark a message with a plus character (+) so that you can come back to it later, first select the message to mark. Then, pull down the Edit menu and select the Mark option. Note that this mark is temporary; when you quit Z-Mail, the mark is removed.

Using the Mark option is identical to marking messages with the **mark** command in the line and fullscreen modes. For more information on **mark**, see Chapter 3.

Removing Marks

The temporary mark characters (+) are removed automatically when you quit Z-Mail; if you want, you can remove them for the current session. To do this, select the marked messages to "unmark." Then, pull down the Edit menu and select Unmark. This removes the plus character (+) from the status indicator field of the selected header summaries.

Specifying Priorities for Messages

Like marking messages temporarily with +, you can mark special messages that you want to reference later with a priority status (A–E, with A having the highest priority). Z-Mail saves the priority settings when you update the folder. Then, you can sort and select messages by priority. We'll explain how to do this later in this chapter.

To set a priority on a message, first select the message to prioritize. Then, pull down the Edit window and select the Priority pull-right menu; select the priority (A through E) from the submenu.

When you let go of the mouse button, the Edit menu disappears and Z-Mail marks the message with the selected priority.

Messages may have both a temporary mark and a priority setting, but can have no more than one priority setting. Remember that, if a message has both a mark and a priority, the plus character (+) takes precedence over the priority-setting character. In addition, when you sort the message list by priority, marked messages appear first, followed by messages with priorities (priority A first, priority E last). (We explain more about priority settings in Chapter 3.)

Removing Priority Settings

Priority settings, unlike marks, are permanent; they remain even after you quit Z-Mail and update the folder. To strip the priority setting from the selected messages, pull down the Edit menu and select the Clear Priorities option.

Picking Messages to Display

If you're looking for messages from one particular person, with a specific `Subject` line or between two dates, you can do this using the last two options on the Edit pull-down menu: Pattern Search and Date Search.

Searching for a Pattern

To find all the messages from one person, select Pattern Search from the Edit menu. Z-Mail displays the Pattern Search window as shown in Figure 7-25.

Messages. Enter the numbers for the messages that you want to search for the pattern in. Use this field to limit the search, or leave it blank to search all the messages.

Search Pattern. Enter the pattern that you want to search for in this field.

Entire Message. Use this option to search the entire message—text and headers—for the pattern specified in the Search Pattern field.

To. Use this option to limit the search to the `To` header. This is equivalent to **pick –t**.

From. Use this option to limit the search to the `From` header (**pick –f**).

Subject. Use this option to limit the search to the `Subject` header (**pick –s**).

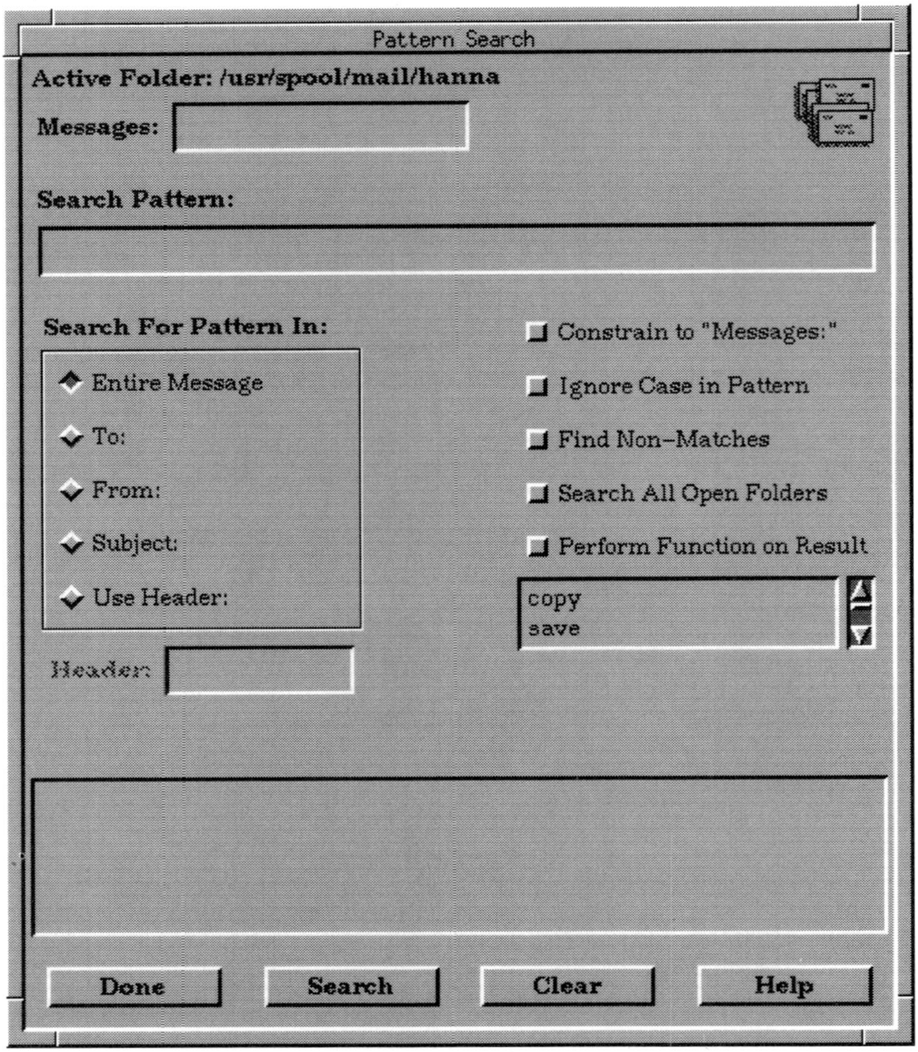

Figure 7-25. Pattern Search window

Use Header. If you want to search in a different header, such as `Message-Id`, select this option and enter the header in the Header field below (**pick –h** *hdr*).

Constrain to "Messages". Use this option to limit the search to a specified list of messages (**pick –r** *msg-list*).

Ignore Case in Pattern. This option tells Z-Mail to ignore the case of the letters when comparing patterns (**pick –i**).

Find Non-Matches. Use this option to find all the messages that don't match the specified pattern (**pick –x**).

Search All Open Folders. Use this option to tell Z-Mail to search for the specified pattern in all the folders that are currently open. (This feature is not available in line or fullscreen modes).

Perform Function on Result. To specify an action to take on the messages that match the pattern, select one of the following actions:

Action	Description
Copy	Save messages to a folder without marking for deletion.
Save	Save messages to a folder, marking it as "saved."
Delete	Delete messages.
Undelete	Restore messages.
Mark	Mark messages with a temporary mark character (+).
Unmark	Remove temporary marks from messages.

The left column, below the Search Pattern field, lets you select the component of the message in which you want to search for the pattern; you can select only one button from this column. Use the right column to specify the limits of the Search; select as many constraints from this column as you want.

Below the two columns is the Search Results list where Z-Mail displays the header summaries for the messages that match the search pattern. At the bottom of the window are the Action area buttons. You're familiar with the Done and Help buttons; we'll explain the Search and Clear buttons in this section.

By default, Z-Mail searches through each message (using the Entire Message option) in the message list for the exact pattern that you specify. You can limit the search to a pattern in the `To`, `From`, or `Subject` lines by selecting a button in the left column.

You want to search for a pattern in a header that's not listed in the left column. For example, you might want to search for a pattern in a personal header, such as `Phone`.

To do this, enter the pattern that you want to search for in this field. Now, select Use Header from the left column; the Header field becomes available. Enter the personal header in this field and click the Search button. Z-Mail searches for the pattern in the specified header and displays the result of the search in the Search Results list.

You might be tempted to use this method to search the **Date** field for messages sent on a specific date. However, it's actually easier (and more precise) to use the Date Search utility that we'll explain in the next section.

If you want to limit the search to a specific message list (for example, you just want to search the most recent message), use the Constrain to "Messages:" option. This means that the search is limited to the messages specified in the Messages field at the top of the window. So, to search in messages 5 through 15, enter **5-15** in the Messages field, specify the pattern in Search Pattern, select the Constrain option, and then click Search.

Because Z-Mail automatically puts the results of the search (message numbers) in the Messages field, you can combine searches by selecting the Constrain option. For example, you might first search for one pattern, then select Constrain and search for another pattern within the list of selected messages.

Searching All the Open Folders

With Z-Mail, you don't have to limit your search to the messages in the current folder; if you have other folders open, you can look in those folders, too. To do this, select the Search All Open Folders option. Remember that you can display the list of open folders by selecting Folders from the File menu and then selecting Show Open Folders from this window.

Searching for Messages That Don't Match

To find all the messages that don't match the pattern in Search Pattern, use the Find Non-Matches option. This is useful for finding the messages that aren't addressed specifically to you. For example, to find all the messages *not* addressed to me, I enter **hanna** in the Search Pattern field, select the To and Find Non-Matches options, and then click Search. Z-Mail puts the header summaries for all the messages that don't contain "hanna" in the **To** line in the Search Results list.

Manipulating the Results of the Search

Once you select a group of messages that contain a specific pattern, you'll probably want to do something with them. For example, if you find all the messages that aren't addressed to you, you can delete them, or save them to another folder to deal with later. To do this, use the Perform Function on Result option.

For example, once you specify the search pattern and options, select the Perform Function option. The Function list becomes available. Select a function (for example, **delete**) from the list. Then, click Search. Z-Mail still finds the messages that match the pattern and displays them in the Search Results list, but first it performs the selected function on them. Thus, if you selected **delete**, the header summaries in the Search Results list show an asterisk (*) to indicate that they've been deleted.

If you've already found the messages that match your pattern, you can still perform the function on them (as long as you haven't clicked Clear in the meantime). Simply select Perform Function and click Search again.

If you select either the **copy** or **save** functions, Z-Mail displays an Input pop-up window like the one in Figure 7-26 when you click Search.

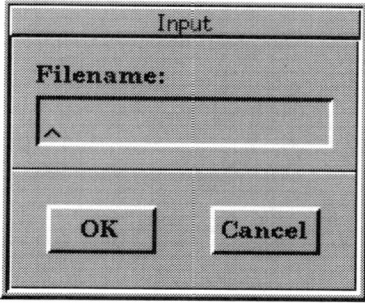

Figure 7-26. Input window

Enter the filename to save (or copy) the messages to and click OK to continue.

Another way to perform functions on the results of a search is to select messages from the Message list. Z-Mail copies these selections to the main Z-Mail window, where you can perform any function you prefer—for example, forward or reply.

Picking Messages by Date

To select messages by the date they were sent, pull down the Edit menu and select Date Search. You see the Date Search window in Figure 7-27.

Many of the options in the right column are familiar from (and are identical to) the Pattern Search window; in this section, we'll discuss the functions that differ. (If you're not already familiar with the other functions, see the section "Searching for a Pattern.") Remember that you can select as many constraints from the right column as you want.

Use Date Message Received. Select this option to search for messages by the date you received them, rather than the date they were sent. This is the default action if you set the **date_received** variable.

On Date Only. This option selects only the messages sent on the specified date. This is equivalent to the line-mode command **pick –d** *date*.

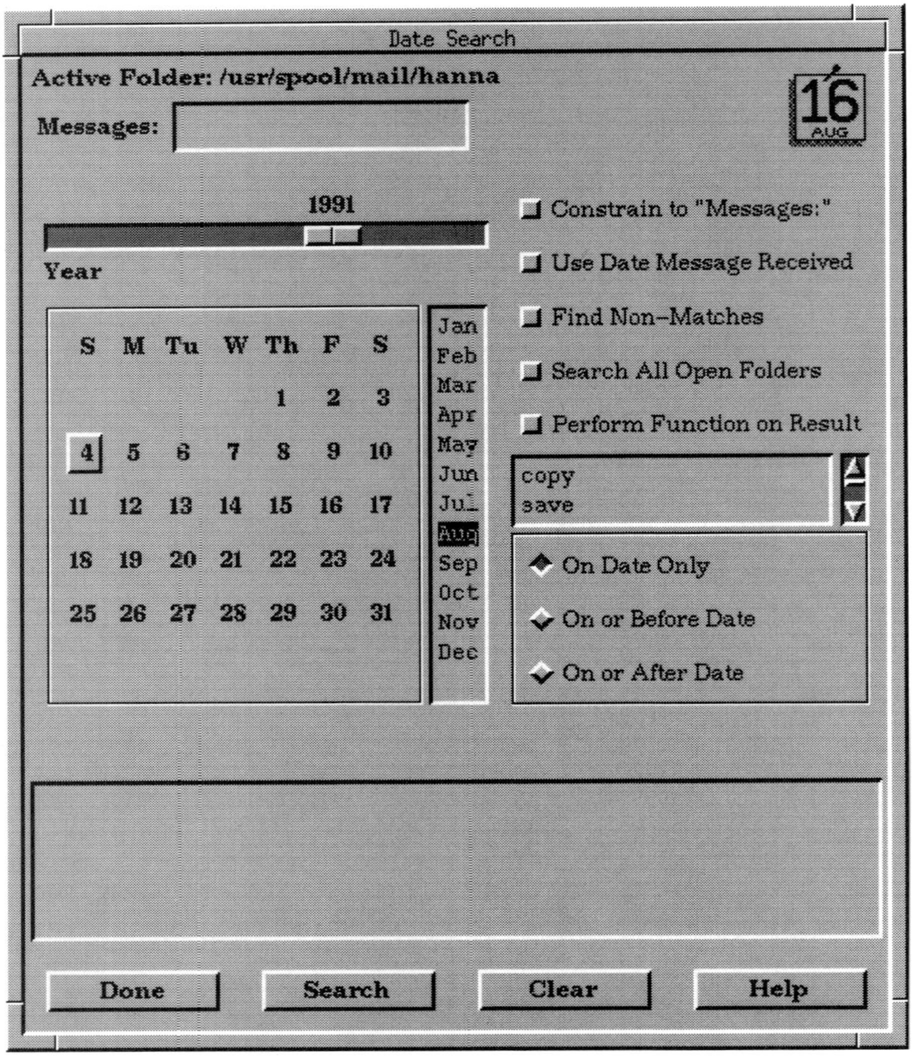

Figure 7-27. Date Search window

On or Before Date. To find all the messages sent on or before the specified date, select this option (**pick –d** *–date*).

On or After Date. Use this option to select messages that were sent on or after the specified date (**pick –d** *date*).

The features in the left column allow you to select specific dates to search for. By default, Z-Mail uses the current date (day, month, and year). To change the year, move the Year thumb exactly as you move scrollbar thumbs. Move it left for an earlier year, right for a later year; the number above the thumb changes as you move it.

To change the day and month, click on a number in the Calendar box or the month name in the Month frame. Z-Mail changes the Calendar box accordingly.

Searching for an Exact Date

To find all the messages that exactly match the date you specify in the left column, select the On Date Only option from the right column.

By default, Z-Mail searches for messages by the date that they were sent; you can change this to the date you received them by selecting the Use Date Message Received option.

Searching for a Relative Date

If you want to search for messages sent on a date relative to a specific date, such as before or after, use the On or Before Date and On or After Date options. This feature is useful for finding old messages to delete.

For example, to find all the messages received on or before November 26, 1990, first select the date from the left column. Then, select the Use Date Message Received and On or Before Date options from the right column. Finally, click Search. Z-Mail puts the results of the search in the Search Results list above the Action area.

Again, you can perform specific functions on the messages that Z-Mail finds using the Perform Function on Result option. We show you how earlier in this chapter in the section "Manipulating the Results of the Search."

Sorting the Message Headers

As in the line and fullscreen modes, the MTA appends new messages to the end of the spool folder (your system mailbox). You can change the order of the messages, using the options on the Sort menu listed in Table 7-21.

Table 7-21. Sort Menu Options

Option	Description
By Date	Sort messages by date sent (most recent last).
By Subject	Order messages alphabetically by `Subject`.
By Author	Sort messages alphabetically by `From` (or `Reply-To`) line.
By Message Length	Order messages by size in number of characters (smallest to largest).
By Priority	Sort messages by priority setting (**A** to **E**).

Table 7-21. Sort Menu Options (continued)

Option	Description
By Status	Sort messages by status indicator character.
Custom Sort	Open the Custom Sort window.

You can use any of the first six options in Table 7-21 either by selecting them from the Sort menu or by selecting the Custom Sort option to open the Custom Sort window. We'll approach each of these options from the Custom Sort window and mention the equivalent Sort menu option where appropriate.

The Custom Sort Window

To bring up the Custom Sort window, pull down the Sort menu and select Custom Sort. Figure 7-28 shows the Custom Sort window.

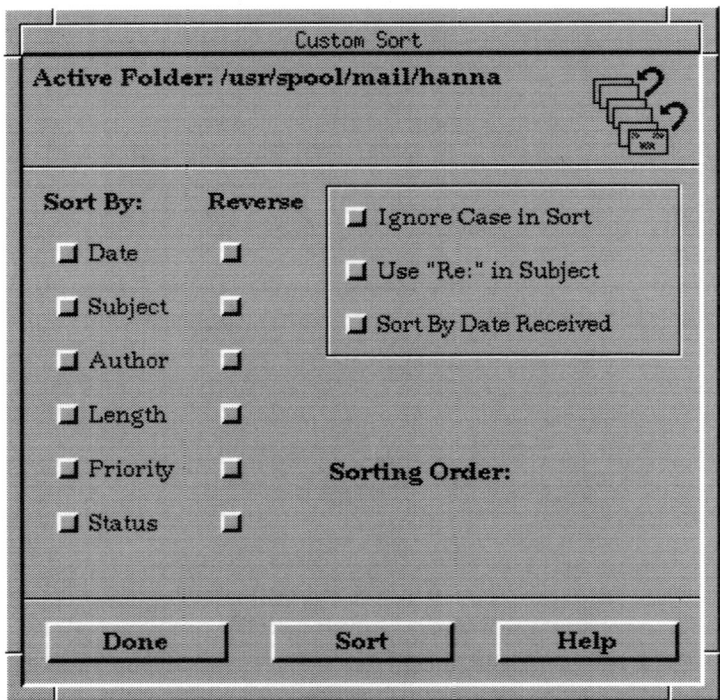

Figure 7-28. Custom Sort window

Use the options in the Sort By column to specify the field to sort by. For example, to order the messages alphabetically using the `Subject` header, use the Subject option. For a complete explanation of the Sort Order options, see Chapter 3.

As in the line mode, you can combine and reverse Sort options. So, if you want to sort alphabetically by author and then order each group of messages by status, first select Author and then select Status. When you select one option in the Sort By column, Z-Mail displays the Sorting Order list in the bottom right. Figure 7-29 shows what the list looks like.

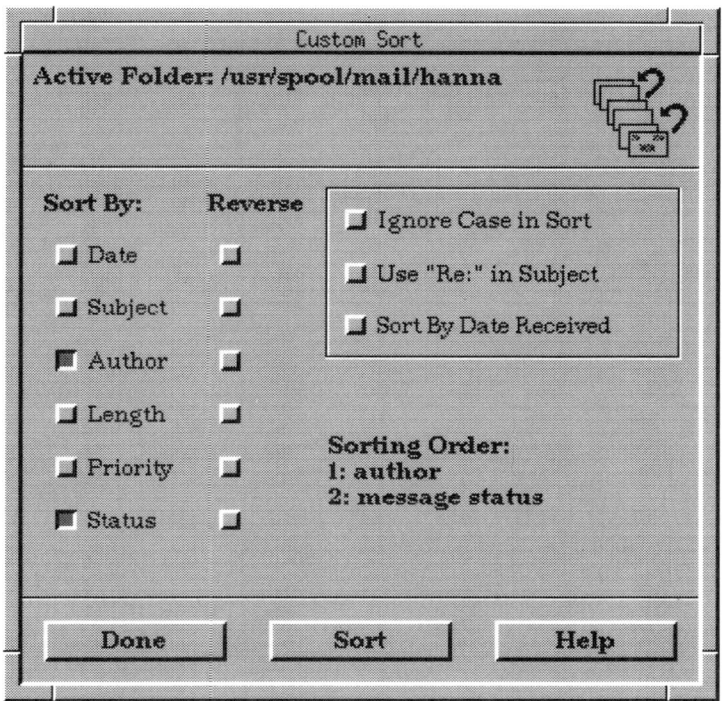

Figure 7-29. Sorting order list

Reverse any of the Sort By options by selecting the corresponding Reverse option. Once you've selected the sort parameters, click the Sort button.

Let's say you want to order messages by the date you received them. To do this, select the Date option from the left column and the Sort By Date Received option in the right column. Then, click Sort. Note that this is the only way to sort messages by the date you received the messages; you can't do this from the Sort pull-down menu. If you always want Z-Mail to sort by date received, set the **date_received** variable.

When you use the Subject and Author options, Z-Mail sorts the messages alphabetically, grouping uppercase together first. If you want all the messages that begin with a specific letter grouped together, regardless of any uppercase letters, select Ignore Case from the Sort menu.

By default, Z-Mail ignores the `Re:` in `Subject` headers. In other words, all the messages whose `Subject` lines begin with "A" appear first, regardless of whether they're replies or not. If you want to group together replies (messages with `Re:` in the `Subject`), use the Use "Re" In Subject option.

Customizing Z-Mail

You can customize the way Z-Mail works by setting specific variables and specifying headers that you want to ignore when reading messages. If you send mail to groups of people or people with long mail addresses, you can create mail aliases to use instead. And, if you're really ambitious, you can even create your own Z-Mail functions and attach buttons to them. These buttons then appear in the main Z-Mail window.

To access these tools, activate the Z-Mail window and pull down the Options menu. Table 7-22 lists the options on this menu.

Table 7-22. Options Menu Options

Option	Description
Variables	Set Z-Mail variables.
Headers	Specify headers to ignore.
Envelope	Create personal headers to appear in outgoing messages.
Aliases	Set mail aliases.
Buttons	Create Z-Mail functions and attach them to buttons.
Toolbox	Access all the important Z-Mail dialog boxes.

We'll explain how to use these options in the next few sections.

Setting Z-Mail Variables

The easiest way to set variables is to include them in your initialization file (`~/.zmailrc`). However, you might want to test out the variables from within Z-Mail before making them permanent in the initialization file. To do this from the main Z-Mail window, pull down the Options menu and select Variables. Z-Mail opens the Variables window; you can see what this looks like in Figure 7-30.

Save/Load Variables Filename. This field contains the current initialization file that Z-Mail read to set up your environment. To read in another file, enter the filename in this field and click the Load button.

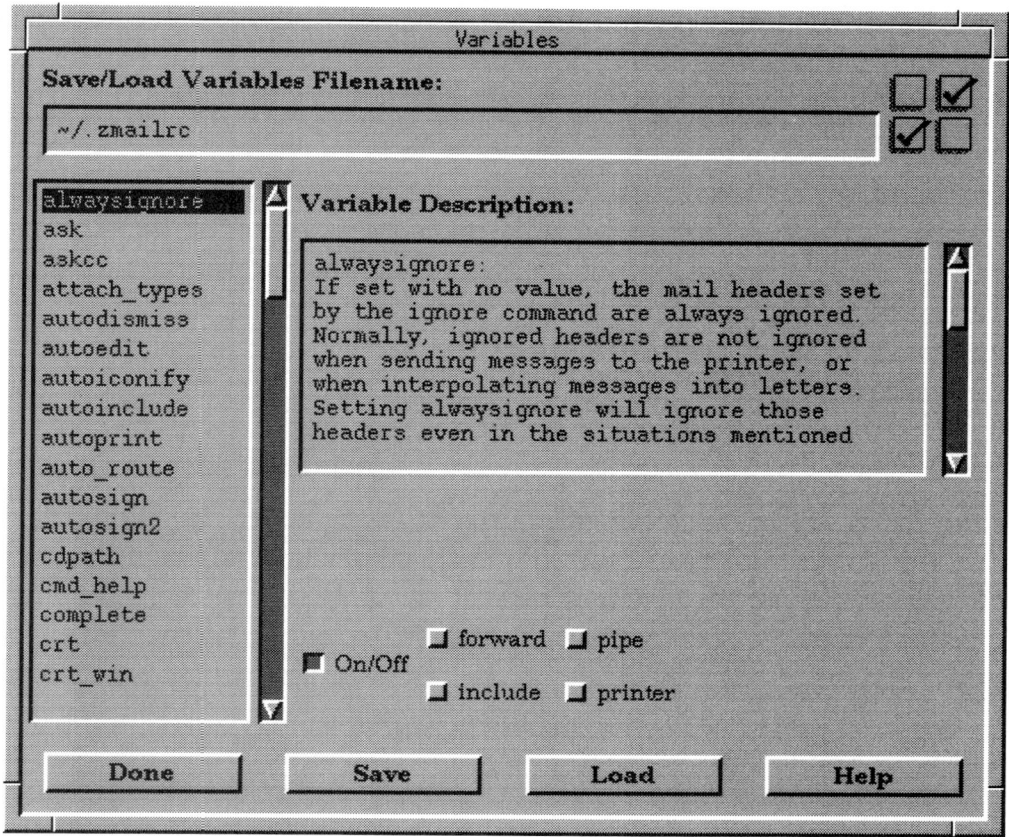

Figure 7-30. Z-Mail Variables window

Variables. This scrollable window contains a list of all the Z-Mail variables. To set a variable, select it from this list.

Variable Description. This frame contains a description of the currently selected variable in the Variables list.

Let's briefly review the different types of Z-Mail variables. Boolean variables can be turned on and off ("toggled"); you don't set them to a particular value. When you select a boolean variable in the Variables frame, Z-Mail displays the On/Off button above the Action area. For example, if you select the **wrap** variable, you can then toggle the On/Off button.

When a string variable is selected, Z-Mail displays the Set/Unset button and a field, such as a Filename field, below the Variable Description frame.

Some variables can be turned on *and* (optionally) set to a value. For example, you can turn on **autosign** and Z-Mail will sign your messages using the ⁓/.*signature* file. Or, you can turn on **autosign** and set it to a string, in which case Z-Mail signs your messages using the specified filename or literal string (see Chapter 4 for more information). In this case, when you select the variable, Z-Mail displays an On/Off button and a field.

You can also set some variables, such as **alwaysignore**, to more than one value. For example, with **alwaysignore**, you can tell Z-Mail to ignore specific headers in some situations and not in others.

At the bottom of the Variables window are the buttons in the Action area. These buttons are listed in Table 7-23.

Table 7-23. Variables Window Buttons

Button	Description
Done	Close the Z-Mail Variables window.
Save	Save the current settings to the specified initialization file.
Load	Load a new initialization file.
Help	Get help about setting Z-Mail variables.

We'll explain these functions in the following sections.

Changing the Value of a Variable

If the Set/Unset (to set or unset a string variable) or On/Off (to toggle a boolean variable) button is depressed, the option is already selected.

To set a boolean variable, select the variable from the Variables frame. Then, select the On/Off option. If the variable is already set, this unsets the variable. For example, let's set the **hold** variable (to prevent messages that have been read from being moved to the ˜/mbox file when you quit Z-Mail). To do this, select **hold** from the Variables frame and then toggle the On/Off option.

To set a string variable, first select the variable name from the Variables frame. Then, select the Set/Unset option and the string field becomes available. Next, enter the value for the string variable in the field and press RETURN or press the Set button to the right of the string field.

For example, let's change the default folder directory by setting the **folder** variable:

1. Select **folder** from the Variables frame.

2. Select the Set/Unset option and the Pathname field becomes available.

3. Enter the full pathname of the new folder directory in the Pathname field and press RETURN or the Set button. Remember to create this directory before you try to save messages to it. For example, change the folder directory to ~/*Folders*.

Now, when you save messages to or switch folders, Z-Mail displays the contents of ~/*Folders* instead of ~/*Mail*.

Using the options in the Variables window is equivalent to setting variables using **set** from line mode and **variable** from fullscreen mode. These variables are set for the current Z-Mail session. When you leave Z-Mail, you'll lose any variable settings that you specified using this method. If you want to save your current variable settings so that you can use the same options the next time you use Z-Mail, the next section explains how to do this.

Saving the New Values

To save the current variable settings to an initialization file, use the Save button. Using Save is equivalent to using the **saveopts** command in either line or fullscreen mode. Z-Mail saves the current variable settings to the filename in the Save/Load Variables Filename field (~/*.zmailrc*, by default). If the filename listed in this field already exists, Z-Mail displays a Warning pop-up window, prompting you to overwrite the current file. This pop-up window looks like the one in Figure 7-31.

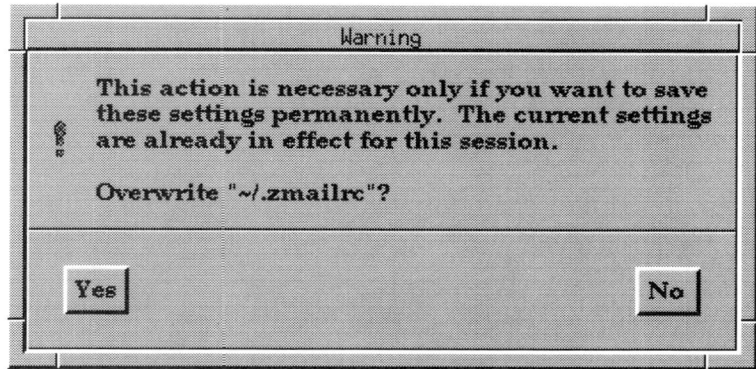

Figure 7-31. Overwrite ~/.zmailrc?

To overwrite the default ~/*.zmailrc* file, click Yes. To cancel the Save request, click No.

CAUTION

If you overwrite your *.zmailrc*, you lose your manually entered **if** statements and commands such as **fullscreen off** (if any). For this reason, be very careful with saving variable values in GUI and with **saveopts** in other modes.

To save your current settings to a file other than the default Z-Mail initialization file, enter the filename in the Save/Load Options Filename field at the top of the Z-Mail Options window *before* clicking Save.

At any time, you can read in Z-Mail settings from an alternate initialization file. This is identical to using **source** from the line and fullscreen modes. To do this from the GUI mode, enter the filename in the Save/Load Options Filename field and then click the Load button. Now the variable settings in the alternate initialization file are in effect. The settings in this file overwrite (or add to) the current settings.

Closing the Variables Window

When you're finished setting and saving variables, you can close the Variables window and return to the main Z-Mail window by clicking the Done button.

Specifying Headers to Suppress

Normally, when you view messages, Z-Mail displays all the headers in the Text frame. In most cases, only a few of these headers are interesting. To tell Z-Mail to ignore specific headers when displaying messages, pull down the Options menu and select the Headers option. You see the Mail Headers window like the one in Figure 7-32.

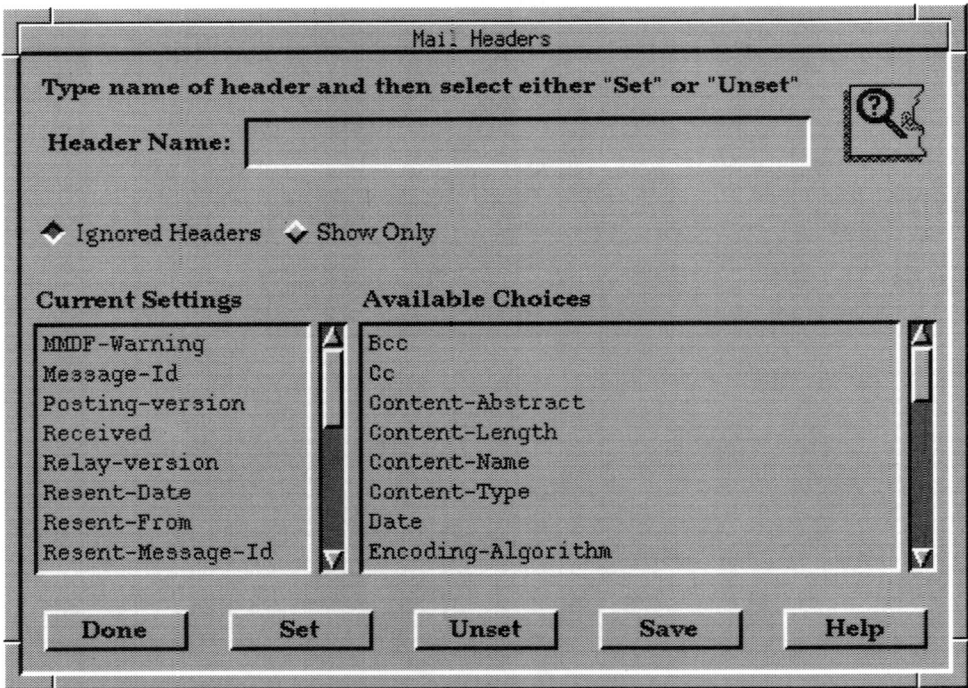

Figure 7-32. Mail Headers window

Header Name field. This field contains the name of the currently selected header. Select a header to ignore or retain and then select either the Ignored Headers or Show Only options.

Ignored Headers. Select this option to tell Z-Mail to ignore the header in the Header Name field. With this option selected, the Current Settings list contains the headers that are currently ignored.

Show Only. Use this option to tell Z-Mail to retain the header in the Header Name field. In this case, Z-Mail lists the headers that are currently retained in the Current Settings list.

In Figure 7-32, you can see that Ignored Headers is selected and that Z-Mail currently ignores five headers: `Message-Id`, `Priority`, `Received`, `Status`, and `Via`.

If you want to see a list of the headers that are retained, select Show Only. Z-Mail replaces the ignored headers in the Current Settings frame with the retained headers.

On the right in the Mail Headers window is the Available Choices frame. The Action area at the bottom of the window contains the Mail Headers buttons. Table 7-24 lists these buttons.

Table 7-24. Mail Headers Window Buttons

Button	Description
Done	Close the Mail Headers window.
Set	Specify a header to ignore or retain.
Unset	Remove an ignored or retained header.
Save	Save the current settings.
Help	Get help about specifying headers to ignore or retain.

To specify headers to ignore, select the header to ignore from the Available Choices list, select the Ignored Headers option, and then click the Set button. If you want to ignore a header that isn't listed, enter the name in the Header Name field before clicking Set. Z-Mail adds the header to the list in the Current Settings frame. This action is identical to using the **ignore** command from either the line or fullscreen mode.

Unsetting Ignored Headers

If you change your mind and decide that you'd really like to see a header that you told Z-Mail to ignore, first select the Ignored Headers option. Then, select the header name from the Current Settings frame and click the Unset button. Z-Mail removes the header from the Current Settings list. In line mode, the equivalent command is **unignore**.

Specifying Headers to Show

If you prefer, you can specify just the headers that you want to see when you view messages. To specify a header to retain, select the Show Only option, select or enter the header, and then click the Set button. Z-Mail adds the header to the Current Settings list. You use the **retain** command in the line and fullscreen modes to accomplish the same thing.

Unsetting Headers

Let's say that you don't want to see a specific header when you read messages, and you want to remove it from the list of retained headers. To do this, first select the Show Only option. Then, select the header that you no longer want to retain from the Current Settings frame and click the Unset button. Z-Mail removes the header from the Current Settings list. To do the same thing from line mode, use **unretain**.

Saving Header Settings

As with their equivalent commands in line and fullscreen mode, when you set headers to ignore or retain using the options in the Mail Headers window, Z-Mail uses the settings for the current session only. To save these settings to your ⁷/.zmailrc initialization file, click the Save button.

If the .zmailrc file already exists, Z-Mail displays a Warning pop-up box. To overwrite the file, click Yes; to cancel the operation, click No.

NOTE

If you decide to overwrite the .zmailrc file, Z-Mail saves *all* of your current settings to this file (not just the modifications to the mail headers). If you had any **if** statements in the initialization, they are lost if you overwrite the file.

Creating Personal Headers

In Chapter 4, *Sending Mail with Z-Mail*, and Chapter 6, *Using the Fullscreen Mode*, we showed you how to create personalized headers to appear in all your outgoing mail messages using the **my_hdr** (in line mode) and **my-hdrs** (in fullscreen mode) commands. To do this from the GUI mode, pull down the Options menu and select Envelope. This opens the Envelope window shown in Figure 7-33.

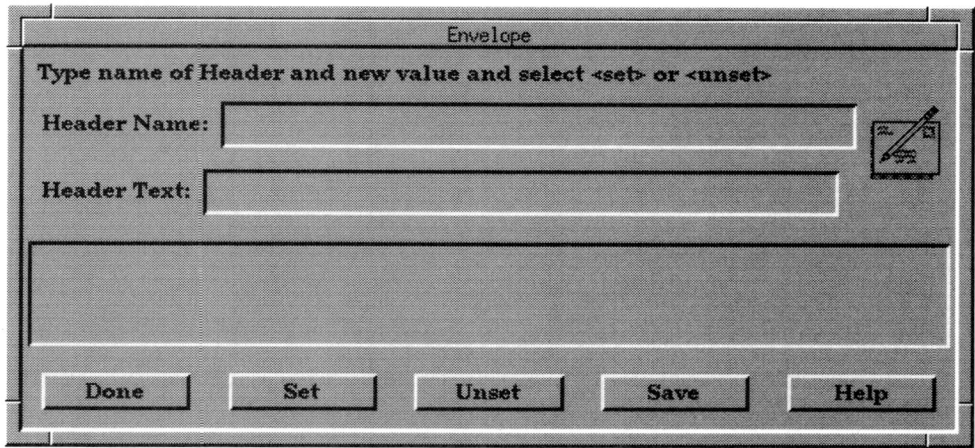

Figure 7-33. Envelope window

Header Name. Enter the name of the personal header, such as `Organization`, that you want to create.

Header Text. Enter the text, such as `Z-Code Software Corp.`, that you want to associate with the header in the Header Name field.

The Header list is where Z-Mail lists your personal headers (if any). At the bottom of the window are the Action area buttons described in Table 7-25.

Table 7-25. Envelope Window Buttons

Button	Description
Done	Close the Envelope window.
Set	Create a personal header.
Unset	Remove a personal header.
Save	Save personal header settings to the initialization file.
Help	Get help about setting personal headers.

To set a personal header, enter the name of the header in the Header Name field and press RETURN. For example, to create an `Organization` header to appear in your outgoing messages, enter **Organization** in this field.

When you press RETURN, the cursor moves to the Header Text field. Enter the text of the header in this field. For example, to set the `Organization` header to the string "Z-Code Software Corp.," enter the string in this field. Now, click the Set button in the Action area.

Z-Mail adds the the new header to the list of personal headers in the Header list. Note that Z-Mail appends a colon character (:) to the header name.

Now, when you send messages, Z-Mail includes this header along with the regular `To` and `Subject` headers. Figure 7-34 shows what this looks like.

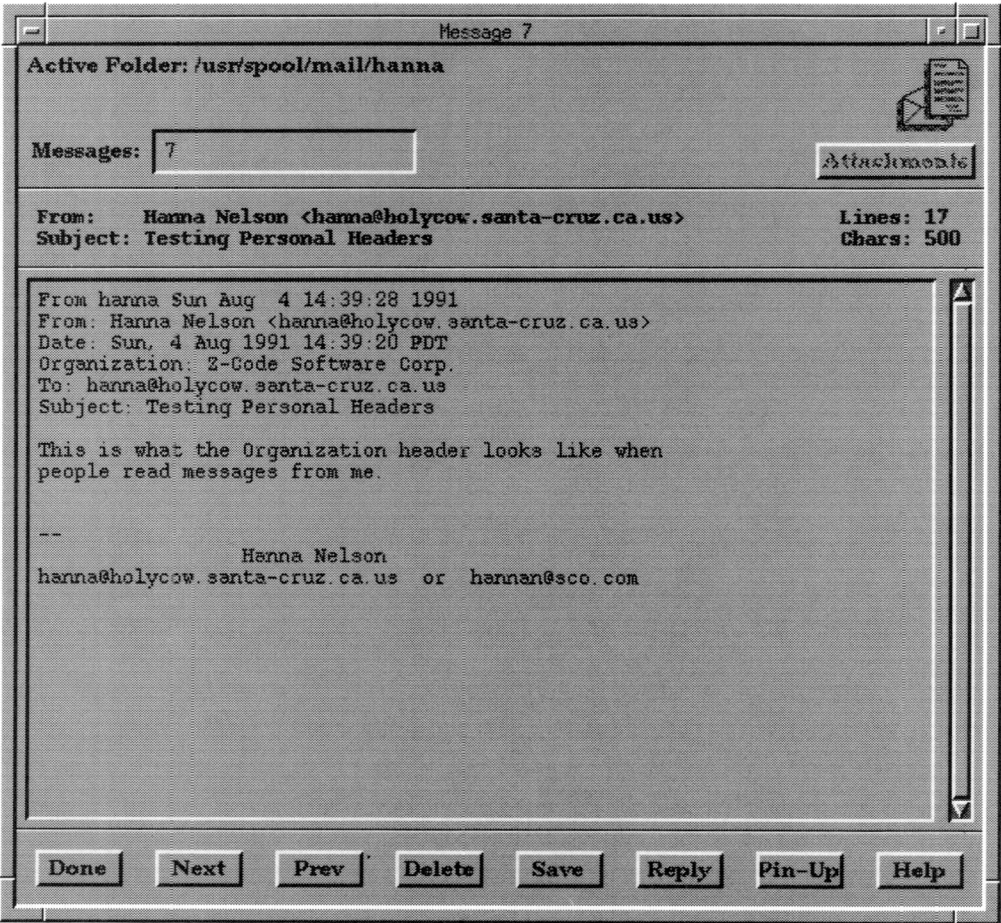

Figure 7-34. Organization header

Removing Personal Headers

If you want to change the text associated with a personal header, simply redefine the header. Enter the name of the header in the Header Name field and put the new value of the header in the Header Text field. Z-Mail replaces the old header with the new header and text in the Header list.

To remove the header from your outgoing messages, select the header in the Header list and then click the Unset button. Z-Mail removes the header from the Header list.

Saving Header Settings

When you create personal headers using the Envelope window options, Z-Mail sets the headers for the current session only. If you want to keep these settings in your initialization file, click the Save button.

If the initialization file (˜/.zmailrc) already exists, Z-Mail prompts you with a Warning pop-up box before saving the settings. As with saving other Options settings, remember that you'll lose any special functions and scripts in your initialization file if you overwrite the file in this way.

Setting Mail Aliases

A mail alias is a short name for a long mail address or group of addresses. Aliases are very handy if you send mail to a large group of people or to people with long addresses. In Chapter 4, *Sending Mail with Z-Mail*, we explain aliases and how you can set and use them. In this section we'll explain how to set them from the GUI mode.

To set up a mail alias, pull down the Options menu and select Aliases. This opens the Mail Aliases window shown in Figure 7-35.

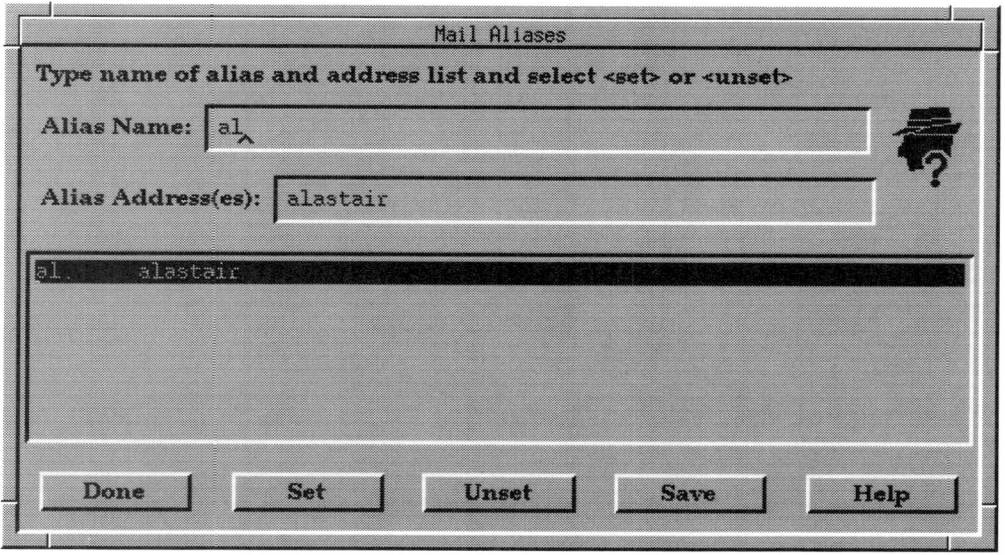

Figure 7-35. Mail Aliases Window

Alias Name. Enter the name of the mail alias that you are creating (for example, *mailmen*) in this field.

Alias Address(es). Use this field to enter the value (the long mail address or a list of addresses) of the alias in the Alias Name field.

The Alias list below these fields lists your current aliases (if any) and values. Table 7-26 describes the buttons on the Action area.

Table 7-26. Mail Aliases Window Buttons

Button	Description
Done	Close the Mail Aliases window.
Set	Set aliases.
Unset	Remove alias settings.
Save	Save alias settings in your initialization file.
Help	Get help on setting aliases.

To set a mail alias, enter the name of the alias in the Alias Name field and press RETURN. For example, to create an alias called *poets*, enter **poets** in this field. The cursor moves to the Alias Address(es) field. Enter the expansion for the alias in this field. For example, to use *poets* as a short name for *mattb*, *tim*, *andreic*, *margaret*, and *sylvia*, enter those names in the Alias Address(es) field. Now, select Set. Z-Mail puts the alias definition (name and expansion) in the Alias list. The *poets* alias is now set.

You can also create alias short names for long mail addresses. See Chapter 4 for more information about creating aliases.

Removing Alias Settings

As with the other settings in the Options menu, the alias is set for the current Z-Mail session only. To remove the alias setting, exit Z-Mail. If you want to remove the setting for the current session, select the alias from the Alias frame and click the Unset button.

Saving Alias Settings

Unless you save the alias settings to your initialization file, you'll lose them when you close the folder or quit Z-Mail. To keep the current settings, click the Save button. Z-Mail prompts you to overwrite the default ˜/.zmailrc initialization, if it already exists.

Creating a Z-Mail Function

Z-Mail provides you with the ability to write your own functions for performing specific tasks. In the line mode, you execute these functions by entering the function name at the line-mode prompt. To access these functions from the fullscreen and GUI modes, attach these functions to "buttons." Z-Mail then displays the buttons in the Action area on the main Z-Mail window. (In fullscreen mode, you display the buttons by executing the **user-button** command.)

Chapter 8, *Customizing Z-Mail*, and Chapter 9, *Writing Scripts and Functions*, discuss the syntax and special commands for creating functions in Z-Mail. In this section, we'll show you how to add functions and bind buttons to these functions from within the GUI mode; to really learn how to write functions, read these chapters.

To create a function in GUI mode, pull down the Options menu and select the Buttons option. Z-Mail opens the Buttons and Functions window like the one in Figure 7-36.

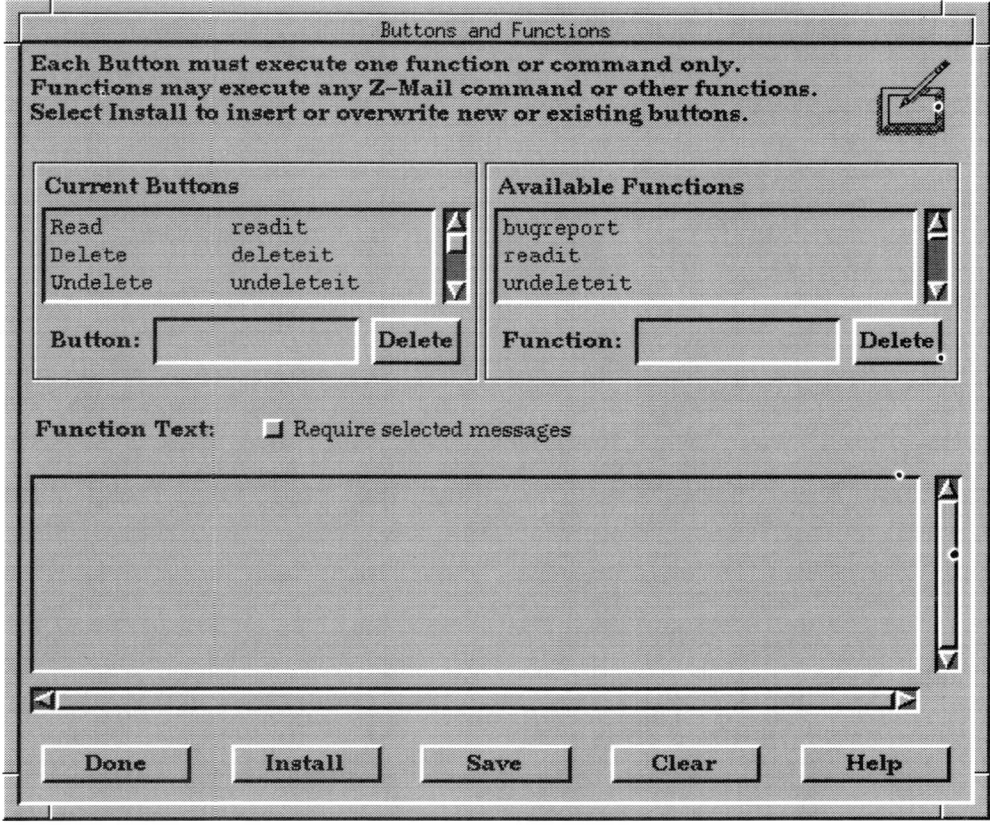

Figure 7-36. Buttons and Functions window

Current Buttons. This list contains the labels for all the buttons that are currently set and the functions that they're bound to.

Button. Enter the label of a button that you want to install or display the text in the Function Text area.

Available Functions. This list contains the names of all the functions that are currently defined. To attach a button to a function, select the function, enter the button label in the Button field, and select Install.

Delete. Use this option to remove the button from the main Z-Mail window. You can also select Delete to remove the function definition for the current Z-Mail session.

Function Text. This area contains the text of the currently selected function in either the Current Buttons or Available Functions lists. If the function that you're attaching a button to requires that you select a message before running the function, select the Require Selected Messages option.

By default, seven buttons appear in the Action area on the main Z-Mail window: Read, Delete, Undelete, Save, Compose, Reply, and Forward. These buttons (and the functions they're bound to) are defined in the default system initialization file for Z-Mail (*/usr/lib/Zmail/system.zmailrc*, by default). If the Action area on your main window doesn't list these buttons (or contains different buttons), it's because your Z-Mail administrator changed the system initialization file.

If you have buttons defined, Z-Mail lists them in the Current Buttons list in the Buttons and Functions window. To the right of this list is the Available Functions list; this is the list of current functions defined in either the system initialization file or your personal initialization file. This list shows *all* the current functions, whether they're attached to buttons or not. For example, you might have created a function to use in line mode but haven't attached it to a button for use in GUI mode yet.

Z-Mail displays the currently selected button name in the Button field, the associated function name appears in the Function field and the text of the specified function appears in the Function Text area below. To display the name and text for another function, simply select a new button from the Current Buttons list.

For example, if you select the Undelete button (this is one of the default buttons from the main Z-Mail window) from the Current Buttons list, the Button field contains "Undelete" and the Function field contains the name of the function that's associated with the Undelete button (**undeleteit**). The Function Text area contains the text of the **undeleteit** function.

Below the Function Text area is the Buttons and Functions window Action area; Table 7-27 describes the buttons in this area.

Table 7-27. Buttons and Functions Window Buttons

Button	Description
Done	Close the current window.
Install	Install the current function or button.
Save	Save the current functions and button settings.
Clear	Clear all the text fields in the window.
Help	Get help on creating functions and attaching buttons.

To create a function and bind it to a button, use this procedure:

1. First, click the Clear button to clear all the text fields in the Buttons and Functions window.

2. Enter the new function name in the Function field.

3. Enter the name of the button that you want to appear in the main Z-Mail window in the Button field.

4. Edit the Function Text area to include the new function.

5. Finally, install the new button by clicking the Install button.

Z-Mail adds the new button name to the Current Buttons list and the function to the Available Functions list.

If you've already created a function (for example, you created it to use in line mode and now you want to use it in GUI mode), you can attach a button to it now. To do this, use the following procedure:

1. Select the function name from the Available Functions list; Z-Mail puts the function name in the Function field and the text in the Function Text area. The Button field is blank.

2. Enter a name in the Button field to attach to the function.

3. Click the Install button.

Z-Mail adds the new button name to the Current Buttons list and puts the button in the Action area on the main Z-Mail window. You can now access that function from GUI mode simply by clicking the button.

Some commands (and by extension, functions) require that you select messages to act upon. For example, if you created a special **reply** function to reply to everyone on the distribution list, you would want to select a message (or messages) to reply to. If your function acts on a message list, select the Require Selected Messages option. Now, if you execute the function without first selecting a message list, Z-Mail displays a warning pop-up box, reminding you to select a message.

Functions and button definitions that you create with the options on this window are only available for the current Z-Mail session; they disappear when you exit Z-Mail. If you want to remove a button setting for the current session without leaving the program, select the button from the Current Buttons list and click the Delete button to the left of the Button field. The procedure is the same for removing function definitions, except that you should use the Available Functions list and the Function field.

Functions that you set by clicking Install are only available for the current Z-Mail session. When you quit Z-Mail, the functions and button settings are lost. To retain these settings, click the Save button. If ~/.zmailrc already exists, Z-Mail prompts you to overwrite the file. Click Yes to save the function settings; No to cancel the Save operation.

You can use any of the icons from the GUI mode (in the Toolbox window) in your own functions using the **dialog** command. For example, if you want your function to pop up the Printer dialog box, include **dialog printer** in your function definition in ~/.zmailrc:

```
function printmessage(){
    dialog Printer
}
```

If you attach the **printmessage** function to a button, Z-Mail installs a new button in the main Z-Mail window. You can then access the Printer dialog by clicking the new button. We'll explain more about creating functions, calling dialogs, and attaching buttons in Chapter 9.

Moving and Resizing Windows

When you perform a function that opens a new window (for example, when you click Read to view a message), the current window might cover previous windows. Let's say you want to look at the main Z-Mail window without closing the Message Display window. You can either move or resize (or both) the window on the top. The following procedures are not specific to Z-Mail but are a function of the window manager you use. Here they are specific to Motif.

Moving a Window

To move the window on the top to another location on your screen so that the window below becomes visible, follow these steps:

1. Move the pointer to the title bar of the window that you want to move.

2. Press and hold down the mouse button. The pointer changes to a cross.

3. Holding down the mouse button, move the window to another location.

4. When the window is where you want it, release the mouse button.

Resizing a Window

To change the size of a Z-Mail window, follow these steps:

1. Move the pointer to any corner or edge of the window that you want to resize.

2. Press and hold the mouse button. The cursor changes to an arrow.

3. While holding down the mouse button, move the pointer, making the window larger or smaller.

4. Release the mouse button when the window is the desired size.

You can also move and resize windows using options on the root pull-down menu. See your window manager documentation for more information about manipulating windows.

Changing Window Colors

The Z-Mail X client is built using the Motif and Open Look programming libraries; these libraries are based on a lower-level library called the X Toolkit (Xt). Xt, Motif, and Open Look define each user-interface object as a *widget*. Some widgets, such as buttons or scrollbars, are things that you see and interact with; other widgets (called managers) control the layout. You can configure the attributes of each widget by specifying *resources*.

You can change the colors of specific Z-Mail windows by specifying the background and foreground (text) colors (resources) of these widgets. The syntax for specifying resource attributes is too complex for the scope of this book; we won't discuss it here. For a more complete explanation, see the *X Window System User's Guide*, Volume Three of the X Window Series from O'Reilly & Associates, by Valerie Quercia and Tim O'Reilly.

However, if you want to change the resource settings for any X client (Z-Mail included), you need to know the names of the particular widgets in the client that you want to change (in addition to knowing how to specify resources). The widgets in the Z-Mail client that you can configure by specifying the resources are listed in Table 7-28.

Table 7-28. Z-Mail Widgets

Z-Mail Widget	Description
main_window	Z-Mail main window.
toolbox_window	Toolbox window.
help_index_dialog	Help window.
message_window	Read window.
pinup_window	Pin-up window.
save_dialog	Save Messages Dialog Box.
printer_dialog	Printer Dialog Box.
compose_window	Compose window.
templates_dialog	Templates Dialog Box.
editor_dialog	Search and Replace Dialog Box.

Table 7-28. Z-Mail Widgets (continued)

Z-Mail Widget	Description
attachments_dialog	Attachments Dialog Box.
folders_dialog	Folders Dialog Box.
search_dialog	Pattern Search Dialog Box.
dates_dialog	Date Search Dialog Box.
sort_dialog	Custom Sort Dialog Box.
variables_dialog	Variables Dialog Box.
headers_dialog	Headers Dialog Box.
envelope_dialog	Envelope Dialog Box.
alias_dialog	Mail Aliases Dialog Box.
buttons_dialog	Buttons and Functions Dialog Box.

One way to change the colors of Z-Mail windows is to place commands in a special file, called *.Xdefaults*, located in your home directory. For example, you can change the background color of all the Z-Mail windows to BlueViolet by adding the following line to your ⁻/.Xdefaults file:

```
Zmail*background:   BlueViolet
```

For a list of the colors available on your X Window system to customize your X clients, see the right-hand column of the */usr/lib/X11/rgb.txt* file.

Reviewing the GUI Mode

In this chapter, we showed you how to use Z-Mail in the X Window based GUI mode. If you're interested in creating your own functions to access from the main Z-Mail window, I recommend that you become familiar with the line-mode commands presented in Chapter 3, *Reading and Managing Mail*, Chapter 4, *Sending Mail with Z-Mail*, and Chapter 5, *Z-Mail Shortcuts, Bells, and Whistles*. Once you're familiar with the line-mode commands, you have the background necessary for learning to create scripts and functions using the Z-Script scripting language. For more information, see Chapter 8, *Customizing Z-Mail*, and Chapter 9, *Writing Scripts and Functions*.

8
Customizing Z-Mail

In previous chapters, we showed you how to use different variables and commands to modify the default behavior of Z-Mail for the current session. As we explained earlier, these modifications are set for the current Z-Mail session only; the settings disappear when you exit the program. However, you can make your customizations permanent by placing the commands and variable settings in your personal initialization file (˜/.zmailrc, by default or .mushrc in MUSH).

In this chapter, we'll show you how to use initialization files to customize Z-Mail. We'll explain the format of the initialization file and introduce you to some of the elements of the Z-Script language. We'll show you how to read in commands at startup time and at any time from within Z-Mail. We'll give you a sample .zmailrc file and explain the different variable settings. Then, we'll describe the variables that we haven't covered in previous chapters. Finally, we'll show you how to use initialization files to emulate other mailers and text editors and how to use filters to manipulate the messages in your folder.

Because we expect you to set the variables described in this chapter in your initialization file rather than at the line-mode prompt, most of the examples included here don't show this prompt.

Modifying Z-Mail Initialization

In this section, we'll discuss how Z-Mail initialization works and how you can change the default behavior of Z-Mail by running commands and setting variables in your initialization file.

Every time you invoke the Z-Mail program, it reads the *system initialization file*. This file is */usr/lib/Zmail/system.zmailrc*, by default or *usr/lib/Mushrc* in MUSH. The system administrator sets up this file with system-wide alias definitions and variable settings that affect all the Z-Mail users on your system. If the system administrator changes the location of the Z-Mail library directory (by default, */usr/lib/Zmail*), you can set the ZMLIB environment variable to the new location.

 Another way to specify the Z-Mail library directory is to set it at the UNIX prompt with the following command:

```
$ zmail —lib /usr/local/lib/Zmail
```

You can customize your own Z-Mail environment by placing macro, alias, and command-line definitions as well as other commands and variable settings in your personal initialization file, ˜/.zmailrc. Then, you set up Z-Mail to read in your personal file automatically when you start up the program. Your own settings overwrite (or add to) the system-wide initialization settings.

Specifying an Initialization File

The easiest way to set up your Z-Mail environment is to create a file called *.zmailrc* in your home directory. Z-Mail automatically reads that file after reading the system initialization file.

You can tell Z-Mail to read another file at initialization time by setting the **ZMAILRC** or **MAILRC** environment variable. (The **MUSHRC** environment variable is in MUSH.) After reading the system initialization file, Z-Mail looks at your environment settings. Environment variables are set in your ˜/.*login* (if you're using C shell) or ˜/.*profile* (for Bourne and Korn shells) files. If you have the **ZMAILRC** or **MAILRC** variable set to a filename, Z-Mail reads the specified file. For example, let's say I have this (Korn or Bourne shell) environment variable setting in my *.profile* file:

```
ZMAILRC=/u/hanna/.zminit
export ZMAILRC
```

When I start up the program, Z-Mail reads the system initialization file and then checks my environment settings. Because **ZMAILRC** is set, Z-Mail then reads the *.zminit* file in my home directory.

If you don't set **ZMAILRC** or **MAILRC**, Z-Mail reads the default initialization file, ˜/.*zmailrc*, if it exists. Otherwise, Z-Mail looks for ˜/.*mushrc*. (MUSH looks for ˜/.*mushrc* and ˜/.*mailrc*). If these files don't exist, Z-Mail uses only the system initialization file to set up the environment.

Command-line Options and Initialization Files

Because Z-Mail interprets the command-line options before reading any initialization files, you can use these options to change the order in which Z-Mail reads the files and even specify other files to read.

For example, to force Z-Mail to source a specified personal initialization file *before* the system initialization file, use the **–init** (**–I**) command-line option:

```
$ zmail —init ˜/.Zinit
```

When you invoke Z-Mail with this command line, Z-Mail first reads ˜/.*Zinit*, then the system initialization file, and finally your ˜/.*zmailrc* file, if it exists. Note that the settings in subsequent files override the previous settings. Thus, if you set a variable in ˜/.*Zinit* that is also set with the system initialization file, you lose your personal setting when Z-Mail reads the second file.

What if you want Z-Mail to read a particular initialization file, but not the system initialization file? Let's say you're on a Berkeley UNIX System and you want to use the default settings for *Mail*. To do this, use the **–init!** (**–I!**) option. For example:

```
$ zmail —init! /usr/lib/Mail.rc
```

We'll explain more about this in the section "Emulating Other Mailers and Editors" later in this chapter.

If you don't want Z-Mail to read the system initialization file at all, use the **–noinit** (**–n**) command-line option:

```
$ zmail —noinit
```

In this case, Z-Mail only reads ⁓/.*zmailrc*.

Use **–noinit!** (**–n!**) to prevent Z-Mail from sourcing *any* initialization files. For example, use the following command to invoke Z-Mail:

```
$ zmail —noinit!
```

In this case, Z-Mail uses only the built-in default settings. To see what these settings are, invoke **zmail** with the **–noinit!** option and then enter **set** at the Z-Mail prompt. As an example, here are the built-in settings on my machine:

```
cmd_help        /usr/lib/Zmail/cmd_help
cwd             /u/hanna
dead            ⁓/dead.letter
escape          ⁓
folder          ⁓/Mail
hdr_format      %25f %7d (%l/%c)
hold
home            /u/hanna
hostname        holycow
indent_str      >
mbox            ⁓/mbox
nonobang
prompt          Msg %m of %t:
realname        Hanna Nelson
tmpdir          /tmp
```

Table 8-1 shows where Z-Mail gets the values for these variables. Built-in default variables are read from the */usr/lib/Zmail/variables* file; if this file can't be read, Z-Mail won't run.

Table 8-1. Z-Mail Default Variables

Variable	Description
cmd_help	Searched for in */usr/lib/Zmail* or **$ZMLIB**.
cwd	Set at startup time.
dead	Built-in default.
escape	Built-in default.
folder	Built-in default.
hdr_format	Built-in default.
hold	Built-in default.
home	**$HOME** environment variable or */etc/passwd*.

Table 8-1. Z-Mail Default Variables (continued)

Variable	Description
hostname	*uname* (or *gethostname* on BSD UNIX).
indent_str	Built-in default.
mbox	Built-in default.
nonobang	Built-in default.
prompt	Built-in default.
realname	*/etc/passwd* or **$NAME** environment variable.
tmpdir	Built-in default.

To read an initialization file *after* the system initialization file and ¯/.*zmailrc* have been read, use the **–source** (**–F**) option:

```
$ zmail —source ˜/.init.file
```

This option reads the file *after* scanning the folder so you can include commands that manipulate messages, such as **sort** and **from**. Note that when you use **–source**, Z-Mail doesn't display the header summaries at startup time.

Sourcing an Initialization File

Once you have invoked Z-Mail and you're in the program, you can read in commands from any initialization file using the **source** command. Use this command if you want to read from a file other than the default file or to re-source the default file after making changes to it. You can also define lengthy or complex commands in a file, called a *script*, to execute using **source**. We'll explain more about scripts later in this chapter and in Chapter 9, *Writing Scripts and Functions*.

The syntax for **source** looks like this:

```
source [ file ]
```

If you don't specify a *file* to source, Z-Mail reads commands from the initialization file described by the **ZMAILRC** or **MAILRC** environment variables, if they're set. If neither is set, Z-Mail reads from .*zmailrc* in your home directory, if it exists.

Saving the Current Settings

If you set variables, or created mail aliases, command-line aliases, or macros from the Z-Mail command line, Z-Mail uses them for the current session. However, once you leave the program, these settings are lost. To save them from within Z-Mail, use the **saveopts** command. This command is most useful for creating an initialization file the first time you use Z-Mail.

Here's the syntax for **saveopts**:

```
saveopts [ filename ]
```

If you don't specify a filename with **saveopts**, this command saves the current settings to the initialization file described by the **ZMAILRC** or **MAILRC** environment variables, if set. If neither are set, the options are saved to the ˜/.zmailrc file, if it exists. If it doesn't exist, Z-Mail creates a file called .zmailrc in your home directory and saves the options to it.

If you specify another file to save the settings to, for example, ˜/.options, Z-Mail displays a message like this:

```
Saved options to ~/.options.
```

If you specify an existing filename, Z-Mail prompts you to confirm:

```
Overwrite "~/options"? (y/n) [n] _
```

If you enter **y**, you overwrite the existing file; otherwise, press RETURN to cancel the **saveopts** command.

CAUTION

If you have any conditional (**if**) statements or other manually-entered comments in the file, they are lost when you use **saveopts**. We'll explain more about these conditional statements later.

Initialization File Format

By default, Z-Mail reads ˜/.zmailrc (or an initialization file that you specify with **$ZMAILRC**) last. So, to override or turn off any system initialization settings, specify your own values in this file.

This section explains the format for including Z-Mail commands, variable settings, and comments in your personal initialization file. In addition, we'll explain some of the basics of the Z-Script scripting language. We'll show you how to use conditional statements to test for certain conditions, such as the current mode, before running commands or setting variables, how to use expression operators to compare variables with constants, how to negate an expression, and how to check to see if a variable is set.

Putting Comments in the Initialization File

Comments are ways to document what the commands are doing in your initialization file. It's a good idea to comment your commands to remind you (and other people who might read and use your initialization file) later what you are thinking of now.

Z-Mail recognizes the pound character (**#**) as a comment character in initialization files. You can place this character in any column on the line; Z-Mail doesn't look at anything following the **#** character on the line. For example:

```
# This is a comment line.
cmd H 'headers +' # Use "H" instead of "headers +"
```

If you want to include a **#** without it being interpreted as a comment, put it in single (') or double (") quotes:

```
set prompt="Message #%m:  "
```

Because the **#** appears within the double quotes, Z-Mail doesn't ignore everything following it. This command sets the prompt to:

```
Message #
```

followed by the current message number. (For more information about the special characters that you can use in your prompt, see the discussion of the **prompt** variable in Chapter 3, *Reading and Managing Mail*.)

Conditional Statements

In initialization files such as ~/.zmailrc (and in Z-Mail scripts), a conditional statement is used to test certain conditions, such as the mode Z-Mail is running in or the value of a particular variable, before executing commands.

Conditional statements begin with an **if** expression and end with **endif**. The syntax looks like this:

```
if expression
        action
else
        alternate_action
endif
```

The *expression* can be any Z-Mail variable, environment variable, user-defined variable, comparison operation, or one of the six mode-testing Z-Mail variables that we'll explain in the next section. The *action* is the Z-Mail command or commands that you want to execute if *expression* evaluates to true. If *expression* evaluates to false, Z-Mail executes the commands specified by *alternate_action*. (We'll explain **else** later in this chapter.) The expression always appears on a separate line from the action and parentheses are not allowed.

 Here's an example that tests to see what the terminal type is before setting the number of lines of message text to display (we'll explain the **==** format later in this chapter):

```
if $TERM == vt100          # if the value of $TERM is "vt100"
        set crt = 24       # set the crt variable to 24
endif
```

All variables, except the mode-testing variables (which we'll get to in the next section), can be referenced by preceding the variable name with a dollar sign ($), such as **$TERM** and **$folder**.

In this case, if the *expression* (**$TERM == vt100**) evaluates to true, then Z-Mail sets the value of **crt** to 24.

You can nest **if** statements as deep as you like; just remember to include an **endif** for each **if**:

```
if expression
    if expression2
```

```
        if expression3
            if expression4
                action
            endif
        endif
    endif
endif
```

In the example above, the *action* is performed only if all four *expressions* are true.

Note that we use indentation to distinguish between each nested level. The format isn't necessary to run the script, but it makes the script easier to read.

More than one action (and action line) is allowed per **if** statement, so you can create a conditional statement that looks like this:

```
if expression
    action1 ; action2 ; action3
endif
```

or like this:

```
if expression
    action1
    action2
    action3
endif
```

However, you can only evaluate one conditional expression on each **if** line. You **cannot** evaluate multiple expressions with "logical AND" (**&&**) or "logical OR" (**||**) expressions.

Using the Mode-testing Variables

Z-Mail includes six variables that you can use in scripts to test the mode in which Z-Mail is running. You can only use these special variables, called *mode-testing variables*, in conditional **if** statements to determine the current mode; you can't reference them in other situations. Table 8-2 lists the mode-testing variables. Note that in MUSH the **is_gui** variable is equivalent to **istool** and **is_fullscreen** is equivalent to **iscurses**.

Table 8-2. Mode-testing Variables

Variable	Evaluates to True if:
is_gui	You are invoking Z-Mail in GUI mode using **zmail** with the **–gui** option from the UNIX command line. In MUSH, the **is_gui** variable is called **istool**.
is_fullscreen	Z-Mail is in or is being invoked in fullscreen mode using the **–fullscreen** (**–V**) option. In MUSH, use the **iscurses** variable in place of **is_fullscreen**.
is_shell	You are in the Z-Mail program. In other words, you aren't calling Z-Mail to send mail from the UNIX prompt.

Table 8-2. Mode-testing Variables (continued)

Variable	Evaluates to True if:
is_sending	You are sending mail from the UNIX command line.
hdrs_only	You invoked Z-Mail with the **–headers** (**–H**) option.
redirect	You are redirecting input to Z-Mail.

Because Z-Mail treats these variables differently in **if** expressions, you do not need to preface them with the dollar sign character (**$**).

Let's write a conditional statement that tests to see if Z-Mail is running in fullscreen mode before setting some common fullscreen-mode variables:

```
if is_fullscreen          # if we're in fullscreen mode,
      set screen = 15      # set value of screen variable to 15
      set fullscreen_help  # and put help information on screen
endif
```

If you're using Z-Mail in fullscreen mode, this statement sets the number of the header summaries to display to 15. This **if** statement also sets **fullscreen_help**, so that Z-Mail shows some common key-bindings at the bottom of the fullscreen-mode display. However, if you enter fullscreen mode from line mode, this script isn't executed. In this case, use the **source** command (the default binding for **source** in fullscreen mode is the left parenthesis character) to read the script from fullscreen mode.

In this situation, using the **if** statement to test the mode before setting variables reduces the number of variables that you set when Z-Mail reads the script file. This can speed up the time it takes for Z-Mail to start up. We'll cover other advantages to the **if** statement using examples in the following sections.

The is_sending Variable

Use the **is_sending** variable to test if you're sending mail. You might want to use this test to set variables that affect Z-Mail only while sending mail. Let's set a few of these variables:

```
if is_sending             # if we're sending mail
      set editor=/bin/vi   # set these variables
      set autoedit edit_hdrs autosign
endif
```

This statement sets the variables only if you send mail from the UNIX command line with **zmail**. (If you send mail with **mail** from the Z-Mail line-mode prompt, **is_sending** evaluates to false so the variables are not set.)

In a situation where you send a message and enter the Z-Mail program in one command like this:

```
$ zmail —f ~/mbox —s "Sending a Message" dan bart
```

is_sending is true until you press CTRL-D to send the message. At that point, you enter Z-Mail and **is_sending** is no longer true. So, if you want to execute commands even after you enter Z-Mail, don't include them in a conditional **is_sending** statement.

The is_shell Variable

Because many commands, such as the ones that manipulate messages and folders, can only be run from within Z-Mail, you can use the **is_shell** variable to test if Z-Mail is ready to accept interactive commands or commands that manipulate messages. (In other words, Z-Mail has read in messages from the folder before running them.) For example, if you want to pick out messages from a certain user (see Chapter 5, *Z-Mail Shortcuts, Bells, and Whistles*), Z-Mail must have already opened the folder.

The **is_shell** variable is false when you enter the program. Once you read an initialization file with the **source** command or with the **–source** (**–F**) option at the command line, the variable becomes true. (Remember, when you use **–source**, Z-Mail reads the specified initialization file *after* reading the system initialization file and *˜/.zmailrc*, and after opening the folder.) So, if you invoke Z-Mail like this:

```
$ zmail —source ˜/.zmailrc
```

or enter the following command from the Z-Mail prompt:

```
Msg 3 of 10: source ˜/.zmailrc
```

then **is_shell** is true. Thus, when you're sending mail from the UNIX command line, **is_shell** is false, but **is_sending** is true.

Let's use **is_shell** to test whether or not Z-Mail has opened the folder, then pick out messages from MMDF (regardless of case), and save them to a file:

```
if is_shell # if Z-Mail has opened the folder
    pick —f —i MMDF | save ˜/mail.error
      # select/save mail error messages
endif
```

Because we placed the **pick** statement within the **if** expression, Z-Mail does not run the commands until **is_shell** is true. So, if you invoke Z-Mail *without* the **–source** option, the messages from MMDF are not saved. Once you read in the initialization file (either by specifying **–source** at the UNIX command line or by entering **source** at the Z-Mail command line), **is_shell** becomes true and Z-Mail saves the messages.

Note that Z-Mail doesn't display the header summaries at startup time when you use **–source** (unless you also use the **–fullscreen** option (**–V**) to enter fullscreen mode). To tell Z-Mail to display the header summaries, include the **headers** command at the end of your script. For example, modify the script in the last example as follows:

```
if is_shell # if Z-Mail has opened the folder
    pick —f —i MMDF | save ˜/mail.error
      # select/save mail error messages
endif
headers   # display the header summaries at startup time
```

Now, Z-Mail opens the folder, picks out and saves the messages from MMDF, and then displays the header summaries in the folder.

The redirect Variable

Ordinarily, when you use command-line redirection, the **redirect** mode-testing variable evaluates to true. In addition, any time you run Z-Mail when not connected to a terminal (for example, with *rsh*), Z-Mail thinks that you're redirecting input. For example, let's say you're sending a file using the following command:

```
$ zmail —subject "Testing Redirection" dan bart < redirect
```

In this example, Z-Mail addresses the message to *dan* and *bart*, puts "Testing Redirection" in the `Subject` line (the –s option), and includes the file *redirect*. This all happens without input from the terminal; when it finishes, all you see is the UNIX prompt. Remember that when you use redirection, Z-Mail doesn't add a signature or fortune to your outgoing mail. In this case, **redirect** evaluates to true.

However, if you use the **–interact** (**–i**) command-line option as in the following example:

```
$ zmail —interact —subject "Testing Redirection" dan bart < redirect
```

Z-Mail echoes the process to your screen:

```
To: dan, bart
Subject: Testing Redirection

Here's the contents of the redirect file.
Let's test and see how it appears with
the —i option.

$
```

In this case, **redirect** evaluates to false. Keep this in mind when using the **redirect** option in your scripts.

Let's say you have **record** set to save all of your outgoing messages to a folder, but you don't want to save the messages when you send files using command-line redirection. Here's where **redirect** comes in handy. Use this script to unset **record** when you redirect input from files:

```
if redirect       # if we're redirecting input from a file
    unset record # don't save the outgoing message
endif
```

This prevents Z-Mail from saving any outgoing messages that you send with command-line redirection.

With this script, Z-Mail unsets the **record** variable only if **redirect** is true (in other words, you don't have to set **record** again after this **if** expression). However, if you use the **–interact** option on your command line, **redirect** is false and thus **record** remains set.

Negating an Expression

Use an exclamation mark (!) to negate a conditional expression in the **if** statement. For example, if you want to set specific variables only if you're *not* running Z-Mail in GUI mode, you can check that **is_gui** is not true. Here's an example:

```
if !is_gui              # if we're not in GUI mode
        set ask askcc # prompt for Subject and Cc when sending mail
        set cmd_help = /usr/lib/zmail.help # set regular help
endif
```

This command sets variables that you don't use in GUI mode only if you are *not* invoking Z-Mail in GUI mode.

Evaluating a String Expression

In our previous examples, we tested variables to see if they evaluated as true or false. You can also evaluate string expressions. String expressions are usually used to compare string variables with *constants* (values that don't change).

Let's say you want to test a variable setting against a value and then base your action on that. To do this, use one of the expression operators in Table 8-3. With the relational operators, you can compare strings and numbers to each other, but you can't compare strings to numbers and vice versa.

Table 8-3. Expression Operators

Operator	Description
==	Equality (the value on the left-hand side equals the value on the right).
!=	Inequality.
=˜	String on the left-hand side matches pattern on the right containing:
	* Match any string of characters.
	? Match a single character.
	[ ] Match any of the characters enclosed in square brackets.
!˜	String on the left-hand side does not match pattern on the right.
<	Value on the left is less than the value on the right.
<=	Left value is less than or equal to the right value.
>	Left value is greater than the right value.
>=	Left value is greater than or equal to the right value.

One common use of string expressions is to test a variable to see if it is equal to a constant. For example, because you might use Z-Mail on different terminals, you can use a string expression to test if the value of a constant, like **$TERM**, is equal to a variable, such as a specific terminal type. The following example shows how to do this:

```
if $TERM == adm3a      # if the terminal is an adm3a
    set pager = more   # use more
else
    set pager = less   # use less
endif
```

This statement checks your terminal type (the value of the **$TERM** environment variable) and compares it (using = =) to the string "adm3a." If the value of **$TERM** is "adm3a," it sets the **pager** variable to the UNIX command *more*; if not, **pager** is set to *less* because the *less* pager doesn't work correctly with the terminal type "adm3a."

Conversely, use the inequality operator **!=** to test for inequality:

```
if $TERM != adm3a      # if the terminal is anything but adm3a
    set pager = less # use less
endif
```

This sets **pager** to *less* if you're using any terminal other than an "adm3a."

 Another common use of the expression operator is to test for the version number of your Z-Mail software. (It's a good idea to include tests like this if you plan to run (or distribute) your scripts for use on MUSH and different versions of Z-Mail.) This script tests the value of **$version** against the current release of Z-Mail:

```
if "$version" !~ *Z*Mail*2.0*
    exit
endif
```

If the value of **$version** does not match ***Z*Mail*2.0*** on the right-hand side, this script exits.

Z-Mail doesn't allow you to compare variables to an empty string; if you try, you get an error message when Z-Mail reads the script. For example, let's say you want to perform an action only if a variable isn't set. You might want to preserve specific messages if **keepsave** isn't set. If you use a conditional statement like this:

```
if $keepsave != ""
    pick -s Z-Mail | preserve
endif
```

 Z-Mail complains that **keepsave** is an undefined variable. However, you can test to see if a variable is set using **$?**:

```
    $?variable_name
```

Use an exclamation mark (!) to negate the expression:

```
! $?variable_name
```

So, in our previous example, to test if **keepsave** is set, use the following format:

```
if ! $?keepsave                 # if $keepsave isn't set
    pick -s Z-Mail | preserve # preserve messages about Z-Mail
endif
```

If **keepsave** isn't set, this statement preserves all the messages with "Z-Mail" in the Subject header. (If **keepsave** is set, this statement doesn't do anything.)

Here's another example that checks to see if the **mbox** variable is set before switching to the folder specified by **$mbox**. If **mbox** isn't set, the statement sets **$mbox** to ~/Mail/mbox and then switches to that folder:

```
if $?mbox                    # if $mbox is set
        folder $mbox         # open $mbox
else
        set folder = ~/Mail  # set folder directory to ~/Mail
        set mbox = +mbox     # open mbox in $folder
        folder $mbox         # open $mbox
endif
```

Use =~ and !~ for matching patterns on the right-hand side. For example, use =~ to test to see if the name of your terminal type begins with a "W" or "w" followed by a "y" and any string of characters (for example, a Wyse) before setting **crt** to 24 (the number of lines on a Wyse terminal):

```
if $TERM =~ [Ww]y*    # if the terminal is any kind of Wyse
    set screen = 24   # set the crt variable to 24
endif
```

Use !~ to test for patterns that do not match. For example, this script tests to see if the **EDITOR** environment variable includes the string "vi." If it doesn't, Z-Mail sets **editor** to vi:[1]

```
if $EDITOR !~ *vi # if the value of $EDITOR doesn't include "vi"
    set editor = "/usr/bin/vi" # set editor to vi
endif
```

Using File Test Operations

When referencing folders in initialization files, you can test to make sure the folders exist and contain information before using them.

 For example, to test if a folder exists before you switch to it, use the −e (−exist) option. This statement tests to make sure we're in Z-Mail and then verifies that the ~/mbox file exists before switching to it:

```
set mbox=~/mbox          # set local mbox variable to $mbox
if is_shell              # if Z-Mail read the folder
    if −e $mbox          # test to see if that $mbox exists
        folder $mbox # switch to $mbox
    endif
endif
```

---

[1] *vi* might be located in a different directory on your system.

In this case, if *mbox* doesn't exist, this statement does nothing and if the *mbox* folder exists, the statement switches you to that folder. However, if *mbox* exists and is empty, you see the following message:

```
Msg 0 of 0: _
```

 Here's where the **–z** (**–zero-length**) option comes in handy. Use **–z** with **–e** to test if an existing file is empty (zero-length) or not. In this example, we test to make sure a folder exists and is *not* empty (using the negation character ! with **–z**) before switching to it:

```
if is_shell
    if -e ~/outgoing.mail          # if outgoing.mail exists,
        if !-z ~/outgoing.mail     # and is not empty,
            folder ~/outgoing.mail # open the folder
        endif
    endif
endif
```

Both of these scripts test to see if *~/outgoing.mail* is empty; if it is, instead of switching to the empty folder, Z-Mail does nothing. If it isn't empty, you switch to the *~/outgoing.mail* folder.

Specifying an Alternate Action

If you want to perform an alternate action to execute in cases where the expression in your conditional statement evaluates to false, use the **else** expression with **if** and **endif**, as in the following:

```
if expression
    action
else
    alternate_action
endif
```

Use **else** on a line by itself.

Here's an example of how to use **else** to specify an alternate action:

```
if hdrs_only # if we're just displaying header summaries
    set hdr_format="%22a %M %-2N %5T  %.33s" # use this format
else
    set hdr_format='%22n %M %-2N %5T (%1) %.25s' # use this format
endif
```

The **else** expression specifies what to do if **hdrs_only** evaluates to false. So, if you invoke Z-Mail by entering this command at the UNIX prompt:

```
$ zmail -H
```

then **hdrs_only** is true and the script sets **hdr_format** like this:

```
set hdr_format="%22a %M %-2N %5T  %.33s"
```

In this case, Z-Mail displays the header summaries in the specified format in your system mailbox without starting the program. The format looks like this:

```
       1  U   cooper@holycow.UUCP   Dec  7 11:22  Re: Z-Mail Chapters
       2  p   albert@ucscc.edu      Dec 13 10:37  Z-Mail
       3      luciem                Dec 21  9:50  phone message
       4    r davidn@castle.edinburg Dec 30 11:31  $$
    >  5  N   dave                  Dec 30 11:31  Chapter 8
       6  N   joyce@dublin.edu      Dec 31  2:23  Ulysses
```

(If you use **zmail –H:n**, Z-Mail displays only the header summaries for the new messages in your system mailbox.)

On the other hand, if you don't use **–H** when entering **zmail** at the UNIX prompt, the script sets a different **hdr_format**, and starts the Z-Mail program. When you enter Z-Mail, the **hdr_format** looks like this:

```
    [0]+ "/usr/spool/mail/hanna":  5 messages, 2 new,  1 unread, 0 deleted
       1  U   Dale Cooper       Dec  7  11:22  (51)   Re: Z-Mail Chapters
       2  p   Albert Einstein   Dec 13  10:37  (88)   Z-Mail
       3      Lucie             Dec 21   9:50  (12)   phone message
       4    r D Neilson         Dec 30  11:31  (98)   $$
    >  5  N   Mr. Dave          Dec 30  11:31  (20)   Chapter 8
       6  N   James Joyce       Dec 31   2:23  (8008) Ulysses
    Msg 5 of 6:  _
```

(Note the different formats for the authors' names.)

When you use **else** in conditional statements, don't forget the **endif**.

The exit Command

Another way to speed up Z-Mail initialization is to include the **exit** command. In line mode, **exit** quits the Z-Mail program; in the initialization file, **exit** tells Z-Mail to stop reading the file. Note that the **exit** command works identically in scripts as it does in functions.

If your statement is:

```
    if is_fullscreen
         set screen=12 fullscreen_help
         exit # Quit reading this file.
    endif
```

Z-Mail tests to see if you're in fullscreen mode, sets the variables and then stops reading the initialization file. Note that if you have any mail aliases or other settings defined *after* this statement, Z-Mail doesn't set them. For this reason, make sure that you include all the general (not mode-specific) initialization *before* any conditional statements that include **exit**.

Another way to exit from a script is to use the **return** command. Because **return** gives you more control over the status of the script when you exit, we encourage you to use **return** in place of **exit**. We'll explain more about **return** in Chapter 9, *Writing Scripts and Functions*.

Z-Mail Commands in the Initialization File

You can use any valid non-interactive Z-Mail commands in the initialization file. (*Interactive commands* are commands that require input from the keyboard).

Z-Mail reads the initialization file *before* reading in messages, so you shouldn't put commands that manipulate the messages, such as **sort** or **from**, in initialization files unless you plan to read in these commands again later (using the **source** command). However, Z-Mail does provide a special command called **filter** that allows you to pick out certain messages and manipulate them with **delete** or **save** before displaying the header summaries. We'll explain more about this command later in this chapter.

You'll probably end up using the initialization file to make certain settings permanent. In other words, you won't include commands such as **print, update,** and **next** which actually perform actions on messages. Your initialization file will contain commands like **set, alias, ignore, map,** and **map!** which change the way Z-Mail works.

If you use the line mode, you'll also want to put any command-line aliases that you create with **cmd** in the initialization file.

If you use the fullscreen mode, you won't use command-line aliases unless you frequently escape to the line mode to run line-mode commands. However, if you change the key-to-command bindings, you'll want to put the new bindings in your initialization file.

To use Z-Mail commands, simply use your favorite editor to enter them in the initialization file as you would type them from the Z-Mail line-mode prompt. We discuss how to use each of the commands in the following sections in Chapter 3, *Reading and Managing Mail*, Chapter 4, *Sending Mail with Z-Mail*, and Chapter 5, *Z-Mail Shortcuts, Bells, and Whistles*.

Mail Aliases

We explain how to create short names (*mail aliases*) for long addresses in Chapter 4; here's the format for making an alias permanent by including it in your initialization file:

```
alias name address_list
```

Suppressed and Retained Headers

In Chapter 5, we discuss how to tell Z-Mail to ignore and retain specific headers when displaying messages. Use this format to make these settings permanent:

```
ignore headers
```

To specify the headers that you want to display, use **retain:**

```
retain headers
```

This command isn't available with MUSH; use the **show_hdrs** variable instead.

Command-line Aliases

We described how to create command-line aliases with **cmd** in Chapter 5. To make your command-line aliases permanent, use this format to add them to the initialization file:

> **cmd** *name command*

Fullscreen-mode Bindings

If you used the **bind** command to change any of the key-to-command bindings in fullscreen mode, make your new bindings permanent by adding them to the initialization file in this format:

> **bind** *key-sequence expansion*

Macro Definitions

In Chapter 10, we'll explain how to create macros in line, fullscreen, and compose modes. After you test them, you'll probably want to keep them for future Z-Mail sessions. The syntax for defining line- or compose-mode macros in the initialization file looks like this:

> **map**[!] *key-sequence expansion*

Use **map** to create line-mode macros and **map!** to create compose-mode macros.

When adding fullscreen-mode macros to the initialization file, use **bind-macro** like this:

> **bind-macro** *key-sequence commands*

Customizing Z-Mail with Variables

We described many of the ways you can modify the behavior of Z-Mail using variables in Chapter 3, *Reading and Managing Mail*, Chapter 4, *Sending Mail with Z-Mail*, and Chapter 5, *Z-Mail Shortcuts, Bells, and Whistles*. Instead of going over this information again in this section, we suggest that you review Table 3-8, Table 4-5, and Table 5-8 for brief descriptions of these variables. You might also want to review the chapters for more complete information about how you can use the variables.

In this section, we'll show you how to make your variable settings permanent by including them in the initialization file, and we'll explain some basic customization that you might want to perform.

Setting Variables in the Initialization File

Any values that you set in your personal initialization file override Z-Mail's built-in settings and the settings in the system initialization file.

The syntax for setting variables in the initialization file is identical to setting variables at the line-mode prompt:

```
set variable [ = value ]
```

As we explained in Chapter 5, some variables are *boolean* (you simply turn them on and off) and others you set to a specific *value*. Remember: when setting a variable to a value, if you put spaces around the equal sign (=), make sure you put them on both sides.

You can set each variable on a separate line:

```
set ask
set askcc
set dot
set editor=/usr/bin/vi
set folder=~/Folder
set complete
```

Or, you can combine variable settings on a line:

```
set ask askcc dot complete
set editor = "/usr/bin/vi" folder = "~/Folder"
```

As you can see, you only need one **set** command on each line. I prefer setting variables on lines by themselves because it's easier for me to distinguish settings from each other. However, you can shorten a long initialization file considerably by combining settings.

Setting Environment Variables

There are some situations where Z-Mail checks the value of an environment variable if the corresponding Z-Mail variable isn't set. For example, when you edit your message using ~v, Z-Mail checks the value of the **visual** variable. If it's not set, Z-Mail uses the value of the **VISUAL** environment variable instead.

If you want, you can set environment variables from within Z-Mail using the **setenv** command, which works the same as the C shell **setenv** command. As an example, you might want to set an environment variable to affect your environment when you execute a shell escape with **sh**. Any environment variable that you set from the shell, you can set from within Z-Mail.

For example, to set the value of the **HOME** environment variable to */tmp/hanna*, use this command:

```
setenv HOME=/tmp/hanna
```

If the variable value contains spaces, enclose the string in double quotes ("). If you don't specify a value for the variable, **setenv** sets it to an empty string.

Here's a list of some common environment variables and corresponding Z-Mail variables:

EDITOR	editor
HOME	home
NAME	realname
PAGER	pager
SHELL	shell
TMPDIR	tmpdir
VISUAL	visual

If you set any of the environment variables on the left in your ˜/.profile or ˜/.login, it has the same effect as if you set the Z-Mail variable on the right in your initialization file (˜/.zmailrc). If you set any of the local variables after starting up Z-Mail, it doesn't change the value of the environment variables. In other words, setting **realname** doesn't change the value of **NAME**.

Normally, Z-Mail converts the name of any local variables to uppercase and then checks the environment before reporting that the variable isn't set. Z-Mail uses some other variables that it doesn't read from the environment at initialization time. Here's a list of these variables:

CRT	crt
ESCAPE	escape
PROMPT	prompt
SCREEN	screen
WRAPCOLUMN	wrapcolumn

If you change these environment variables with **setenv** or in your .profile or .login files, it won't affect the value of the internal variable that Z-Mail uses. The only way to modify these variables is to use **set**.

 You can list the current environment variable settings with **printenv**. To display the value of a particular variable, use **printenv** with the variable name. For example, to display the value of **NAME**, enter the following:

```
Msg 3 of 10: printenv NAME
```

Z-Mail displays something like this:

```
NAME=Hanna Nelson
```

To remove an environment variable setting for the current Z-Mail session, use **unsetenv** followed by the variable name.

Basic Customization Settings

Here are some basic customization settings from a sample initialization file (˜/.zmailrc for Z-Mail or ˜/.mushrc for MUSH).

```
set ask
set askcc
set dot
set editor=ex
```

```
set visual=vi
set pager=more
set hold
set keepsave
set history=24
set nonobang
set unix
set complete
set record=+outbox
```

Everyone might customize Z-Mail a little differently; in the next few sections, I'll give you the rationale behind these basic settings.

The ask and askcc Variables. In my experience, most people prefer to have their mail program prompt them for the **Subject** and **Cc** when they send mail. If Z-Mail doesn't prompt for these headers, set the **ask** and **askcc** variables. We discuss these variables in detail in Chapter 4.

The dot Variable. Set the **dot** variable if you want to be able to send messages by pressing the dot character (.) on a line by itself in compose mode. We explain more about **dot** in Chapter 4.

The editor and visual Variables. Use **editor** and **visual** to specify the default text editors to use when you enter the ˜e and ˜v tilde-escapes or when you use −e at the command line. We explain the distinction between the two in Chapter 4.

The pager Variable. Use **pager** to specify the pager program for Z-Mail to call if a message has more than 24 lines of text. Chapter 3 explains the details of **pager**.

The keepsave Variable. If you don't want Z-Mail to delete messages that you've saved when you update the system mailbox, set the **keepsave** variable. See Chapter 3 for a discussion of **keepsave**.

The history and nonobang Variables. If you want to display and re-execute previous commands, the **history** and **nonobang** variables are essential. The **history** variable indicates how many previous commands you want to save; **nonobang** tells Z-Mail to ignore any history-referencing errors. See Chapter 5 for details.

The unix Variable. Set the **unix** variable to tell Z-Mail to interpret any commands that it doesn't recognize as UNIX commands. We discuss this variable in detail in Chapter 5.

The complete variable. The **complete** variable enables Z-Mail filename completion. See Chapter 5 for more information.

The record Variable. Use **record** to tell Z-Mail to save all your outgoing mail messages to the specified filename. We discuss this variable in Chapter 4.

Sample Initialization Files

Z-Mail includes several sample initialization files in the */usr/lib/Zmail* directory. These files, *novice.zmailrc*, *sample.zmailrc*, and *expert.zmailrc*, are intended to set up initialization files for the different levels of Z-Mail users. For example, if you're new to Z-Mail, you might want to use the *novice.zmailrc* file as your initialization file until you become more familiar with the way Z-Mail works.

You can use any of these files as your personal initialization file by copying the file from */usr/lib/Zmail* to *˜/.zmailrc* in your home directory. For example, to use *novice.zmailrc*, enter the following command at your UNIX prompt:

```
$ cp /usr/lib/Zmail/novice.zmailrc ˜/.zmailrc
```

If you don't have permission to copy files from the */usr/lib/Zmail* directory, consult with your system administrator.

You can also read these files at startup time like this:

```
$ zmail −init /usr/lib/Zmail/novice.zmailrc
```

Additional Z-Mail Variables

We've already discussed most of the Z-Mail variables in the context of the function that they modify; see Chapters 3, 4, 5, 6, and 7 for details. In this section, we'll cover the variables available in Z-Mail that we haven't already covered elsewhere.

Wrapping the Message Pointer

Normally, when you delete the last message in a folder, the current message pointer remains pointing to the last message. For example, if you delete message 10, Z-Mail displays:

```
Msg 10 of 10: _
```

You can tell Z-Mail to move the current message pointer, wrapping to the first undeleted message in the folder automatically by setting the **wrap** boolean variable. Now, when you delete the last message or enter the **next** (or **+**) command after displaying the last message, Z-Mail wraps the message pointer to the beginning of the message list. Now, the prompt looks like this:

```
Msg 1 of 10: _
```

Specifying Alternate Home or Temporary Directories

When you invoke Z-Mail, the program checks the value of the **$tmpdir** variable and copies the specified folder (your system mailbox, by default) to a temporary file in that location (*/tmp*, by default). Z-Mail also uses this directory to store temporary files when you edit outgoing messages.

If **tmpdir** isn't set, Z-Mail uses the location specified by **$home** (by default, the directory specified by the **HOME** environment variable). Z-Mail also uses the value of **$home** as the default value when you use the **cd** and **chdir** commands in line and fullscreen modes.

To change the directory that Z-Mail uses as your home directory, set the **home** variable to another directory. Let's say you want to use a temporary directory in */tmp* as your home directory. To do this, use a **home** setting like this:

```
set home = /tmp/hanna
```

Now, Z-Mail uses */tmp/hanna* as my home directory.

If the permissions on your home directory (as specified by **$HOME** or **home**) deny Z-Mail read or write access, Z-Mail uses */tmp* instead.

If you don't want Z-Mail to use the */tmp* directory, change the location of the temporary directory with the **tmpdir** variable. If **tmpdir** isn't set, Z-Mail uses the value of the **TMPDIR** environment variable.

For example, let's say your home directory is on on the */usr* file system that has very little free disk space. In this situation, you might want to set **tmpdir** to a directory in a file system with more space, for example:

```
set tmpdir = /y/hanna/tmp
```

Now, Z-Mail stores your temporary files on the */y* file system. Note that the directory must exist and you must have write permission.

NOTE

On some systems, you can't override the default location (*/tmp*) for certain temporary information. If this is the case on your system, you might see error messages, such as `file system full` even if you set **tmpdir** to a directory in a partition other than that of */tmp*.

Setting the Search Path for cd

If you use **cd** (in line mode) or **chdir** (%) (in fullscreen mode) without specifying a directory to change to, Z-Mail changes to the directory specified by **home**. When you use **cd** without specifying an absolute pathname, Z-Mail searches the current directory for the directory that you specify. Then, Z-Mail checks the value of **cdpath** and searches the directories listed there. To set the list of pathnames for Z-Mail to search, set **cdpath** like this:

```
set cdpath = "/ ~/ora ~/bin /bin /usr/bin"
```

Remember, Z-Mail expands the tilde character (˜) to your home directory.

Let's say I'm in */u/hanna/Mail* when I use this command:

```
Msg 3 of 10: cd chapters
```

Z-Mail checks the current directory for *chapters*. If it doesn't find the directory, Z-Mail checks the value of *cdpath* and searches those directories for the specified directory. When Z-Mail finds *chapters* (in */u/hanna/ora*), it changes to that directory.

Note that Z-Mail always checks the current directory before any directory that you specify in **cdpath**.

Suppressing Z-Mail Messages

By default, when you invoke Z-Mail, you get a message like this one displaying the version of your Z-Mail software before the list of header summaries:

```
Z-Mail (2.0.0 7/1/91): Type '?' for help.
```

You can suppress this message, as well as messages in other situations, using the **quiet** variable. Use either of these **quiet** settings to suppress the version message at startup time:

```
set quiet
set quiet = startup
```

If you set **quiet** to a list of keywords, you can suppress messages in other situations. To use one or more keywords, separate the keywords by spaces or commas. Table 8-4 lists these keywords.

Table 8-4. quiet Variable Keywords

Keyword	Description
autosign	Suppress messages when appending a signature file to messages.
complete	Suppress the bell that sounds when you use word completion and a prefix is not unique.
fortune	Suppress messages when appending a fortune to messages.
newmail	Suppress messages when new mail arrives (MUSH uses the **await** keyword).
pick	Suppress the description of searches with **pick**.
save	Suppress description when you **save**, **write**, or **copy**.
startup	Suppress the startup message.
gui	Suppress the bell that sounds when new mail arrives in GUI mode.

These **pick** and **save** keywords are particularly useful when you use these commands in scripts and functions; we'll give you some examples in this chapter and in Chapter 9, *Writing Scripts and Functions*.

By default, when you receive new mail while you are using Z-Mail, you see a message like this:

```
New mail (#5) Dale Cooper Dec 25 11:00 (848) Fine Coffee
```

To suppress this message, set **quiet**:

```
set quiet = newmail
```

This doesn't prevent Z-Mail from including the new mail in your system mailbox; this command simply suppresses the new mail message.

For example, suppose you set **autosign** and **fortune** to sign your name and include a random fortune in all your outgoing mail. Every time you send a message, you get messages like these:

```
Signing letter... /u/hanna/.signature: 2 lines
You may be fortunate... added 3 lines
```

To suppress these messages, set **quiet** like this:

```
set quiet = "autosign fortune"
```

In this case, Z-Mail still displays any errors with signatures and fortunes. For example, if Z-Mail can't find the UNIX program *fortune* on your system, you'll still see an error like this:

```
sh: /usr/games/fortune: not found
```

GUI Specific Variables

This section covers the variables and other customization features that are specific to GUI mode.

Removing GUI-mode Dialogs Automatically

When you use the GUI mode, you can specify whether to remove specific dialog boxes after the operation is complete. For example, you can tell Z-Mail to close the Save Messages dialog box after Z-Mail finishes saving the messages. To do this, set the **autodismiss** variable. If you set **autodismiss** like this, Z-Mail closes the Compose window when you finish sending your message:

```
set autodismiss
```

You can also set **autodismiss** to one or more keywords (separated by spaces or commas) to close dialog boxes in other situations. These keywords are listed in Table 8-5.

Table 8-5. autodismiss Variable Keywords

Keyword	Action
buttons	Buttons and Functions window after installing a button.
compose	Compose window after sending the message.
folder	Find Folders window after changing folders.
message	Message Display window after deleting the message.*
print	Print Messages window after printing.
save	Save Messages window after saving.
sort	Custom Sort window after sorting.
templates	Form Templates window after selecting a template.

*The Message Display window also closes automatically when you delete the message if either **show_deleted** or **autoprint** is set.

For example, let's tell Z-Mail to close the Save Messages dialog box after saving a message and the Custom Sort dialog after performing the sort:

```
set autodismiss = "save,sort"
```

 You can also set the **autoiconify** variable to tell Z-Mail to iconify specific windows after performing an operation, instead of removing them. Set **autoiconify** to one of the keywords in Table 8-6.

Table 8-6. iconify Variable Keywords

Keyword	Description
compose	Iconify the Compose window after sending the messsage.
message	Iconify the Message Display window after you delete the displayed message. If you also set **autoprint**, Z-Mail displays the next message (instead of iconifying the window), if available.

Note that if you set both **autodismiss** and **autoiconify** for the same window, **autoiconify** takes precedence.

Changing the Z-Mail Icon

When you convert the main Z-Mail window to an icon, Z-Mail uses the default **mail_icon**. If you have another icon that you want to use in place of this one, set the **mail_icon** to the pathname of a file containing an alternate icon to use when the Z-Mail window is closed. For example:

```
set mail_icon = ~/icons/zmail_icon
```

Now, when you convert the Z-Mail window to an icon, you see the icon that you specified with **mail_icon**.

You can change the icon that is displayed when you have new mail in your folder by setting the **newmail_icon** variable to the pathname of a file containing an alternate icon. For example, set **newmail_icon** like this:

```
set newmail_icon = ~/icons/new_mail
```

Z-Mail now uses the icon in the *new_mail* file for the icon to display when new mail arrives.

Emulating Other Mailers and Editors

In this section, we'll explain how to make Z-Mail emulate other screen-oriented environments, such as electronic mail programs and visual editors, by reading a different system initialization file at startup time.

The default line-mode interface functions very much like other mail programs, such as the Berkeley Software Distribution (BSD) UNIX *Mail* and UNIX System V *mailx*. If you're familiar with one of these mailers, you might want to configure the Z-Mail line mode to act like it. Z-Mail includes two special system initialization files for doing just this.

When you use Z-Mail in fullscreen mode, the default key-to-command bindings are very similar to those in the visual editor, *vi*. If you're more familiar with the *emacs* editor, you might prefer that Z-Mail act like it instead. We'll show you how to do this by reading a special initialization file included with Z-Mail.

BSD UNIX Mail

 If you're using Z-Mail on a Berkeley UNIX System and you want it to emulate UCB *Mail*, you can source a special system initialization file that customizes your environment to look like *Mail*. To do this, source the *Mail.zmailrc* system initialization file instead of *system.zmailrc* using this command to invoke Z-Mail:

```
$ zmail —init! /usr/lib/Zmail/Mail.zmailrc
```

In this case, Z-Mail sources the special *Mail* initialization file *instead of* Z-Mail's system initialization file (*system.zmailrc*). This sets your environment to look and act like *Mail*. Z-Mail reads */usr/lib/Zmail/Mail.zmailrc*, which automatically reads your personal initialization file for *Mail*, ˜/.mailrc. Remember that, if you have a ˜/.zmailrc file in your home directory, Z-Mail sources this file automatically. If you want to read your personal ˜/.mailrc file *instead*, set the **MAILRC** or **ZMAILRC** environment variable to ˜/.mailrc.

UNIX System V mailx

 If you're using UNIX System V and you want Z-Mail to emulate *mailx*, use this command to source the special *mailx* system initialization file:

```
$ zmail —init! /usr/lib/Zmail/mailx.zmailrc
```

As with emulating *Mail*, you'll probably want to set **MAILRC** or **ZMAILRC** to ˜/.mailrc so that Z-Mail reads it instead of ˜/.zmailrc.

emacs Editor

If you use fullscreen mode and you'd prefer that Z-Mail behave like *emacs* instead of *vi*, use the following command to read the *emacs* initialization file:

```
$ zmail —init! /usr/lib/Zmail/emacs.zmailrc
```

Z-Mail sources the */usr/lib/Zmail/emacs.zmailrc* file instead of the default system initialization file (*/usr/lib/Zmail/system.zmailrc*), setting your fullscreen-mode environment to behave like *emacs* instead of *vi*. The *emacs* initialization file provides *gnuemacs*-style bindings. Note that the *emacs* emulation isn't perfect.

Filtering Messages

By default, if you put commands that manipulate messages like **delete, pick,** and **save** in the initialization file, Z-Mail doesn't execute them. This is because Z-Mail reads the initialization file before reading in the messages in your system mailbox (or folder). Ordinarily, this means that you can't "prefilter" messages before you see them. However, Z-Mail does include a special initialization command called **filter** that lets you execute certain commands on the messages before displaying them. (MUSH does not support the **filter** command.) This is useful for saving messages from a particular person or on a specific subject to folders that you read separately.

The syntax for **filter** looks like this:

```
filter [ -n ] filter_name command [ pick_options ]
```

The **filter** command creates a filter called *filter_name* that runs a *command*. To run the command on a subset of the messages, use any of the options (*pick_options*) that you normally give to **pick,** listed earlier in Table 3-3. If the command contains spaces, surround it in double quotes (").

By default, Z-Mail applies filters to all new messages that arrive while you're running Z-Mail. These newly arrived messages are marked with an exclamation mark (!). If you want Z-Mail to apply filters to all the messages currently in a folder at startup time as well as filter new mail as it arrives, you must specify the **–filter** option on the command line. For example, use this command to start up Z-Mail from the UNIX command line:

```
$ zmail -filter
```

Make sure that your **filter** definitions are read when you start Z-Mail by putting **filter** definitions in your ~/.zmailrc file.

If you're already in the Z-Mail program and you want to open a new folder and apply filters to it, use the **–f (filter)** option to the **folder** or **open** commands like this:

```
Msg 3 of 10: open -f +zmail.book
```

In both of these cases, Z-Mail applies the filters in your initialization file to all the messages currently in the folder and any new messages that arrive. You can restrict filters to affect just the new mail as it arrives by specifying the **–n** option when you create the filter using **filter.**

NOTE

With **filter –n**, filters are *not* run when you first load the folder, even if you specify **zmail –filter** or **folder –f**.

For example, to tell Z-Mail to notify you each time you receive new mail from a particular person, use a filter like the following:

```
filter -n bossmail 'echo "New mail from the Boss."' -f linda
```

Now, when you receive new mail from *linda*, Z-Mail displays:

```
New mail from the Boss.
```

Let's say you want to save all the messages sent to the *docland* alias currently in your folder to a file called +*work/doc.mail*. Use a command like this in your initialization file and specify the –f option when you open each folder:

```
filter save-doc-mail "save +work/doc.mail" -t docland
```

This creates the **save-mail-doc** filter that finds all the messages with "docland" in the **To** line (using the –t option to **pick**) and saves them to +*work/doc.mail*. If there are any messages to the *docland* alias in your system mailbox, you see messages like the following when you start up Z-Mail with the **–filter** option:

```
Saving msg 6 ... (12 lines)
Saving msg 10 ... (22 lines)
Saving msg 24 ... (100 lines)
Appended 3 msgs to ~/Mail/work/doc.mail
```

You can suppress these messages by setting the **quiet** variable to include the string "save." The saved messages still appear in your header summary display (marked with an **S**). If you want to remove them before displaying the header summaries in your mailbox, add another filter such as the following:

```
filter delete-doc-mail delete -t docland
```

Now, the mail messages no longer appear when you start Z-Mail. Note that they haven't been removed; you can still recover them with the **undelete** command.

You might want to use a filter to set priorities on certain messages at startup time. For example, you're working on a high-priority project and you want to mark all the messages that pertain to it with priority "A" and then sort your messages so they appear at the top of the list. To do this, create a filter like the following and put it in your initialization file:

```
filter set-priorities "mark -A" -s -i Z-Mail
```

The **set-priorities** filter catches all occurences of "Z-Mail," regardless of case.

Now, add the following line to your initialization file (*~/.zmailrc*) to sort your system mailbox so the priority messages appear first:

```
set sort = -p
```

The following is an example of a filter you can use to remind yourself to clean out your system mailbox. This filter finds and lists all the messages that are one week old each time you start Z-Mail (I used the backslash character (\) to break the line):

```
filter oldmail \
    'set match; echo "These messages are one week old: "$match"' -a 1w
```

Now, when you start Z-Mail with the **–filter** option, Z-Mail prompts you with a message like the following:

```
These messages are one week old: 20-26
```

Now, you can delete these old messages with the following command:

```
Mse 3 of 10: d $match
```

You can run many Z-Mail commands with **filter,** but there are a few exceptions. Table 8-7 lists these exceptions.

Table 8-7. filter Command Exceptions

await	display	filter	next
previous	print	quit	read
sort	type	update	

Z-Mail runs the filtering command on messages only when you first open a folder; if the folder is already open, filters don't take effect when you switch to it using **folder**.

Any new mail that arrives after you start Z-Mail is also affected by the filter. If you only want to filter new mail as it arrives in the system mailbox, specify the **-n** option like this:

```
filter -n save-zmail "save ~/zmail.book" -s -i Z-Mail
```

As new messages arrive, this command picks out the ones with "Z-Mail" in the Subject line (regardless of case) and saves them to the file ~/zmail.book.

Removing Filter Definitions

To remove the filter definition for the current Z-Mail session, use **unfilter**. For example, to turn off the **save-zmail** filter so that new mail *isn't* filtered, use this command:

```
Msg 5 of 10: unfilter save-zmail
```

To turn off all filtering action for the current session, use the following command (the asterisk (*) specifies *all* filters):

```
Msg 5 of 10: unfilter *
```

To remove a filter permanently, delete the filter definition from the initialization file.

Filtering Messages in Other Folders

By default, Z-Mail doesn't filter messages when you open and switch to folders. However, you can force Z-Mail to filter those folders using the **-f** (**filter**) option to **folder** (or **open**, if you prefer):

```
Msg 5 of 10: open -f +work/doc.mail
```

If you want Z-Mail to always filter your messages, regardless of the folder, you might want to create a command-line alias for **folder**:

```
cmd open open -f
```

With this command-line alias, you can suppress filtering by entering this command when you switch folders:

```
Msg 4 of 10: open -F
```

Here's what the command line that Z-Mail interprets looks like in this case:

```
Msg 4 of 10: open -f -F
```

The Z-Mail Handbook

The **–F** (don't filter messages) option overrides the **–f** (filter messages) option.

If you start Z-Mail reading a folder other than your system mailbox, use these options to activate filters on the messages in that folder:

```
$ zmail -filter -folder ~/Mail/work/doc.mail
```

In this example, we start Z-Mail reading the messages in +*work/doc.mail*. If you don't want to filter messages in the system mailbox or other folders when you invoke Z-Mail, don't specify the **–filter** option.

Filtering in a .forward File

Some MTAs, such as *sendmail*, read the *.forward* file in your home directory for instructions on routing your mail or running commands. For example, you might use a *.forward* file to send copies of messages to yourself both at home and at work. Another way you might use *.forward* is to run the **vacation** filter that sends replies explaining that you are away for awhile (see the section "Using the Vacation Filter" later in this chapter for an example).

If you use a ~/*.forward* file, you can tell Z-Mail to run the filters in your initialization file on your incoming messages. Generally, you use the *.forward* file to specify that your messages get sent to another folder instead of (or in addition to) your system mailbox. You can also use *.forward* to run another program (such as the BSD *vacation* program).

To use *.forward* to run Z-Mail filters on all your incoming messages, add this line to the beginning of ~/*.forward*:

```
|"/usr/bin/zmail -filter -folder -"
```

In this case, the MTA runs the **zmail –filter** command and then any other forwarding instructions in the *.forward* file. The result is that your mail messages are filtered before they are delivered to your system mailbox (or other destination).

If the Z-Mail library directory is not in */usr/lib/Zmail*, you might have to specify the library location in *.forward* using the **–lib** (**–L**) option. For example, you might use a line like the following in your *.forward* file:

```
|"/usr/bin/zmail -lib /usr/local/lib/Zmail -filter -folder -"
```

Filtering in a .maildelivery File

If the MTA on your system is MMDF, you can use a file called ~/*.maildelivery* to route your mail. This file is useful for routing messages from specific people or about a particular subject to different mail folders instead of your system mailbox. As with ~/*.forward*, you can run the **vacation** filter from within ~/*.maildelivery*; for more information about **vacation**, see the next section.

With the ˜/.*maildelivery* file, you can tell Z-Mail to run your filters on the incoming messages before they are delivered to your system mailbox. To use this feature, add the following line to ˜/.*maildelivery*:

```
*   -   pipe   ?   /usr/bin/zmail -filter -folder -
```

For more information on the format of the .*maildelivery* file, see your operating system documentation or ask your system administrator.

As with ˜/.*forward*, if the Z-Mail library directory is not in /usr/lib/Zmail, specify the location in ˜/.*maildelivery* with the **-lib** option:

```
*   -   pipe   ?   /usr/bin/zmail -lib /usr/local/lib/Zmail -filter -folder -
```

Using the Vacation Filter

Z-Mail includes a **vacation** filter that you can use to reply to messages automatically. This feature is useful for telling people that you won't be answering their mail because you're on vacation.

When you enable the **vacation** filter, Z-Mail sends a vacation message to each person who sends mail to you. If you receive more than one message from a person while you're gone, Z-Mail sends a response no more than once per week. In addition, Z-Mail tries to avoid replying to mailing lists and junk mail.

To use the **vacation** filter, create the message that you want to send and put it in a file in your home directory called .*vacation.msg*. For example, if you are vacationing in Japan, you might include a message like the following:

```
Hi.  I'm vacationing in Japan until June 30th.
This is an automated reply to your mail message;
I'll send you a personal reply when I get back.

Hanna Nelson - hanna@holycow.santa-cruz.ca.us
```

By default, Z-Mail uses "I am on vacation" as the `Subject` for your replies. You can change this by setting the **v_subject** variable in your ˜/.*zmailrc* file. For example, change the `Subject` to "I am in Japan through June" using the following command:

```
set v_subject = "I am in Japan through June"
```

Avoid using double quotes (") in your **v_subject** setting except to enclose the `Subject` string.

Now, enable the **vacation** filter by including the following command in your ˜/.*forward* file (if your MTA is *sendmail*):

```
|"/usr/bin/zmail -init /usr/lib/Zmail/vacation -filter -folder -"
```

If your MTA is MMDF, use the following line in ˜/.*maildelivery*:

```
*  -  pipe  ?  /usr/bin/zmail -init /usr/lib/Zmail/vacation -filter
-folder -
```

In either case, use the appropriate pathname for **zmail**; and the **vacation** filter (by default, *usr/lib/Zmail*) on your system. If the Z-Mail library directory (as specified by the ZMLIB variable) isn't *usr/lib/Zmail*, use **–lib** to specify its location.

With these commands in your ˜/*.forward* or ˜/*.maildelivery* files, Z-Mail runs the **vacation** filter on every message that you receive. When someone sends you a message, they receive an automatic reply like the following example:

```
From hanna Sun May  5 11:52:36 1991
X-Mailer: Z-Mail (2.0.0 7/1/91)
To: andreic
Subject: I am in Japan through June
Date: Sun, 5 May 91 11:52:35 PDT
From: Hanna Nelson <hanna@holycow.santa-cruz.ca.us>
Message-ID:  <9105051152.aa05627@holycow>
Status: O

Hi.  I'm vacationing in Japan until June 30th.
This is an automated reply to your mail message;
I'll send you a personal reply when I get back.

Hanna Nelson - hanna@holycow.santa-cruz.ca.us
```

For more information on the **vacation** filter, see the *usr/lib/Zmail/vacation* file on your system.

Creating Customized Help Files

One way to customize Z-Mail is to create your own help file or otherwise add information to the default help file. The easiest way to do this is ask your system administrator for a copy of the default file and then modify it to suit your needs. This section covers the format of the different help files in the Z-Mail library directory (usually */usr/lib/Zmail*). The GUI-mode help file is either *motif_help* or *ol_help* (depending on your window manager) and the help file for line- and fullscreen-modes is *cmd_help*.

Help File Format

To create your own help file entries, copy the help file for the mode that you're using to another location, add the new help entries and then set the **cmd_help** or **gui_help** variable to the new location.

The format for the entries in the Z-Mail help files is as follows:

```
%index entry string%
%other key strings%
text of help entry
[%%<continuation entry]
%%
```

Do not use TAB characters in this file; use spaces for all text formatting.

The *continuation entry* can be a *key string* for another entry in the current help file. For example, here's the **saveopts** entry from the */usr/lib/Zmail/cmd_help* file:

```
%Commands: saveopts%
%saveopts%
%%<source
%%
```

In this case, the **%%<source** line specifies that you want to display the help text for **source** whenever you enter the following command:

```
Msg 3 of 10: help saveopts
```

In this case, the help text for **source** also contains the information for **saveopts**.

You can also specify that Z-Mail look up the key string in another help file named by a Z-Mail variable. The syntax looks like this:

```
%index entry string%
%other key strings%
text of help entry
%%<variable>continuation entry
%%
```

For example, the following is the default help text for the Header Format entry in the */usr/lib/Zmail/motif_help* file:

```
%Header Format%
%%<cmd_help>Header Format
%%
```

The **%%<cmd_help>Header Format** line tells Z-Mail to look in the file specified by the **cmd_help** variable for the entry that describes the Header Format. This variable is generally set in the system initialization file as **/usr/lib/Zmail/cmd_help**, but you can change the location by setting **cmd_help** to another location. We'll explain how in the next section.

Changing the Location of Help Files

Once you copy the default help file to a new location and modify it to suit your own needs, you must tell Z-Mail where to look for the new file. To do this, set either the **cmd_help** or **gui_help** variables to the new location.

To change the location of the GUI mode help file, set **gui_help** to the new filename in your initialization file (*.zmailrc*).[2] For example, if the file is called ~/.gui.help, set **gui_help** like this:

```
set gui_help = ~/.gui.help
```

----

[2] Z-Mail only recognizes the **gui_help** variable on systems capable of running Z-Mail in GUI mode.

Now, whenever you click a Help button in one of the windows, Z-Mail looks for the *.gui.help* file in your home directory.

To change the location of the help file for line and fullscreen modes, set **cmd_help**:

```
set cmd_help = ~/.new.help
```

With this **cmd_help** setting, Z-Mail uses the information in *~/.new.help* whenever you request help in line and fullscreen modes. For more information, see the section, "Getting Help with Z-Mail Commands," in Chapter 3, and the section, "Getting Help in Fullscreen Mode," in Chapter 6.

Adding Attachment Types

 When you attach files to mail messages, Z-Mail uses the information in the attachment types description file, *attach.types*, to describe the attachment. This file is located in */usr/lib/Zmail* ($ZMLIB), by default.

The *attach.types* file describes the type of data (the "attachment type") that the attachment contains and any conversion processes necessary to transmit and present ("encoding" and "decoding") the data in the attachment. Depending on the type of data, the conversion process might include compressing or encoding. This file also gives the location of the programs that Z-Mail needs to perform encoding, determines how to match the attachment type with the appropriate encoding, and provides a default encoding process if the attachment type requires encoding but you don't specify one.

You can add attachment types to this file as needed. For example, you might find yourself frequently sending a particular type of file, such as the output from a particular spreadsheet or desktop publishing program, as an attachment. In this case, instead of explaining what type of attachment it is and what program the recipient should use to decode it each time you send the attachment, you can create a new attachment type telling Z-Mail to include this information automatically. When you define an attachment type, you place the information about the attachment in the *attach.types* file and let Z-Mail include the information about it each time you send that type of attachment.

The best way to create and use a new attachment type is to copy the *attach.types* file to another location, add the new attachment type, and then set the **attach_types** variable to the file in the new location.

NOTE

Z-Mail always reads the system *attach.types* file first and appends the information from any attachment types description file that you specify with **attach_types**.

In this section, we'll discuss the format of the attachment types description file.

Attachment Types Description File Format

The attachment types description file contains five keywords that describe an action for Z-Mail to take. Table 8-8 describes these keywords.

Table 8-8. attach.types Keywords

Keyword	Description
PATH	Describes the PATH environment variable where the programs specified by the TYPE and CODE entries are located.
	If you specify a PATH, Z-Mail appends the directories you specify to the current list in the system *attach.types* file. This is important because the directories specified in the system file are always searched before the ones in your PATH definition. If you want to substitute a program that has the same name as a program in the system PATH, enter the full name of the program in your TYPE or CODE definition.
TYPE	Defines the type of the attachment, the program to use when viewing the attachment, the editor to use when editing the attachment, and a comment describing the attachment type.* This keyword is required to declare a new attachment type. Note that the editor field is not currently used.
CODE	Specifies a key that indicates what program the recipient has to use to convert the attachment back to its original form. This keyword also specifies the program to use to encode the attachment and a comment describing the encoding program. This keyword is required for declaring a new encoding type.
ENCODE	Specifies the default encoding for a particular attachment type.
DEFAULT	Specifies the encoding to use if encoding is necessary (the attachment data is not ASCII) and the user doesn't specify an encoding process.

*Future versions of Z-Mail might use information in the comment field to identify the attachment type automatically.

The only required keyword when you declare a new attachment type is TYPE (and, unless you have already defined the pathname to the attachment programs earlier in *attach.types*, PATH).

The PATH Keyword

Use the PATH keyword to add directories to the default PATH in */usr/lib/Zmail/attach.types*. To declare the PATH, use the following syntax:

PATH *directory1:directory2:...*

For example, if the viewing and encoding programs that you want to use with a particular attachment are located in */u/hanna/bin* and */usr/local/bin*, declare PATH like this:

PATH /u/hanna/bin:/usr/local/bin

The TYPE Keyword

Use the TYPE keyword to define a new attachment type. The syntax for TYPE looks like this:

TYPE *type_key* "*viewer_program*" "*editor_program*" "*comment*"

The *type_key* defines the name of the attachment type. Z-Mail includes this information with the attachment so that the Z-Mail that the recipient is using knows what method to use to display it. This is also the same string that Z-Mail displays when you enter **?** at the Attachment type prompt and places (or displays) in the **X-Zm-Data-Type** header.

This string should not include spaces or tabs, but you can use other non-alphabetic characters. For example, if you define the *type_key* as **xwd**, Z-Mail includes the word "xwd" in the list of attachment types.

The *viewer_program* describes the program that the recipient uses to display the contents of the attachment; *editor_program* describes the editor to use with the attachment. (Note that, in the current version of Z-Mail, the *editor_program* field is not used.)

To specify that the *viewer_program* or *editor_program* process a particular file, put an **%s** (the *printf* format character) wherever the program normally expects a filename. Z-Mail inserts the specified filename at that point. For example, the *bitmap* program takes a filename as input; to display a bitmap file called *zm.icon*, you enter the following command:

bitmap zm.icon

To tell Z-Mail how to display a bitmap file, create a TYPE definition for the **bitmap** program that looks something like the following:

TYPE bitmap   "bitmap %s"   None   "X11 bitmap"

In this case, if you tell Z-Mail to display an attachment that is of the type **bitmap** and you specify the filename as *zm.icon*, Z-Mail substitutes "zm.icon" for the **%s**, writes the attachment to *zm.icon*, and then runs **bitmap zm.icon** to display the attachment.

When you're sending an attachment, the *type_key* "bitmap" appears when you display the list of possible attachment types.

In the example above, note that the attachment type doesn't have an *editor_program*; the reason for this is that you generally wouldn't edit a bitmap file with a regular editor. In any case, where it's inappropriate to edit the attachment type, simply enter "None" in the *editor_program* field.

To direct standard input to either the *viewer_program* or *editor_program*, insert a leading pipe character (|). For example, the following TYPE definition specifies that the *nroff* program read from standard input, rather than accept input from a file:

```
TYPE roff   "|nroff —mm"   "vi %s"   "An nroff document"
```

If you're using Z-Mail in GUI mode, you won't be able to display the output from *nroff* under X Windows, so you might want to modify this attachment type slightly as follows:

```
TYPE roff   "|ditroff —mm|xditview"   "xedit"   "An nroff document"
```

In this case, *ditroff* accepts input from standard input and outputs it to *xditview*; the *editor_program* is *xedit*.

In both these examples, the *viewer_program*s (*nroff* and *ditroff*) are post-processing operations; they process the data and then display the output on the screen. In the TYPE **TarMail** below, the *viewer_program* is a post-processing operation using *atob*:

```
TYPE TarMail     "|atob|uncompress|tar xvf -"   None   "Tar Archive"
```

The leading pipe tells Z-Mail to redirect input to the *atob* program (and then to *uncompress* and *tar*). In this case, the files aren't displayed, but rather they're extracted into the local directory tree.

If you don't include either a leading pipe character or a trailing %s, Z-Mail executes the specified program without giving a file to read. In this case, the user has to load the input file manually.

If you are specifying a GUI-oriented program or a program that does not produce screen output (such as a post-processor), you can include a trailing ampersand character (**&**) to tell Z-Mail to run the program in the background (so that you don't have to wait for the program to execute before continuing).

The CODE Keyword

Use the CODE keyword to define a new encoding procedure that you want to perform. CODE is similar to TYPE, except that you use this keyword to define the encoding and decoding programs to use. Here's the syntax for CODE:

```
CODE code_key "encoding_program" "decoding_program"   "comment"
```

The *code_key* string is similar to *type_key* in the TYPE definition except that it defines the name of the encoding and decoding process. This information is included with the attachment to tell the recipient what program to use to convert the attachment back to its original state. This is also the string that Z-Mail displays when you enter **?** at the Encoding prompt and is placed (or displayed) in the **X-Zm-Data-Type** header.

Again, don't include spaces or tabs in this string, but other non-alphabetic characters are fine. For example, if you define the *code_key* as **compress**, Z-Mail includes the word "compress" in the list of encoding options.

As with the TYPE definition, use a leading pipe character (|) to tell Z-Mail to redirect input to the *encoding_program* or *decoding_program*. Use the %s to indicate that the program processes a particular file.

In addition, you can use a trailing pipe character to indicate that the program writes to standard output. For example, the following CODE definition indicates that both the *encoding_program* (*btoa*) and the *decoding_program* (*atob*) read from standard input and write to standard output:

```
CODE btoa "|btoa|" "|atob|" "Binary to ASCII"
```

Note that this differs from the TYPE definition; the *viewer_program* and *editor_program* in the TYPE definition should never have a trailing pipe character because Z-Mail doesn't provide special treatment for viewer and editor programs that write to standard output. The standard output from these programs goes to the same place as standard output from Z-Mail: the screen. In line and fullscreen mode, this might work fine; however, in GUI mode, Z-Mail might not have a place for the program to write to. In this case, you should specify that the command in TYPE declarations redirect the output somewhere (like a file).

With both a leading and trailing pipe character, the program reads from standard input and writes to standard output. If you give a trailing %s and pipe, the program reads the file and writes to standard output. With the leading pipe and trailing %s, the program reads from standard input and writes to the specified file. With just the trailing %s, the program reads the specified file and then writes back to the same file.

The CODE *encoding* and *decoding* programs must have either both a leading and trailing pipe character (|); a trailing %s and |; a leading pipe and trailing %s; or a trailing %s.

Note that the *encoding_program must* produce ASCII output. Thus, if you use *compress* as the *encoding_program*, you must also pass the output from *compress* to a program, such as *btoa*, that converts it to ASCII. For example:

```
CODE compress "|compress|btoa|" "|atob|uncompress|"
"Compress/convert to ASCII"
```

In this case, *compress* reads from standard input and then writes to standard output; *btoa* reads the output from *compress* (non-ASCII), converts it to ASCII, and writes to standard output.

The ENCODE Keyword

Use ENCODE to specify a default encoding for a particular attachment type. The syntax for ENCODE is as follows:

```
ENCODE   type_key   code_key
```

Use the ENCODE keyword to specify that the default encoding for *type_key* is *code_key*.

NOTE

Both *type_key* and *code_key* must be declared somewhere in the attachment types description file.

For example, if you always want attachments of type **Folder** to be encoded using the *code_key* "compress," use this ENCODE declaration:

```
ENCODE Folder compress
```

The DEFAULT Keyword

Use the DEFAULT key to specify the default encoding if the attachment requires encoding (in other words, if the attachment data is non-ASCII) and the user doesn't specify an encoding process. The syntax is:

    DEFAULT code_key

Because the system *attach.types* file includes a DEFAULT declaration, you don't have to define one unless you want to change the default encoding.

For more information about the format of the attachment description file, see */usr/lib/Zmail/attach.types* .

Summary

In this chapter, we showed you how to modify the behavior of Z-Mail at initialization time by modifying the initialization file. In discussing the format of the initialization file, we introduced you to some of the elements of the Z-Script scripting language. Using these special commands, we showed you how to test for certain conditions (such as the current mode) before running commands or setting variables, how to use expression operators to compare variables with constants, and how to check to see if a variable is set. You'll need this information as background when learning how to create functions in Chapter 9, *Writing Scripts and Functions*.

This chapter also covered some of the variables that aren't covered elsewhere in the book, how to to emulate a different mail program or editor by sourcing a different initialization file, and how to "pre-filter" messages using the **filter** command.

Finally, this chapter explained the format of the different help files and the *attach.types* file so that you can further customize Z-Mail by adding or modifying help entries and attachment types.

9
Writing Scripts and Functions

One of the most powerful features of Z-Mail is the ability to manipulate messages using your own customized scripts and functions; Z-Mail provides a scripting language, Z-Script, for creating these scripts. Generally, you put a script in a file and then read in the commands using **source** or a command-line option. Like shell scripts in UNIX, Z-Mail scripts allow you to test to see if certain conditions are true before executing commands. This gives you control over exactly when you want to execute a given set of commands. In fact, scripts are so versatile that you can literally run an entire mail session without ever interacting with the Z-Mail program.

Functions are similar to scripts except that, instead of sourcing them, you invoke them like the command-line aliases that you create with **cmd**. (Functions are not available in MUSH.) Unlike command-line aliases, however, you can create complex functions that run interactive commands, prompt for input from the keyboard, and manipulate command-line arguments.

In Chapter 8, *Customizing Z-Mail*, we covered many of the elements of the Z-Script scripting language when we discussed the format of the initialization file. To review, Chapter 8 describes the following concepts:

- Using comments in scripts.

- Using conditional (**if**) statements and specifying an alternate action (**else**).

- Negating expressions with **!**.

- Using mode-testing variables, such as **is_gui** and **is_sending**.

- Evaluating string expressions with expression operators.

- Using file test operations to make sure files exist and contain information before manipulating them.

If you aren't already familiar with this information, we suggest that you read these sections before continuing.

In this chapter, we'll begin by describing some additional commands and variables that you'll find useful when creating scripts. Then, we'll use this information, along with the information from Chapter 8, as background for writing functions.

Special Variables

In addition to the regular and read-only variables, Z-Mail recognizes the three special variables in Table 9-1. As with read-only variables, these variables are useful for obtaining information from within Z-Mail scripts. Using $[%fmt], for example, you can get the same information as from **hdr_format**: the current date or subject of a message. Then, you can use this in your scripts and functions to create filenames or your own variables.

Table 9-1. Special Variables

Variable	Description
$$	The process ID (PID) number of the Z-Mail process.
$[%fmt]	The format from **hdr_format** (see Table 3-6).
$(%c)	The format from **prompt** (see Table 3-7).

NOTE

The distinction between square brackets and parentheses ([ ], ()) is very important; use square brackets to reference **hdr_format** formatting characters and parentheses for **prompt** characters.

The $$ variable is used to reference the process ID (PID) of the Z-Mail process. For example, when you type the following:

```
Msg 4 of 13: echo $$
```

Z-Mail displays the PID number like this:

```
4110
```

You can use this variable for creating temporary files that are unique to the current Z-Mail process. For example, here's the command-line alias **bounce** (from Chapter 5) that you used to resend mail that the mailer-daemon "bounced" back to you. In this example, we've modified the alias so that it creates a temporary file, using the PID of the current Z-Mail process in the name:

```
cmd bounce 'Pipe -p From: "cat > $tmpdir/b$$" ; \
    m -euh $tmpdir/b$$ ; sh rm $tmpdir/b$$'
```

In this example, we use the backslash character (\) to break the line because it is too wide to fit on the page. You can use the command as displayed or put the entire command on one line and eliminate the backslash.

This command-line alias sends the current message, beginning with the pattern "From" to the UNIX *cat* command. Then, *cat* puts the message in a filename consisting of "b" followed by the PID of the current Z-Mail process in the temporary directory (specified by the **tmpdir** variable). For example, if the temporary directory is */tmp* and the current Z-Mail PID is "4110," the filename is */tmp/b4110*.

Next, this command-line alias executes the **mail** command with the −**e** (enter the editor), −**u** (don't append signature or fortune), and −**h** (to read in the *b4110* file as a prepared draft with headers) options. When you quit the editor and send the message, **bounce** then removes the temporary file *b4110*.

The names of these temporary dot (or hidden) files that Z-Mail creates always contain the number of the Z-Mail process. For example, let's say the current Z-Mail process is 4110. The temporary directory contains filenames that look like this:

```
.ed0041100
.zma0041100
.zma0041101
```

In this example, the *.ed0041100* file is created while you edit a message. The second file, *.zma0041100*, contains a copy of the first open folder; *.zma0041101* contains the messages in the second open folder. If you edit more messages or open new folders, Z-Mail creates new files in the temporary directory and increments the last digit in the name it assigns.

 Once you understand the connection between the Z-Mail PID and the temporary filenames, you can use the $$ special variable in other ways. For example, use this command to list all the temporary files for the current Z-Mail session:

```
Msg 3 of 10: sh "ls -a $tmpdir | grep $$"
```

Note that we use the **sh** command to escape to the UNIX shell to run this command because you're piping the output of one UNIX command (the list of files) to another (*grep*).

Note that you can't use the variable substitution modifiers (:) from Table 5-1 to select arguments from the $$ special variable.

Use $[*%fmt*] to reference a header formatting string (listed in Table 3-6) and have Z-Mail expand it using the header information from the current message. Note that the formatting string doesn't have to appear in your current **hdr_format** setting. For example, this variable reference:

```
Msg 3 of 10: save $[%6a]:u
```

saves the current message to a filename that is the first six characters of the author's address, converted to uppercase. (You can use the variable substitution modifiers (colon modifiers) with this special variable.) So, if the current message is from *george@vegan.edu*, this command saves the message to a file called *GEORGE*.

I like to use this variable to display the value of specific header format strings for the current message that don't appear in my **hdr_format** setting. For example, my **hdr_format** setting shows the date the message was sent, but doesn't include the day of the week (%W). To display this information for the current message, enter the following:

```
Msg 4 of 13: echo $[%W]
```

So, for a message sent on June 28, 1991, the result looks like this:

```
Fri
```

Here's another way to use the $[%fmt] special variable. Use this construction to search for messages that are similar to the current message. For example, create a variable named **subject** and set its value to the Subject line of the current message:

```
Msg 4 of 13: set subject = "$[%s]"
```

Let's say the current header summary looks like this:

```
> 4   Bart    Feb 14 11:09  (890)  Special Variables
```

 You can now search for all the messages with this Subject using this command:

```
Msg 4 of 13: pick -s "$subject"
```

Note that we surround the **$subject** variable in double quotes (") in case the variable includes single quotes ('). You see something like this:

```
Searching for messages that contain "Special Variables" in subject line
```

Here's another example of how you can extract and use parts of the Subject header of the current message. Let's say someone sent you three chapters to a book and the header summaries look like this:

```
> 6   Andrei  Feb 14 10:49  (200)  Commentary - Part1 of 3
  7   Andrei  Feb 14 11:37  (280)  Commentary - Part2 of 3
  8 N Andrei  Feb 14 11:48  (308)  Commentary - Part3 of 3
```

Use this command to save the first message to a file called *Part1*:

```
Msg 6 of 12: save $[%s]:3
```

This command uses the third word in the Subject header as the filename to save the current message to. Z-Mail displays this message:

```
saving message 6 to Part1 ...
```

Now, move the current message pointer to message 7 with the following command:

```
Msg 6 of 12: from +
```

With the current message pointer on message 7, you can execute this command again to save Part 2 of "Commentary" to a file called *Part2*. Use command history to do this:

```
Msg 7 of 12: !s
```

The $(%c) variable is similar to $[%fmt] except that you use it to refer to the **prompt** format (from Table 3-7). Note that you **can** use variable substitution modifiers (colon modifiers) with it. This variable is useful for obtaining general information about the status of the current folder. For example, use this command to display the current folder name: Note that this is equivalent to the value of the **$thisfolder** variable.

```
Msg 7 of 12: echo $(%F)
```

Throughput is equivalent to the value of the **$thisfolder** variable.

 This variable construction is also useful for getting information about the current date and time. Thus, to save messages to a file that contains the current date, set a variable as follows:

```
set filename = rcvd-$(%M)-$(%N)-$(%y)
```

Now, save messages with this command:

```
Msg 7 of 12: s * $filename
```

This saves all the messages in the current folder to a file called *rcvd-Jun-28-91* (if today is June 28, 1991).

 You can also use this variable in initialization files. For example, if you want Z-Mail to save your outgoing mail messages to a folder with the name of the current month, set **record** in your initialization file:

```
set record = +$(%M)-$(%y)
```

Now, when you initialize Z-Mail, the **record** variable is set to the name of the current month. If you send a message on April 1, 1991, Z-Mail saves it to the folder *Apr-91* in the folder directory. Use this command to switch to the current month's outgoing message folder:

```
Msg 7 of 12: fo $record
```

 In general, you'll probably use this variable in scripts to check the status of a folder before doing something. This command displays the number of messages (%t) in the folder:

```
echo "There are $(%t) messages in the current folder."
```

Here's an example of how to check for new messages (%n) in a folder:

```
if $(%n) == 0
    echo "There are no new messages"
endif
```

Using the eval Command

If you find yourself using more than one **$[%fmt]** or **$(%c)** variable in a single command, you should probably use the **eval** command with **–h** (to expand **hdr_format** strings) or **–p** (to expand **prompt** strings) options instead. It's generally better to use the **eval** construction in scripts (commands that you don't change very often) and the **$[%fmt]** and **$(%c)** forms for commands that you enter at the Z-Mail prompt.

The **eval** command performs variable substitution and then rescans the line, executing the commands. This is useful if you want to set variables within variable settings.

Here's an example of how you might use this:

```
set newprompt='"$thisfolder:t-$cwd:t>"'
eval set prompt=$newprompt
```

These two commands set your prompt to include the current folder name and the current directory (the **:t** specifies the tail of each pathname). If the current folder is ⁻/*mbox* and the current directory is */u/hanna/zmail.book/chapters*, the prompt is:

```
mbox–chapters>
```

If you didn't use **eval** to expand the variable settings in the **newprompt** variable, here's what the prompt would look like:

```
$thisfolder:t-$cwd:t>
```

The **eval** command expands the variables before executing the **set** command.

With the **–p** and **–h** options, you can include (and expand) **prompt** and **hdr_format** strings before executing the command. (Remember that the **hdr_format** strings are listed in Table 3-6; the **prompt** strings are in Table 3-7.)

So, instead of using **thisfolder:t** in the example above, you can use the **prompt** string %**f**:

```
set newprompt='"%f-$cwd:t> "'
eval set prompt=$initprompt
```

Note that **hdr_format** strings are expanded using information from the current message. Thus, instead of using these commands to display all the messages with the same Subject header as the current one:

```
set subject = "$[%s]"
pick —s $subject
```

use this command instead:

```
eval —h pick —s %s
```

You can also use this format in command-line aliases. For example, put this command in your initialization file:

```
cmd delsub "eval —h pick —s %s | delete"
```

 Now, you can delete all the messages in the current folder that have the same Subject as the current message by entering **delsub** at the line-mode prompt. Note that you can't use both **–h** and **–p** in the same **eval** command line.

The **eval** command is mostly used in functions; for more examples, see the */usr/lib/Zmail/sample.lib* file on your system.

Creating Your Own Variables

With Z-Mail, you can create your own variables and manipulate them as you do the built-in Z-Mail variables. For example, you might want to set a temporary variable to use in a script or function. Use the following syntax to create your own variables:

```
set variable_name = variable_value
```

For example, you can create a temporary file (like the one in the **bounce** command-line alias earlier in this chapter) like this:

```
Msg 3 of 10: set tmpfile = /tmp/tmp$$
```

This uses the value of the special variable **$$** (the process ID (PID) number of the Z-Mail process) in the name of a temporary directory. To display the value of **tmpfile**, enter the following command:

Z-Mail displays:

    /tmp/tmp4110

This command creates a variable called **monthfile** and sets it to a file, using the current month and year for the name.

    Msg 3 of 10: set monthfile = $(%M)-$(%y)

In this example, if the current date is July 4, 1991, the value of **monthfile** is **July-91**.

You can also use pipes to create your own variables to store information about the last command or the results of a particular **pick** operation. For example, here's how to create a variable and set its value to a list of messages:

    Msg 7 of 12: pick —s Status Reports | set reports

This creates the new variable called **reports** and sets it to a message list (all the messages that contain "Status Reports" in the `Subject` header). To see the numbers of these messages, enter the following:

    Msg 7 of 12: echo $reports

Z-Mail displays the value of **reports**:[1]

    4,6-8,12

Now you can use the variable as the message list for any command that accepts one. Let's say you want to save those messages to a file. Use this command:

    Msg 7 of 12: save $reports +status.reports

This saves the value of the **reports** variable (the list of messages) to the file *status.reports* in the folder directory. Z-Mail displays messages like the following:

    Saving message 4 ... (96 lines)
    Saving message 6 ... (19 lines)
    Saving message 7 ... (55 lines)
    Saving message 8 ... (89 lines)
    Saving message 12 ... (12 lines)
    Saved 5 messages to +status.reports

Here's another way you can use this new variable:

    Msg 7 of 12: mail —i $reports linda

This mails the text of all the messages in the **reports** variable to *linda*.

Although you can create and set your own variables, these variables don't show up when you list all the possible variables and help text with **set ?all**; Z-Mail only displays the Z-Mail internal variables with this command. To display your current variables (including the ones you created), use **set**.

---

[1] MUSH uses spaces instead of commas to separate the message numbers. For this reason, it's generally a good idea to put quotes around the variable reference, in this case "**$reports**".

In the following sections, we'll give more examples that show how to create and use your own variables in some sample scripts and functions.

Z-Mail Scripts

A Z-Mail script is a file containing Z-Mail commands. You can include these commands in your ~/.zmailrc initialization file so that Z-Mail reads them automatically each time you invoke Z-Mail, or you can put them in other files, called *script files*, and read them in manually. Either way, scripts are similar in format to the ~/.zmailrc (or .mushrc) initialization file; Chapter 8, *Customizing Z-Mail*, contains a complete description of this format.

Keep in mind that history-referencing is disabled in script files except for use in **cmd** command-line aliases. In addition, some older versions of MUSH don't allow you to use the exclamation mark (!) to reference arguments in **cmd** command-line aliases either.

In Chapter 8, we discuss the format of initialization and script files. In the following sections, we'll discuss the different ways you can run scripts and then give you some sample scripts and explain how they work.

Running Scripts

Basically, scripts are like initialization files. You can source them at startup time with the **–source (–F)** option like this:

```
$ zmail –source ~/.init.script
```

 or you can read them from within Z-Mail with the **source** command:

```
Msg 3 of 10: source ~/.init.script
```

Unlike regular initialization files, you can include commands that manipulate or search through messages. Because Z-Mail reads the regular initialization file, ~/.zmailrc, *before* scanning the folder, there are no messages to manipulate until after the folder is scanned. The **–source** option tells Z-Mail to read the specified file *after* scanning the folder. (If you use the **–init (–I)** option instead, Z-Mail reads the specified file before scanning the folder.) To execute the script without entering the Z-Mail program, use the **source!** option from the UNIX command line.

Let's say ~/.init.script contains commands that sort all the messages in the folder into separate folders. To run the script, use the following command:

```
$ zmail –source! ~/.init.script
```

In this case, Z-Mail runs the commands in *init.script* on your system mailbox and returns you to the UNIX command line.

Another way to read scripts is to redirect the input from a script file to your folder using **–interact (–i)** like this:

```
$ zmail –interact < ~/.init.script
```

Note that, if the ˜/.init.script file contains comments (lines that begin with the pound character (#)), you can't direct input from them to Z-Mail.

The **–interact** option forces Z-Mail to run interactively in situations where it wouldn't ordinarily; for example, if you're running Z-Mail remotely using *rsh*. This situation isn't very common, but Z-Mail provides **–interact** for backwards-compatibility with UCB *Mail*.

When you run Z-Mail with the **–interact** command-line option, Z-Mail reads the commands in the initialization file as if you entered them at the command line (or in compose mode). For this reason, Z-Mail doesn't treat the pound character (#) as a comment.

Sample Scripts

Here's a Z-Mail script file called *cleanrecord* for cleaning out your outgoing messages folder. (This script uses some commands and variables not available in MUSH, but there is a similar script for MUSH later in this section.) Put this script in a file and then run it (using **source**) at the end of each month to sort the outgoing messages in your **record** file to a filename indicating the current month and year.

```
set quiet = "pick save"
# don't display messages during picks and saves
set outmail = $record
# set local $outmail variable to $record
set monthfile = +old.mail/$(%M)-$(%y)
# set the filename to save to
if —e $+old.mail        # test to see if the directory exists,
     if —e $outmail   # and the file exists
          if —z $outmail # and is not empty
               exit        # exit the script if it's empty
          endif
          open —N $outmail # open the file
          pick —ago —1 month | save $monthfile | delete
          # select, save, and delete messages
          close  # update and close the folder
          unset outmail monthfile quiet
          # unset the local variables
     endif
endif
```

First, the script sets **quiet** to "pick save" to suppress any messages that the **pick** and **save** commands display. Then, the script sets the **outfile** variable to the value of **$record** and **$monthfile** to a filename located in the directory *old.mail* in the default folder directory. The value of **monthfile** depends on the special variables $(%M), for name of the current month and $(%y), the number of the current year. So, if you run the script on February 28, 1991, the value of **monthfile** is **Feb-91**.

The script tests to make sure the *old.mail* directory exists. Then, the script tests to see if **outfile** exists and contains messages. If any of these conditions is not true, the script exits. If **outfile** contains messages, the script opens the folder (using the **–N** option to **open** to suppress the header summary display), picks out all the messages older than one month, saves them to **monthfile**, and deletes them. Then, the script runs the **close** command to update and close the current folder and switch back to the previous folder. Finally, it unsets the local variables (**outfile**, **monthfile**, and **quiet**).

You can change the script so that it displays progress messages as it selects messages and saves them by unsetting the **quiet** variable. However, you might not want to use the default verbose **pick** and **save** messages. You can create your own progress messages with the **echo** command and use the **verify** variable to prompt before updating the folder, as shown in the following example script:

```
set quiet = "pick save"
set outmail = $record
set monthfile = +old.mail/$(%M)-$(%y)
set verify = update
# prompt for verification when you update
if -e $+old.mail
      if -e $outmail
            if -z $outmail
                  exit
            endif
            open -N $outmail
            pick -ago -1 month | set messages
            # store messages in variable
            echo Saving messages $output to $monthfile...
            # print progress message
            save $messages $monthfile # save messages
            echo Deleting messages $messages...
            # print progress message
            delete $messages  # remove messages
            close
            unset outmail monthfile
      endif
endif
```

Now, when you run the script, Z-Mail selects the messages that are more than one month old and stores this information in **$message**. Then, **echo** displays a message like the following, immediately before saving the messages to **$monthfile**:

```
Saving messages 1-12 to May-91...
```

Setting the **quiet** variable doesn't suppress all the messages from **save**; you still see a message like the following:

```
Saved 12 msgs to May-91
```

Immediately before deleting the messages, **echo** displays a message like the following:

```
Deleting messages 1-12...
```

Before updating and closing the folder, **verify** prompts:

```
Update ~/.out.mail? (y/n/c) [y] _
```

If you decide you don't want to delete all the messages, enter **n** to cancel the update and Z-Mail displays the following (if you press **c**, Z-Mail doesn't close the folder):

```
Close anyway? (y/n) [y] _
```

Press **y** to close the folder without updating or **n** to remain in the folder.

Running the cleanrecord Script

Put the Z-Mail script in a file and call it *cleanrecord*. To run this file at the end of the month, read the file from within Z-Mail using this command:

```
Msg 3 of 10: source cleanrecord
```

Later in this chapter, we'll show you how to create Z-Mail functions from scripts like this so that you can execute them by name, instead of using **source**.

A MUSH Script

The previous scripts in this section do not work with MUSH because they use **open** and **close**, commands that are not available in MUSH. In addition, MUSH doesn't support the **update** keyword to **verify** or the **save** keyword to **quiet**.

While you can't suppress **save** messages and prompt before updating, you can still create a MUSH script that accomplishes (mostly) the same things as the Z-Mail script. So, if you're using MUSH, use the following script instead:

```
set quiet = pick
set outmail = $record
set monthfile = +old.mail/$(%M)-$(%y)
if —e $+old.mail
     if —e $outmail
            if —z $outmail
                  exit
            endif
            folder -N $outmail
            pick —ago —1 month | set messages
            echo Saving messages $output to $monthfile...
            save $messages $monthfile
            echo Deleting messages $messages...
            delete $messages
            update       # update the folder manually
            folder "#"   # switch to previous folder
            unset outmail monthfile quiet
      endif
endif
```

First, the script sets **quiet** to suppress messages from **pick**; it then sets the **$outfile** and **$monthfile** variables just as in the Z-Mail script. The script performs the same tests—verify that the *old.mail* directory exists and that **$outfile** exists and contains messages. If so, it updates the current folder, switches to **$outfile**, picks out all the messages older than one month and saves them to **$messages**. Then **echo** displays the following message and MUSH saves the messages to **monthfile**:

```
Saving messages 1–12 to May-91...
```

The **echo** command displays:

```
Deleting messages 1–12...
```

and then deletes them. Finally, MUSH updates the current folder, switches back to the previous folder with the **folder "#"** command, and unsets the local variables.

Note that when we to refer to the previously active folder, we enclose the pound character (**#**) in double quotes ("). This is because Z-Mail interprets this character as a comment in script files; use the double quotes to prevent this from happening. Chapter 5, *Z-Mail Shortcuts, Bells, and Whistles*, has more information on the options to **folder**.

Using the #! Syntax in Scripts

If you're running BSD UNIX, you can use the "**#!**" syntax to turn your script into an executable program. (This syntax is generally not supported on System V UNIX systems earlier than Release 4.) To use this feature, add a line like the following as the first line in the script file:

```
#! /usr/bin/zmail —source
```

This invokes Z-Mail (instead of the shell) to run the script.

NOTE

The total length of the string on the **#!** is usually limited to 32 characters and can contain exactly one argument to the command. To stay within this character limit, you might need to use the **–F** command-line option instead of **–source**.

Now, make the script file executable. For example, make *cleanrecord* executable with this command:

```
$ chmod +x cleanrecord
```

If you don't have a *bin* subdirectory in your home directory, create one and add it to your **PATH** environment variable setting (in ˜/.*profile* or ˜/.*login*). Now, put *cleanrecord* in the *bin* subdirectory. To run the commands in the *cleanrecord* program on your system mailbox, enter this command:

```
$ cleanrecord
```

This invokes Z-Mail, reads commands from *cleanrecord*, and executes them on the messages in your system mailbox. Then, it enters the Z-Mail program.

Running Scripts Non-interactively

If you want to run the commands in the *cleanrecord* script on the folder without interacting with Z-Mail, use this **#!** line at the beginning of the *cleanrecord* file instead:

```
#! /usr/bin/zmail —source!
```

You should also use **–source!** if you plan to run the script in the background using the ampersand character (**&**). For example, run *cleanrecord* in the background with this command:

```
$ cleanrecord&
```

Use **–source!** in any other situation where you can't enter commands from the terminal and the script contains all the commands that you want to execute.

For example, you might want to set up a *cron* job to run *cleanrecord* automatically each month. In this case, do not add the **#!** line at the beginning of *cleanrecord*. Instead, add these lines to your file in the */usr/spool/cron/crontabs* directory:[2]

```
0    0    1,3,5,7,8,10,12    31    *    /usr/bin/zmail —source! ./bin/cleanrecord
0    0    2                  28    *    /usr/bin/zmail —source! ./bin/cleanrecord
0    0    4,6,9,11           30    *    /usr/bin/zmail —source! ./bin/cleanrecord
```

With these lines in the */usr/spool/cron/crontabs/hanna* file, *cron* runs **zmail** (which runs the commands in */u/hanna/bin/cleanrecord*) at midnight on the last day of each month. (Note that this *crontabs* entry doesn't work in Leap Years.) Make sure that you use **—source!** (rather than **—source**), otherwise *cron* enters the Z-Mail program.

 You might want to create a different script for cleaning out your *mbox* folder. For example, instead of saving messages to folders by month name, this script deletes messages that are older than three months:

```
set quiet = pick
set mailbox = $mbox
if —e $mailbox
    if —z $mailbox
        exit
    endif
    open $mailbox
    pick —ago —3 months | delete
    # delete messages older than 3 months
    close
    unset mailbox quiet
endif
```

In this script, note that instead of selecting messages from the current month, we select messages that are three months old (**pick —ago 3 months**) and pipe the results directly to **delete**.

To run this script without interacting with Z-Mail, put this script in an executable file called *cleanmbox* in your *bin* directory and add this line to the beginning of the script:

```
#! /usr/bin/zmail —F!
```

If you want to run *cleanmbox* automatically with *cron*, remove the **#!** line and use this *crontab* line to run the script:

```
0    0    1    1,4,7,10    *    /usr/bin/zmail —source! ./bin/cleanmbox
```

With this line in your *crontabs* file, *cron* runs Z-Mail, which runs *cleanmbox* at midnight every three months, on the first day of January, April, August, and October.

---

[2] If you're not familiar with the format of the *crontabs* file, refer to your operating system documentation. Also, note that many BSD UNIX systems do not have per-user *cron*; check with your system administrator for more information.

Building Functions

Now that you know how to write scripts to run Z-Mail commands and the different ways you can run them, we'll show you how to use the Z-Script scripting language to build your own *functions*. (Functions are a new feature of Z-Mail and are not available in MUSH.)

If you're using Z-Mail (as opposed to MUSH), all the commands in this section are available to use in scripts as well as in functions. The only difference between these commands and the commands presented in the "Z-Mail Scripts" section earlier in this chapter and the "Initialization File Format" section in Chapter 8 is that the commands in this section are not available in MUSH.

Z-Mail functions are similar to functions in the C programming language (and in the Bourne and Korn shells) in that both consist of a group of logically connected commands that perform a specific task. With each function performing a task, you can combine them to create scripts.

So, when would you use a function instead of a script (or vice versa)? In general, the distinction is how you intend to use it. One way is to distinguish between commands that you run often or that you plan to run interactively (we'll explain more about prompting for input later in this section). In these cases, you create a function so that it is available simply by entering a command (or pressing a button in the GUI mode). Put functions in your initialization file; Z-Mail reads in the function definitions automatically at startup time and stores them in memory.

On the other hand, you might plan to run the commands every once in awhile or you want Z-Mail to run it automatically in the background (for example, *cron* runs our *cleanmbox* script every three months). In these situations, create a script (in a file other than your initialization file) and then run it with *cron* or source it manually with **source**. Z-Mail doesn't load the script into memory each time you start the program; instead, Z-Mail reads the commands at the time that you source the script file.

One limitation of functions is that you cannot define a function inside another function. However, you can call functions from both scripts and functions. So, if you have several tasks that you want to perform, create a function for each task, and then call each of the functions from a script or function.

The simplest way to create a function is to use the **function** command to attach a name to a script. Then use this name, instead of reading a file with **source**, to run the commands in the script. As you'll see in this section, Z-Mail provides additional commands (for use in scripts as well as functions) that you can use to prompt for input, provide defaults, force a selection, select arguments from the command line, and attach functions to buttons so that you can run them in each of the different interfaces.

The function Command

Here's the syntax for creating functions with the **function** command:

```
function function_name() {
        script
}
```

When you define a function, you must include a pair of empty parentheses, (), immediately after the *function_name*. The last argument on the **function** line must be a left curly brace ({).[3] The right curly brace (}) at the beginning of a line signifies the end of the current function. The *script* can be any series of conditional statements and commands that you use to create scripts or set up the initialization file. As we describe each of the commands in this section, we explain how to use them in functions; keep in mind that you can convert many of these functions to scripts by removing the function syntax from around the script text. You can use the # character for comments and spaces and tabs to indent lines.

Creating Help for Functions

 You can also create special help text for your functions. This text is displayed when you enter the function name followed by –? at the Z-Mail command line (in line mode) or you press the Help key on a button for your function (in GUI mode).

To include help text, place a line beginning with **#%** immediately following the first line of the function declaration. Now, enter the help text as comment lines (lines beginning with the pound character). Finally, end the help text with another line beginning with **#%**. The format looks like this:

```
function function_name() {
#%
# Some help text.
# Some more help text.
# The last line of help text.
#%
        script
}
```

If the *function_name* in this case is **cleanrecord**, when you enter the following command in line mode:

```
Msg 3 of 10: cleanrecord -?
```

you see the following help message:

```
cleanrecord is a user-defined function

Some help text.
Some more help text.
The last line of help text.
```

---

[3] Note that this differs from the Bourne and Korn shell functions, which allow a newline before the left curly brace ({).

Note that, if you place the help text outside the function declaration (between the left and right curly braces), Z-Mail can't find the help text. In this case, you see this message when you request help:

```
cleanrecord is a user-defined function
```

Function Naming Conventions

Note that function names cannot contain any of the following characters: $| ; 1 2 3 4 5 6 7 8 9$ $0 * ^ \$$. In addition, function names cannot contain any whitespace (blanks or tabs).

The *function_name* can be any word you prefer, but watch out. If you name your function the same name as a Z-Mail command, whenever you use that name, you'll execute your function, not the Z-Mail command. For example, if you have a function called **delete**, whenever you execute **delete**, Z-Mail runs your function. In this case (if you set the **warning** variable), you'll see a message like this when you start Z-Mail or source your initialization file:

```
Warning: "delete" is the name of a builtin command.
```

You might want to use this feature to replace some of the Z-Mail commands with your own functions; to do this, write your functions and then use the names of Z-Mail commands to name them.

If you redefine the default Z-Mail commands by creating functions with the same names, you might have problems when you use those names in other functions. For example, if you want to call the Z-Mail **delete** command instead of your **delete** function, use the **builtin** command. The **builtin** command calls default Z-Mail commands instead of your functions. For example, if you want to call **delete** from within the function, call **builtin delete** instead.

As in scripts and initialization files, the **exit** command in a function means to exit the current function. (However, it's better to use **return** to exit functions because you have more control over the exit status of the function; we'll explain **return** in the next section.) If you want the function to exit the Z-Mail program, use **x** or **builtin exit** instead.

Creating a Simple Function

Here's an example of a simple function for sending a file to a specific person (you might find it handy for submitting a weekly status report to your boss):

```
function mailreport() {
    mail -H report -s "Status Report" -U linda
}
```

Try creating this function at your line-mode prompt. First, enter:

```
Msg 3 of 10: function mailreport() {
```

When you press RETURN, the Z-Mail prompt changes to:

```
>
```

Now, enter the second and third lines:

```
> mail —H report —s "Status Report" —U linda
> }
Msg 3 of 10: _
```

Once you enter the closing right curly brace (}), Z-Mail returns you to line mode and you've created the **mailreport** function. As with **cmd**s and variable settings, **mailreport** only exists for the current session; to save it to your ~/.zmailrc file, use **saveopts**. Use this method to build and test your functions before saving them to files.

When you enter **mailreport** at the line-mode prompt, Z-Mail sends the file called *report* to *linda* with the subject "Status Report." The **—U** option tells Z-Mail to send the file immediately, without further editing.

The **mailreport** function is very simple, intended only to introduce you to the form of **function**. You could easily do the same thing by creating a command-line alias with **cmd** like this:

```
Msg 3 of 10: cmd mailreport 'mail —H report —s "Status Report" —U linda'
```

Both the **mailreport** function and **cmd** definitions accomplish the same thing; however, with **cmd**, you are limited to one line to define your command-line alias. With **function**, you can use as many lines as you like; just remember to use the proper syntax. Notice that, using **function**, you don't need the extra pair of quotes required with **cmd**.

As you'll see, functions can be much more powerful than command-line aliases. For instance, you can modify **mailreport** to prompt you for a file, test to verify that it exists and is not empty, prompt for a list of addresses, send the file, and then display a status message. We'll explain these features in upcoming sections.

Turning Scripts into Functions

You can create functions out of existing scripts using the **function** command. For example, let's use the contents of the *cleanrecord* script to create a function that you can run by entering **cleanrecord**. Put the following function definition in your ~/.zmailrc:

```
function cleanrecord(){
    set quiet = "pick save"
    set outmail = $record
    set monthfile = +old.mail/$(%M)-$(%y)
    set verify = update
    if —e $monthfile
        if —e $outmail
            if —z $outmail
                exit
            endif
            open —N $outmail
            pick —ago —1 month | set messages
            echo Saving messages $output to $monthfile...
            save $messages $monthfile
            echo Deleting messages $messages...
            delete $messages
            close
```

```
                unset outmail monthfile
            endif
        endif
    }
```

We simply add the "`function cleanrecord( ){`" line at the top of the script and the left curly brace ({) at the bottom (and adjust the indentation to make it easier to read). Now, if you put this function in your initialization file (*~/.zmailrc*) or another file that you source at startup time, Z-Mail automatically loads the function into memory. You can call **cleanrecord** from within Z-Mail at any time by entering the following command at the prompt:

```
Msg 3 of 10: cleanrecord
```

Here's another simple function for saving messages from an alias to another folder. For example, if you're on the *mush-users* alias, you get the postings from the *comp.mail.mush* newsgroup mailed directly to you.

 You can create a function that automatically moves all these messages from your system mailbox to a separate folder. This function, called **savemush**, saves all the messages with the string "comp.mail.mush" in the **Newsgroups** header to a folder called *comp.mail.mush*:

```
function savemush() {
    if -e +News
    # make sure $folder/News directory exists!
        set mushnews = +News/comp.mail.mush
        # name the file
        if $thisfolder == /usr/spool/mail/hanna
        # make sure we're in the system mailbox
            pick -h Newsgroups comp.mail.mush | set mushmesg
            # select messages and store in mushmesg variable
            save $mushmesg $mushnews
            # save messages
            delete $mushmesg
            # delete messages
            update
            # update current folder to get rid of deleted messages
            unset mushnews mushmesg
            # unset local variables
        endif
    endif
}
```

Enter **savemush** at your Z-Mail prompt to run the script. First, **savemush** tests to see that the directory *+News* exists (remember that the plus character (+) refers to the value of the **folder** variable). If the directory exists, Z-Mail sets the **mushnews** variable to the file *comp.mail.mush* in **+News**. The function verifies that the current folder (**$thisfolder**) is the system mailbox, selects all the messages with "comp.mail.mush" in the **Newsgroups** header and saves them to *+News/comp.mail.mush*. Finally, this function deletes those messages from the system mailbox, updates the system folder, and unsets the local variables, **mushnews** and **mushmesg**.

The return Command

You can use the **return** command, as well as **exit**, to exit from a function. While **exit** simply stops running the function, **return** allows you to set the value of **$status** when the function exits. Because of this added control, **return** is preferable to **exit**.

With **return**, you can set **$status** to one of the values in Table 9-2.

Table 9-2. status Variable Values

Value	Response
0	Yes (or a valid response).
1	No (yes/no/cancel only).
−1	Cancel.

You might want to create **true** and **false** functions for setting the **status** variable. Here's an example:

```
function true( ) {
    return 0
}
function false( ) {
    return -1
}
```

In this case, you can set the **$status** to −1 using the **false** function. In the following example, if the value of **$selection** is **c**, this executes the **false** function to set **status** to −1:

```
if $selection == c
    false
endif
```

Note that this doesn't necessarily cause the current function to return; the function returns whatever the final value of **$status** is.

Argument Variables

When you call a function, the arguments from the command line are passed to that function. Each word from the command line represents a parameter. To refer to specific words on the command line, use the special variables in Table 9-3. These variables are not available in scripts. (In shells, such as the Bourne shell (*sh*), these variables are also known as *positional parameters*.)

Table 9-3. Special Argument Variables

Variable	Description
$*	The entire list of command-line arguments.
$#	The total number of command-line arguments.
$0	Function name.
$1-$N	Individual arguments on the command line.

For example, you can use the value of $* (all the command-line arguments) inside your function. For example, if you have a function that takes a filename as a command-line argument (for example, a **savemsg** function), you can use $* to refer to the filename entered at the prompt (we'll explain the **ask** command in the next section):

```
ask -i _filename "Save: $*\nFilename:" $_choices
```

When you call the function that includes this line: Z-Mail displays the prompt `Save:`, followed by the filename that you gave on the command line:

```
Save: from_dale
```

The sections that follow give more examples of how to use the special argument variables in Table 9-3.

The ask Command

The **ask** command is used inside functions, scripts, and command-line aliases (with **cmd**) to prompt for input from the keyboard. As we stated earlier, you might prefer to use scripts to run commands in the background; in this case, you probably don't want to put interactive commands, like **ask**, in your scripts.

For example, you might want to create a function that prompts you for confirmation when you enter the **quit** command or that prompts for a list of people to whom you want to forward a message. In line and fullscreen mode, **ask** prints a prompt; in GUI mode, **ask** generates a prompt box. Here's what the syntax for **ask** looks like:

```
ask [-i variable [-m]] [-d default] "question" [choices]
```

We'll explain more about these options in the following sections.

Yes, No, or Cancel?

If you don't specify a *choice*, **ask** assumes that *question* requires a "yes," "no," or "cancel" response with "yes" as the default choice. This is commonly used to prompt for confirmation before performing an action, as in the following example:

```
ask "Do you really want to Quit?"
```

In this example, **ask** displays the prompt like this:

```
Do you really want to Quit? (y/n/c) [y] _
```

The choices (**yes**, **no**, or **cancel**) appear in parentheses; the default action (the action that occurs if you simply press RETURN) appears in square brackets. You can change the default action using the –d option. For example, if you want the default to be **n** instead of **y**, use this command:

```
ask -d n "Do you really want to Quit?"
```

The prompt looks like this:

```
Do you really want to Quit? (y/n/c) [n] _
```

Now, to select **n**, simply press RETURN.

Z-Mail stores the response to the question in the **status** variable, where **$status** is one of the values in Table 9-2. In this case, if you specifically enter **c** or anything other than **u**, **q**, or **e**, or you cancel the **ask** question by pressing CTRL-C or DEL (the interrupt character on your system), Z-Mail sets the **$status** variable to **–1** to indicate that the last command failed.

One common use of the **$status** variable in scripts and functions is to test the value of **$status** before performing an action. For example, to build the **quit** confirmation function, use the equality operator (= =) to test if **$status** evaluates to 0 (the response is **y**) before executing the **quit** command. Here's how to do this:

```
function Quit() {
ask -d n "Do you really want to Quit?"  # set default to "n"
if $status == 0                         # if "yes"
        builtin quit                    # quit Z-Mail
endif
}
```

Again, when you enter **Quit**, you see this prompt:

```
Do you really want to Quit? (y/n/c) [n] _
```

If you enter **y**, this function executes the **quit** command (to exit from Z-Mail). If you enter anything other than **y** (or press RETURN), the value of **$status** is nonzero (1 or –1) and the **Quit** function does nothing.

Prompting for a String

Not all questions require yes or no answers. For example, let's say you want to write a function that forwards the current message to another person; you can use **ask** to prompt for that person's name. In this case, you'll need a place to store the response to the question. To do this, use the –i option to specify a *variable*. For example, this **ask** command prompts for the people to forward the message to and stores that information in *$recipients*:

```
ask -i recipients "Forward current message to: "
```

The prompt looks like this:

```
Forward current message to: _
```

Anything that you enter at this prompt is stored in the **recipients** variable. You can then pass this information on to other commands, such as **mail**, in the function.

For example, here's how to create a simple function called **Forward**:

```
function Forward( ) {
    ask -i recipients "Forward current message to: "
    # store response in "recipients"
    if $status == 0              # if answer is valid
        mail -U -f $recipients # forward message to recipients
    endif
}
```

Notice that the function still tests to see if the value of **$status** is 0 before continuing. The status of the **ask** command is still stored in the **status** variable; the function returns 0 if you enter a valid response, −1 if you cancel. (The **ask** function only returns 1 if you enter **n** to a yes/no/cancel prompt.)

If you don't cancel the function, the **Forward** function passes the contents of $recipients to the **mail** command.

Going back to our **mailreport** function from earlier in the chapter, let's use **ask** to add a prompt for the filename to send. While we're at it, we should also add some tests to verify that the file exists and isn't empty:

```
function mailreport( ) {
    ask -i filename "Send which file? "
    # store response in "filename"
    if -e $filename                 # if $filename exists
        if !-z $filename            # and $filename isn't empty
            if $status == 0         # if answer is valid
                mail -H $filename -s "Status Report" -U linda
                # send file to linda
            endif
        else
            echo "$filename is empty."
        endif
    else
        echo "$filename does not exist."
    endif
}
```

In this case, when you enter **mailreport**, **ask** displays the following prompt:

```
Send which file? _
```

When you press RETURN after entering the filename, Z-Mail includes the file and sends the message. You see the following:

```
Msg 3 of 10: mailreport
Send which file?  8.3.status
To: linda
Subject: Status Report

65 lines
Cc:
Msg 3 of 10: _
```

If the filename doesn't exist or is empty, you'll see an error message.

You can have more than one **ask** command in your functions. For example, if you don't always send the report to the same person, you can modify **mailreport** to prompt for the recipients (instead of automatically sending it to *linda*):

```
function mailreport( ) {
    ask -i filename "Send which file? "
    # store response in "filename"
    ask -i recipients "To whom? "
    # store response in "$recipients"
    if -e $filename
    # if $filename exists
        if !-z $filename
        # and $filename isn't empty
            if $status == 0
            # if answer is valid
                mail -H $filename -s "Status Report" -U $recipients
                # send file to $recipients
            endif
        else
            echo "$filename is empty."
        endif
    else
        echo "$filename does not exist."
    endif
}
```

Now, **mailreport**, also displays this prompt:

```
To whom? _
```

When you press RETURN after entering the address list, Z-Mail includes the file and sends the message to the people that you specify.

Providing a Selection

You can also provide a selection of options to choose from when answering the prompt. For example, to write a function for saving messages that prompts you for the filename and provides a choice, simply add the list of choices after the prompt.

So, to list *mbox* and *~/Mail/function* as choices with **ask**, use a command like the following:

```
ask -i filename -d $mbox "Save this message to:" +function $mbox
```

Note that this command uses the value of the **mbox** variable. The *function* folder is located in the folder directory (+), in other words, whatever is specified by the **folder** variable.

When you invoke the function, the prompt looks like this:

```
Save message to:[+function, ~/mbox] ~/mbox_
```

If you don't specify a default (in this case, the default is *mbox*), **ask** uses the first word following the prompt as the default choice. If, when answering the prompt, you don't want to use any of the provided selections, you can erase the default selection, using DEL, BACK-SPACE, word-erase (usually CTRL-W), or line-erase (usually CTRL-U), and then enter a new value. To cancel the **ask** question, erase the default choice and enter the **EOF** character (usually CTRL-D), or type the interrupt character.

Here's an example of a function that lists the value of the **mbox** variable if it is set:

```
function Save( ) {
        if $?mbox                    # if mbox is set
             set choice = $mbox  # then, set choice to mbox
        else
             set choice = " "    # set choice to empty string
        endif
        ask -i filename "Save message to:" $choice
        # put $choice in "filename"
        if $status == 0            # if valid response
             save $filename         # save to specified file.
        endif
}
```

First, the **Save** function tests to see if **mbox** is set; if it is, this function sets the **choice** variable to the value of **mbox**. If **mbox** isn't set, then **choice** is set to a blank string. Then, the **ask** command prompts for the file to save the message to, giving the value of **choice** as a selection. So, if **mbox** is set to *˜/mbox*, the prompt is:

```
Save message to:  ˜/mbox _
```

If **mbox** isn't set, the prompt is:

```
Save message to: _
```

The string that you enter at the prompt is stored in $**filename**. If you enter a valid response, this function saves the current message to the *filename* file.

Forcing a Selection

What if you want to restrict the selection to the choices you provide? Let's say you've got a function called **Bye** that prompts whether to update the folder (thus leaving any new and unread messages marked as new and unread), write back all changes before quitting, or exit without modifying the folder. In this case, you have three specific choices; you don't want to allow for any others.

To limit the selection, use the **−m** (for "match") option. For example, let's say you give three choices:

```
ask -i selection -m "Update, Quit or Exit? " u q e
```

Here's what the prompt looks like:

```
Update, Quit or Exit? [u, q, e] u_
```

If you enter any command other than the three listed commands, you get the following error message and Z-Mail displays the prompt again:

```
You must select one of the choices.
```

With **−m**, you have to select one of the choices or press the interrupt character (CTRL-C or DEL) to cancel the function. For this reason, you might want to make Cancel one of the choices. Here's an example:

```
function Bye( ) {
        ask -i selection -m "Update, Quit, Exit or Cancel?" u q e c
             if $status == 0                # if a valid response
```

```
                        if $selection == u    # if "update"
                             builtin update    # run Z-Mail update command.
                        endif
                        if $selection == q    # if "quit"
                             builtin quit      # run Z-Mail quit command.
                        endif
                        if $selection == e    # if "exit"
                             builtin exit      # run Z-Mail exit command.
                        endif
                        if $selection == c    # if "cancel"
                             return -1         # exit Bye, return -1.
                        endif
                else
                        if $status != 0       # if invalid response
                             return -1         # cancel, exit Bye, return -1.
                        endif
                endif
        }
```

In this example, **Bye** calls the builtin **update** command if you respond with **u** to the prompt. If you enter **q** or **e**, **Bye** calls the builtin Z-Mail commands, **quit** or **exit**, and you exit the program entirely. If you enter **c** or anything other than **u**, **q**, or **e**, **Bye** calls the **return** command.

Manipulating Function Arguments with the shift Command

If you tested the **mailreport**, **Save**, or **Forward** functions in the earlier examples, you probably noticed that they ignore any arguments (such as a message list, filename, or a list of recipients) that you give on the command line. Thus, you can't use **Forward** like this:

```
Msg 3 of 10: Forward 3-8 george
```

The function still prompts you for the recipients and then forwards the current message, regardless of what you specify on the command line.

If you want to create a function that expects arguments from the command line, you'll need to use the **shift** command to distinguish between the message list and any other arguments. Here's the syntax for **shift**:

```
shift [ -m | N ]
```

The **shift** command allows you to remove arguments from the beginning of the list of words on the command line. By itself, **shift** removes the first word from the list. Use **shift** with the **-m** argument to remove any leading message list from the list of command-line arguments. You can then use the pipe character (|) to store this information in a variable to use later. Here's a simple example of how to do this:

```
function replyinclude() {
    shift -m | set msg_list      # sets the messages to reply
    reply $msg_list -i $msg_list  # replies to, including the messages
}
```

When you enter **replyinclude** followed by a message list, this function saves the message list in the *msg_list* variable. Then, the function invokes the **reply** command to reply to the messages in *msg_list* and includes them with the **–i** option. So, in other words, this command:

```
Msg 3 of 10: replyinclude 8-10
```

is equivalent to entering this command:

```
Msg 3 of 10: reply 8-10 -i 8-10
```

In the latter case, you have to specify the messages that you are including in addition to the messages which you are replying to.

Let's go back to the arguments that we tried to pass to our **Forward** function:

```
Msg 3 of 10: Forward 3-8 george
```

In this example, the total number of command-line arguments (the value of **$#**) is 2 (**$1** is "3-8" and **$2** is "george") and the value of the first argument (**$0**) is Forward. To refer to the message list (the first argument on the command line), use **$1**.

Our **Forward** command line is a more complex example. The **shift –m** removes the first ("3-8") argument, leaving one argument (the new **$1**).

Once you strip the message list argument from the command line, you can test for the number of remaining arguments. If there are no arguments remaining, then the function should prompt for a list of recipients. However, if there is one (as in our **Forward** example), then the recipients have already been specified on the command line and the function should use that information, rather than prompt for it.

Let's take a look at the **Forward** function now. The new function uses the message list and recipients from the command line, if specified; otherwise, it prompts for the recipients and forwards the current message:

```
function Forward( ) {
    shift -m | set messages
    if ! $?messages
        set messages = "."
    endif
    if $status == -1
        return
    endif
    if $# == 1
        ask -i recipients "Forward message(s) to:"
        if $status == -1
            return
        endif
    else
        set recipients = "$*"
    endif
    mail -Uf $messages $recipients
    unset recipients messages
}
```

Forward first removes the message list from the list of command-line arguments and stores it in **$messages**. Then, the function tests to see if **messages** is set; if not, the function sets **messages** to the current message. (The reason for this is the **set** command does not set **messages**

if there is no list of messages for **shift –m** to remove; you have to set **messages** manually in this case.) Then, it tests to see if the function was canceled (remember, a function returns –1 and stores this value in **$status** if you cancel it). If the value of **$status** is –1, the function stops and returns.

The function then tests **$#**. Now, if there are no arguments on the command line, it prompts you for the people to forward the message to and stores this information in **$recipients**. Then, the function checks the value of **$status** again and returns if canceled.

If the value of **$#** is not 0, the function sets the value of **recipients** to **$*** (all the remaining arguments on the command line). Then **Forward** invokes **mail** with the –U and –f options, followed by the list of messages and recipients to forward to. Finally, the function unsets the local variables, **$msg_list** and **$recipients**.

If the original command line looked like this:

```
Msg 3 of 10: Forward 3-8 george
```

the **Forward** function creates a command line like this:

```
mail -Uf 3-8 george
```

You can also use **shift** by itself to remove the first single argument from the list of command-line arguments. If you use **shift** followed by a number (*n*), this command removes the first *n* arguments from the command line.

For example, let's say you want to shift two arguments (such as a command name and an option) on the command line. Here's one way to do this:

```
if $1 == -f          # if the first argument is "-f"
    shift            # remove "-f"
    set file = $1    # set file variable to new first argument
    shift            # remove new first argument
endif
```

Another way to do the same thing is to use **shift** with a number argument:

```
if $1 == -f          # if the first argument is "-f"
    set file = $2 # remove first 2 arguments
    shift 2
endif
```

In this case, you don't have to remove each argument separately with **shift**, but the results are the same.

The msg_list Command

The **msg_list** command is similar to **from**, except that it doesn't print the header summaries for the messages that match. Use **msg_list** to parse message lists (either numbers or the special message list characters) in your functions. Here's the syntax:

```
msg_list [+ | - ][msg_list]
```

For example, you can use **msg_list** to evaluate a symbolic message list and use the actual numbers. If the *msg_list* argument is syntactically correct, Z-Mail evaluates the list, places

the numbers in **$output** and sets **$status** to 0. If the list is incorrect, Z-Mail sets **$status** to
–1; in this case; **$output** is empty.

Here's a review of the special message list characters:

*	All the messages in the list.
^	The first message in the list.
$	The last message in the list.
.	The current message.
n-m	A range of messages between *n* and *m*, inclusive.

Remember that you can specify ranges using the other special message list metacharacters
and that the range must be in ascending order.

You can use plus (+) and minus (–) to move the current message pointer to the next and previous messages in the list. If you use + with a list of messages, Z-Mail moves the pointer to
the last message in the message list; with –, Z-Mail moves the pointer to the first message.
For example, this command moves the current message pointer to the last message (message
8) in the range 8-12:

```
Msg 3 of 10: msg_list + 8-12
```

You can also negate a message list using curly braces ({}). For example, to manipulate all
the messages in the list except messages 10 and 12, use this command:

```
Msg 3 of 10: msg_list * {10,12}
```

Here's an example function that uses **msg_list** to test if the current message is deleted:

```
function is_deleted(){
     set deleted = ""
     :d | set deleted
     msg_list . { $deleted } | set current
     if $?current == 0
          return
     endif
}
```

First, the **is_deleted** function finds all the deleted messages and stores them in **deleted**.
Then, using **msg_list**, the function sets the value of the **current** variable to the current message (.) if it's not included in the value of **deleted**. If the value of **$current** is 0, the function
returns successfully.

Another way you can use **msg_list** is in a function that finds all the messages with the same
`Subject` as the current (or currently selected in fullscreen and GUI modes) message:

```
function find_subject() {
     msg_list - $*
     # set current message to message currently selected.
     eval -p pick -s %s | msg_list .
     # eval -p expands the prompt string (%s) of the selected message
     # and "msg_list ." includes selected message in the output list.
}
```

The each Command

With the **each** command, you can execute a specified command once for each message in a list. Here's the syntax:

```
each msg_list command
```

If you want to use options to the *command*, enclose the entire string in double quotes (") or single quotes ('). Thus, to reply to a series of messages, for example, messages 1 through 6 and 10, excluding 2 and 5, use this command:

```
each 1-6 {2,5} 10 reply
```

In this example, **each** passes each number as an argument to **reply** and Z-Mail executes the following commands:

```
reply 1
reply 3
reply 4
reply 6
reply 10
```

Here's another example of how to use **each** to execute a separate command on each message in a list. Let's say you have a multi-part archive (for example, three parts of one Usenet posting) that you want to **pipe** to *sh*. Because **pipe** sends each argument to the same UNIX process, you can't use the following command:

```
Msg 3 of 10: pipe 3,8,12
```

This **pipe** command only affects message 3. To execute **pipe** separately on all three messages, use this command:

```
Msg 3 of 10: each 3,8,12 pipe
```

In this case, Z-Mail runs **pipe** once for each of the messages 3, 8, and 12.

Because Z-Mail passes each number in the message list separately to the command, be careful with multiple commands using pipelines and semicolons. If you want to use complex commands, create a command-line alias (with **cmd**) or a function (with **function**) to use with **each**.

Let's say you also want to include the message that you're replying to; do this with a command-line alias:

```
Msg 3 of 10: cmd replyinclude 'reply \!* -i'
```

Now, use **each** like this:

```
Msg 3 of 10: each 1-5 {3,4} 6 replyinclude
```

In this case, **each** executes four different **reply** commands:

```
reply 1 -i
reply 2 -i
reply 5 -i
reply 6 -i
```

Note that if any of the commands returns a nonzero exit status (the **status** variable is set to **-1**), Z-Mail terminates the loop. However, if the command used with **each** is a user-defined function, the entire function must return –1 to break the loop. This is because command-line aliases and functions return the status of the last command that they execute and **each** only sees the final value of **$status**; the alias or function might reset the value of **$status** before returning.

Here's another example of using a command line to run complex commands with **each**. Let's say you create this command-line alias to pipe messages:

    Msg 3 of 10: cmd pipem 'pipe \!$ \!1-'

Here's an example of how you'd use **pipem** with **each** to send messages to *patch*:

    Msg 3 of 10: each * "pipem patch"

This command executes **pipem** on each message in the folder (*) like this:

    pipe 1 patch
    pipe 2 patch
    pipe 3 patch

And so on.

Another way to do this is with the **foreach** command:

    Msg 3 of 10: foreach msg * 'Pipe $msg patch'

We'll explain **foreach** in the next section.

The same restrictions on the Z-Mail commands that you can run with **filter** apply to the commands that you can run in an **each** loop. For this list of restrictions, see Table 8-7.

The foreach Command

Similar to **each**, the **foreach** command allows you to set variables to each item (filenames or messages) in a list and then execute a command on each item. Unlike **each**, which only allows you to execute the command for each message in the list, **foreach** allows you to execute commands for filenames as well.

Here's the syntax for using **foreach** with a file:

    foreach variable_name (file-list) 'command using $variable_name'

In **foreach**, both *variable_name* and *$variable_name* refer to the same variable name. You must place the *file-list* in parentheses for **foreach** to treat them as filenames. The **foreach** command expands any metacharacters inside the parentheses, such as * and ?, as the C shell does (see Table 5-5 for details).

The **foreach** syntax with messages look like this:

    foreach variable_name msg_list 'command using $variable_name'

Again, *variable_name* and *$variable_name* are the same variable name.

Note the absence of parentheses characters around the *msg_list*; if you put *msg_list* in parentheses, **foreach** treats them as filenames. With no parentheses, **foreach** treats metacharacters as message-list special characters (see Table 3-1 for a list).

In the previous section, we showed you how to run the **pipe** command once for each message in a list. To do the same thing with **foreach**, use this command:

```
Msg 3 of 10: foreach msg 3,8,12 'pipe $msg'
```

This creates the **$msg** variable and sets it to the list of messages (3, 8, and 12). Now, you can run **pipe** on each of the messages in **$msg**. Note that the single quotes (') prevent **$msg** from expanding until **foreach** runs the **pipe** command.

Suppose you want to specify the program for **pipe** to use (instead of the default, *sh*). You can try this with **each** as in the following example:

```
Msg 3 of 10: each 3,8,12 'pipe patch'
```

In this case, **each** tries to pipe *patch* to each of the messages (using the command **pipe patch 3**) instead of piping each of the messages to *patch* (**pipe 3 patch**). The *patch* utility responds with the following for each message that you pipe *patch* to:

```
Hmm...  I can't seem to find a patch in there anywhere.
Hmm...  I can't seem to find a patch in there anywhere.
Hmm...  I can't seem to find a patch in there anywhere.
```

To specify the program to use with **pipe**, use **foreach** instead of **each**. For example:

```
Msg 3 of 10: foreach msg 3,8,12 'pipe $msg patch'
```

This passes the message numbers to *patch* correctly. Z-Mail executes the following commands:

```
pipe 3 patch
pipe 8 patch
pipe 12 patch
```

Here's an example of how to use **foreach** to select a pattern from different headers. First, use **ask** to prompt for a pattern to search for and then run **foreach** using the list of headers:

```
ask -i pattern "Pattern:"
foreach header (From To Cc) 'pick -h $header -e $pattern'
```

In this case, **ask** prompts for a pattern and stores the value in *pattern*. Then, **foreach** takes a list of the headers (**From**, **To**, and **Cc**) and stores the list in **$headers**. Finally, **pick** selects searches for *pattern* in each of the headers in **$header**.

Note that if you want to run a command on each file in a list, you must use **foreach** because **each** only works with messages.

Recursive Functions

Z-Mail usually refuses to allow a user-defined function to call itself; this is to prevent unintentional looping. If you want your functions to be able to call themselves recursively, set the **recursive** variable like this:

```
Msg 3 of 10: set recursive
```

Here's an example of a recursive function. The **watch** function uses the **await** command to watch for new mail and then report when new mail arrives. Note that you must set **recursive** for this function to work because **watch** calls itself.

```
function watch( ) {
    if $?1                  # If an interval was given, pass it to "await".
        await -T $1         # wait the specified time period, then check.
    else
        await               # wait 30 seconds, then check.
    endif
    if $status == 0         # If no interrupt, keep watching.
        watch $1            # watch calls itself recursively.
    endif
}
```

By default, **watch** checks for new mail every 30 seconds; you can specify the number of seconds between checks by giving a number argument to **watch**. For example, to specify the interval between checking for new mail to five minutes (300 seconds), invoke **watch** like this:

```
Msg 3 of 10: watch 300
```

You don't need this function in GUI mode because Z-Mail automatically collects new mail every 30 seconds, whether you're actively using the program or not. However, if you're using line or fullscreen modes, Z-Mail only collects new mail after you execute a command. If you want Z-Mail to process your new mail (for example, to run your new mail filters) even while you're away from your desk, use **watch**. When you return, enter the interrupt character to terminate the **watch** function.

NOTE

To prevent infinite loops, Z-Mail limits the number of recursive calls. In this case, if you plan to be away from your desk for a long time, specify a larger time interval between new mail checks so that **watch** runs longer.

Listing Your Functions

When you create functions in an initialization file, Z-Mail doesn't know about them until you read the file with **source**. (If you put functions in the default initialization file, Z-Mail reads them in automatically when you start the program.) To display all the your function definitions, use the **function** command; to display only the names of the user-defined functions, use **functions**.

When displaying function definitions, Z-Mail converts any leading tabs to eight spaces. When you enter **function** to list your functions, you get a display like the following:

```
function Forward( ) {
    shift -m | set messages
    if $status == -1
        return
```

```
            endif
            if $# == 1
                ask -i recipients "Forward message(s) to:"
                if $status == -1
                    return
                endif
            else
                set recipients = $*
            endif
            mail -Uf $messages $recipients
            unset recipients messages
    }
```

If you have more than one function, Z-Mail lists them all, one page at a time.

If you know the name of a function, but you can't remember exactly what it does, use the **function** command followed by the function name to list the contents of the function. For example, to list the contents of **savemush**, enter the following:

```
Msg 3 of 10: function savemush
```

Z-Mail displays:

```
savemush( ) {
        if -e +News # make sure $folder/News directory exists
            set mushnews = +News/comp.mail.mush # name the file
            if $thisfolder == /usr/spool/mail/hanna
            # make sure we're in the system mailbox
                    pick -h Newsgroups comp.mail.mush | set mushmesg
                    # select messages and store in mushmesg variable
                    save $mushmesg $mushnews # save messages
                    delete $mushmesg          # delete messages
                    update
                    # update the current folder to get rid of deleted messages
                    unset mushnews mushmesg  # unset local variables
            endif
        endif
    }
```

Notice that **function** lists the contents of your function, comments and all.

Removing Function Definitions

What if you've created a function with the same name as a default Z-Mail command and you want to turn off the function definition temporarily? For example, let's say you have a function called **delete** that prompts you for confirmation each time you delete a message. (This function might look something like the **Quit** function we described earlier.) If you're going through a folder, deleting a lot of old messages, you might find it intrusive for Z-Mail to prompt you each time you delete a message.

To remove the function definition for the current Z-Mail session, use the **unfunction** command:

```
Msg 3 of 10: unfunction delete
```

This returns the behavior of the **delete** command back to the Z-Mail default. Now, if you use **function** to list the contents of **delete**, Z-Mail does nothing.

Binding Functions to Buttons

As you know, you execute your functions from the Z-Mail line-mode command line by entering the function name. In addition, Z-Mail provides you with a way to run these functions from the GUI and fullscreen modes. Using the **button** command, you can create a "button" that runs the commands in a function when you select it.

In GUI mode, the button appears in the Action panel (under the Header Summary list) of the main Z-Mail window. You see buttons like the one in Figure 9-1.

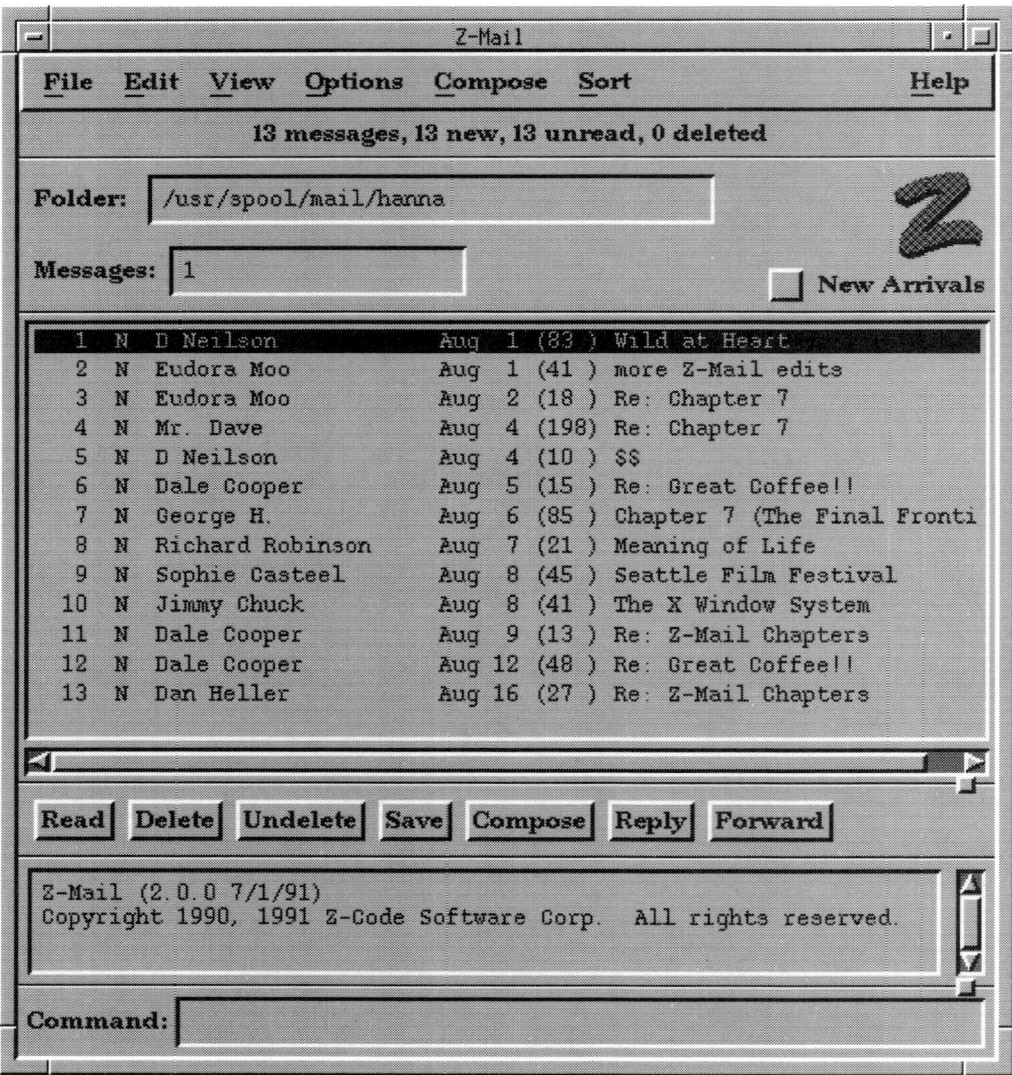

Figure 9-1. Buttons in the Main Z-Mail window

The Action panel on the main Z-Mail window contains seven buttons by default: Read, Delete, Undelete, Save, Compose, Reply, and Forward. If you bind a function to a button with the **button** command, the new button appears to the right of the Forward button. To execute the function in GUI mode, click the button with the mouse pointer.

In fullscreen mode, the button appears in a menu at the bottom of the screen when you select **user-button** (\). The buttons look like this:

```
Bounce  Compose Forward Reply
```

To execute the function in fullscreen mode, enter the first character of the button name or move the highlight to the button and press RETURN. As in other fullscreen-mode menus, if you decide not to select an option, simply press ESCAPE.

Buttons have no effect when you use Z-Mail in line mode. To execute a function, simply enter the function name at the line-mode prompt.

Here's the syntax for creating buttons with **button**:

```
button [ -n ] label function_name
```

The *label* is the descriptive text that appears on the button (as an example, the label on the Save button is "Save"). If your label has spaces, enclose the entire string in double quotes ("). Button labels cannot contain double quote characters or equal sign characters (=). In addition, if you want to refer to a button as an X resource, you can't use the dot character (.) in the button label. You can specify the button name in a resource specification file (such as *~/.Xdefaults*) using this format: **Zmail*Clean**. For more information on resources, see Chapter 7, *Using the Graphical User Interface*, and the *X Window System User's Guide*, Volume Three of the X Window Series from O'Reilly & Associates, by Valerie Quercia and Tim O'Reilly.

When creating buttons to use in fullscreen mode, keep in mind that you can select buttons using the first character; try to use unique labels for your buttons. The *function_name* is the name of your function.

For example, here's how to create a button using the **cleanrecord** function:

```
button -n Clean cleanrecord
```

The **-n** option allows you to call a function that doesn't require a message list. If you don't use **-n**, Z-Mail displays a pop-up box with this warning when you click the Clean button:

```
Select one or more messages.
```

With the **button** command in your initialization file, Z-Mail puts a button labeled "Clean" in the Z-Mail window Figure 9-2 shows how the Action panel looks now.

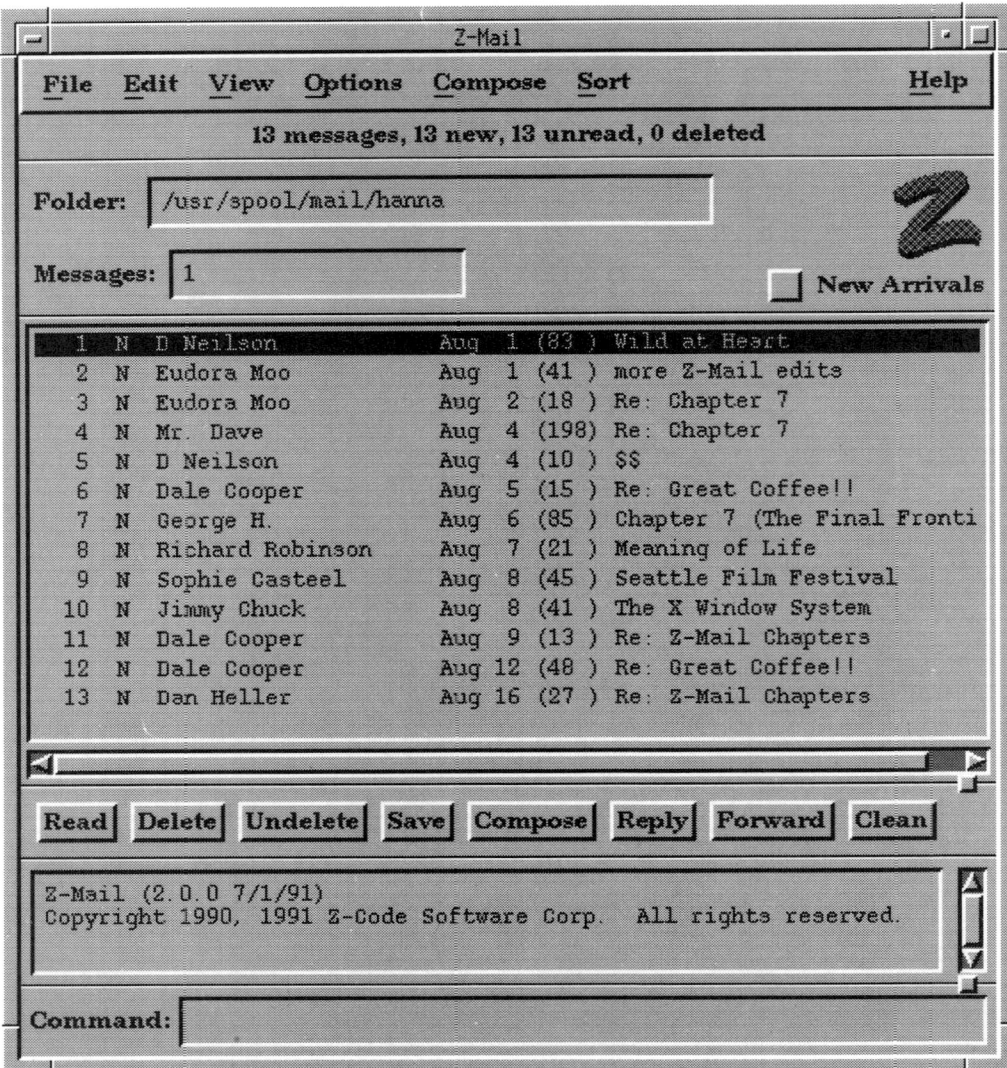

Figure 9-2. Clean button

When you click the Clean button, Z-Mail calls the **cleanrecord** function which cleans out old messages from your outgoing record folder.

If your function requires a message list (for example, **reply** and **delete**), don't include the **-n** option to **button**. By default, **button** requires that you select messages for your function to act on and displays the Warning pop-up window if you don't select a message.

Calling a Dialog Box

In functions designed for use in the GUI mode, you can open dialog boxes from within the function. For example, in a function that prompts for a pattern to search in messages, you can call the Search dialog box. Use the **dialog** command to do this. Table 9-4 lists the dialog boxes that you can open in GUI mode.

Table 9-4. GUI Mode Dialogs

Dialog	Description
Help	Get help about Z-Mail.
Folders	Open, switch to, and list folders.
Variables	Set and remove variables.
Buttons	Create functions and attach buttons.
Aliases	Create mail aliases.
Headers	Ignore and retain Z-Mail headers.
Dates	Search for messages by date.
Sort	Sort messages in the folder.
Compose	Create and send a new message.
Envelope	Create and use personal headers.
Search	Select messages by patterns.
Templates	Create and use form letters.
Printer	Send messages to the printer.
Save	Organize messages in files and folders.

For example, you can create a function that pops up the Search dialog box:

```
function searchpattern(){
    if is_gui
        dialog Search
    else
        ask -i pattern "Enter pattern to search for: "
        if $status == 0
            pick $pattern
        endif
    endif
}
```

This function checks to see what mode Z-Mail is running in. If Z-Mail is in GUI mode, **searchpattern** pops up the Search dialog box; otherwise, this function prompts the user to enter a pattern and then runs the **pick** command using that pattern as input.

Now, attach this function to a button so that you can access it from the GUI mode:

```
button -n Search searchpattern
```

This puts a button labeled "Search" in the Action panel on the main Z-Mail window. When you click Search, **searchpattern** function pops up the Search dialog.

Using the **dialog** command, you can create buttons for any of the dialogs in the Toolbox window that you use frequently. Use **button** to display them on the main Z-Mail window for easy access.

Listing Buttons

To see a list of the current button-to-function bindings in fullscreen mode, select **user-button** (\). The buttons appear in a menu at the bottom of the screen like this:

> █Bounce█ Compose Forward Reply

In GUI mode, the current buttons are always listed in in the Action panel of the main Z-Mail window. You can display the functions attached to those buttons by opening the Buttons and Functions window. (To display this window, pull down the Options menu on the main Z-Mail window and select the Buttons option.) For more information, see Chapter 7. To see the current list of functions in fullscreen mode, use the **user-button** (\) command to display them at the bottom of the header summary list (press BACKSPACE to exit the menu without selecting a button).

From line mode, you can list the buttons and corresponding functions by running **button** alone like this:

```
Msg 3 of 10: button
```

From fullscreen mode, use the **line-mode** command to run **button**:

```
:button
```

You get a display like this:

```
Read          readit
Delete        deleteit
Undelete      undeletit
Compose       composit
Reply         replyinclude
Search        searchpattern
```

Now, you can use **function** to see what each of the buttons do. For example, type the following:

```
Msg 3 of 10: function searchpattern
```

and Z-Mail displays this:

```
function searchpattern( ){
     if is_gui
         dialog Search
     else
         ask -i pattern "Enter pattern to search for: "
         if $status == 0
            pick $pattern
         endif
     endif
}
```

Removing Buttons

To remove a button from the window, use the **unbutton** command and specify the button label. For example, to remove the Reply button from the window use this command in your initialization file:

```
unbutton Reply
```

To remove all the buttons at once, include the following:

```
unbutton *
```

In GUI mode, you can remove the button by opening the Buttons and Functions window, selecting a button from the Current Buttons list, and then clicking the Delete button. You can also do this by entering the **unbutton** command line in the Command field on the main Z-Mail window. To remove a button in fullscreen mode, escape to the line-mode command line using **line-mode** (:) and enter a command like this:

```
:unbutton Reply
```

Reviewing Scripts and Functions

In this chapter, we reviewed the Z-Script elements discussed in Chapter 8, *Customizing Z-Mail*, explained how to use the special variables and how to create your own variables and use them in scripts and functions. We finished up the discussion of scripts by explaining the different ways to run the script: as an executable file (if you're using BSD UNIX), by sourcing it from within Z-Mail (using the **source** command) or from the UNIX command line (with the **–source** option), and from a *crontabs* file.

Then, we explained how to build functions using the information presented in Chapter 8 and the scripts section. You can use the commands such as **ask, shift**, and **foreach** in scripts and functions; we presented these commands in the context of functions because they, like the **function** command, are available in Z-Mail only (and not in MUSH). Finally, we showed you how to call GUI dialog boxes from within a function and how to attach buttons to functions so you can access them from GUI mode.

For more examples, see the sample functions in file *sample.lib* in the Z-Mail library directory (*/usr/lib/Zmail* by default).

10
Creating and Using Macros

In Chapter 5, *Z-Mail Shortcuts, Bells, and Whistles*, we discussed several areas where you can use shortcuts in Z-Mail to manage your mail more efficiently. However, the shortcuts presented in Chapter 5 are only available in the line mode. In this chapter, we'll show you some other shortcuts, by creating *macros* to customize and streamline your mail management tasks. Macros are available in line, fullscreen, and compose mode.

A *macro* is a shorthand definition for a longer command or string. The main difference between command-line aliases and macros is that command-line aliases are like commands—to execute the commands, you have to press RETURN after entering the alias. To execute the macro command, simply press the key or key-sequence associated with that macro; you don't have to press RETURN.

Macros consist of a *key-sequence* and an *expansion*; you create macros by *mapping* the key-sequence to the string expansion. When you enter the macro key-sequence, Z-Mail *expands* the macro and then interprets it as if you had entered the string. For example, suppose you create a macro with the key-sequence CTRL-P that expands to the command **pick**. Now, instead of entering **pick** at the command line prompt, you can press the CTRL and P keys simultaneously.

Macro Types

Z-Mail includes mechanisms for creating macros to use in several different modes: line mode, compose mode, and fullscreen mode. *Line-mode macros* are similar to command-line aliases; you use them to map key-sequences to longer command lines. *Compose-mode macros* are used to expand strings of text while editing messages in compose mode. Finally, use *fullscreen-mode* macros when using Z-Mail in fullscreen mode.

You can't use macros while using or composing messages from the GUI mode. You also cannot use macros if you invoke Z-Mail with the **–echo** (**–E**) command-line option. When you use **–echo**, Z-Mail doesn't process input from the keyboard until you press RETURN. You might use **–echo** when the system is heavily loaded and slow—that way, you don't have to wait for Z-Mail to echo back each character.

Macro Key-sequence Restrictions

Macro key-sequences generally consist of one or two *control characters* (keys that you press simultaneously with the **CTRL** key) or a sequence of characters sent by one of the function keys on your terminal. However, you can create macros using almost any key-sequence that you want.

There are three restrictions for choosing key-sequences:

- You cannot use keys that generate a signal or an end-of-file from the keyboard.[1]

- You cannot begin a line-mode macro with any of the special key-sequences listed in Table 6-10. These include DEL, CTRL-C, and CTRL-D.

- Macros that you create on one kind of terminal might not work on another, particularly if you use a key-sequence associated with a function key on your terminal.

To avoid confusion when entering commands or composing messages, you should choose unusual characters or combinations of characters, rather than individual lowercase letters for macros.

You must enter macro key-sequences quickly for Z-Mail to recognize them as keys in a sequence. For this reason, keep key-sequences very short or use strings that are automatically generated by pressing a special key on the terminal. You can use this characteristic of macros to prevent them from expanding.

 Simply enter the first character of the macro, then wait for it to echo before typing the next.

When testing new macros, you may want to start Z-Mail in read-only mode so that you don't lose or alter messages unintentionally. To do this, use the **–readonly** (**–r**) option to **zmail**:

```
$ zmail —readonly
```

Z-Mail displays a message like the following to let you know you're in read-only mode:

```
"/usr/spool/mail/hanna" [read only]: 5 messages, 3 new, 2 unread
```

---

[1] On BSD (Berkeley Software Distribution) UNIX systems, CTRL-Z generates a TSTP signal and CTRL-D generates end-of-file.

Creating Line-mode Macros

Line-mode macros are useful for accessing frequently used commands with a keystroke or two. The **map** command creates line-mode macros. Note that the macros that you create using **map** from the Z-Mail prompt are effective for the current Z-Mail session only—when you leave the program, you lose your macro settings. To make them permanent, you must include them in your initialization file.

Here's the syntax for **map**:

```
map [ key_sequence [ expansion ] ]
```

The *key_sequence* can be almost any key or combination of keys; in these first examples, we'll use non-alphabetic characters. If the *expansion* contains tabs, spaces, the tilde character (˜), or single quotes ('), enclose the entire string in double quotes ("); if it includes double quotes, use single quotes around the string. So, if the string contains a single quote, put double quotes around it.

Let's say that you often use the **mark** command to mark messages with a plus character (+). There is no abbreviation for **mark**; each time you use the command, you have to enter the entire word "mark." If you don't use the + command very often, it might be useful to map this character to the **mark** command. (By default, the plus character (+) displays the next message in the message list.) To do this, enter the following:

```
Msg 3 of 10: map + mark
```

Now, when you enter +, Z-Mail expands the macro and displays this message:

```
Msg 3 of 10: mark_
```

Press RETURN to mark the current message or mark another message by entering the message number.

If you just want to mark the current message each time you press +, you can include a RETURN, so that the macro executes **mark** immediately. To do this, enter \n at the end of the macro expansion, as shown in the following example:

```
Msg 3 of 10: map + mark\n
```

Now, when you press +, Z-Mail marks the current message. You see something like this:

```
Msg 3 of 10: mark
Msg 3 of 10: _
```

Here's another situation where you might want to create a macro. Let's say you often switch back and forth between line mode and fullscreen mode. Currently, if you want to switch to fullscreen mode from line mode, you have to enter the word "fullscreen" and press RETURN. You can make it easier by creating a line-mode macro for the **fullscreen** command. For example, map the colon character (:) to **fullscreen** like this:

```
Msg 3 of 10: map : fullscreen\n
```

Now, when you press the : key, Z-Mail interprets this as if you entered "fullscreen." (Now you can toggle back and forth between fullscreen and line mode using the : character.)

Using Control Characters in Key-sequences and Expansions

Z-Mail provides a special syntax for using control characters and other nonprinting characters in macro key-sequences and expansions. We've already seen this format in our examples when we used "\n" to execute RETURN. Table 10-1 shows the format that you should use to refer to these special keys.

Table 10-1. Z-Mail Control-character Syntax

Key	Syntax
CTRL-*X**	^*X*
ESCAPE	\E
RETURN	\n
TAB	\t

*The ^*X* syntax means that you either enter the caret character (^) followed by almost any uppercase letter or that you press the uppercase letter while holding down the **CTRL** key.

For example, if you want to create a macro that executes when you press these key-sequences:

CTRL-G CTRL-H

(Hold down the CTRL key while pressing first the G and then the H.) Enter this key-sequence to create the macro:

^G^H

To insert a newline (RETURN) in a macro expansion, include the **\n**. If you want to be able to change your mind after beginning a line-mode macro, don't include **\n** in the macro expansion. Without it, Z-Mail doesn't execute the macro immediately; you can then erase the line (or part of it) and enter something different or add to the current line.

In Chapter 5, *Z-Mail Shortcuts, Bells, and Whistles,* we explained how to use templates; now let's create a macro for sending a "phone message." This macro automatically loads the **phone** template and enters the editor:

    Msg 3 of 10: map ^P mail —e —p phone\n

Note the special syntax for referring to CTRL-P and the **\n** at the end of the macro expansion.

When you press CTRL-P (you don't have to press RETURN because the macro includes the **\n** character), Z-Mail displays the **phone** template for you to fill out. Fill out the form, exit the editor, and press CTRL-D to send the message.

Let's say you want to create a macro that forwards the current message to *james* when you press CTRL-F. Create the macro like this:

    Msg 3 of 10: map ^F mail —f . james\n

This macro invokes **mail** with the **–f** option to forward the current message (**.**) to *james*. So, when you press CTRL-F, you see the following:[2]

```
Msg 3 of 10: mail —f . james
To: james

forwarding message 3 ...(600 lines)
(continue editing letter)
```

Let's say you want to create a macro that lets you forward a message list to *james* instead of just the current message. You can use special functions to pause the macro for input from the keyboard. We'll discuss macro functions in the next section.

Using Special Functions in Macro Expansions

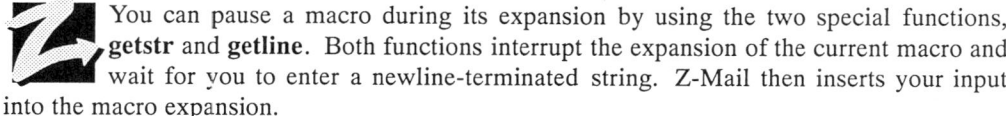 You can pause a macro during its expansion by using the two special functions, **getstr** and **getline**. Both functions interrupt the expansion of the current macro and wait for you to enter a newline-terminated string. Z-Mail then inserts your input into the macro expansion.

To use these functions, you must surround them with square brackets ([ ]). (Include only the function name within the square brackets; no whitespace is allowed.) The **getline** function retains the newline (RETURN) at the end of the input string. When you press RETURN after your input, **getline** echoes the complete macro, including your input, and then executes it immediately.

For example, if you often use **pick** to search for messages from certain people, you can create a macro that pauses for you to enter their names:

```
Msg 3 of 10: map ^W pick —i —f [getline]
```

Now, when you press CTRL-W, you see this:

```
Msg 3 of 10: pick —i —f _
```

The **getline** function then waits for you to enter the names to search for. Let's say you want to search for messages from David. To do this, enter the following:

```
Msg 3 of 10: pick —i —f Dav
```

When you press RETURN at the end of your input, Z-Mail immediately executes the **pick** command and searches for "Dav" (ignoring the case). You see the following:

```
Searching for messages that contain "Dav" from author names.
    2    D Neilson <davidn@> Mar 21 10:49  (16)  Z-Mail
    3    Doc Williams <dave> Mar 21 11:37   (28)  Floppy disks
    5    Mr. Dave <mrdave@c> Mar 21 12:37   (20)  Polyester
```

This **getline** function executes the command immediately because the RETURN at the end of the input string is retained.

---

[2] If you're using MUSH, this command sends the message immediately, without entering compose mode.

The **getstr** function strips off the newline. When you press RETURN to terminate your input, **getstr** echoes the complete macro, including your input, and then Z-Mail waits for you to press RETURN again before executing the command.

Let's see what happens if you use the **getstr** function, instead of **getline**, in the example above:

```
Msg 3 of 10: map ^W pick -f -i [getstr]
```

Now, when you press CTRL-W, you see this:

```
Msg 3 of 10: pick -f -i _
```

As before, enter **Dav** when the macro pauses for your input:

```
Msg 3 of 10: pick -f -i Dav
```

Now, when you press RETURN, you see the following:

```
Msg 3 of 10: pick -f -i Dav
pick -f -i Dav_
```

The **getstr** function echoes the macro and then Z-Mail pauses, waiting for you to enter more input. When you press RETURN, Z-Mail executes the **pick** operation.

Use the **getstr** function if you want to be able to change your mind after pressing RETURN to terminate your input.

Here's another example of how to pause macro expansion with **getstr**. This is similar to the macro that we created to forward the current message to *james* except that now we can pause the macro and enter a message list. To do this, enter the following:

```
Msg 3 of 10: map ^L mail -f [getstr] james\n
```

Now, when you enter CTRL-L, the macro displays this line:

```
Msg 3 of 10: mail -f _
```

Then, the macro pauses for you to enter a message list to forward. Let's say you want to forward the first and last message to *james*:

```
Msg 3 of 10: mail -f ^,$
```

When you press RETURN, the macro forwards the messages that you specified to *james*:

```
Msg 3 of 10: mail -f ^,$
mail -f ^,$ james
To: james

forwarding message 1 ...(54 lines)
forwarding message 5 ...(22 lines)
(continue editing letter)
```

Remember, if you don't want Z-Mail to execute the macro immediately, leave out the \n.

NOTE

When using these special functions, Z-Mail doesn't allow you to backspace past the beginning of a **getline** function. You can backspace past the beginning of a **getstr** function only after terminating your input with a RETURN.

If you want to cancel a macro at the **getstr** or **getline** prompt, press the interrupt character (CTRL-C or DEL).

In fullscreen mode, you can create additional functions out of almost any fullscreen-mode command. We show you how to do this later in this chapter.

Nesting Macros

Macros are *recursive*. This means that if you use the key-sequence from one macro in the expansion of another (or even the same macro), the second key-sequence is expanded when the first key-sequence expansion reaches the nested key-sequence.

 For example, you can create a macro that marks all the messages that have a specific string in the **Subject** line. First, let's create a macro to find the messages:

```
Msg 3 of 10: map ^T 'pick -s -i [getstr] | +'
```

Now, let's use our macro for +:

```
Msg 3 of 10: map + mark\n
```

When you press CTRL-T, the macro executes the **pick** command and you see the following:

```
Msg 3 of 10: pick -s -i _
```

Enter the string to search for (for example "Z-Mail Book") and press RETURN. Then, you see this:

```
Msg 3 of 10: pick -s -i Z-Mail Book
pick -s -i Z-Mail Book | mark
Msg 3 of 10: _
```

The macro marked all the messages with "Z-Mail Book" (ignoring case) in the **Subject** line:

```
1 + Dale Cooper      Apr 10 12:19    (16)   Z-Mail book
4 + Doc Williams     Apr 20 17:17    (28)   Re: Z-Mail Book
```

If you created the + macro first, when you enter + in the ^T macro definition, Z-Mail expands the + character and you see this:

```
Msg 3 of 10: map ^T 'pick -s -i [getstr] | mark
Unmatched '.
Msg 3 of 10: _
```

Because + has a newline at the end, the cursor returns before you can add the final single quote (') character and Z-Mail displays the error message above.

You can prevent the key-sequence from expanding by entering a special *literal-next* character before the key-sequence. We'll explain these characters in the next section.

When you create macros, make sure that you don't create recursive macros unintentionally. It's a bad idea, for example, to use any of the special characters that you use to refer to message lists as the key-sequence for a macro. For example, let's say you map the . character to a command like this:

```
Msg 4 of 10: map . sort —d\n
```

If you ever want to use the . character to refer to the current message, the macro will produce some unexpected results. For example, you previously defined this CTRL-F macro:

```
map ^F mail —U —f . james
```

Now, when you press CTRL-F to forward the current message to *james*, you see the following:

```
Msg 4 of 10: mail —U —f sort —d
To: sort, —d

forwarding message 4 ...(3 lines)
Msg 4 of 10: james
james: command not found.
type '?' for valid commands, or type 'help'
Msg 4 of 10: Saved letter in ~/dead.letter.
```

This is a relatively minor problem compared to others you can have. So, make sure that you don't use special characters like caret (^), dot (.), and dollar sign ($) for macro names. When you do call macros from within other macros, make sure that you know what you're doing.

Preventing Macros from Expanding

If you want to prevent the key-sequence for a macro from expanding, you need to precede the macro name with a special *literal-next* character. These special characters remove the significance of the next character, preventing Z-Mail from interpreting it as part of the key-sequence. Z-Mail recognizes the backslash (\) and CTRL-V as literal-next characters. You can enter literal-next characters from the keyboard or use them in macro expansions. Be careful using the backslash character in expansions because Z-Mail also uses this character to refer to special control characters, such as \n.

In our example, when you have this macro definition:

```
map + mark
```

and you want to include the + in another macro, without having it expand while you enter it, prevent the expansion by entering a \ before the key-sequence:

```
Msg 3 of 10: map ^T pick —s —i [getstr] | \+
```

This keeps the macro from expanding while you enter it. However, when you press CTRL-T, the macro still expands the "+" to "mark."

If you want to use the key-sequence in a macro without having it expand when you execute it, insert two backslashes (\\) before the sequence. For example, if you want to create the **H** macro that executes the **headers +** command, enter the following:

```
Msg 3 of 10: map H 'headers \\+\n'
```

When you press **H**, you see this:

```
Msg 3 of 10: headers \+
```

and Z-Mail runs the **headers +** command. If you only specify one \, when you enter **H**, you see this message:

```
Msg 3 of 10: headers mark
```

Literal-next Characters

If your system has the new BSD device driver, Z-Mail recognizes the *lnext* escape character from your terminal settings. To see if your BSD system uses the *lnext* character, try either of these commands at your system prompt:

```
$ stty -a
$ stty all
```

If the output includes an *lnext* character in the display, then Z-Mail recognizes that character. Here's sample BSD 4.2 output from **stty all**:

```
new tty, speed 38400 baud, 44 rows, 80 columns; -tabs
crt
decctlq
erase kill werase rprnt flush lnext susp  intr quit stop  eof
^?   ^U   ^W    ^R    ^O    ^V   ^Z/^Y ^C   ^    ^S/^Q ^D
```

Thus, if you change the stty literal-next character, Z-Mail still recognizes it.

With this device driver, when you type literal-next characters from the keyboard, you must enter two, because the *tty* driver strips off the first one. However, when using the literal-next character in a macro expansion, you don't need to specify two unless you want the second literal-next character to be literal.

If you don't have the device driver (when you entered one of the **stty** commands above, the output didn't include the *lnext* character), Z-Mail recognizes CTRL-V (^V) as the literal-next character.

For examples on how to use the ^V and backslash characters from the keyboard or in macro expansions, see the sections in this chapter on creating macros.

Listing the Current Line-mode Macros

If you want to display the current list of line-mode macros, use the **map** command. When you see this prompt, press RETURN to display the current map settings:

```
map [<CR>=all, -?=help]: _
```

For example:

```
Current map settings:
+           mark\n
:           fullscreen\n
^F          mail -f . james\n
^L          mail -f [getstr] james\n
^W          pick -f -i [getline]
^T          pick -s -i [getstr] | +
```

To print the expansion of a particular macro, enter the key-sequence at the **map** prompt. So, if you wanted to find out what happens when you press CTRL-L, without having to actually execute the macro, use the special control-character format (from Table 10-1) to enter the key-sequence, like this:

```
Msg 3 of 10: map ^L
```

and you see this:

```
"^L" is mapped to "mail -f [getstr] james\n".
```

You can enter the actual control-key-sequence from the keyboard if you want. To do this, first enter either the \ character or CTRL-V. For example:

```
Msg 3 of 10: map ^V^L
```

In this example, hold down the **CTRL** key while pressing the **V** and then the **L** keys. The CTRL-V sequence prevents the CTRL-L macro from expanding when you enter it at the keyboard. Note that if the *tty* driver *lnext* character is CTRL-V, you'll have to type **^V^V^L**—in this case, it's probably easier to use the backslash character (\ ).

To use backslash instead, enter the following:

```
Msg 3 of 10: map \^L
```

If you don't use the special format or escape the key-sequence with the \ or CTRL-V, the macro is expanded when you enter it.

Creating Compose-mode Macros

Compose-mode macros are similar to line-mode macros except that they expand while you enter messages in compose mode. (Compose-mode macros are not available in GUI mode.) If you frequently enter a word or a phrase while composing messages, you can create a compose-mode macro that expands to the phrase. For example, let's say you want to create a macro that inserts the word "percent" into your message whenever you press the % key. To do this, create a macro with the **map!** command.

Note that when you create a compose-mode macro using **map!**, it's effective only for the current Z-Mail session. To make it permanent, include it in your initialization file using the information in the section "Making Macros Permanent" later in this chapter.

The syntax for using **map!** is identical to **map**:

```
map! [ key_sequence [ expansion ] ]
```

Here's how to create the % macro:

Msg 3 of 10: map! % percent

Now, when you press % in compose mode, Z-Mail enters the word "percent" into the message text.

I use compose-mode macros in the same way that I define strings in *troff*. I define a short name and let the macro expand the string. For example, the word "Z-Mail" has been coming up a lot lately in my outgoing mail messages. So, I've created this compose-mode macro to write the string for me:

Msg 3 of 10: map! zM Z-Mail

Now, when I enter "zM" while composing a message, the macro expands to include the word "Z-Mail" in my message text. It's a good idea to use unusual character combinations (like a lowercase letter followed by an uppercase one), otherwise, you'll have your compose-mode macros expanding when you least expect it.

You might want to use compose-mode macros to expand acronyms or when you enter long company names. For example, create a macro that expands to "O'Reilly and Associates, Inc." whenever you press CTRL-O in compose mode by entering the following:

Msg 3 of 10: map! ^O "O'Reilly and Associates, Inc."

Note that I use double quotes (") to enclose the expansion of the CTRL-O macro because the expansion contains a single quote ('). If I use single quotes, Z-Mail complains:

Unmatched '.

Be careful not to use a string for the key-sequence that you might need to use in compose mode. Recently, I created a compose-mode macro called "ora" that expands to "O'Reilly and Associates, Inc." Now, whenever I use the string "ora" in common words (such as "temporary" and "corporate") or I try to send mail to people at *ora.com* by entering the address using the tilde-escape commands ~t or ~c, Z-Mail expands the macro for me. For example, if

I try to send mail to *lenny* at *ora.com*, when I type the string "ora," Z-Mail expands it to "O'Reilly and Associates:"

```
~t lenny@O'Reilly and Associates, Inc.
```

(That address won't work very well!) In this case, you can always set up an alias that doesn't include "ora" and use it to add addresses to your message with ˜t. Another way to deal with this problem is escape "ora" with a backslash like this:

```
~t lenny@\ora.com
```

Note that the backslash doesn't appear in the address when you enter the "ora" macro.

You can create a compose-mode macro that simulates the indentation feature of a text editor. For example, when you press CTRL-T, this macro inserts four spaces into the text:

```
Msg 4 of 10: map! ^T '    '
```

Note that, to retain the spaces, you have to put the expansion in quotes (single or double).

What if your tilde key (˜) is located in an awkward place on your keyboard and you have a hard time executing tilde-escape commands? You can change the character that executes the tilde-escape character (by setting the **escape** variable to another character), or you can create your own macros to call tilde-escape characters. As an example, I'll create a macro that invokes the editor when I press a function key. The F6 function key on my Wyse WY60 terminal sends this control-key-sequence:

```
^AE
```

You can figure out what control-key-sequence the function keys on your terminal send simply by pressing the function key; your terminal echoes the control-key-sequence to your screen. Be careful with this, however; the function key might echo a character that means something to Z-Mail.

To create a macro that invokes the editor when I press F6, I enter the following:

```
Msg 3 of 10: map! ^AE  '\n~v\n'
```

Now, when I press F6, this macro prints a newline (to make sure that the tilde-escape command appears at the beginning of a line) and then enters ˜v and another newline to start the editor.

NOTE

The macros that depend on the control-key-sequences from function keys for one terminal might not work on other terminals.

You can create similar macros to execute other tilde-escape commands.

Because macros that you create with **map!** work only when you execute them in compose mode, you can re-use these key-sequences with line-mode macros. For example, if you have a compose-mode macro that executes when you press CTRL-F, you can create a line-mode macro with the same key-sequence. However, I don't recommend this practice because remembering which macro does what, in which mode, can get confusing.

There might be times when you want to prevent a macro from expanding in the text of your message. Let's say you want to use the percent sign without it expanding to "percent." In this case, precede the percent sign (%) with a backslash or CTRL-V, like this:

```
\%
^V%
```

When you use either format, Z-Mail doesn't expand the %—the backslash or CTRL-V does not appear in text.

You can include tilde-escape commands in your compose-mode macros. For example, you can create a macro to keep a copy of the message you're composing automatically. To do this, create the following compose-mode macro:

```
Msg 3 of 10:  map! cC "~c hanna"
```

Now, whenever I enter **cC** in compose mode, this macro expands to:

```
~c hanna
(continue editing letter)
```

This inserts the following line in my outgoing message:

```
Cc: hanna
```

If you want to prompt for the **Cc** line, include the **[getstr]** function in your macro:

```
Msg 3 of 10:  map! cC "~c [getstr]\n"
```

NOTE

Because Z-Mail uses special processing for tilde-escape commands, you can't use **[getline]** to wait for input to these commands **[getstr]\n** instead. With **[getline]**, Z-Mail does not recognize the tilde (~) as a special character and enters the entire line as message text instead. However, if you use **[getstr]**, Z-Mail recognizes the tilde and the tilde-escape works as expected.

Listing the Current Compose-mode Macros

To display the current list of compose-mode macros, enter the **map!** command at the line-mode prompt:

```
Msg 3 of 10: map!
```

To list the current compose-mode macros from within compose mode, enter the following command:

```
~:map!
```

In either case, press RETURN when you see this prompt:

```
map! [<CR>=all, -?=help]: _
```

You see a list like the following:

```
Current map! settings
%                 percent
zM                Z-Mail
^O                O'Reilly and Associates, Inc.
^AE               \n~v\n
```

If you just want to display the expansion for one macro name without having to enter compose mode and press the key-sequence, enter **map!**. At the **map!** prompt, enter the macro key-sequence. If it's a control-key-sequence, use the special format in Table 10-1 for referring to control keys. For example, to display the expansion for the CTRL-O macro, enter the following:

```
Msg 3 of 10:  map!  ^O
```

and you see this:

```
"^O" is mapped to "O'Reilly and Associates, Inc.".
```

If you want to enter the actual control-key-sequence at the line-mode prompt, precede it with either \ or CTRL-V. For example:

```
Msg 3 of 10: map!  ^V^O
```

To do this, hold down the **CTRL** key while you press the **V** and then the **O** keys. CTRL-V prevents the CTRL-O macro from expanding when you enter it at the keyboard. If you don't use the special format or escape character, the macro expands when you enter it and you see this:

```
Msg 3 of 10: map! O'Reilly and Associates, Inc.
```

(Remember that it might be easier to use the backslash character (\) if the *tty* driver *lnext* character is CTRL-V). To use backslash instead of CTRL-V, enter the following command:

```
Msg 3 of 10: map \^O
```

Mixing Line- and Compose-mode Macros

A *mixed-mode* macro is one that causes the mode to change before the expansion completes. Normally, you can't mix macros across different modes. However, if the expansion causes the mode to change (for example, by running the **mail** or **fullscreen** commands), the rest of the macro expansion continues in the new mode.

For example, let's say you create a macro that executes a tilde-escape command to start the editor when you press F6 (on a Wyse WY60 terminal):

```
Msg 3 of 10: map!  ^AE '\\en~v\\en'
```

(Note that we put the expansion in single quotes because it includes a tilde character (~). Now, create a line-mode macro that calls this macro:

```
Msg 3 of 10: map # 'reply -i [getline]~t[getstr]\n^AE'
```

When you press **#** from line mode, the macro displays this message:

```
Msg 3 of 10: reply -i _
```

and then the **getline** function waits for you to enter a list of messages. Let's say you want to reply to message 5 (from *dan*). You enter the following:

```
Msg 3 of 10: reply -i 5_
```

When you press RETURN, the macro executes **reply** with the **-i** option (automatically including message 5). Then you see the following:

```
To: dan
Subject: Mixing Macros

including message 5 ...(3 lines)
~t_
```

The **[getstr]\n** waits for you to enter more addresses. When you press RETURN, the **#** macro expands the CTRL-A CTRL-E macro recursively to start the editor.

When using macros that change modes, be very careful not to expand recursive macros accidentally. To prevent macros from expanding, use backslash (\) and CTRL-V.

Creating Fullscreen-mode Macros

A *fullscreen-mode macro* is a shorthand definition for a series of fullscreen-mode commands. These macros only work when you use Z-Mail in fullscreen mode. When you enter the macro, Z-Mail interprets it as if you entered the series of commands. Macros are particularly useful in fullscreen mode because you can include key-to-command bindings and fullscreen-mode commands as well as other macros in the expansion of the macro.

Creating Macros with bind

Use the **bind** (**b**) command with the special **macro** command to create fullscreen-mode macros. To include control characters in macros, use the same special syntax that you used with key-to-command bindings as explained in Table 10-1.

When you create a macro with **bind**, you can use the macro during the current Z-Mail session only. To make the macro permanent, you must include it in your initialization file. We'll show you how to do this in the section "Making Macros Permanent" later in this chapter.

To create a macro with **bind**, use these steps:

1. Enter **bind** (the default key binding is **b**). Z-Mail displays the following prompt:

   ```
   bind [<CR>=all, -?=help]: _
   ```

2. Enter the key-sequence that you want to use to invoke the macro. For example, to create a macro that executes when you press the CTRL and **E** keys simultaneously, enter ^E.

   Z-Mail displays:

   ```
   "^E" = <unset>: New binding [<CR> for list]: _
   ```

3. Enter the special **macro** command at the prompt. Z-Mail displays:

```
"^E" = <unset>
New macro: _
```

4. Enter the macro expansion that you want to associate with the key-sequence. For example, you can use the following expansion to sort the messages in your current folder by date and then send the most recent one to the printer:

```
New macro: od$|
```

Now, when you press CTRL-E, this macro first invokes the **sort** command (the default binding is **o**), using **date** (**d**) as the sort criteria. Then, the macro moves the current-message pointer to the last message (**$**) and sends the contents of the message, using **lpr** (|), to the default printer.

This macro uses the default key-to-command bindings in the macro expansion. You may want to use the actual fullscreen-mode commands instead; we'll show you how to do this in the next section.

Using Functions in Fullscreen Macro Expansions

You can use key-to-command bindings to execute fullscreen-mode commands in your macro expansions. The problem with this is that, unless you are very familiar with the bindings, it's hard to tell what the macro does just by looking at it. As an example, our CTRL-E macro looks like the following:

```
^E          macro          od$|
```

Can you tell what happens when you press CTRL-E?

Another problem with this macro definition is that it depends upon the default key bindings for **o**, **$**, and |. If you rebind any of these keys, you'll probably get unexpected results when you press CTRL-E.

It's less confusing to use the actual command names instead. To use command names instead of key bindings, use fullscreen-mode *functions*. To create a function, simply enclose any one of the fullscreen-mode commands (except **macro**) in square bracket characters ([]). (Include only the function name (no whitespace) within the square brackets.) Using functions, the CTRL-E macro looks like this:

```
^E          macro          [sort]d[last-msg][lpr]
```

Now (if you're familiar with the fullscreen-mode commands), it's clear that CTRL-E sorts the message list by date, then goes to the last message and sends it to the printer. With this macro definition, you can also change any of the default bindings for **sort**, **last-msg**, and **lpr** without breaking the macro.

You can only use fullscreen commands in fullscreen-mode functions; don't use line-mode commands. You can't use the special **macro** command as a function because it doesn't have a key binding; use this command for creating macros with **bind** only.

You can also use two special functions, **getstr** and **getline**, in fullscreen-mode macros.[3] Both of these functions interrupt the expansion of the current macro and wait for you to enter a string terminated by a newline. When you press RETURN, Z-Mail then includes the text that you entered in the macro expansion.

Here's an example of a macro that uses the **getline** function. You can use this macro to clean out your mailbox. First, it prompts you for a pattern, then it goes to the next message with that pattern, displays the contents of the message, and finally deletes it:

```
"^F" = <unset>
New macro: [search-next][getline][display][delete]
```

First, this macro invokes a forward search through the `Subject` lines in the header summary display. Then, you see the following prompt and the **getline** function pauses the macro for your input:

```
forward search: _
```

After entering the pattern that you want to search for, press RETURN. Z-Mail finds the first message that matches the pattern, displays it, and then deletes it.

Here's another way to use functions in fullscreen-mode macros. This macro forwards the current message to *albert*:

```
"^B" = <unset>
New macro: [mail-flags]-f\nalbert\n
```

This macro invokes **mail-flags** command and enters **-f** to forward the current message to *albert*:

```
flags [-?]: -f
To: albert

forwarding message 5 ...(35 lines)
  5  P  Dale Cooper   Apr 22 18:11  (12)  Z-Mail Chapters
Msg 5 of 10: ...continue... _
```

Creating Macros with bind-macro

You can also create macros using the **bind-macro (&&)** command. This command accomplishes the same thing as **bind** with the **macro** function, but some of the steps are different.

As with **bind**, macros that you create with **bind-macro** are effective during the current Z-Mail session only. Make them permanent by including them in your initialization file. For information on how to do this, see the section "Making Macros Permanent" later in this chapter.

---

[3] The **getstr** and **getline** functions are available in line- and compose-mode macros, as well. For more information on these special functions, see the section, "Using Special Functions in Macro Expansions," earlier in this chapter.

To use **bind-macro**, follow these steps:

1. Enter **bind-macro** and Z-Mail displays this prompt:

   ```
   bind-macro [<CR>=all, -?=help]: _
   ```

2. Enter the key-sequence that you want to use to invoke the macro. For example, to create a macro that executes when you press the CTRL and **T** keys simultaneously, enter **^T**.

   Z-Mail displays:

   ```
   "^T" = <unset>
   New macro: _
   ```

3. Enter the series of commands that you want to associate with the key-sequence. Let's say you want to display the current date and time. To do this, create a macro that escapes to the UNIX shell, runs the *date* command, and returns to continue mode:

   ```
   New macro: [shell-escape]date\n
   ```

   Note that this macro uses the macro **shell-escape** function instead of the key-binding. If you use the default binding, the macro looks like this:

   ```
   New macro: !date\n
   ```

Now, when you press CTRL-T, you see something like the following:

```
Shell command: date
Sat Mar 09 19:03:08 PST 1991
Msg 3 of 6: ...continue... _
```

You can display the current list of fullscreen-mode macros (without the list of key-bindings) using **bind-macro**. To do this, enter **bind-macro** and press RETURN at this prompt:

```
bind-macro [<CR>=all, -?=help]: _
```

Z-Mail displays the list:

```
Current bind-macro settings:
^E          od$|
^F          [search-next][getline][display][delete]
^B          [mail-flags]-f\nalbert\n
^X          [sort]d[last-msg][lpr]
^T          [shell-escape]date\n
```

Both the **^E** and **^X** commands in the example above accomplish the same thing (if you haven't changed the default bindings for those fullscreen-mode commands). Note that **bind-macro** alone displays only the bind-macro settings; **bind** displays both the current key-to-command bindings and the macro settings.

Using Macros to Run Line-mode Commands

You can use macros to escape to the line mode to execute commands that are not available in fullscreen mode. For example, when you run **reply** in line mode, you can use any of the **mail** command-line options. You can also use **reply** to respond to a list of messages. While fullscreen mode has the **mail-flags** command that allows you to specify command-line options to **mail**, there is no equivalent "reply-flags" command. In addition, the fullscreen-mode **reply** command only allows you to respond to the current message.

To get around these problems, use these steps to create a macro that executes the line-mode **reply** command when you press CTRL-O:

1. Enter **bind-macro**.

2. When you see this prompt, enter ˆ**O**:

   ```
   bind-macro [<CR>=all, -?=help]: ˆo
   ```

3. At the prompt, enter these commands:

   ```
   "ˆO" = <unset>
   New macro: [line-mode]reply _
   ```

   Note that the **reply** command is not in square bracket characters ([]). In this example, **reply** functions as a line-mode command, rather than a fullscreen-mode function.

Now, when you press CTRL-O to execute the macro, Z-Mail escapes to the line-mode prompt and enters the **reply** command, followed by a space:

```
:reply _
```

At this point, you can enter any options to **reply** or specify a list of messages. You can even backspace, using CTRL-H or BACKSPACE, over the **reply** command and enter a new command (for example, **mail**) at the line-mode prompt. If you backspace over **reply** and press RETURN, you return to the line mode. You can backspace past the line-mode prompt (:) to return to fullscreen mode.

You can add options to **reply** in your macro. For example, if you like to include the current message in your response and then enter the editor, use these options in the macro:

```
New macro: [line-mode]reply —ei _
```

Now, when you execute the macro, you see the following:

```
:reply —ei _
```

This passes the **−e** and **−i** options to **reply** and waits for you to enter a list of messages to include. To include messages 1 and 6, enter the following:

```
:reply —ei 1,6
```

When you press RETURN, Z-Mail replies to the current message, includes messages 1 and 6 (without headers), and automatically enters the editor.

If you use the **getline** or **getstr** functions in a line-mode escape, you can't erase the text that appears before the **get** function. For example, in the previous example, you use a **getline** in the macro expansion:

```
New macro: [line-mode]reply —ei [getline]
```

In this example, you can't change or remove the **–ei** options.

Creating Line-mode Macros from Fullscreen Mode

You can create line-mode macros from fullscreen mode using the **map (&:)** command. Line-mode macros are different from fullscreen-mode macros that escape to the line mode to run commands; to use line-mode macros, you *must* be in line mode. The **map** command is identical to the line-mode **map** command. In this section, we'll briefly cover how to create line-mode macros while in fullscreen mode; for more information on creating line-mode macros, see the section, "Creating Line-mode Macros," earlier in this chapter.

1. First, select **map**. Z-Mail displays this line:

```
map [<CR>=all, -?=help]: _
```

2. When you see this prompt, enter the key-sequence. For example, enter ˆ**A** to create a macro that executes when you press CTRL-A:

```
map [<CR>=all, -?=help]: ˆA
```

Z-Mail displays this message:

```
"ˆA" = <unset>
New macro: _
```

3. Enter the line-mode commands. For example, create a line-mode macro that picks out all the messages from *Cron* and then deletes them:

```
New macro: pick —f Cron | delete\n
```

To display the current value of a line-mode macro, enter the macro name when you see this prompt:

```
map [<CR>=all, -?=help]: ˆA
```

Z-Mail displays this expansion:

```
"ˆA" = <pick —f Cron | delete\n>
New macro: _
```

To retain the current value of the macro, press DEL or CTRL-C (in MUSH, use the BACK-SPACE key); otherwise enter a new value and press RETURN.

You can display the current list of line-mode macros by pressing RETURN when you see this prompt:

```
map [<CR>=all, -?=help]: _
```

You see a display like the following:

```
Current map settings:
^A                pick -f Cron | delete\n
^G                set ?all\n
^X                set ?[getline]
```

Note that the commands in these macros are line-mode commands; you can't use these macros from fullscreen mode. If you try to use line-mode macros in fullscreen mode, Z-Mail sounds the terminal bell.

Creating Compose-mode Macros from Fullscreen Mode

From fullscreen mode, you can create macros to use while entering messages in *compose mode*. Use compose-mode macros while you edit messages. (Note that compose-mode macros are not available in GUI mode.) For example, if you frequently enter a long string, such as "UNIX in a Nutshell," you can create a macro to do this for you.

From fullscreen mode, use the **map! (&!)** command to create compose-mode macros. Use these steps:

1. Enter **map** and Z-Mail displays the following:

   ```
   map! [<CR>=all, -?=help]: _
   ```

2. Enter the macro key-sequence at this prompt. For example, enter **^O**:

   ```
   "^O" = <unset>
   New macro: _
   ```

3. Now, enter the macro expansion and press RETURN. In our example, enter the following:

   ```
   New macro: UNIX in a Nutshell
   ```

Now, when you press CTRL-O in compose mode, this macro inserts the string "UNIX in a Nutshell" into your message.

To display the current value of a compose-mode macro, enter **map!**. When you see this prompt, enter the macro name:

```
map! [<CR>=all, -?=help]: ^O
```

Z-Mail displays the expansion:

```
"^O" = <UNIX in a Nutshell>
New macro: _
```

To keep this macro, press the interrupt character. (Change it by entering a new expansion at the prompt.)

To display the current list of compose-mode macros, use **map!**. At this prompt, press RETURN:

```
map! [<CR>=all, -?=help]: _
```

You see a display like the following:

```
Current map! settings:

^O          UNIX in a Nutshell
mE          Hanna Nelson (hanna@holycow.santa-cruz.ca.us)
SCO         The Santa Cruz Operation, Inc.
zM          Z-Mail
```

Listing the Current Fullscreen-mode Macros

To display the current list of fullscreen-mode macros, enter **bind** and press RETURN at the prompt. Z-Mail displays the macro settings at the top of the list. For example:

```
bind [<CR>=all, -?=help]: _

Current key to command bindings:

^E      macro      od$|
*       mark
n       display-next
p       display
t       display
T       top
.       display
m       mail
...
```

The first item in the list is the **^E** macro that we created earlier; the others are examples of the default key-to-command fullscreen-mode bindings.

Removing Macro Definitions

If you want to change a macro key-sequence to use a different expansion, you don't need to remove the macro; instead, simply redefine the key-sequence to the new expansion.

To remove a macro definition completely, use **unmap** (for line-mode macros), **unmap!** (for compose-mode macros), or **unbind-macro** (for fullscreen-mode macros). Remember that the macros you create at the line-mode prompt using the **map**, **map!**, and **bind-macro** commands aren't permanent. To remove them, simply quit from Z-Mail. If you want to make them permanent, include them in your initialization file; see the next section for more information.

For example, let's say you decide you want to use **+** to display the next message instead of to mark messages. Unset the **+** line-mode macro by entering the following:

```
Msg 3 of 10: unmap \+
```

To unset a macro with a control-key-sequence, use the special format from Table 10-1 to refer to the key-sequence. For example, unset CTRL-T by entering this:

```
Msg 3 of 10: unmap \^T
```

Use CTRL-V or backslash (\) to prevent the macro from expanding.

When I stop using the string "Z-Mail" so much in my mail messages, I can remove the compose-mode macro. To do this, enter the following:

```
Map 3 of 10: unmap! zM
```

Making Macros Permanent

When you create macros with **map**, **map!**, and **bind-macro** from the Z-Mail prompt, the macros are temporary; when you quit Z-Mail, you lose the macro settings. You'll probably want to save some of your macros after you've tested them. To make the macros permanent, add them to your initialization file, *.zmailrc*.

The format for line-mode macro settings is this:

```
map key-sequence expansion
```

For compose mode, use **map!**:

```
map! key-sequence expansion
```

For fullscreen mode, use **bind-macro**:

```
bind-macro key-sequence expansion
```

For example, let's make our CTRL-O compose-mode macro permanent. Add this line to your initialization file:

```
map! ^O "O'Reilly and Associates, Inc."
```

Here's an example of how to save the CTRL-L line-mode macro:

```
map ^L mail —f [getstr] james\n
```

To save the CTRL-T fullscreen-mode macro, use this command:

```
map ^T [shell-escape]date\n
```

When you add these macros to your initialization file, your definitions are read in automatically each time you start Z-Mail. If you edit the initialization file from within Z-Mail, read in the definitions using the **source** command like this:

```
Msg 3 of 10: source ~/.zmailrc
```

Now, if you want to remove a macro, simply delete the macro definition line from your initialization file and read in your changes (either with **source** or by invoking Z-Mail again).

11
Z-Mail Addressing

In this chapter, we'll talk about mail addresses and how Z-Mail interprets them. We'll introduce you to such concepts as UUCP and Internet addresses and the different options for specifying them with Z-Mail. However, we won't attempt to explain everything about using networks and mail addressing; we'll just give you the basics so you understand how Z-Mail interprets and handles mail addresses.

Addressing Outgoing Messages

When you send mail to someone, you specify that person's *address*. An address is usually the person's login name on the computer where she receives mail, combined with the name of that computer. An address can also be a sequence of letters or numbers, or even special characters, depending on the network that each computer uses to transfer mail. In the simplest case, when you send mail to someone on the same computer that you're using, you don't need to specify the name of the computer, just the person's login name. Thus, if *lisa* and I are on the same machine, I can send her a message like this:

```
Msg 3 of 10: m lisa
```

When you send mail to more than one person, separate the login names with commas or spaces. If you use spaces, like this:

```
Msg 3 of 10: m lisa faith tracy
```

Z-Mail interprets each login name as a separate address and inserts commas like this:

```
To: lisa, faith, tracy
```

Comments in Mail Addresses

People's mail addresses don't necessarily match with their names in real life. For this reason, you might want to include a comment in their mail address showing the recipient's real name. (This is particularly useful for referring back to outgoing messages that you saved in a **record** file.)

To use comments in addresses, follow these guidelines:

- Put the comments in parentheses ( ); everything else is considered the address.

- Enclose the address in angle brackets (< >); everything else is interpreted as a comment. In this case, you must use a comma (,) between the addresses.

WARNING

The angle brackets (< >) are also used to redirect input on the UNIX command line. If you want to use these characters for specifying the address at the UNIX command line, precede them with the backslash character (\ ):

```
$ zmail Laurie Anderson \<laurie\>
```

If you follow these guidelines when using comments, they won't affect the destination of the message you're sending.

Here's an example of an address within angle brackets:

```
Sophie Casteel <sophie@film.com>
```

This address, *sophie@film.com*, is an example of an *Internet* address. We'll explain more about this address format in the section "Using Internet (Domain) Addresses" later in this chapter.

Note that the order of the address and comment doesn't matter.

Here's an example of the same address, with the comment appearing within parentheses:

```
sophie@film.com (Sophie Casteel)
```

If the comment includes special characters, such as single quotes ('), you must put the entire string in double quotes. For example, enclose the following address in double quotes:

```
"laurie (Gravity's Angel)"
```

If you don't include the double quotes, Z-Mail displays an error like the following:

```
Unmatched '.
```

You might want to create *mail aliases* with these comments and include them in your initialization file. We explain mail aliases in Chapter 4, *Sending Mail with Z-Mail*.

If you address the message to more than one person, make sure that you follow the same guidelines. For example, to include *karl* (with no comment) on the distribution, use:

```
Sophie Casteel <sophie@film.com>, <karl>
```

In these cases, you'll probably want to separate the addresses with a comma (,) to avoid confusion. If you include a comma, you don't need to surround the second address in angle brackets (< >).

If you forget one of the parentheses or angle brackets, you get an error like this:

```
Warning! Malformed address: "Jeffie <jeff"
```

In this case, Z-Mail prompts you with the **To** line again so that you can enter the address correctly this time.

If you want to use a comma character within the comment field, you must enclose the entire comment in double quotes or parentheses. (Remember, Z-Mail uses the comma to separate mail addresses.) For example, use this format:

```
"Hanna Nelson, Documentation" <hanna>
```

If you forget the double quotes (or parentheses, if you prefer), as in this example:

```
Msg 3 of 10: m Hanna Nelson, Documentation <hanna>
```

Z-Mail attempts to send mail to "Hanna" and "Nelson" and disregards everything that follows:

```
To: Hanna, Nelson
```

If you want, you can use angle brackets and parentheses together. For example, you might want to include a special nickname in your comment and have it appear in parentheses. In this case, put the address in angle brackets. Thus, mail addressed like this:

```
Hanna (Wacker) Nelson <hanna>
```

is delivered to *hanna* and appears on the **To** line like this:

```
To: Hanna (Wacker) Nelson <hanna>
```

Remember, if you're sending the message with **zmail** from the UNIX command line, you must escape the metacharacters; in this case, use:

```
$ zmail Hanna \(Wacker\) Nelson \<hanna\>
```

You probably won't find yourself entering comments each time you send mail at the Z-Mail command line, but they're useful in alias definitions in your initialization file. For example, include the following line in *.zmailrc*:

```
alias dale Dale Cooper <cooper@tp.com>
```

Remember that you can include aliases within alias definitions. So, to create an alias called *peaks* that includes *dale*, use a command like this:

```
Msg 3 of 10: alias peaks dale, audreyh, harry
```

When you send mail to *peaks*, this alias expands to:

```
To: Dale Cooper <cooper@tp.com>, audreyh, harry
```

However, when you send mail to an alias, you can't specify a comment at the same time. In this example, Z-Mail loses the comment "Twin Peaks" when it expands the *peaks* alias:

```
Msg 3 of 10: m Twin Peaks <peaks>
```

This appears on the **To** line like this:

```
To: Dale Cooper <cooper@tp.com>, audreyh, harry
```

If you set the *no_expand* variable, the alias isn't expanded and the comment is retained.

Sending Mail to Other Computers

Let's say *lisa* is on another computer in the same network. For example, we both work at a company where there are hundreds of computers linked together. If I know which computer *lisa* is on, I can send her a message. Here's where UUCP and Internet addresses come in.

Using UUCP Addresses

 If your system uses UUCP (UNIX to UNIX CoPy) to send mail to other UNIX sites, you will most likely use UUCP addresses.[1] If you're not sure how your system communicates with other systems, ask your system administrator.

To specify a UUCP address, preface the person's login name with the system name followed by an exclamation mark (!). In UNIX-speak, the ! character is called a "bang," thus a UUCP address is often referred to as a "bang address."

The format looks like this:

```
host![host2]!login
```

So, let's say *lisa* is on the machine *cocoa* and our machines communicate with UUCP. To send mail to her from *holycow*, I would use this command:

```
Msg 3 of 10: m cocoa!lisa
```

Remember that, unless you have **nonobang** set or you have history referencing turned off (by setting the **ignore_bang** variable), you'll have to escape the bang with a backslash character (\).

You can find out which computers are connected to yours (via UUCP) using the *uuname* command:

```
$ uuname
```

For example, when I use *uuname* at home, I get this list:

```
sco
ucscc
peren
```

This means that I can send mail (using UUCP addresses) to people on each of the listed computers. So, to send mail to *james* on the machine *peren*, use this command:

```
Msg 3 of 10: m peren!james
```

Let's say you want to send mail to a computer that's not directly connected to your computer. If your computer and the other computer both connect to a third computer using UUCP, you can build a UUCP mail path using the names of those computers. Each machine name in the path is known as a "hop." For example, let's assume that *sco* communicates with *rosebud*

---

[1] For information about UUCP, see the Nutshell Handbooks, *Using UUCP and Usenet*, by Grace Todino and Dale Dougherty and *Managing UUCP and Usenet*, by Tim O'Reilly and Grace Todino.

and your machine connects directly to *sco*. To send mail to *orson* on *rosebud*, build the following mail address:

    Msg 3 of 10: m sco!rosebud!orson

This message makes two hops to arrive at its destination.

Sending Mail Using Backbone Computers

To send mail to people on computers that aren't connected directly to your computer, you're going to have to do a little research to find out the path on which to send your message.

Sometimes, these mail paths can get long and complex. For example, when I send mail to my friend Matt in Grenoble, France, my message makes four hops before it gets to him. If your machine connects to a machine on the Usenet network, you can reduce the number of hops your message takes. Usenet is a large, informal network of UNIX computers that agree to exchange mail and netnews.

On the Usenet network, there are large sites that connect with other larger sites; these computers are known as *backbone* computers. For example, *ucscc* (a computer at the University of California at Santa Cruz or UCSC) is a backbone computer. Backbone computers serve as major mail transfer connections for a particular area or company. In this case, most of the mail sent to and from the Santa Cruz County area is transferred to other sites via this computer.

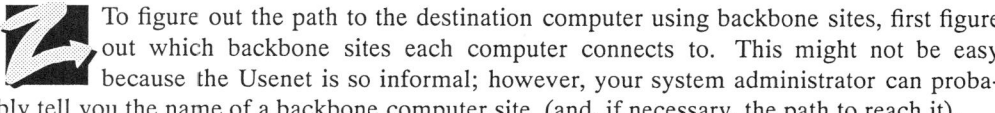 To figure out the path to the destination computer using backbone sites, first figure out which backbone sites each computer connects to. This might not be easy because the Usenet is so informal; however, your system administrator can probably tell you the name of a backbone computer site (and, if necessary, the path to reach it).

Once you know the path from your computer to a backbone computer and the path from the destination computer to another backbone, construct a path like the following to the destination computer:

    host1!backbone1!backbone2!host2

where *host1* is a computer directly connected to your system and *host2* is directly connected to your friend's system.

Let's say your computer (*holycow*) is connected directly to *ucscc* (*backbone1*). You want to send mail to *jeff* on the machine *couscous* that is directly connected to *papadam* (*host2*); *papadam* is directly connected to *indiana* (*backbone2*). To send mail to *jeff*, construct this path:

    Msg 3 of 10: m ucscc!indiana!papadam!couscous!jeff

(Remember, you can create a mail alias so that you don't have to enter long pathnames each time you send mail; see Chapter 4 for more information.)

Figuring Out Your UUCP Email Address

What if someone at a remote site wants to send you mail via UUCP? If you're not sure of the name of your machine, use this command (for UNIX System V):

```
$ uname -n
```

If you're on a Berkeley BSD UNIX system, use the following command (you can also use *hostname* on BSD systems):

```
$ uuname -l
```

For example, when I use **uname –n**, I see:

```
holycow
```

Let's say my friend *jeff* who gets his mail on *couscous* wants to send me a message at *holycow*. Using the path to each backbone described in the previous section, he constructs an address like the following:

```
Msg 3 of 10: m papadam!indiana!ucscc!holycow!hanna
```

Setting the Name of Your Machine

If your MTA does not create a correct **From** header on your outgoing mail messages, Z-Mail creates one using the system name or *hostname* of your computer. This makes it easier for other people to respond to your messages (with **reply** or **replyall**).

Generally, Z-Mail gets the hostname from the system (the same information as when you use *uuname*). However, if Z-Mail can't get this information from the system (or the system name is incorrect), the MTA on your system won't create the correct **From** header and people might have problems responding to your messages. In this case, the system administrator on your system can set the hostname manually using the **hostname** variable in the system-wide Z-Mail initialization file (*/usr/lib/Zmail/system.zmailrc*). (You can also set this variable in your personal initialization file.)

Note that setting **hostname** doesn't change the system name, just the hostname as it appears in the **From** line of outgoing mail on your system. Only the system administrator can change the system name.

Using Internet (Domain) Addresses

The Internet is a group of interconnected networks that form one large network. Machines on the Internet are connected directly, using TCP/IP (Transmission Control Protocol/Internet Protocol) to transfer mail, Usenet news, and files, and to run remote login sessions. The Internet also provides gateways to other networks, such as networks in Europe.

If your site is connected to the Internet, you won't use UUCP addressing to send mail to people on other machines on the Internet.[2] In this case, you'll use Internet addresses to send

---

[2] If your machine isn't on the Internet, you can still use UUCP to connect with a machine on the Internet (and thus with all the other machines on the Internet).

mail to other people. (Internet addresses are also known as domain, fully qualified, RFC822, and Arpanet addresses.) Internet addresses use the at sign (@) to separate the login name from the computer name. The format looks like this:

> *login@host[.subdomain].domain*

Here, *login* is the login name of the person you're sending mail to, *host* refers to the actual machine where that person receives mail, and *domain* is a *domain name*. A domain name is the location, for example, a corporation or university, where people get mail.

Domain names are divided into top-level domain names and subdomain names. For example, the Internet uses the *COM* top-level domain name to refer to commercial organizations; the *EDU* domain is used for educational facilities, such as universities and research institutions; *GOV* is reserved for government facilities. (You can use either uppercase or lowercase letters when referring to domain names.) In addition, the Internet recognizes country codes, such as *US* for the United States, *JP* for Japan, and *UK* for the United Kingdom, as top-level domain names.

A subdomain name is a company, university, or other organization under the top-level domain. For example, *ucsc* is a subdomain under the *EDU* domain. Subdomains can also be divided into smaller subdomains. For example, a department in a company or university might be a subdomain under the main subdomain; the department *lit* is a subdomain under the *ucsc* subdomain (which is in the *EDU* domain).

The fully-qualified domain name is the full name of the machine, beginning with the machine name and ending with the top-level domain name. For example, the fully-qualified domain name for someone on a machine at UCSC might look like this:

    james@grafix.ucsc.edu

My (fully-qualified) Internet address where I work looks like this:

    hannan@sco.com

Thus, anyone on the Internet can send me mail using this command:

    Msg 3 of 10: m hannan@sco.com

My machine at home uses another format, including the country code (US), that the Internet recognizes:

    hanna@holycow.santa-cruz.ca.us

Thus, instead of sending me mail via UUCP by "hopping" from one UNIX machine to another with an address like this:

    Msg 3 of 10: m ora!ucscc!holycow!hanna

someone on the Internet can send me mail with this command:

    Msg 3 of 10: m hanna@holycow.santa-cruz.ca.us

(The mail actually goes to the Internet host, in this case *ucscc*, which holds onto it until *holycow* calls up to transfer it with UUCP.)

Because UUCP and Internet addressing schemes are different, and not necessarily compatible, it's best that you not "mix bangs and ats," as we say, or ! and @.

If your machine is connected, as mine is, to a machine on the Internet via UUCP, when addressing mail to sites on the Internet, you should convert the at signs (@) to bangs (!). Thus, if *ora.com* is on the Internet, don't use a construction like the following to send mail via UUCP to *dale* on the computer *ora.com*:

```
Msg 3 of 10: m ucscc!dale@ora.com
```

Instead, convert everything to bang form. To do this, first enter the machine name closest to your site, followed by an exclamation mark, followed by the machine name where *dale* receives his mail, followed by another exclamation mark, followed by *dale*'s login. The address now looks like the following:

```
Msg 3 of 10: m ucscc!ora.com!dale
```

You don't need to specify the complete domain address for *ora.com* when using bang addresses; in other words, this address works just as well:

```
Msg 3 of 10: m ucscc!ora!dale
```

How Z-Mail Creates a Return Address

When you respond to a message (using **reply**), Z-Mail uses information in certain headers of the original message to construct the most efficient return address. Some headers that include useful information are: `From`, `Reply-To`, `Return-Path`, and `Sender`. Not all MTA's insert all these headers in outgoing messages.

By default, Z-Mail looks for these headers in this order:

1st `Reply-To`*
2nd `From`
3rd `Return-Path`

*The `Reply-To` header is not a default Z-Mail header; however, you can create this header in your outgoing messages using the **my_hdr** command.

For more information, see Chapter 4, *Sending Mail with Z-Mail*. Do not create a `Return-Path` header with **my_hdrs**; the MTA on your system should create this if it's necessary.

So, if you get a message with these headers:

```
From: ucscc!sun.com!nancyl
Reply-To:  Nancy Levin <nancyl@eng.sun.com>
```

Z-Mail uses the `Reply-To` header to construct the return address. When you reply to the message, Z-Mail creates the following `To` header:

```
To: Nancy Levin <nancyl@eng.sun.com>
```

If there was no `Reply-To` header in the original message, when you reply, Z-Mail uses the `From` line:

> `From: ucscc!sun.com!nancyl`

If the message doesn't have any of these three headers, Z-Mail tries to use the information in the first line of the message, the line beginning with `From` (without the colon character). This header is called the "From_" header (because it doesn't include a colon, but does contain the return address of the author of the message) and is created by most (but not all) mail delivery systems. (Some versions of MMDF don't create this header.)

If none of these headers exist, you might get an error like this one when you try to respond to the message:

> `Warning: unable to find who msg 9 is from!`

and the `To` line looks like this:

> `To: <>`

You can tell Z-Mail to search the default headers in a different order (or search for different headers) when constructing the return address using the **reply_to_hdr** variable.

To specify the headers (and the order) that you want Z-Mail to search, set **reply_to_hdr** to a list of headers, as always, separated by spaces or commas:

`Msg 3 of 10 set reply_to_hdr = "from_ reply-to from return-path sender"`

Now, when you respond to a message, Z-Mail searches for the headers specified in the list. In this example, the special `From_` header is listed first because it almost always succeeds. If Z-Mail can't find this header, it searches for `Reply-To` header (regardless of case), then `From`, and so on.

Note that, in cases where you receive a message forwarded from another person, the `Reply-To` header might be from the original sender. Be sure to double-check the `To` line when responding to forwarded messages to verify that your message is addressed to the right person. (Z-Mail omits the `Reply-To` header when forwarding messages, but MUSH and other MUA's do not.)

If Z-Mail doesn't find any of these headers in the message you are replying to, it prints a message like this:

> `Warning: message contains no `reply_to_hdr' headers.`

In this case, Z-Mail uses the default headers (`Reply-To`, `From`, and `Return-Path`) to construct the return address.

Telling Z-Mail About UUCP Connections

Even though Z-Mail checks the value of **reply_to_hdr**, it still might not construct the most efficient return address. Think of a situation where someone sends you a message in a roundabout way (instead of sending it directly though a backbone machine that your system talks to). Or, sometimes when a message is a reply, to a reply, to a reply, the `From` header gets long and jumbled (and there might not be a **Reply-To** header). In such cases, the materials that Z-Mail has available for creating a return address are not ideal.

You can help create efficient return addresses by telling Z-Mail which sites your computer talks to using the information from *uuname*. For example, let's say I receive a message with this **From** line:

    From: sco!sun!ucscc!ora!dale

If *dale*'s mail doesn't include a more direct address in another header, such as **Reply-To**, when I respond, the **To** line looks like this:

    To: sco!sun!ucscc!ora!dale

Because my machine talks directly to both *ucscc* and *sco* (and mail that I send through *sco* goes through *ucscc* anyway), there's no need for my response to go back through *sco* and *sun*. I can send mail directly with this address:

    Msg 3 of 10: m ucscc!ora!dale

If you want **reply** to use an efficient address like this one, you have to tell Z-Mail about the machines that your machine talks to via UUCP. When **reply** removes redundant UUCP addresses, you avoid unnecessary UUCP connections and thus speed up mail delivery.

If you notice that your mail isn't taking the most efficient route, tell your Z-Mail administrator. The administrator can tell Z-Mail about your system's direct connections by setting the **known_hosts** and **auto_route** variables in the system-wide Z-Mail initialization file (*/usr/lib/Zmail/system.zmailrc*). For example, use the output of the *uuname* command to set these variables:

    set known_hosts = "ucscc sco peren"
    set auto_route

The hostnames are separated by spaces, tabs, or commas.

With **known_hosts** and **auto_route** set, whenever you respond to mail, Z-Mail checks this list and constructs the shortest path back to the person by removing any unnecessary (redundant) hostnames. When I respond to the message from *dale*, the **To** line now looks like this:

    To: ucscc!ora!dale

In this case, **auto_route** removes *sco* from the path, but does not remove *ucscc* because it is the right-most host in the path that also appears in the **known_hosts** setting).

If **auto_route** is set to a system name like *ucscc*, Z-Mail appends that system name to all your nonlocal outgoing mail, in effect, forwarding it to that system for delivery. You can override this using the **-r** option to specify a path with **reply** or **replyall**; we'll explain this option in the next section.

How Z-Mail Creates Addresses with replyall

When you respond to a message with **replyall**, Z-Mail uses the original author's To and Cc lines to construct the new To and Cc lines. For example, let's say I get a message with these headers:

```
From: ucscc!ora!dale
To: ucscc!holycow!hanna
Cc: ucscc!apple!mc, zip!bart
```

If I use **replyall**, Z-Mail constructs the reply addresses by copying addresses unchanged from the original lines and I end up with:

```
To: ucscc!ora!dale
Cc: ucscc!apple!mc, zip!bart
```

However, from the original headers, (with the bang addresses) you can see that *dale*'s machine (*ora*) talks via UUCP to *ucscc* (a backbone computer), which in turn talks to my machine, *holycow* and *apple*. His machine also uses UUCP to talk directly to *zip*.

 When constructing the reply address, Z-Mail checks to see if **auto_route** is set. In this case, Z-Mail first constructs this header to route mail to *mc* and *bart* through *ora* (using the path in the original mail through *ucscc*):

```
To: ucscc!ora!dale
Cc: ucscc!ora!ucscc!apple!mc, ucscc!ora!zip!bart
```

The **auto_route** setting optimizes the path by removing any redundant UUCP hostnames so we end up with:

```
To: ucscc!ora!dale
Cc: ucscc!apple!mc, ucscc!ora!zip!bart
```

If **auto_route** is set, Z-Mail also checks the value of **known_hosts** to determine which UUCP hosts our machine talks to. Let's say **known_hosts** is set to "apple" and "ucscc." With this setting, Z-Mail constructs a return address that looks like this:

```
To: ucscc!ora!dale
Cc: apple!mc, ucscc!ora!zip!bart
```

Because we talk directly with *apple*, there's no need to go through *ucscc*.

If you want, you can also specify that your messages go through one host (or path) with **auto_route**. By setting **auto_route** to a specific pathname, you can tell Z-Mail to always use a specific path when you use **replyall**. This is useful if your system uses UUCP to communicate with a host that is connected to the Internet. In this case, your machine is one hop away from all other hosts. As an example, my machine *holycow* connects to *ucscc* via UUCP; *ucscc* is on the Internet. This means that the mail that I send from *holycow* makes one hop (to *ucscc*) to get to any machine on the Internet.

So, let's say you get a message with these headers:

```
From: ora!maggie
To: hanna@holycow terre@zip.com
Cc: ucscc!suzzy
```

To route mail through the machine *ucscc*, set **auto_route** like this:

```
Msg 3 of 10: set auto_route = ucscc
```

Now, instead of using the original author's pathname, Z-Mail appends the specified pathname to all of the addresses:

```
To: ucscc!ora!maggie, ucscc!zip.com!terre
Cc: ucscc!suzzy
```

Note that Z-Mail converts the at sign (@) construction on the original **From** line to a bang (**!**). Whenever Z-Mail changes the routing path, it converts the at characters to bangs. The original **Cc** line doesn't change because **auto_route** removes any redundant pathnames from the address.

Specifying the Return Path

If you want to route your response through a particular machine or with a particular path, you can specify the path using the **–r** option to **reply** and **replyall**. For example, the current message contains the following address lines:

```
From: sun!albert, cooper@fbi.gov
Cc: ucscc!audreyh
```

When you respond with **replyall**, you can add another address to the beginning of a pathname. For example, I usually route mail through the machine *ucscc*. To add the address *ucscc* to the beginning of each address, use the following command:

```
Msg 3 of 10: R -r ucscc
```

When you specify the return path with **–r**, Z-Mail uses the following return addresses:

```
To: ucscc!sun!albert, ucscc!fbi.com!cooper
Cc: ucscc!audreyh
```

Z-Mail converts the at (@) construction on the original **From** line (*cooper@fbi.gov*) to UUCP-style exclamation mark character (**!**) format (*ucscc!fbi.com!cooper*). The original **Cc** line does not change because Z-Mail removes any redundant pathnames from the address.

The **–r** option is identical to and overrides the value of the **auto_route** variable, if set.

Shortening Internet Addresses

The **auto_route** variable checks for redundant UUCP addresses and the **known_hosts** variable allows **auto_route** to shorten any redundant paths. If you frequently get mail with long domain addresses, you can use the **domain_route** variable to shorten these addresses when you reply. Use **domain_route** in conjunction with **auto_route**. So, if you set **domain_route** as a boolean variable like this:

```
Msg 3 of 10: set domain_route
```

Z-Mail shortens any addresses that contain a fully-qualified domain name to the rightmost fully-qualified domain name. Thus, if you have a message with this header:

```
From: ucscc!sun.com!dan@zip.com
```

when you respond, **domain_route** shortens the address to:

```
To: dan@sun.com
```

(This is the last fully-qualified domain name in the address.) Now, instead of making two UUCP hops to get to the Internet, the message uses the most direct (fully-qualified) address.

If you set **domain_route** to a string value, this variable acts like **auto_route** (remember, if you set **auto_route** to a string, Z-Mail puts the string at the beginning of all your responses). In this case, Z-Mail converts the Internet address (at format) to UUCP format (bang). For example, let's say you set **domain_route** like this:

```
Msg 3 of 10: set domain_route = ucscc
```

In this case, Z-Mail converts the addresses of *all* your responses to UUCP style and adds "ucscc" to the beginning. In our previous example, this:

```
ucscc!sun.com!dan@zip.com
```

becomes this:

```
ucscc!sun.com!dan
```

With **domain_route** set to a specific path, Z-Mail shortens the response path regardless of whether you specify a path with the **–r** option to **reply** or **replyall**. In addition, even if you specify a different path with **auto_route**, Z-Mail uses the path indicated by **domain_route**.

Internet addressing is much more complex than I can explain here; if you need more information, talk to your system administrator or take a look at the Nutshell Handbook, *!%@:: The Directory of Electronic Mail Addressing & Networks*, by Donnalyn Frey and Rick Adams.

Telling Z-Mail About Your Alternate Addresses

Normally, when you use **replyall** to reply to a message, Z-Mail removes your name from the list of recipients. Thus, when you reply to all the recipients of the message with these headers:

```
From: george@vegan.edu
To: hanna@holycow, faith
Cc: james@espresso.uucp, lisa@cocoa.com
```

Z-Mail creates headers like this, omitting your name from the original **To** line:

```
To: george@vegan.edu, faith
Cc: james@espresso.uucp, lisa@cocoa.com
```

If you want to keep your name on the **To** line, set the **metoo** variable:

```
Msg 3 of 10: set metoo
```

Now, when you use **replyall**, Z-Mail sends a copy of the message to you.

However, even if you don't set **metoo**, if you have accounts on more than one machine and you receive mail with more than one of those addresses on the **To** line, Z-Mail includes those other account names when you use **replyall**. For example, let's say the headers look like this:

```
From: george@vegan.edu
To: hanna@holycow, hannan@sco.com
Cc: james@espresso.uucp, lisa@cocoa.com
```

When you use **replyall**, Z-Mail removes your login name on the current system, but not any login names you might have on any other systems. (Unless, of course, you set **metoo**; then Z-Mail doesn't remove your name on the current system.) The outgoing headers would look like this:

```
To: george@vegan.edu, hannan@sco.com
Cc: james@espresso.uucp, lisa@cocoa.com
```

You can see that Z-Mail doesn't know that *hannan@sco.com* is another address for me. If you don't want to send copies of messages to other accounts where you receive mail, you can tell Z-Mail about the hostnames where you have other accounts using the **alternates (alts)** command. Using **alternates**, you can prevent multiple responses from going to your accounts on several machines.

Here's the syntax for **alternates**:

```
alts [host_list] [!path!login] [user@host] [*[login] ]
```

Let's say your name is the same on all the machines where you receive mail (only the hostname distinguishes them). To tell Z-Mail about all these accounts, use **alts** like this:

```
Msg 3 of 10: alts *
```

In this case, Z-Mail matches your name against all pathnames and local addresses, removing any addresses with the same login name from the **To**, **Cc**, or other headers. (Any accounts with different login names remain.) However, if you add your address to the distribution later, Z-Mail doesn't remove it.

What if your address on the current machine is different from your name on another machine where you get mail? As an example, my address at home is *hanna*; at work, it's *hannan*. To tell Z-Mail to ignore the address on the other system, append that name to * like this:

```
Msg 3 of 10: alts *hannan
```

In this case, Z-Mail matches the specified name (*hannan*) instead of my name on the current machine (*hanna*) and ignores *hannan*.

If you have different login names on the local or remote machines, you can tell Z-Mail to ignore them all using either the UUCP (bang) or Internet (at) addressing format. Look at the following example:

```
Msg 3 of 10: alts espresso holycow hannan@sco.com !root
```

In this example, Z-Mail matches the address in these cases:

- *hanna* on *espresso* or *holycow*.

- *hannan* at *sco.com*.

- *root* on the local machine only.

So, if the local machine is *espresso* and I respond to a message with the following headers:

```
From: faith@sco.com
To: hanna, hannan@sco.com, james
```

Z-Mail ignores both the *hanna* and *hannan@sco.com* headers and constructs the following **To** line:

```
To: faith@sco.com, james
```

If you use UUCP format when defining alternate addresses, you must specify the leading bang character to differentiate paths ending in a login name from paths to which the login name should be appended. In the previous example, *!root* is an example of a UUCP path ending in a login name. If you specify *root* instead, Z-Mail cannot distinguish between a user named *root* and a system named *root*.

To display the list of alternate names, use **alts** with no arguments:

```
Msg 3 of 10: alts
```

Z-Mail displays:

```
alts espresso holycow !sco.com!hannan !root
```

Any names that you specified in Internet format are displayed in UUCP format. In the example above, Z-Mail converts the original Internet address *hannan@sco.com* to *!sco.com!hannan*.

Note that the names that you specify with subsequent **alts** commands are *not* cumulative; these new names replace the current list. So, let's say you have the previous **alts** setting and you enter this command:

```
Msg 3 of 10: alts cocoa
```

Now, Z-Mail only matches your current address on *cocoa*.

At this point, you might want to customize your Z-Mail environment by adding some of the information from this chapter to your personal initialization file. For example, you might want to add comments to your alias definitions, create aliases for long mail paths, set up a primary route machine with **auto_route**, or tell Z-Mail about your other account names with **alts**. If you haven't already set up your personal initialization file, this is a good time to do so. For more information, refer back to Chapter 4, *Sending Mail with Z-Mail*, and Chapter 8, *Customizing Z-Mail*.

If you're interested in learning more about how mail is routed and the different addressing schemes, I highly recommend The Nutshell Handbook, *!%@:: The Directory of Electronic Mail Addressing & Networks*, by Donnalyn Frey and Rick Adams (O'Reilly & Associates, 1989).

A
Useful Tips and Hints

Throughout the book, we give you suggestions for how you can use Z-Mail to your greatest advantage. Because these tips are discussed in the context of the Z-Mail features that they illustrate, they are scattered throughout the book and thus difficult to refer back to. However, they are marked by the following icon:

This appendix is a collection of these suggestions and serves as an index to all the helpful tips presented in the book. Note that this appendix is not intended to replace the Table of Contents or Index; rather, it points you to places within the other sections where these hints are discussed.

Z-Mail Commands

Table B-1 lists all the Z-Mail commands in alphabetical order. Commands followed by an asterisk are not available in MUSH.

Table B-1. Z-Mail Commands

Command	Abbreviation	Description
about		Display information about Z-Mail.
alias		Define a short name for a long address or a list of mail addresses.
alternates	alts	Specify alternate addresses.
ask*		Ask a question and wait for a reply (for **cmds**, functions, and scripts).
await		Tell Z-Mail to wait for new mail to arrive.
bind		Bind keystrokes to a command.
bind-macro		Create fullscreen-mode macros.
button*		Bind functions to buttons in fullscreen and GUI modes.
cd		Change the current working directory ($HOME, by default).
close*		Close an open folder.
cmd		Define a command-line alias for a Z-Mail command.
copy	co	Copy a message (current by default) to a specified file (or ~/*mbox*) without marking it for deletion.
delete	d	Mark messages to delete when updating the current folder.
detach*		Extract an attachment from a message.
dialog*		Display a dialog box in GUI mode (for use in functions).
display		Display the contents of a message.
Display		Display the contents of a message (including any ignored headers unless **alwaysignore** is set).
dp		Delete the current message and display the next message.
dt		Same as **dp**.
each*		Execute a command on each message in a message list.
echo		Echo arguments on the command line, expanding variables and history references.
edit	e, v	Edit the messages in the folder.

Command	Abbreviation	Description
error*		Identical to echo; used in GUI mode to pop up a dialog. Returns **$status** of **−1**.
eval		Execute the arguments as a Z-Mail command.
exit	x, xit	Return to login shell without updating the folder.
expand		Expand mail alias lists on command line.
filter*		Create filters to run on folders.
flags		Set the status indicator characters on messages.
folder	fo	Change or print the name of the current folder.
folders		Display a list of folder names in the folder directory (*$HOME/Mail*, by default).
foreach*		Execute a command on each message in a message list or each file in a file list.
from	f	Print specified header summaries.
fullscreen		Switch to fullscreen mode from the line mode.
function*		Create functions to run Z-Mail commands.
group		Same as **alias**.
headers	h, z	Print a screenful of header summaries.
help		Print help information.
history		Display command history in chronological order.
iconify*		Iconify all the windows in GUI mode.
ignore		Set headers to ignore in message header display.
jobs*		Display a list of suspended message compositions.
lpr		Send a message list to a specified printer.
ls		Display the contents of directory (identical to the UNIX command *ls*).
mail	m	Send a mail message.
map		Create line-mode macros.
map!		Create compose-mode macros.
mark		Mark messages with a plus (**+**) or priority setting (A-E).
merge		Read messages from a specified folder into the current folder.
msg_list*		Use in functions to interpret message list metacharacters.
my_hdr		Create personalized headers in outgoing mail.
next	n,+†	Display the next message in the list (**+** doesn't use the pager).
open*		Open and switch to a new folder without updating the current folder.
pick		Select message from the current folder by pattern.
pipe		Send the message (text and headers) to a UNIX command.
Pipe		Send the text only of messages to a UNIX command.

†These commands are provided for UCB Mail (BSD) compatibility.

Command	Abbreviation	Description
preserve	pre	Save a message list in spool directory, unless marked for deletion.
previous	−†	Display the previous message (− doesn't use the pager).
print	p	Display the contents of the message.
Print	P	Display the contents of a message (including any ignored headers unless **alwaysignore** is set).
printenv		Display the current environment settings.
pwd		Print the current working directory.
quit	q	Update the system folder and exit Z-Mail.
reply	r	Send a response to the author of a specified message.
replyall	R	Send mail to the author and all the recipients of a specified message.
resume*		Bring suspended composition to the foreground.
retain*		Specify headers to display (opposite of **ignore**).‡
save	s	Save a message to a specified file (˜/*mbox*, by default).
saveopts		Save current settings (variables, mail aliases, and command aliases) to the initialization file.
search*		Same as **pick**.
set		Set variables.
setenv		Set an environment variable.
sh		Invoke an interactive Bourne shell.
shift*		Remove the arguments from the argument list in functions.
shut*		Close an open folder (same as **close**).
sort		Sort messages according to specific sort criteria.
source		Read commands and variables from a file (*.zmailrc*, by default).
stop		Suspend the Z-Mail process (on systems with job control). In GUI mode, performs **iconify**.
top		Print the top few lines (defined by *toplines* variable) of a message.
type	t	Same as **print**.
Type	T	Same as **Print**.
un_hdr		Remove a personal header setting.
unalias		Remove a mail alias definition.
unbind		Remove a binding definition.
unbind-macro		Remove a fullscreen-mode macro.
unbutton*		Remove a fullscreen- or GUI-mode button binding.
uncmd		Remove a command-line alias definition.
undelete	u	Recover messages marked for deletion (before updating the folder).

†These commands are provided for UCB Mail (BSD) compatibility.
‡The equivalent to the **retain** command is setting the **show_hdrs** variable.

Command	Abbreviation	Description
undigest		Burst a collection of messages ("digest") into separate messages.
unfilter*		Remove a filter definition.
unfunction*		Remove a user-defined function definition.
unignore		Include previously ignored message headers when displaying messages.
unmap		Remove line-mode macro definition.
unmap!		Remove compose-mode macro definition.
unmark		Remove marks from messages.
unpreserve	unpre	Remove preserved status from message.
unretain*		Remove headers when displaying messages.
unset		Unset variable definitions.
unsetenv		Remove an environment variable setting.
update		Save changes to the current folder without exiting Z-Mail.
version		Display the version number of your software.
write	w	Save the message (without headers) to a specified file.

C
Z-Mail Variables

Table C-1 lists all the Z-Mail variables in alphabetical order. Variables marked by an asterisk are not available in MUSH.

Table C-1. Z-Mail Variables

Variable	Description
alwaysignore	Ignore the message headers on the "ignored" list.
ask	Prompt for **Subject** on outgoing mail.
askcc	Ask for Carbon-copy (**Cc**) recipients when you send mail.
attach_types*	Specify filename for defining attachment keywords.
autodismiss*	Close windows automatically in GUI mode.
autoedit	Automatically edit all outgoing messages.
autoiconify*	Iconify windows automatically in GUI mode.
autoinclude	Include copy of author's message in your reply.
autoprint	Display the next message in the list when you delete a message.
auto_route	Remove redundant UUCP addresses when you reply to messages.
autosign	Add file (~/.signature) to the end of letters.
autosign2	Signature to use for specific addresses.
cdpath	Path to search for directories when you use **cd**.
cmd_help	Location of the general help file for line and fullscreen modes.
complete	The character you type to complete words.
crt	The number of lines a message must have to invoke *pager*.
crt_win	The number of lines in the GUI-mode Text frame.
cwd	Your current working directory.
date_received	Display date received in message headers.
dead	File in which to store dead mail (~/dead.letter).
deletesave*	Delete saved messages from *any* mailbox.
domain_route	Send fully-qualified domain addresses directly.
dot	Send letters with a dot (.) on a line by itself.
edit_hdrs	Edit headers with messages.
editor	Editor to use when editing messages (EDITOR or *vi*).
escape	Another character to begin tilde-escape commands.
fignore	Filename extensions or patterns to ignore when completing words.
folder	Full pathname to the directory where you keep mail folders.
fortunates	People to receive fortunes if you set *fortune*.

Table C-1. Z-Mail Variables (continued)

Variable	Description
fortune	Append fortune to outgoing messages.
fullscreen_help	List of fullscreen-mode command bindings that appear in the help display. In MUSH, this variable is called **curses_help**.
gui_help	Location of the GUI mode help file. List of fullscreen-mode command bindings that appear in the help display. In MUSH, this variable is called **tool_help**.
hdr_format	Format to display header summaries (see Table 8-2).
history	Number of commands to remember in the history list.
hold	Save messages that you read in system mailbox (not ˜/*mbox*).
home	Your home directory.
hostname	The name of your machine.
ignore_bang	Ignore ! as a history reference.
ignoreeof	Don't exit with CTRL-D.
indent_str	String to indent included messages when you send mail.
in_reply_to	Add **In-Reply-To** header to outgoing messages (see Table 8-2).
keepsave	Don't delete messages that you saved from your system mailbox.
known_hosts	List of hosts that your site knows with UUCP.
logfile	Log the headers only of your outgoing mail messages.
mail_icon	Change the icon that appears when you convert the Z-Mail window to an icon.
mbox	Default mailbox (instead of ˜/*mbox*).
metoo	Keep your name on distribution when sending replies.
mil_time	Use 24-hour military time format when printing the time.
msg_win	Number of lines in the Compose frame.
newline	Ignore RETURN (or execute a command when you press RETURN).
newmail_icon	Alternate icon to display when new mail arrives.
no_expand	Prevent aliases from expanding in outgoing messages.
no_hdrs	Don't insert personal headers in outgoing mail.
no_reverse	Disable reverse video in fullscreen mode.
nonobang	Suppress errors from unsuccessful history references.
nosave	Don't save canceled mail in ˜/*dead.letter*.
output	Output of the last command (a message list).
pager	Program to use to page through message text (instead of *more*).
picky_mta*	Tell Z-Mail not to pass specific headers to the MTA.
post_indent_str	String that appears after included message.
pre_indent_str	String that appears before included message (see Table 8-2).
print_cmd	Program to send messages to the printer.
printer	Default printer to send messages to.
prompt	Your prompt (see Table 8-4).
quiet	Turn off messages and bells in various situations.
realname	Your real name.
record	Save all outgoing mail in specified filename.
record_users*	Save outgoing mail to specific users.
recursive*	Allow functions to call themselves recursively.

Table C-1. Z-Mail Variables (continued)

Variable	Description
reply_to_hdr	Headers to use when constructing reply addresses.
save_empty	Save empty folders when you update.
screen	Number of header summaries to display in fullscreen and line mode.
screen_win	Size of the Header frame.
sendmail	Program to deliver mail (instead of *sendmail*).
show_deleted	Display deleted messages in header summary listings.
sort	Sort messages when you invoke Z-Mail.
squeeze	When reading mail, squeeze all blank lines into one.
status	Status (success or failure) of the most recent command.
templates*	Specify the directory to store form letters.
thisfolder	Current folder name.
title*	Set title for the top of your active folder in GUI or fullscreen mode.
tmpdir	Directory to store temporary files.
toplines	Number of lines to display when you execute **top**.
unix	Interpret non-Z-Mail commands as UNIX commands.
verbose	Set verbose mode (if available on your system).
verify	Prompt before acting in specific situations.
version	Display the current version of your Z-Mail software.
visual	Default visual editor (instead of *vi*).
warning	Print warning messages for nonfatal errors.
window_shell*	Specify program to use when a *tty* window is needed for input or output in GUI mode.
wrap	Current message pointer wraps to beginning of header summary list.
wrapcolumn	Wraps lines (at a specified column) in compose mode.
$$	The process ID (PID) of the Z-Mail process.
$[*%hdr_format*]	The format from **hdr_format** (see Table 8-2).
$(*%prompt_format*)	The format from **prompt** (see Table 8-4).

D
Tilde-escape Commands

This appendix lists the tilde-escape commands that you can use in compose mode while sending mail. Arguments are displayed in *italics*; those arguments that appear in square brackets ([ ]) are optional. Tilde-escape commands not available in MUSH are marked by an asterisk.

Table D-1. Tilde-escape Commands

Command	Description
˜a *file*	Append the message to the specified *file*.
˜A *file**	Attach the specified *file* to the message; Z-Mail prompts for attachment information.
˜A! *file*	Remove an attachment.
˜b [*Bcc-list*]	Modify (or set) the blind carbon copy recipients (**Bcc** header).
˜c [*Cc-list*]	Modify (or set) the carbon copy recipients (**Cc** header).
˜e [*editor*]	Start the default (or specified) editor to edit the message.
˜E[!]	Save (or don't save) the message buffer to ˜/*dead.letter*, then erase the message buffer.
˜f [*message-list*]	Forward the current (or specified) message without indenting, marking as "forwarded mail."
˜F[!]	Add (or don't add) a fortune to the end of the message.
˜h	Modify all the message headers.
˜i [*message-list*]	Include the body of the current message (or messages), indented with *indent_str*.
˜I [*message-list*]	Include the body and header information of the current (or specified) message, indented by *indent_str*.
˜p [*pager*]	Page through the message body (using the default or specified pager).
˜q	Cancel the message, saving it to ˜/*dead.letter* (if *nosave* variable is not set).
˜r *file*	Include the specified file.
˜R[!]	Request (or don't request) a return-receipt.
˜s [*subject*]	Modify (or set) the **Subject** header.
˜S[!]	Include (or don't include) a signature at the end of the message.
˜t [*recipients*]	Change (or set) the list of recipients (**To** header).
˜u	Edit the previous line in the message.
˜v [*editor*]	Start the default or specified fullscreen (visual) editor.
˜w *file*	Save the message to the specified file without headers.

Command	Description
~x	Exit message without saving to *dead.letter*.
~z²	Suspend current message composition; use **resume** to continue editing.
~$*variable*	Insert the string value for *variable* into the current message.
~:*command*	Run the Z-Mail *command*.
~?	Print a list and description of available tilde-escape characters.
~|*command*	Pipe the message through the UNIX *command*.
~~	Begin a line with a single tilde character.

Fullscreen-mode Bindings

This appendix contains a complete list of the fullscreen-mode commands and their default bindings. The fullscreen-mode commands marked by an asterisk are not available in MUSH.

Table E-1. Fullscreen-mode Commands

Command	Default Binding	Description
alias	a	Set a mail alias.
back-msg	-, k, K, ^K	Go back to the previous message.
bind	b	Set a key-to-command binding.
bind-macro	&&	Create a fullscreen-mode macro.
bottom-page	}	Move the cursor to the bottom of the page.
chdir	%	Change the current directory.
copy	c	Save a message, without marking it for deletion, to a folder (~/mbox, by default).
copy-list	C	Like copy, only save a list of messages.
delete	d	Delete a message.
delete-list	D	Delete a list of messages.
display	., p, t	Display the contents of a message.
display-next	n	Display the contents of the next message in the list.
exit	x	Exit Z-Mail without updating the current folder.
exit!	X	Exit Z-Mail from continue mode without updating the current folder.
first-msg	^	Move the cursor to the first message in the list.
folder	f	Switch to another folder.
folder-menu*	F	Display a menu for manipulating folders.
goto-msg	g, *n*	Move the cursor to the specified message number *n*.
help	?	Display help information about fullscreen mode.
ignore	i	Set headers to ignore when displaying the contents of a message.
jobs-menu*	J	Display a menu for listing and restarting background compositions.
last-msg	$	Move the cursor to the last message in the list.
line-mode	:	Exit the fullscreen mode and continue in line mode.
lpr	|	Send a message to the printer.

Command	Default Binding	Description
mail	m	Send a mail message.
mail-flags	M	Send a mail message, prompting for command-line flags to give to the **mail** command.
map	&:	Create a line-mode macro.
map!	&!	Create a compose-mode macro.
mark	*	Mark (or unmark) a message.
my-hdrs	h	Set personal headers in outgoing mail messages.
next-msg	+, j, RETURN	Move the cursor to the next message in the list.
preserve	^P	Preserve (or unpreserve) a message.
quit	q	Update the current folder and exit Z-Mail.
quit!	Q	Update the current folder and exit Z-Mail from continue mode.
redraw	^L	Redraw the screen.
reply	r	Send a reply to the author of a message.
reply-all	R	Send a reply to the author and all the recipients of a message.
reply-menu*	^R	Display a menu for replying to messages. The default binding for **reverse-video** in MUSH is **^R**.
retain*	I	Specify headers to display when reading messages.
reverse-video	~	Turn the current message indicator (reverse video) on (or off). The default binding for **reverse-video** in MUSH is **^R**.
save	s	Save a message to a folder.
save-list	S	Save a message list to a folder.
saveopts	)	Save the current settings to a filename.
screen-back	Z	Display the previous screenful of header summaries.
screen-next	z	Display the next screenful of header summaries.
search-again	N	Repeat the last search pattern.
search-back	^/	Search for a pattern backwards through the message list.
search-next	/	Search for a pattern forward in the message list. Note that some terminals use ^_ for ^/e.
shell-escape	!	Escape to the UNIX shell.
sort	o	Sort messages.
sort-reverse	O	Sort messages in reverse order.
source	(	Source the specified file.
top	T	Display the first few lines of a message (specified by the *crt* variable).
top-page	{	Move the cursor to the top of the screen.
unbind	B	Unset command bindings.
undelete	u	Restore a message.
undelete-list	U	Restore a list of messages.

Table E-1. Fullscreen-mode Commands (continued)

Command	Default Binding	Description
update	^U	Update the current folder without exiting Z-Mail.
user-button*	\	Display a menu of user-defined functions.
variable	v	Set a Z-Mail variable.
version	V	Display the version number of the Z-Mail software.
write	w	Save a message (without headers) to a file.
write-list	W	Save a list of messages (without headers) to a file.

F
Command-line Options

Tables F-1 through F-5 list the command-line options that you can use with Z-Mail. We've placed the options, based on the functions that they control, into five categories. Arguments are displayed in *italics*; those arguments that appear in square brackets ([]) are optional. The options marked by an asterisk are not available in MUSH.

Table F-1. Specifying the Mode

Option	Short Option	Description
−fullscreen	−V	Start Z-Mail in fullscreen mode. To start MUSH in fullscreen (or "curses") mode, use the **−curses** (**−C**) command-line option.
−gui		Start Z-Mail in GUI (X Window) mode (must be the first option on the command line). To start MUSH in graphics tool mode on Sun Workstations running the SunView windowing system, use the **−tool** (**−t**) command-line option.
−interact	−i	Force interactive mode even if you redirect input to the Z-Mail program.
−shell	−S	Start up Z-Mail even if the system mailbox or specified folder is empty or doesn't exist.

Table F-2. Initializing Z-Mail

Option	Short Option	Description
−echo	−E	Tell Z-Mail to process input from the keyboard only after pressing RETURN.
−eval *command**	−e	Execute *command* immediately before starting the Z-Mail program.

Table F-2. Initializing Z-Mail (continued)

Option	Short Option	Description
−headers[:adfmnoprsu]	−H	Display specified mail header summaries without entering Z-Mail.
−init[!] *filename*	−I	Reads the specified initialization file before default Z-Mail initialization files. The **!** character tells Z-Mail not to read the default system initialization file.
−lib *library-directory* *		Specify the Z-Mail library directory location.
−mailbox *mailbox-path*	−m	Use specified *mailbox-path* instead of your system mailbox.
−noheaders	−N	Start Z-Mail without displaying message headers.
−noinit[!]	−n	Don't read the default system initialization file at startup time. The **!** character also tells Z-Mail not to read your personal ZMAILRC initialization file.
−picky*	−P	Prevent Z-Mail-generated **From** and **Date** headers from being passed to the MTA (the MTA supplies these headers).
−source[!] *filename*	−F	Read commands from the specified initialization file after scanning the folder. The **!** character tells Z-Mail not to start after reading the file.
−timeout *seconds*	−T	Set the length of time between checking for new mail in GUI mode.

Table F-3. Sending Mail

Option	Short Option	Description
−attach [*type*:] *file* *	−A	Attach a *file* to the message and (optionally) specify the *type* the recipient should use to read the file.
−bcc *Bcc-list*	−b	Specify the people to receive blind carbon copies.
−cc *Cc-list*	−c	Specify people to receive carbon copies of the message.
−direct*	−D	Sends redirected or piped file directly to the MTA.
−draft *draft-file*	−h	Reads in and sends a *draft* file that includes a **To** header.

Table F-3. Sending Mail (continued)

Option	Short Option	Description
—send[!]	—U	Use with **—draft** to send the draft immediately without editing. The ! character tells Z-Mail not to include signatures or fortunes.
—subject *Subject*	—s	Specify the `Subject` of the message.
—template *template-name**		Use a template for your message.
—verbose	—v	Turn on your MTA's verbose mode, if available.

Table F-4. Managing Folders

Option	Short Option	Description
—filter*		Runs *filters* (specified in an initialization file) on the specified folder (or the system mailbox, if none is specified).
—folder [*folder*]	—f	Open the specified *folder* (or *mbox*, if none is specified) instead of the system mailbox.
—nofilter*		Don't run filters (specified with the **filter** command in your initialization file) on the folder when you start Z-Mail.
—readonly	—r	Start up Z-Mail with the folder in read-only mode, preventing you from modifying the folder.
—user [*user*]	—u	Tell Z-Mail to act as if the specified *user* (or *root* if not specified) is running the program. Z-Mail sets the home directory, system mailbox, real name, and login name as the specified user.

Table F-5. Miscellaneous

Option	Description
—debug	Activate verbose debugging output.
—help*	Prints the Z-Mail usage message.
—register[!] *password* [*users*]*	Register the host's license information.

Important Z-Mail Files

Table G-1 lists the files that Z-Mail uses.

Table G-1. Z-Mail Files

File	Description
*/usr/spool/mail/**	Default directory for storing incoming mail.
˜/Mail	Default folder directory.
˜/mbox	File where Z-Mail automatically saves old mail.
˜/.zmailrc	Personal Z-Mail initialization file.
˜/.mailrc	Alternate initialization file.
˜/.edPIDY	File where Z-Mail stores temporary outgoing messages.
˜/.zmaPIDY	Temporary files containing copies of open folders. The filename is described as above.
/usr/lib/Zmail/system.zmailrc	Z-Mail system initialization file. You can change the location of /usr/lib/Zmail by setting the ZMLIB environment variable to a different pathname.
/usr/lib/Zmail/Mail.zmailrc	Initialization file to make Z-Mail emulate BSD *Mail*.
/usr/lib/Zmail/mailx.zmailrc	Initialization file to make Z-Mail emulate System V *mailx*.
/usr/lib/Zmail/emacs.zmailrc	Initialization file to make Z-Mail emulate *emacs*.

*PID is the process ID of the Z-Mail process and Y is a digit to make the name unique if you open multiple files.

Index

executing in initialization file, 284

help, 26

my_hdr, 380

output in GUI, 204

re-executing, 129

reply, 384

replyall, 384

testing output status, 124

UNIX, 154

comments, in mail addresses, 373

initialization file, 273

metacharacters, 274

pound character (#), 148, 317, 323

complete keyword, quiet variable, 142

complete variable, 141

enabling filename completion, 137

completion character, changing, 141

defined, 137

completion listing character, changing, 141

defined, 137

comp.mail.mush newsgroup, 2

Compose area, changing height, 222

Compose button, 204

Compose dialog, 205, 345

Compose Frame, editing commands, 221

Compose menu, Templates option, 224

Z-Mail window, 200

Compose Message window, buttons, 221

example, 217

compose mode, about, 11

editing keys, 73

running Z-Mail commands, 85

wrapping lines automatically, 73

compose-mode escapes, (see tilde-escapes)

compose-mode macros, creating, 359-361, 369-370

displaying, 369

listing, 361-362

map! command, 359

saving, 285

syntax, 371

compose_window widget, 267

computer, backbone, 377

conditional statements, 274

continue mode, 167

exiting, 168, 192

control characters, macros, 352

control keys, binding, 194

macros, 363

conventions, xxii

copies, (see carbon copies)

copy command, 47, 178

Copy option, 225

copy-list command, 179

country codes, domains, 379

cron, running scripts, 321

crontabs file, 321

crt variable, 30, 169, 176

crt_win variable, 210

˜c tilde-escape, 71

CTRL key, macros, 352

CTRL-C key, canceling messages, 12

CTRL-C key sequence, 194

CTRL-D key, default completion listing character, 137

ignoring, 56

sending messages, 12

CTRL-V key, compose-mode macros, 362

literal-next character, 356

CTRL-Z key, job control, 160

curly brace characters ({ }), filename completion, 140

msg_list command, 336

curly brace characters ({ }) , 25

current message pointer, 13

defined, 14

current working directory, 123

curses command, 163

curses mode, MUSH, 2

using, 163

-curses command-line option, 163

cursor, moving in fullscreen mode, 166

Custom Sort option, 250

Custom Sort window, 250

Cut option, 225

cwd variable, 123

D

dash character (-), 24
  personalized headers, 103
  picking messages, 38
  signature, 107, 158
  sorting messages, 52
date, exact, 249
  relative, 249
  selecting messages, 40, 247
  sorting, 184
date command, 87
date format, specifying, 41
Date Search window, 247
date_received variable, 53, 251
Dates dialog, 205, 345
dates_dialog widget, 268
dead.letter file, 77
dead.letter folder, 12
DEL key, canceling messages, 12
Delete button, 204, 210, 212
delete command, 17, 180
Delete option, 241
deleted messages, displaying, 18, 35
  reading, 30, 213
  recovering, 18
  restoring, 181, 213
delete-list command, 180
deletesave variable, 147
deleting messages, automatically, 30
  basic concepts, 17-18
Deliver menu, 227
Detach button, 212, 230
detach command, options, 95
  syntax, 95
dialog boxes, about, 201
  accessing from Toolbox, 204
  calling in functions, 345-346
  GUI mode, 345
  Toolbox window, 204
dialog command, 266, 345
digests, (see mail digests)
-direct command-line option, 96
directories, changing, 47, 179-180
display command, 175
displaying, mail aliases, 98
  message tops, 31
distribution list, checking, 83
  (see address)

dollar sign character ($), macros, 356
  message list characters, 209
  referring to variables, 121
domain, about, 379
domain address, (see Internet address)
domain_route variable, 384
Done button, 210
dot character (.), sending messages, 12, 89
dot variable, 89
double quote character, alias expansion, 96
  button labels, 343
  command-line aliases, 133, 135
  comments, 274
  creating personalized headers, 103
  each command, 337
  filter command, 296
  macros, 351, 359
  referencing variables, 312
  setting variables, 121
  v_subject, 300
double quote character (") in personalized headers, 174
double-click, 209
draft files, including, 223
  sending, 89-90
-draft command-line option, 89
-draft option, sending files, 82
dt command, 30

E

each command, 337-338
-echo command-line option, 142, 349
ed editor, 74
edit command, 146
Edit menu, Format option, 228
  Z-Mail window, 200
Edit menu options, 241
edit_hdrs variable, 76, 97
editor, default, 74
EDITOR environment variable, 74, 146
Editor option, 227
editor variable, 74, 146, 227

editor_dialog widget, 268
editors, emulating, 294
EDU domain, 379
electronic mail, (see e-mail)
elm, 1
else expression, 282
emacs editor, 74, 294
  emulating, 295
emacs.zmailrc file, 295
e-mail, communicating with, 1
endif expression, 274
end-of-file, 350
end-of-file character, ignoring, 56
Envelope dialog, 205, 345
Envelope option, 252
Envelope window, 258
envelope_dialog widget, 268
environment settings, default, 9
environment variables, EDITOR,
    74, 146
  HOME, 47
  MAILRC, 270, 272, 295
  MUSHRC, 270
  PAGER, 31
  PATH, 320
  SHELL, 154
  TMPDIR, 290
  VISUAL, 74, 146
  ZMAILRC, 270, 272, 295
  ZMLIB, 92, 224, 269, 301, 411
equal sign character (=), setting
    variables, 120
error message, event not found,
    132
  file system full, 291
  suspended compositions, 55
  unknown ˜ escape, 68
  unmatched ', 103
error messages, displaying in
    GUI, 204
errors, 21
escape character, backslash (\),
    131
ESCAPE key, default completion
    character, 137
  macros, 352
escape variable, 360
˜e tilde-escape, 74
˜E tilde-escape, 78
eval command, 313
event not found, error message,
    132

ex editor, 74
exclamation mark character (!),
    addresses, 384
  command-line aliases, 316
  history referencing, 127
  in cmds, 136
  negating an expression, 279
  new mail, 15, 234, 296
  re-executing commands, 129
  UUCP address, 376
-exist option, scripts, 281
exit! command, 192
  closing folders, 187
exit command, 18, 54, 168, 192
  closing folders, 187
  functions, 324
  scripts, 283
exiting Z-Mail, 18-19
  about, 54-56, 240
expansion, macros, 351
expression, negating, 279
expression operators, 279

F

field-width specifier, defined, 59
fignore variable, 140
File menu, Z-Mail window, 200
file system full error message,
    291
filename completion, changing
    completion character, 141
  enabling, 137
  excluding patterns, 140
  using, 137-140
filename metacharacters,
    defined, 45
  filename completion, 138
files, draft, 89
  hidden, 311
  including in messages, 82, 222
  saving messages, 46, 178, 213
  sending, 12, 89-96
  sending as attachments, 92, 228
  temporary, 311
filter command, 296, 298
  initialization file, 284
  limitations, 297
  removing definitions, 298
  syntax, 296

G

fullscreen-mode macros, 365
goto-msg command, 166
GOV domain, 379
Graphical User Interface, (see GUI)
(see GUI)
grep, UNIX command, 311
GUI help file location, 302
GUI mode, about, 6-8
   creating functions, 263-266
   customizing, 204, 252
   dialog boxes, 345
   entering line-mode commands, 204
   removing buttons, 266
-gui command-line option, 200
gui_help variable, 302
GUI-mode interface, xix

M

macro command, 363
macros, about, 349-371
  canceling, 355
  compose mode, 285, 369
  creating, 363
  creating with bind, 363-364
  creating with bind-macro,
    365-366
  defined, 349
  executing immediately, 353
  expanding unintentionally, 359
  expansion, 351
  fullscreen mode, 285
  function keys, 360
  getline function, 363
  getstr function, 363
  interrupting expansion, 353
  key-sequence, 351-352
  line mode, 285, 351, 368
  listing, 358, 370
  listing current, 366
  literal-next character, 356
  mixed mode, 362
  nesting, 355-356
  pausing, 353
  preventing expansion, 356-357
  recursive, 355
  removing, 370-371
  restrictions, 350
  running line-mode commands,
    367
  saving, 285, 371
  special keys, 352
  types, 349
  using functions, 353-355,
    364-365
  using metacharacters, 351, 359
mail, sending from fullscreen
  mode, 172
mail address, (see address)
mail aliases, about, 96-99
  creating, 96
  displaying, 98-99
  removing, 174, 262
  saving, 262
  setting, 173-174, 261-262, 284
  unsetting, 99
Mail Aliases window, 261
Mail command, 1, 3, 9

mail command, 65, 152, 172
Mail command, 294
  emulating, 295
mail digests, bursting, 152
  reading, 152
Mail Folders window, 236
Mail Headers window, example,
  256
mail keyword, verify variable, 89
Mail program, 271
Mail Transport Agent, (see MTA)
Mail User Agent, (see MUA)
Mail User's Shell, (see MUSH)
mailbox flag, 234
-mailbox command-line option,
  142
.maildelivery file, 300
  filtering messages, 299
˜/Mail directory, 45, 49
mailer-daemon, 158
mailers, emulating, 294
mail-flags command, 172
  command-line options, 172
mail.log folder, 114
MAILRC environment variable,
  270, 272, 295
.mailrc file, 270, 272
  sourcing, 295
mailreg command-line alias, 106
mailreport function, 330
mailx command, 1, 3, 9, 294
  emulating, 295
mailxrc.zmailrc file, 295
Mail.zmailrc file, 295
main mailbox, (see mbox folder)
Main Mailbox button, 214
main_window widget, 267
malformed address error, 374
map! command, 284, 369
  listing compose-mode macros,
    361
  syntax, 285, 359
map command, 284, 351, 368
  listing macros, 358
  syntax, 285, 351
˜, map! command, listing compose-mode macros, 361
mark command, 43, 182, 242,
  351
  using, 189
Mark option, 241-242

Sort menu, 249
Options menu, 252
  Z-Mail window, 200
organizing messages, 45
outgoing messages, saving, 83-84, 113-114, 223
Output area, displaying command output, 204
output variable, 123
Overwrite File option, 214

P

pager, specifying, 31
PAGER environment variable, 31
pager variable, 31
parentheses characters (()), comments, 374
  functions, 323
  special variables, 310
Paste option, 225
PATH environment variable, 320
pattern, non-matching, 246
  searching, 182-183
  searching by, 243
Pattern Search window, 243
percent character (%), switching to system mailbox, 144
Perform Function on Result option, 246
period character (.), macros, 356
permanent marks, (see priority marks)
personal initialization file, specifying, 270
personalized headers, creating, 174, 258
  picking by, 245
  removing, 106, 175, 260
  saving, 261
  (see headers)
pf command-line alias, 134
phone command-line alias, 91
phone noise, updating folder, 57
phone template, 90, 225
pick command, 86
  -e option, 38
  ignoring case, 39
  non-matching patterns, 40
  options, 37, 296

selecting by author, 38
  selecting by date, 40
  selecting by pattern, 38
  selecting by recipient, 40
  selecting by subject, 39
  specifying another header, 40
  suppressing descriptions, 42
  syntax, 37
  using, 37-44, 167, 189
pick keyword, quiet variable, 43
PID, Z-Mail process, 310
Pin-Up button, 210
Pin-Up messages, 209
pinup_window widget, 267
pipe character (|), 155
  combining commands, 39, 126
  command-line aliases, 133, 135
  output variable, 124
Pipe command, 156
pipe command, 156
  specifying a pattern, 157
pipelines, defined, 126
plus character (+), 30
  active folder, 238
  creating aliases, 98
  folder directory, 45
  macros, 351
  marking messages, 182, 242
  msg_list command, 336
  precedence, 242
  suspended compositions, 85
  temporary mark, 43
pointer, mouse, 201
  (see message pointer)
-p option, eval command, 313
positional parameters, (see special argument variables
post_indent_str variable, 101
pound character (#), comments, 273, 317, 323
  functions, 148
  previously active folder, 145
  scripts, 320
pre_indent_str variable, 101
prepared drafts, including, 223
preserve command, 55, 181, 241
Preserve option, 241
Prev button, 210-211
previous command, 30, 298
previous commands, modifying, 130

re-executing, 129
previous line, editing, 74
Print button, 216
print command, 15, 29
Print command, 152
print command, 298
    changing, 36
Print Message option, 215
print_cmd variable, 36
printer, default, 35
    specifying, 36
Printer dialog, 206, 345
Printer Name field, 216
printer variable, 36
Printer window, example, 215
printer_dialog widget, 267
priority marks, 44, 242
    picking messages, 44
Priority option, 241
Priority pull-right menu, 242
priority settings, removing, 243
prompt variable, format, 310
pS command-line alias, 39, 134
pt command-line alias, 134
˜p tilde-escape, 83, 85
pull-right menu, 201, 232, 242
    Reply, 217
pwd command, 47, 123

Q

q command-line alias, 160
˜q command, 173
˜q tilde-escape, 77, 85
question mark (?), displaying
        help, 27
    filename completion, 139
quiet variable, 142, 160
    suppressing pick descriptions, 43
    suppressing save descriptions,
        297
    update keyword, 186
quit! command, 192
quit command, 18, 54, 168, 192,
        298
Quit option, 240

R

Read button, 204
reading mail, basic concepts,
        13-16
reading messages, 29
read-only mode, switching fold-
        ers, 144, 236
    testing macros, 350
read-only variables, using,
        122-125
-readonly command-line option,
        350
realname variable, 87
recipients, changing, 69
    specifying, 69
record file, 373
record variable, 98, 113, 134, 313
record_users variable, 114
recursive macros, 356
recursive variable, 339
redirect variable, 276, 278
redirection, (see command-line
        redirection)
redraw command, 168
refresh time, fullscreen mode, 164
Replace Text option, including
        files, 223
Reply button, 204, 210, 232
    Message Display window, 217
reply command, 16, 66, 152, 177,
        384
Reply pull-right menu, 232
    options, 217
Reply to All option, 217
Reply to Sender option, 217
replyall command, 16, 66
reply-all command, 177
replyall command, 384
ReplyAll/IncludeMessage option,
        217
replying to mail, basic concepts,
        16
reply-menu command, 178
replyreg command-line alias, 106
**ReplySender/IncludeMessage
        option**, 217
Reply-To header, creating, 104
    return address, 380
reply_to_hdr variable, 381
restoring messages, 30

About the Author

Hanna Nelson majored in English Literature at the University of California at Santa Cruz where she first met Dan Heller, *Mush*'s creator. After graduating, she went into Technical Writing (mostly to prove to everyone that you can make a decent living with a Liberal Arts degree). She currently works at the Santa Cruz Operation, Inc., documenting operating system software, where she uses *Mush* to manage her mail.

In her free time (what's that?), she likes to read (20th Century fiction), write (anything but technical documentation), study film and feminism, promote transportation alternatives and ride her custom-built purple-striped bicycle.

Colophon

Our look is the result of reader comments, our own experimentation, and distribution channels.

Distinctive covers complement our distinctive approach to UNIX documentation, breathing personality and life into potentially dry subjects.

The image featured on the cover of *Z-Mail Handbook* is a chariot. Chariots were developed by the Sumerians in 2000 B.C. for use in war. The early chariots were heavy, four wheeled wagons drawn by a team of four oxen or asses. The lighter, two-wheeled, horse-drawn chariot did not emerge until 1500 B.C. when it was used by the Hyksos to subdue the Egyptians, and subsequently by the Egyptians to overthrow the Hyksos. These vehicles were typically drawn by a two-horse team and were designed to carry a driver and warrior. In battle, they were rarely used in the front lines but instead kept to the flanks and rear.

Once introduced, the chariot spread throughout China, the Middle East, Greece, and Rome. In Greece and Rome it quickly fell out of use as a machine for war. However, it remained useful in processionals and racing. Racing became very popular; in the Olympic Games early in the 7th century B.C. the chariot race was the first and most exciting event. As chariot racing increased in popularity, chariots moved to a four horse team and races became a daily event in the capital.

Edie Freedman designed this cover. The image is adapted from a 19th-century engraving from the Dover Pictorial Archive.

The text of this book is set in Times Roman; headings are Helvetica; examples are Courier. Text was prepared using SortQuad's sqtroff text formatter. Figures are produced with a Macintosh. Printing is done on a Tegra Varityper 5000.

Books That Help People Get More Out of Computers

If you want more information about our books, or want to know where to buy them, we're happy to send it.

❏ Send me a free catalog of titles.

❏ What bookstores in my area carry your books (U.S. and Canada only)?

❏ Where can I buy your books outside the U.S. and Canada?

❏ Send me information about consulting services for documentation or programming.

Name _____

Address _____

_____

City _____

State, ZIP _____

Country _____

Books That Help People Get More Out of Computers

If you want more information about our books, or want to know where to buy them, we're happy to send it.

❏ Send me a free catalog of titles.

❏ What bookstores in my area carry your books (U.S. and Canada only)?

❏ Where can I buy your books outside the U.S. and Canada?

❏ Send me information about consulting services for documentation or programming.

Name _____

Address _____

_____

City _____

State, ZIP _____

Country _____

NAME _____

COMPANY _____

ADDRESS _____

CITY _____ STATE _____ ZIP _____

BUSINESS REPLY MAIL

FIRST CLASS MAIL PERMIT NO. 80 SEBASTOPOL, CA

POSTAGE WILL BE PAID BY ADDRESSEE

O'Reilly & Associates, Inc.

632 Petaluma Avenue
Sebastopol, CA 95472-9902

NAME _____

COMPANY _____

ADDRESS _____

CITY _____ STATE _____ ZIP _____

BUSINESS REPLY MAIL

FIRST CLASS MAIL PERMIT NO. 80 SEBASTOPOL, CA

POSTAGE WILL BE PAID BY ADDRESSEE

O'Reilly & Associates, Inc.

632 Petaluma Avenue
Sebastopol, CA 95472-9902